THE COLLECTED WORKS OF
WALTER BAGEHOT

VOLUME FOUR

THE COLLECTED WORKS OF
WALTER BAGEHOT

EDITED BY

Norman St John-Stevas

The Historical Essays
(in two volumes) with an introduction by
Jacques Barzun

VOLUME FOUR

HARVARD UNIVERSITY PRESS
CAMBRIDGE, MASSACHUSETTS
1968

The Collected Works of Walter Bagehot
This volume first published 1968
This edition © The Economist 1968

PRINTED IN ENGLAND

THE COLLECTED WORKS OF
WALTER BAGEHOT

VOLUMES I & II · LITERARY ESSAYS
VOLUMES III & IV · HISTORICAL
VOLUMES V & VI · POLITICAL
VOLUMES VII & VIII · ECONOMIC
VOLUME IX · LETTERS & MISCELLANY

CONTENTS

Volume Four

Walter Bagehot and Napoleon III

by Norman St John-Stevas

THE two foreign nations which engaged Bagehot's consistent interest throughout his career as a journalist were France and the United States. France in particular attracted him and from the time of his first visit to Paris in 1851 he was fascinated by Louis Napoleon whom he considered intrinsically more interesting than his famous uncle Napoleon I. He watched him closely throughout his career with what his sister-in-law, Mrs. Russell Barrington, called 'a strange, almost personal interest'. He followed him from triumph through adversity to his death at suburban Chislehurst in January 1873. His early admiration faded and he grew more critical, but in the end his assessment was by no means entirely unfavourable and certainly sympathetic. It was a misfortune that they never met.

Bagehot, as has been noted,[1] was an eyewitness of the *coup d'état* of 1851 and in contrast to most educated Englishmen of the time passed favourable judgment. In England the feeling against Napoleon was intense, and Palmerston was forced to relinquish the premiership because of his premature public approval of the new régime. Bagehot helped to build the republican barricades in Paris but his sentiments were on the side of Napoleon. 'I wish for the President decidedly myself', he wrote to his mother, 'as against M. Thiers and his set in the Parliamentary World; even I can't believe in a Government of barristers and newspaper editors, and also as against the Red party, who, though not insincere, are too abstruse and theoretical for a plain man. It is easy to see what they would abolish, but horribly hard to say what they would *leave*, and what they would *find*. I am in short what they call here a reactionnair, and I think I am with the majority—a healthy habit for a young man to contract.'[2]

He expressed his views for the public in seven brilliant letters published in the *Inquirer*, the unitarian paper edited by Langton Sanford, and in which his friends Hutton, Roscoe and Osler had a

[1] See Volume I of this edition, pp. 50–1.   [2] Letter of December 7 1851.

hand. The letters are an extraordinary combination of rollicking cynicism and profound good sense. They outraged the *Inquirer*'s readers by eulogising the Catholic Church, defending Louis Napoleon's use of force, attacking the freedom of the French press and maintaining that the country was totally unfitted for parliamentary government. 'They were light and airy, and even flippant, on a very grave subject,' wrote Hutton. 'They made nothing of the Prince's perjury; and they took impertinent liberties with all the dearest prepossessions of the readers of the *Inquirer*, and assumed their sympathy just where Bagehot knew they would be most revolted by his opinions.'

Bagehot's 'fast' politics, as Hutton called them, were more than racy, they contained in embryo some of the fundamental ideas of his maturity, his Burkeian concern for the preservation of the social fabric, his belief in the importance of national character, and his conviction that British parliamentary institutions could not be exported indiscriminately. 'Only this much is most certain,' he writes in the third letter, 'all men and all nations have a character, and that character when once taken, is, I do not say unchangeable—religion modifies it, catastrophe annihilates it—but the least changeable thing in this ever-varying and changeful world. . . . When you hunt with greyhounds and course with beagles, then, and not till then, may you expect the inbred habits of a thousand years to pass away, that Hindoos can be free, or that Englishmen will be slaves.'

'I fear you will laugh,' he writes in the second letter, 'when I tell you what I conceive to be about the most essential mental quality for a free people, whose liberty is to be progressive, permanent, and on a large scale: it is much *stupidity*.' The dull, bovine, English charac-ter was in this respect well endowed and thus ideally suited for parlia-mentary government, and Bagehot contrasted it in this respect with that of the mercurial French. The essence of the French character was 'a certain mobility; that is, as it has been defined, a certain "exces-sive sensibility to *present* impressions," which is sometimes *levity*,—for it issues in a postponement of seemingly fixed principles to a momentary temptation or to a transient whim; sometimes *impatience*, as leading to an exaggerated sense of existing evils; often excitement—a total absorption in existing emotion; oftener *inconsistency*—the sacrifice of old habits to present emergencies; and yet other unfavour-able qualities.' Such a character could support only a small degree of civil liberty and needed a strong executive to keep its worst excesses in check. A 'strong, vigorous, anti-barricade executive' had at whatever risk or cost to be established, and it was for doing this that Bagehot praised Louis Napoleon.

Louis Napoleon's character was a subject of perennial interest to Bagehot. Writing in *The Economist* in March 1870, a few months before the Emperor's fall, he ventured the prophecy that posterity would find him a more interesting man than Napoleon I and pointed out that already he had reigned for five years longer than his uncle: 'To us at all events there seems to be something much more rare and unique in the slow and pondering intellect which has so curiously studied and so perseveringly measured—almost as it were by the successive tentative instalments and gradual approximation of some mathematical formula,—the political wants and needs of France, than in that of the far swifter and more self-willed genius which flashed with an irregular lustre over Europe and fell through the excess of the very qualities by virtue of which it rose.'[3] Nearly twenty years earlier Bagehot had praised him in similar terms in the first of his letters on the *coup d'état*, when he extolled the fact that he was neither a professor, a journalist nor a litterateur but was capable of 'observing facts rightly, of reflecting on them simply, and acting on them discreetly'. Bagehot denied him any great intuitive gifts, there was no divination of genius, no instinctive sympathy with French feeling, but he expressed the people's will by 'deep meditation on its phenomena.' As to the morality of his seizure of power Bagehot hardly discussed it on that level but dismissed the issue with these words: 'Six weeks ago society was living from hand to mouth: now she feels sure of her next meal. And this, in a dozen words, is the real case—the political excuse for Prince Louis Napoleon.'[4] But not even Bagehot could stomach the vindictive confiscation of the Orleanist property and this with Louis Napoleon's dismissal of Monsieur de Morny were major points of criticism.

For Bagehot Louis Napoleon was 'un homme de caractère', by which he meant a man with 'a singular preponderance of peculiar qualities, an accomplished obstinacy, an inveterate fixedness of resolution and idea that enable him to get done what he undertakes'. He had 'the instinctive habit of applied calculation which is essential to a merchant and extremely useful to a statesman'. As one of his primary

---

[3] See *The Economist*, March 26 1870, pp. 379–80.
[4] See Second Letter on the *Coup d'État*.

qualities he singled out his 'restlessness' but this was held in check by an equally pronounced caution. 'To sum up all', he wrote in 1863, 'he has a restless, scheming, brooding *cavernous* mind; daring in idea— hesitating when it comes to action; a singular mixture of tenacity and inconsistency; recoiling before the difficult and hazardous; shrinking from the irrevocable; and certain not to venture on the desperate. For the rest, unusually farseeing and forecasting; thoroughly understanding his nation, his day and his position; and perhaps beyond any other statesman in the world acting with a purpose and on a system.'[5]

As the years passed Bagehot became increasingly critical of the Empire but the seeds of a major indictment were already present in the Letters of 1851. The government of Louis Napoleon did not rest on 'the moral power of civilised opinion'. 'You may put down newspapers,' wrote Bagehot, 'dissolve parliaments, imprison agitators, almost stop conversation, but you can't stop thought.' Louis Napoleon's government would always be uneasy because it would always be conscious of a conspiracy against it, 'a conspiracy of *mind*'.[6] It could not influence thought, because it had stopped the teaching apparatus of government; the newspaper article and the popular speech were both forbidden.[7] As a result of this suppression of discussion the government had no means of ascertaining public opinion. Napoleon ruled over the middle classes, in defiance of the educated classes, and with the support of the lower classes and the army. When a crisis came he would be unable to free himself from domination by the most unthinking section of his subjects.

Another radical defect of the Empire was that it centred on the life of one man or one family.[8] 'It is a system which, by concentrating all power in single persons, makes the future incalculable, destroys all reliance upon it, and so prevents those who trade from being able to borrow, and those who save from being able to lend.' Although despotism favours property it kills credit. The Emperor himself might manage but what would come after him? The problem of all despotisms, declared Bagehot, was simple, 'first *catch* your despot'.

[5] See 'The Emperor of the French,' *The Economist*, November 28 1863, pp. 1322–3.
[6] See 'France or England', *The Economist*, September 5 1863, pp. 982–3.
[7] Even *The Economist* was occasionally banned. 'If *The Economist* would make a revolution, what would not make a revolution?' asked Bagehot. See 'The Gravity and Difficulty of Affairs in France', *The Economist*, August 7 1869, pp. 926–7.
[8] 'Caste may be a bad principle. But no caste is so bad as a caste containing virtually only a single family.' See 'The Collapse of Caesarism', *The Economist*, August 20 1870, pp. 1028–9.

'The present happiness of France,' he concluded in 1865, 'is happiness on a short life lease; it may end with the life of a man who is not young, who has not spared himself, who has always thought, who has always *lived*.'⁹ This ever present danger lay at the centre of the imperialist idea which centred on the personal ability of the sovereign embodying it. The chances of personal ability of this order being transmitted by heredity were slight. Bagehot's mature view of the Empire five years before it crumbled was succinctly expressed in an *Economist* article of 1865: 'It is an admirable government for present and coarse purposes, but a detestable government for future and refined purposes.'¹⁰

Bagehot praised Napoleon for the prosperity he had brought to France and his moves towards freer trade, his principal reservation being the restrictions on credit which the nature of the Empire imposed: Paris 'is a great place of pleasure,—she is an inferior place of lending business'. To the liberal Empire he was sympathetic but detached and a little sceptical of its likelihood of success; yet it was infinitely preferable to the only alternative, a socialist republic, and through *The Economist* Bagehot advised French liberals to accept the shadow of Empire if they could obtain the substance of freedom. He regarded the Emperor's surrender of power as without parallel in history. Whether the liberal Empire would have worked long term will never be known: its life was cut short by the Franco-Prussian war and the disaster of Sedan. Bagehot had thought that liberal Empire might well last for the Emperor's lifetime.

Bagehot and *The Economist* were more critical of the Emperor's foreign policy. It reflected not only national aspirations but the idiosyncratic nature of the Emperor himself. His character meant trouble for England and for Europe. 'He is,' he wrote in 1863, 'essentially *restless*. He has a busy mind rather than a prompt and active will. He broods much; and he broods in silence and in darkness. He is ever full of schemes and projects, which from time to time he throws out to disturb and dismay Europe. Occasionally he puts them forth in a tentative form, and when they have only reached the nebulous and floating stage in his brain. At other times he waits till he has matured them. It is the *incalculable* nature of his restlessness that renders it so peculiarly pernicious. He is for ever breaking out in a fresh place. You never know what he will do or say next. You only know that he will

⁹ See *The Economist*, March 4 1865, pp. 249–50.   ¹⁰ *Ibid.*

not be long quiet. He is, and will always be as long he lives the vol-canic and rémuant element in the cauldron of European politics.'[11] This suited France well since she loved two things above all others 'gain and glory'. 'France demands of him that he shall exhibit her increasingly in the blended attitude and colours of the peacock and the eagle.'[12] The result was that under his leadership France counted for more in Europe than at any time (the reign of Napoleon I apart) since the days of Louis XIV but she was not so much 'influential' as 'disturbing'. The judgment was shrewd and today could be applied with equal justice to the effect of the foreign policy of General de Gaulle. Indeed much of what Bagehot wrote about the France of his day still has relevance today. The parallels between Napoleon III and President de Gaulle are striking.

Bagehot singled out a number of principles which directed imperial foreign policy. A cardinal point was the preservation of the friendship with England: another was support for the principle of nationalities. Bagehot saw that Napoleon was a despot with a difference, quite different from his feudal and legitimist predecessors. 'The old monar-chies claim the obedience of the people upon grounds of duty. They say they have consecrated claims to the loyalty of mankind. They appeal to conscience and even to religion. But Louis Napoleon is a Benthamite despot. He is for the 'greatest happiness of the greatest number'. He says, 'I am where I am, because I know better than anyone else what is good for the French people, and they know that I know better'. He is not the Lord's anointed; he is the people's agent.'[13] Napoleon was the 'crowned democrat' or the 'democratic despot' embodying not constitutional principles but the spirit of 1789. Hence he supported the national movement in Italy but was careful for domestic reasons not to be manoeuvred into a position of hostility to the Papacy. Bagehot praised him for having added two provinces to France (Nice and Savoy) and having created one kingdom (Italy) and one empire (Mexico). Strangely enough for so sharp an observer, Bagehot failed to see the dangers of Napoleon's Mexican adventure, which he mildly commended but which turned out to be a fatal turning point in the fortunes of the régime. He thought that Maximilian would bring stability to Mexico and that the Mexican

---

[11] See *The Economist*, November 28 1863, pp. 1322–3.
[12] See *The Economist*, December 5 1863, pp. 1348–9.
[13] See *The Economist*, March 4 1865, pp. 249–50.

Empire would form a barrier to the expansion of the Union. His judgment seems to have been clouded by the claims of the Mexican bondholders. 'Napoleon,' he wrote in 1863, 'has contrived to obtain a splendid position upon the American continent without incurring all the responsibility a colony would have imposed.'[14]

Bagehot foresaw the possibility of a Franco-Prussian conflict and the threat to the European leadership of France of a united Germany, but felt that Napoleon would tilt the balance towards peace. As early as 1863 he noted that 'in a cause which really touched the German nation, Germany by herself would be at least her equal—perhaps more than her equal'.[15] In the same article he was prophetically pessimistic about the future peace of Europe: 'If she (France) *means* to fight for her old place in Europe,—and at present it looks as if she did mean it,—the life of the present generation will be very different and far sadder than that which we had hoped for it.' When the Franco-Prussian war did break out in 1870 Bagehot, like most contemporaries, held France responsible, knowing nothing of Bismarck's perfidy. He feared for the future of Europe and condemned the declaration of war by France in the strongest terms. 'The most desperate act of a mid-night conspirator,' he wrote in *The Economist*, 'is not morally worse than a breach of the peace of Europe in this manner on a sudden, and with no object which anyone can state.'[16] Nothing that can be said, he added in the same article, 'is adequate to the meaning of this most awful and painful event, and it is most melancholy that with all our boasts of civilisation, and after so many centuries of Christianity, so great a crime (for it is no less) should be possible in the world'. Napoleon, thought Bagehot, had abandoned all his statecraft and staked everything on a gambler's throw.

If the war took Europe by surprise the sudden collapse of the Empire was found even more astonishing. Bagehot too was taken aback by the French disintegration but he was able to explain it. Caesarism contained within itself the seeds of its own decay: it was 'the abuse of the confidence reposed by the most ignorant in a great name to hold at bay the reasoned arguments of men who both know the popular wish and also are sufficiently educated to discuss the best means of gratifying those wishes. A virtually irresponsible power

---

[14] See 'The New Mexican Empire', *The Economist*, August 22 1863, pp. 925–6.
[15] See 'France and The Money Market', *The Economist*, December 14 1867, pp. 1405–6.
[16] See 'The Declaration of War by France', *The Economist*, July 16 1870, pp. 877–8.

obtained by one man from a vague preference of the masses for a particular name,—that is Caesarism, and that is a system which has undoubtedly undergone a sudden and frightful collapse such as none but the very worst hereditary monarchies of Europe have sustained'.[17] The collapse was no accident; it came from the nature of the system itself which provided massive scope for corruption: 'the absence of all intermediate links of moral responsibility and co-operation which such a system necessarily leaves between the throne and the people. It is the very object of the plebiscite to give the Emperor an authority which reduces all intermediate powers to comparative insignificance if they come into collision with his own. Consequently everything must depend on him, and if he be not practically omniscient there is no substantial check at all on the creatures whom he sets up to execute his will. This has evidently been the ruin of the great military power of France'.[18] Bagehot contrasted 'Prussianism' with 'Caesarism'. The King of Prussia, in relation to the army was only the head of a ruling caste, itself bound by strict traditions and etiquettes, the organic growth of many generations. 'Had he been as incompetent and negligent as the Emperor of the French seems to have been, there could still have remained a thousand checks against the dishonesty and corruption which seems to have undermined the French military system.'[19] By contrast the French régime needed 'angels' to make it work. This intrinsic defect was made worse by Napoleon's inability to pick talented ministers, partly Bagehot thought, because of his innate self-distrust, which made him jealous of a capacity greater than his own. Eventually he brought on his own downfall by his inability to remain 'quiet'.

When assessing Napoleon's abilities during his career Bagehot did not know the extent to which during the latter years he was ravaged by disease, but he was able to take this into account when he wrote his obituary in *The Economist* for January 11 1873. In fact this did not radically alter his assessment, a compound of admiration and condemnation. Napoleon he concluded was not a great administrator, or especially farsighted, but he was the most '*in*sighted' of the modern statesmen of France. 'To declare him a great man,' concluded Bagehot, 'may be impossible in the face of his failures, but to declare him a small

[17] See 'The Collapse of Caesarism', *The Economist*, August 20 1870, pp. 1028–9.
[18] *Ibid.*
[19] *Ibid.* In 1865 Bagehot had commented on the corruption of the Empire: 'All that follows from the misuse of the *two* temptations of civilisation, money and women is concentrated round the imperial court'.—*The Economist*, March 4 1865, pp. 249–50.

one is ridiculous. Small men dying in exile do not leave wide gaps in the European political horizon'.[20]

After the collapse of the Empire Bagehot observed curiously the revival of imperialism in France and assessed the chances of the young Napoleon with a cool and unsentimental eye. Yet the bases of his thought on French politics remained unchanged, and in two articles written in *The Economist* in the summer of 1874 the wheel came full circle. The judgments in the articles are substantially identical with those he had passed as an exuberant young man in Paris nearly a quarter of a century before. 'There is something to a Frenchman,' he wrote, 'dearer than free thought, much dearer than parliamentary government, dearer even than successful foreign policy, and that is *fixity*. He wants to be sure that he will have the same government to-morrow as today, next month as this month, next year as this year. He lives in the constant presence of a revolutionary force: he is always imagining an outbreak of it; he has heard of the terrors of '93 and he has seen the losses of the Commune; above all things he desires a sufficient and incessant force which is able to prevent revolutions and make them impossible.'[21]

In the second article, cumbrously but revealingly entitled 'Why an English Liberal may look without disapproval on the progress of Imperialism in France', the echoes of 1851 are even clearer, although the tone is sober. An ordinary Frenchman, he wrote, regards parliamentary government as more unstable than any other. The French are 'naturally excitable, uncontrollable, and sensitive to risk; they have been so used to political misfortune that they are now scared at any shadow. There are generally two simultaneous but contrary excitements; one of the revolutionist who wants to revive the *Commune*: the other of the peasant or the shopkeeper who fears the *Commune*. And the passion of each tends to intensify the passion of the other. These frenzies—for on both sides they are often little better—work on the most inflammable and least stoical of national characters. There is no soil so unsuitable to parliamentary government'.[22] There was nothing inconsistent therefore, Bagehot concluded, with a firm alle-

[20] Looking back to Bagehot's visit to Paris in 1851 it is interesting to recall the fear he expressed at the time in the third letter as to the judgment of Paris on Louis Napoleon: 'Napoleon the Little, as I fear the Parisian multitude may learn to call him.' It was not until the following year 1852 that Victor Hugo published his scathing indictment of Louis Napoleon, entitled 'Napoléon le Petit'.
[21] 'The Prospects of Bonapartism in France', *The Economist*, May 30 1874, pp. 650-1.
[22] See *The Economist*, June 6 1874, pp. 681-3.

giance to parliamentary government, where parliamentary government is possible, and looking on the 'rapid revival of Imperialism in France without dismay and even with satisfaction'.

Yet there was to be no Napoleonic restoration. In 1879 Bonapartist hopes perished for ever when the young and gallant Prince Imperial fell under African spears in an obscure kraal in Zululand. Bagehot himself had already been dead two years. We have had to wait until our own time to see his judgments on France vindicated.

Napoleon III

Introductory note

Charles Louis Napoleon (1808–1873) was born in Paris, the third son of Louis, brother of Napoleon, and of Hortense de Beauharnais. One of his brothers died young, the other died without issue. After the final abdication of Napoleon I, all Bonapartes had been banished from France, and the boy was brought up in Germany by his mother, who was separated from her husband. In 1832, upon the death of the Duke of Reichstadt, the only son of Napoleon I, Louis Napoleon became heir to the Napoleonic tradition and had already developed a romantic Napoleonic liberalism. In 1836 he plotted in Strasbourg in an attempt to gain the throne but was arrested and forced onto a ship which took him to New York; in 1840 he was again arrested for an attempted insurrection in Boulogne, sentenced to life imprisonment, and placed in the fortress of Ham. In 1846 he escaped to England. After the revolution of 1848 he was elected to the National Assembly and in December of the same year to the Presidency of the Republic. His ultimate goal was the re-establishment of the Napoleonic Empire, and he made careful preparations for it during the next few years. Profiting from the growing discredit of parliamentary government, he staged the *coup d'état* of 1851. On December 2 he ordered the arrest of 20,000 of his opponents, dissolved the Assembly, and appealed to the people for virtually dictatorial powers. After a plebiscite on December 20 he was made autocratic President for the next ten years, and a year later another plebiscite made him Napoleon III, Emperor of the French. (Napoleon's only son, who never reigned, was considered to have been Napoleon II.) The new Emperor instituted an authoritarian régime: the press was censored; the legislature was deprived of the right to amend or initiate laws. These repressive measures were counterbalanced by the encouragement of economic prosperity and public works. Napoleon III strove to enhance the prestige of France by successes in foreign affairs. France participated in the Crimean War, 1854–6; in 1859 she assisted Piedmont in the war against Austria, which was a decisive step in Italy's struggle for independence, and France was able to annex Nice and Savoy. A treaty with Britain in 1860 provided for free trade. Napoleon's ambitions were growing, and he envisaged a Catholic empire in the New World, guided by the French.

For this reason he pressed the Mexican expedition of 1863–7, but it ended in complete failure, as did his attempt to intervene in the Polish insurrection of 1863. His Italian policy, moreover, had alienated the Catholics in France, and he was soon faced by a strengthened Prussia. There was a growing opposition to his despotism at home; through the growth of industry and commerce the *bourgeoisie* had become increasingly powerful and the working classes less and less willing to submit to his repressive measures. A third party came into being from the ranks of the government deputies, and Napoleon was obliged to liberalise his régime through parliamentary reform and through concessions with respect to the liberty of the press and public meetings. In 1870 Napoleon gave up most of his power to a ministry under the liberal leader Emile Ollivier but still sought to maintain his rule by an external success and declared war on Prussia in July. On September 2 he was forced to capitulate at Sedan, and the fall of the empire was proclaimed in Paris. Napoleon III was released in March 1871, and settled with his wife and son in England, at Chislehurst, where he died in 1873.

Letters on the French *Coup d'État* of 1851

Letter I.— The Dictatorship of Louis Napoleon[1]

Paris, January 8, 1852.

M Y D E A R S I R,—You have asked me to tell you what I think of French affairs. I shall be pleased to do so; but I ought perhaps to begin by cautioning you against believing, or too much heeding, what I say. However, I do not imagine that I need do so; for with your experience of the public journals, you will be quite aware that it is not difficult to be an 'occasional correspondent.' Have your boots polished in a blacking-shop, and call the interesting officiator an intelligent *ouvrier*; be shaved, and cite the *coiffeur* as 'a person in rather a superior station;' call your best acquaintance 'a well-informed person,' and all others 'persons whom I have found to be occasionally not in error,' and— abroad, at least—you will soon have matter for a newspaper letter. I should quite deceive you if I professed to have made these profound researches; nor, like Sir Francis Head, 'do I no longer know where I am,' because the French President has asked me to accompany him in his ride. My perception of personal locality has not as yet been so tried. I only know what a person who is in a foreign country during

1 These letters were addressed to the editor of the *Inquirer*, and were published in that journal during 1852. They all appeared in Volume XI, 1852. Letter I is found on page 19 (January 10): Letter II on pages 34–5 (January 17); Letter III on pages 51–2 (January 24); Letter IV on pages 67–8 (January 31); Letter V on pages 83–4 (February 7); Letter VI on page 99 (February 14); Letter VII on pages 145 and 147 [*sic*] (March 6). In the case of Letter VII the true pagination should be pages 145–6, but page 146 does not appear in the *Inquirer*. All except Letter V are dated from Paris.
    From the first the editor seems to have been in some doubt about Bagehot's views. The first letter is preceded by the following note: 'We have much pleasure in being able to lay before our readers the First of a Series of Letters from a Correspondent, present in Paris, during the late tragic scenes. It will be seen that his opinion on those events differs widely from our own, but as conveying the impressions of an intelligent unbiased eye-witness, his communication is entitled to attention and serious consideration.' Letter II 'The Morality of the Coup d'État' apparently pleased the editor even less and is preceded by the brusque note: 'The sentiments expressed in this letter render it advisable that we should again declare our own entire dissent from the views of the writer.' Despite this expression of editorial displeasure the entire series of seven letters was published in the *Inquirer*.

an important political catastrophe cannot avoid knowing, what he runs against, what is beaten into him, what he can hardly help hearing, seeing, and reflecting.

That Louis Napoleon has gone to Notre Dame to return thanks to God for the seven millions and odd suffrages of the French people—that he has taken up his abode at the Tuileries, and that he has had new Napoleons coined in his name—that he has broken up the trees of liberty for firewood—that he has erased, or is erasing (for they are many), *Liberté*, *Egalité*, and *Fraternité* from the National buildings,—all these things are so easy and so un-English that I am pretty sure with you they will be thought signs of pompous impotence, and I suppose many people will be inclined to believe the best comment to be the one which I heard—'Mon Dieu il a sauvé la France: la rue du Coq s'appelle maintenant la rue de l'Aigle!'*

I am inclined, however, to imagine that this idea would be utterly erroneous; that, on the contrary, the President is just now, at least, really strong and really popular, that the act of 2nd of December did succeed and is succeeding, that many, that most, of the inferior people do really and sincerely pray *Domine Salvum fac Napoleonem*.

In what I have seen of the comments of the English press upon recent events here, two things are not quite enough kept apart—I mean the temporary dictatorship of Louis Napoleon to meet and cope with the expected crisis of '52, and the continuance of that dictatorship hereafter,—the new, or as it is called, the *Bas*-Empire—in a word, the coming Constitution and questionable political machinery with which 'the nephew of my uncle' is now proposing to endow France. Of course in reality these two things *are* separate. It is one thing to hold that a military rule is required to meet an urgent and temporary difficulty: another to advocate the continuance of such a system, when so critical a necessity no longer exists.

It seems to me, or would seem, if I did not know that I was contradicted both by much English writing and opinion, and also by many most competent judges here, that the first point, the temporary dictatorship, is a tolerably clear case; that it is not to be complicated with the perplexing inquiry what form of government will permanently suit the French people;—that the President was, under the actual

---

* The general reader may not before have read, that the Rue du Coq l'Honoré is an old and well-known street in Paris, and that notwithstanding the substitution of the eagle for cock, as a military emblem, there is no thought of changing its name.

facts of the case, quite justified in assuming the responsibility, though of course I allow that responsibility to be tremendous. My reasons for so believing I shall in this letter endeavour to explain, except that I shall not, I fancy, have room to say much on the moral defensibility or indefensibility of the *coup d'état*; nor do I imagine that you want from me any ethical speculation;—that is manufactured in Printing-house-square; but I shall give the best account I can of the matter-of-fact consequences and antecedents of the New Revolution, of which, in some sense, a resident in France may feel without presumption that he knows something hardly so well known to those at home.

The political justification of Louis Napoleon is, as I apprehend, to be found in the state of the public mind which immediately preceded the *coup d'état*. It is very rarely that a country expects a revolution at a given time; indeed it is perhaps not common for ordinary persons in any country to anticipate a revolution at all; though profound people may speculate, the mass will ever expect to-morrow to be as this day at least, if not more abundant. But once name the day, and all this is quite altered. As a general rule the very people who would be most likely to neglect general anticipation are exactly those most likely to exaggerate the proximate consequences of a certain impending event. At any rate, in France five weeks ago, the tradespeople talked of May '52, as if it were the end of the world. Civilisation and socialism might probably endure, but buying and selling would surely come to an end; in fact, they anticipated a worse era than February '48, when trade was at a standstill so long that it has hardly yet recovered, and when the government stocks fell 40 per cent. It is hardly to be imagined upon what petty details the dread of political dissolution at a fixed and not distant time will condescend to intrude itself. I was present when a huge *Flamande*, in appearance so intrepid that I respectfully pitied her husband, came to ask the character of a *bonne*. I was amazed to hear her say, 'I hope the girl is strong, for when the revolution comes next May, and I have to turn off my helper, she will have enough to do.' It seemed to me that a political apprehension must be pretty general when it affected that most non-speculative of speculations, the *reckoning* of a housewife. With this feeling, everybody saved their money: who would spend in luxuries that which might so soon be necessary and invaluable! This economy made commerce,—especially the peculiarly Parisian trade, which is almost wholly in articles that *can* be spared—worse and worse; the more depressed trade became, the more the traders feared, and the more they feared, the worse all trade inevitably grew.

I apprehend that this feeling extended very generally among all the classes who do not find or make a livelihood by literature or by politics. Among the clever people, who understood the subject, very likely the expectation was extremely different; but among the stupid ones who mind their business, and have a business to mind, there was a universal and excessive tremour. The only notion of '52 was 'on se battra dans la rue.' Their dread was especially of socialism; they expected that the followers of M. Proudhon, who advisedly and expressly maintains 'anarchy' to be the best form of government, would attempt to carry out their theories in action, and that the division between the legislative and executive power would so cripple the party of order as to make their means of resistance for the moment feeble and difficult to use. The more sensible did not, I own, expect the annihilation of mankind: civilisation dies hard; the organised sense in all countries is strong; but they expected vaguely and crudely that the party which in '93 ruled for many months, and which in June '48 fought so fanatically against the infant republic, would certainly make a desperate attack,—*might* for some short time obtain the upper hand. Of course it is now matter of mere argument whether the danger was real or unreal, and it is in some quarters rather the fashion to quiz the past fear, and to deny that any socialists anywhere exist. In spite of the literary exertions of Proudhon and Louis Blanc, in spite of the prison quarrels of Blanqui and Barbés—there are certainly found people that question whether anybody buys the books of the two former, or cares for the incarcerated dissensions of the two latter. But however this may be, it is certain that two days after the *coup d'état* a mass of persons thought it worth while to erect some dozen barricades, and among these, and superintending and directing their every movement there certainly were, for I saw them myself, men whose physiognomy and accoutrements exactly resembled the traditional Montagnard, sallow, stern, compressed, with much marked features, which expressed but resisted suffering, and brooding one-idead thought, that from their youth upward had for ever imagined, like Jonah, that they did well—immensely well, to be angry,—armed to the teeth, and ready, like the soldiers of the first Republic, to use their arms savagely and well in defence of theories broached by a Robespierre, a Blanqui, or a Barbés, gloomy fanatics, *over*-principled ruffians. I may perhaps be mistaken in reading on their features the characters of such men, but I know that when one of them disturbed my superintendence of barricade-making with a stern *allez vous en* it was not too slowly that I departed, for I *felt* that he would rather shoot me than not. Having seen these people, I conceive that they exist.

But supposing that they were all simply fabulous, it would not less be certain that they were believed to be, and to be active; nor would it impair the fact that the quiet classes awaited their onslaught in morbid apprehension, with miserable and craven, and I fear we ought to say, *commercial* disquietude.

You will not be misled by any highflown speculations about liberty or equality. You will, I imagine, concede to me that the first duty of a government is to ensure the security of that industry which is the condition of social life and civilised cultivation;—that especially in so excitable a country as France it is necessary that the dangerous classes should be saved from the strong temptation of long idleness; and that no danger could be more formidable than six months' beggary among the revolutionary *ouvriers*, immediately preceding the exact period fixed by European as well as French opinion for an apprehended convulsion. It is from this state of things, whether by fair means or foul, that Louis Napoleon has delivered France. The effect was magical, like people who have nearly died because it was prophecied they would die at a specified time, and instantly recovered when they found or thought that the time was gone and past. So France, so timorously anticipating the fated revolution, in a moment revived when she found or fancied that it was come and over. Commerce instantly improved; New Year's Day, when all the boulevards are one continued fair, has not (as I am told) been for some years so gay and splendid; people began to buy, and consequently to sell; for though it is quite possible, or even probable, that new misfortunes and convulsions may be in store for the French people, yet no one can say when they will be, and to wait till revolutions be exhausted, is but the best Parisian for our old acquaintance *Rusticus expectat*. Clever people may now prove that the dreaded peril was a simple chimera, but they can't deny that the fear of it was very real or painful, nor can they dispute that in a week after the *coup d'état* it had at once, and apparently for ever, passed away.

I fear it must be said that no legal or constitutional act could have given an equal confidence. What was wanted was the assurance of an audacious government, which would stop at nothing, scruple at nothing, to secure its own power and the tranquillity of the country. That assurance all now have; a man who will in this manner dare to dissolve an assembly constitutionally his superiors, then prevent their meeting by armed force; so well and so sternly repress the first beginning of an outbreak, with so little misgiving assume and exercise sole power,—may have enormous other defects, but is certainly a bold ruler—most probably an unscrupulous one—little likely to flinch from any inferior trial.

Of Louis Napoleon, whose personal qualities are, for the moment, so important, I cannot now speak at length. But I may say that, with whatever other deficiencies, he has one excellent advantage over other French statesmen—he has never been a professor, nor a journalist, nor a promising barrister, nor, by taste, a *littérateur.* He has not confused himself with history; he does not think in leading articles, in long speeches, or in agreeable essays. But he is capable of observing facts rightly, of reflecting on them simply, and acting on them discreetly. And his motto is Danton's, *De l'audace et toujours de l'audace,* and this you know, according to Bacon, in time of revolution, will carry a man far, perhaps even to ultimate victory, and that ever-future millennium '*la consolidation de la France.*'

But on these distant questions I must not touch. I have endeavoured to show you what was the crisis, how strong the remedy, and what the need of a dictatorship. I hope to have convinced you that the first was imminent, the second effectual, and the last expedient. I remain yours,   AMICUS.

Letter II.—The Morality of the *Coup d'État*

Paris, January 15, 1852.

My Dear Sir,—I know quite well what will be said about, or in answer to, my last letter. It will be alleged that I think everything in France is to be postponed to the Parisian commerce—that a Constitution, Equality, Liberty, a Representative Government, are all to be seaside if they interfere even for a moment with the sale of *étrennes* or the manufacture of gimcracks.

I, as you know, hold no such opinions: it would not be necessary for me to undeceive you, who would, I rather hope, never suspect me of *that* sort of folly. But as St. Athanasius aptly observes, 'for the sake of the women who may be led astray, I will this very instant explain my sentiments.'

Contrary to Sheridan's rule, I commence by a concession. I certainly admit, indeed I would, upon occasion, maintain *boutons* and bracelets to be things less important than common law and constitutional action. A *coup d'état* would, I may allow, be mischievously superogatory if it only promoted the enjoyment of what a lady in the highest circles is said to call 'bigotry and virtue.' But the real question is not to be so disposed of. The Parisian trade, the jewellery, the baubles, the silks, the luxuries, which the Exhibition showed us to be the characteristic industry of France, are very dust in the balance if weighed against the hands and arms which their manufacture employs—the industrial habits which their regular sale rewards—the hunger and idle weariness which the certain demand for them prevents. For this is the odd peculiarity of commercial civilisation. The life, the welfare, the existence of thousands depend on their being paid for doing what seems nothing when done. That gorgeous dandies should wear gorgeous studs—that pretty girls should be prettily dressed—that pleasant drawing-rooms should be pleasantly attired—may seem, to people of our age, sad trifling. But grave as we are, we must become graver still when we reflect on the horrid suffering the sudden cessation of large luxurious consumption would certainly create, if we imagine such a city as Lyons to be, without warning, turned out of work, and the population feelingly told 'to cry in the streets when no man regardeth.'

The first duty of society is the preservation of society. By the sound work of old-fashioned generations—by the singular pains-taking of the slumberers in churchyards—by dull care—by stupid industry, a certain social fabric somehow exists—people contrive to go out to their work, and to find work to employ them actually until the evening, body and soul are kept together, and this is what mankind have to show for their six thousand years of toil and trouble.

To keep up this system we must sacrifice everything. Parliaments, liberty, leading articles, essays, eloquence,—all are good, but they are secondary; at all hazards, and if we can, mankind must be kept alive. And observe, as time goes on, this fabric becomes a tenderer and a tenderer thing. Civilisation can't bivouac; dangers, hardships, sufferings, lightly borne by the coarse muscle of earlier times, are soon fatal to noble and cultivated organisation. Women in early ages are masculine, and, as a return match, the men of late years are becoming women. The strong apprehension of a Napoleonic invasion has, perhaps, now caused more substantial misery in England than once the Wars of the Roses.

To apply this 'creed of doctrine' to the condition of France. I do not at all say that, but for the late *coup d'état*, French civilisation would certainly have soon come to a final end. *Some* people might have continued to take their meals. Even socialism would hardly abolish *eau sucrée*. But I do assert that, according to the common belief of the common people, their common comforts were in considerable danger. The debasing torture of acute apprehension was eating into the crude pleasure of stupid lives. No man liked to take a long bill; no one could imagine to himself what was coming. Fear was paralysing life and labour, and as I said at length, in my last, fear, so intense, whether at first reasonable or unreasonable, will, ere long, invincibly justify itself. May, 1852, would, in all likelihood, have been an evil and bloody time if it had been preceded by six months' famine among the starvable classes.

At present all is changed. Six weeks ago society was living from hand to mouth: now she feels sure of her next meal. And this, in a dozen words, is the real case—the political excuse for Prince Louis Napoleon. You ask me, or I should not do so, to say a word or two on the moral question and the oath. You are aware how limited my means of doing so are. I have forgotten Paley, and have never read the casuists. But it certainly does not seem to me proved or clear, that a man who has sworn, even in the most solemn manner, to see another drown, is therefore quite bound, or even at liberty, to stand placidly on the bank. What ethical philosopher has demonstrated this? Coleridge said it was difficult to advance a new error in morals,—yet this, I think, would be one; and the keeping of oaths is peculiarly a point of mere science, for Christianity in terms, at least, only forbids them all. And supposing I am right, such certainly was the exact position of Louis Napoleon. He saw society, I will not say dying or perishing— for I hate unnecessarily to overstate any point,—in danger of incurring extreme and perhaps lasting calamities,—and calamities, likely not only to impair the happiness, but moreover to debase the character of the French nation, and these calamities he could prevent. Now who has shown that ethics require of him to have held his hand?

The severity with which the riot was put down on the first Thursday in December has, I observe, produced an extreme effect in England; with our happy exemption from martial bloodshed, it must, of course, do so. But better one *émeute* now than many in May, be it ever remembered. There are things more demoralising than death, and among these is the sickly-apprehensive suffering for long months of an entire people.

Of course you understand that I am not holding up Louis Napoleon as a complete standard either of ethical scrupulosity or disinterested devotedness; veracity has never been the family failing—for the great Emperor was a still greater liar. And he has been long playing what, morality apart, is the greatest political misfortune to any statesman— a visibly selfish game. Very likely, too, the very high heroes of history —a Washington, an Aristides, by Carlyle profanely called 'favourites of Dryasdust,' would have extricated the country more easily, and perhaps more completely, from its scrape. Their ennobling rectitude would have kept M. de Girardin consistent, and induced M. Thiers to vote for the revision of the Constitution; and even though, as of old, the mountain were deafer than the uncharmed adder, a sufficient number of self-seeking Conservatives might have been induced by perfect confidence in a perfect president, to mend a crotchety performance, that was visibly ruining, what the poet calls, 'The ever-ought-to-be-conserved-thing,' their country.

I remember reading, several years ago, an article in the *Westminster Review*, on the lamented Armand Carrel, in which the author, well known to be one of our most distinguished philosophers, took occasion to observe, that what the French most wanted was, '*Un homme de caractère.*' Everybody is aware—for all except myself know French quite perfectly—that this expression is not by any means equivalent to our common phrase, a 'man of character,' or 'respectable individual,' it does not at all refer to mere goodness; it is more like what we sometimes say of an eccentric country gentleman, 'He is a character;' for it denotes a singular preponderance of peculiar qualities, an accomplished obstinacy, an inveterate fixedness of resolution and idea that enables him to get done what he undertakes. The Duke of Wellington is '*par excellence, homme de caractère;*' Lord Palmerston rather so; Mr. Cobden a little; Lord John not at all. Now exactly this, beyond the immense majority of educated men, Louis Napoleon is, as a pointed writer describes him;—'the President is a superior man, but his superiority is of the sort that is hidden under a dubious exterior; his life is entirely internal; his speech does not betray his inspiration; his gesture does not copy his audacity; his look does not reflect his ardour; his step does not reveal his resolution; his whole mental nature is in some sort repressed by his physical: he thinks and does not discuss; he decides and does not deliberate; he acts without agitation; he speaks, and assigns no reason; his best friends are unacquainted with him; he obtains their confidence, but never asks it.' Also his whole nature is, and has been, absorbed in the task which he has undertaken. For many months, his habitual expression has been exactly that of a gambler who is playing for his highest and last stake; in society it is said to be the same—a general and diffusive politeness, but an ever-ready reflection and a constant reserve. His great qualities are rather peculiar. He is not like his uncle, a creative genius, who will leave behind him social institutions, such as those which nearly alone, in this changeful country, seem to be always exempt from every change; he will suggest little; he has hardly an organising mind; but he will coolly estimate his own position and that of France; he will observe all dangers and compute all chances. He can act—he can be idle: he may work what is; he may administer the country. Any how—*il fera son possible*, and you know, in the nineteenth century, how much and how rare that is.

I see many people are advancing beautiful but untrue ethics about his private character. Thus I may quote as follows from a very estimable writer:—'On the 15th of October, he requested his passports and left Aremberg for London. In this capital he remained from the end of 1838, to the month of August 1840. In these twenty months, instead of learning to command armies and govern empires, his days and nights, when not given to frivolous pleasures, were passed on the turf, in the betting-room, or in clubs where high play and desperate stakes roused the jaded energy of the *blasé* gambler.'*

The notion of this gentleman clearly is, that a betting man can't in nature be a good statesman; that horse-racing is providentially opposed to political excellence; that 'by an interesting illustration of the argument from design, we notice an antithesis alike marvellous and inevitable,' between turf and tariffs. But, setting Paley for a moment apart, how is a man, by circumstances excluded from military and political life, and by birth from commercial pursuits, really and effectually to learn administration. Mr. Kirwan imagines that he should read all through Burke, common-place Tacitus, collate Cicero, and annotate Montesquieu. Yet take an analogous case. Suppose a man, shut out from trading life, is to qualify himself for the practical management of a counting-house. Do you fancy he will do it 'by a judicious study of the principles of political economy,' and by elaborately re-reading Adam Smith and John Mill? He had better be at Newmarket, and devote his *heures perdues* to the Oaks and the St. Leger. He may learn there what he will never acquire from literary study—the instinctive habit of applied calculation, which is essential to a merchant and extremely useful to a statesman. Where, too, did Sir Robert Walpole learn business, or Charles Fox, or anybody in the 18th century? And after all, M. Michel de Bourges gave the real solution of the matter. 'Louis Napoleon,' said the best orator of the Mountain, 'may have had rather a stormy youth—(laughter). But don't suppose that any one in all France imagines you, you *Messieurs*, of the immaculate majority, to be the least better (sensation). I am not speaking to saints —(uproar).' If compared with contemporary French statesmen, and the practical choice is between him and them, the President will not seem what he appears when measured by the notions of a people who exact at least from inferior functionaries *a rigid decorum in the pettiest details of their private morals.* I have but one last point to make about this *coup d'état*, and then I will release you from my writing.

* A. V. Kirwan, Esq., barrister-at-law, in *Fraser's Magazine*.

I do not know whether you in England rightly realise the French socialism.

Take, for instance, M. Proudhon, who is perhaps their ideal and perfect type. He was *représentant de la Seine* in the late Assembly, elected, what is not unimportant, after the publication of his books and on account of his opinions. In his 'Confessions d'un Révolutionnaire,' a very curious book—for he writes extremely well—after maintaining that our well-known but, as we imagine, advanced friends, Ledru Rollin, and Louis Blanc, and Barbês, and Blanqui are all *réactionnaires*, and clearly showing, to the grief of mankind, that once the legislator of the Luxembourg wished to preserve 'equilibrium,' and the author of the provincial circulars to maintain the 'tranquillity,' he gives the following *bona fide* and amusing account of his own investigations:—'I commenced my task of solitary conspiracy by the study of the socialisms of antiquity, necessary, in my judgment, to determine the law, whether practical or theoretical, of progress. These socialisms I found in the Bible. A memoir on the institution of the Sabbath—considered with regard to morals, to health, and in its relation to the family and the city—procured for me a bronze medal from my academy. From the faith in which I had been reared, I had precipitated myself head-long, head-foremost, into the pure reason, and already, what was wonderful and a good omen, when I made Moses a philosopher and a socialist, I was greeted with applause. If I am now in error, the fault is not merely mine. Was there ever a similar seduction?

'But I studied, above all, with a view to action. I cared little for academical laurels. I had no leisure to become *savant*, yet less a *litterateur* or an archæologist. I began immediately upon political economy.

'I had assumed as the rule of my investigations that every principle which, pushed to its consequences, should end in a contradiction, must be considered false and null; and that if this principle had been developed into an institution, the institution itself must be considered as factitious, as utopian.

'Furnished with this criterion, I chose for the subject of investigation what I found in society the most ancient, the most respectable, the most universal, the least controverted,—property. Everybody knows what happened; after a long, a minute, and, above all, an impartial analysis, I arrived, as an algebraist, guided by his equations, to this surprising conclusion. Property, consider it as you will,—refer it to what principle you may, is a contradictory idea; and as the denial of property carries with it of necessity that of authority, I deduced immediately from my first axiom also this corollary, not less paradoxical, the true form of government is *anarchy*. Lastly, finding by a mathematical demonstration that no amelioration in the economy of society could be arrived at by its natural constitution, or without the concurrence and reflective adhesion of its members; observing, also, that there is a definite epoch in the life of societies, in which their progress, at first unreflecting, requires the intervention of the free reason of man, I concluded that this spontaneous and impulsive force (*cette force d'impulsion spontaneé*), which we call Providence, is not everything in the affairs of this world: from that moment, without being an Atheist, I ceased to worship God. He'll get on without your so doing, said to me one day the *Constitutionnel*. Well; perhaps he may.' These theories have been expanded into many and weary volumes, and condensed into the famous phrase, 'La Proprieté c'est le vol;' and have procured their author, in his own sect, reputation and authority.

The *Constitutionnel* had another hit against M. Proudhon, a day or two ago. They presented their readers with two decrees in due official form (the walls were at the moment covered with those of the 2nd of December), as the last ideal of what the straitest sect of the socialists particularly desire. It was as follows:—'Nothing any longer exists. Nobody is charged with the execution of the aforesaid decree. Signed, Vacuum.'

Such is the speculation of the new reformers—what their practice would be I can hardly tell you. My feeble income does not allow me to travel to the Basses Alpes and really investigate the subject; but if one quarter of the stories in circulation are in the least to be believed (we are quite dependent on oral information, for the government papers deal in asterisks and 'details unfit for publication,' and the rest are devoted to the state of the navy, and say nothing) the atrocities rival the nauseous corruption of what our liberal essayist calls 'Jacobin carrion,' the old days of Carrier and Barère. This is what people here are afraid of; and that is why I write such things,—and not to horrify you, or amuse you, or bore you—anything rather than that; and they think themselves happy in finding a man who, with or without whatever other qualities or defects, will keep them from the vaunted millennium, and much-expected *Jacquerie*. I hope you think so too—and that I am not, as they say in my native Tipperary, 'Whistling jigs to a milestone.' I am, my dear sir, yours truly,

AMICUS.

P.S.—You will perhaps wish me to say something on the great event of this week, the exile of the more dangerous members of the late Assembly, and the transportation of the socialists to Cayenne. Both measures were here expected; though I think that both lists are more numerous than was anticipated; but no one really knew what would be done by this silent government. You will laugh at me when I tell you that both measures have been well received; but, properly limited and understood, I am persuaded that the fact is so. Of course among the friends of exiled *Représentants*, among the *littérateurs* throughout whose ranks these measures are intended to 'strike terror and inspire respect,' you would hear that there never was such tyranny since the beginning of mankind. But among the mass of the industrious classes—between whom and the politicians there is internecine war— I fancy that on turning the conversations to either of the most recent events, you would hear something of this sort:—'*Ca ne m'occupe pas*' 'What is that *to me.*' '*Je suis pour la tranquillité, moi.*' 'I sold four brooches yesterday.' The socialists who have been removed from prison to the colony, it is agreed were 'pestilent fellows perverting the nation,' and forbidding to pay tribute to M. Bonaparte. Indeed they can hardly expect commercial sympathy. 'Our national honour rose—our stocks fell' is Louis Blanc's perpetual comment on his favourite events, and it is difficult to say which of its two clauses he dwells upon with the intenser relish. It is generally thought by those who think about the matter, that both the transportation, and, in all cases, certainly, the exile will only be a temporary measure, and that the great mass of the people in both lists will be allowed to return to their homes when the present season of extreme excitement has passed over. Still I am not prepared to defend the *number* of the transportations. That strong measures of the sort were necessary I make no doubt. If socialism exist, and the fear of it exist, something must be done to re-assure the people. You will understand that it is not a judicial proceeding either in essence or in form; it is not to be considered as a punishment for what men have done, but as a perfect precaution against what they may do. Certainly it is to be regretted that the cause of order is so weak as to need such measures; but if it *is* so weak, the government must no doubt take them. Of course however 'our brethren' who are retained in such numbers to write down Prince Louis, are quite right to use without stint or stopping this most un-English proceeding; it is their case, and you and I from old misdeeds know pretty well how it is to be managed. There will be no imputation of reasonable or humane motives to the government, and no examination of the existing state of France;—let both these come from the other side—but elegiac eloquence is inexhaustibly exuded— the cruel corners of history are ransacked for petrifying precedents— and I observe much excellent weeping on the Cromwellian deportations and the ten years' exile of Madame de Staël. But after all they have missed the tempting parallel—I mean the 'rather long' proscription-list which Octavius—*l'ancien neveu de l'ancien oncle'*— concocted with Mark Antony in the marshes of Bononia, and whereby they thoroughly purged old Rome of its turbulent and revolutionary elements. I suspect our estimable contemporaries regret to remember of how much good order, long tranquillity, *'beata pleno copia cornu'* and other many 'little comforts' to the civilised world that very 'strong' proceeding, whether in ethics justifiable or not, certainly was in fact the beginning and foundation.

The fate of the African generals is much to be regretted, and the government will incur much odium if the exile of General Changarnier is prolonged any length of time. He is doubtless 'dangerous' for the moment, for his popularity with the army is considerable, and he divides the party of order; he is also a practical man and an unpleasant enemy, but he is much respected and little likely (I fancy) to attempt anything against any settled government.

As for M. Thiers and M. Emile de Girardin—the ablest of the exiles —I have heard no one pity them; they have played a selfish game— they have encountered a better player—they have been beaten—and this is the whole matter. You will remember that it was the adhesion of these two men that procured for M. Bonaparte a large part of his *first* six millions.[1] M. de Girardin, whom General Cavaignac had discreetly imprisoned and indiscreetly set free, wrote up the 'opposition candidate' daily, in the *Presse*, (he has since often and often tried to write him down,) and M. Thiers was his privy councillor. *'Mon cher Prince,'* they say, said the latter, 'your address to the people won't

---

[1] Votes.—Ed.

do at all. I'll get one of the *rédacteurs* of the *Constitutionnel* to draw you up something tolerable.' You remember the easy patronage with which Cicero speaks in his letter of the 'boy' that was outwitting him all the while. But, however, observe I do not at all, notwithstanding my Latin, insinuate or assert that Louis Napoleon, though a considerable man, is exactly equal to keep the footsteps of Augustus. A feeble parody may suffice for an inferior stage and not too gigantic generation. Now I really *have* done.

Letter III.—On the New Constitution of France, and the Aptitude of the French Character for National Freedom

Paris, January 20, 1852.

MY DEAR SIR,—We have now got our Constitution. The Napoleonic era has commenced; the term of the dictatorship is fixed, and the consolidation of France is begun. You will perhaps anticipate from the conclusion of the last letter, that, *apropos* of this great event, I should gratify you with bright anticipations of an Augustan age, and a quick revival of Catonic virtue, with an assurance that the night is surely passed and the day altogether come, with a solemn invocation to the rising luminary, and an original panegyric on the 'golden throned morning.'

I must always regret to disappoint any one; but I feel obliged to entertain you instead with torpid philosophy, constitutional details, and a dull disquisition on national character.

The details of the new institutions you will have long ago learnt from the daily papers. I believe they may be fairly and nearly accurately described as the Constitution of the Consulate, *minus* the ideas of the man that made it. You will remember that, besides the First Magistrate, the Senate, the House of Representatives, the Council of State, (which we may call, in legal language, the 'common form' of continental constitution), the ingenious Abbe Sieyés had devised some four principal peculiarities, which were to be remembered to all time as masterpieces of political invention. These were the utter inaction of the First Magistrate, copied, as I believe, from the English Constitution—the subordination to him of two Consuls, one to administer peace and the other war, who were intended to be the real hands and arms of the government—the silence of the Senate—the double and very peculiar election of the House of Representatives. Napoleon the Great, as we are now to speak, struck out the first of these, being at the moment working some fifteen hours a day at the reorganisation of France. He said plainly and rather sternly that he had no intention of doing

45

nothing—the *ideologue* went to the wall—the 'excellent idea' put forth in happy forgetfulness of real facts and real people was instantly abandoned—for the Grand Elector was substituted a First Consul, who, so far from being nothing, was very soon the whole government. Napoleon the Little, as I fear the Parisian multitude may learn to call him, has effaced the other three 'strokes of statesmanship.' The new Constitution of France is exactly the 'common form' of political conveyancing, *plus* the *Idée Napoléonienne* of an all-suggesting and all-administering mind.

I have extremely little to tell you about its reception: it has made no 'sensation,' not so much as even the 'fortified camps' which his grace is said to be devising for the defence of our own London. Indeed, *'Il a peur'* is a very common remark (conceivable to everybody who knows 'the Duke,') and it would seem even a refreshing alleviation of their domestic sorrows. In fact, home politics are not now *the* topic; geography and the state of foreign institutions are not, indeed, the true Parisian line—but it has, in fine, been distinctly discovered that there are no *salons* in Cayenne, which, once certain, the logical genius of the nation, with incredible swiftness, deduced the clear conclusion that it was better not to go there. Seriously, I fancy—for I have no data on which to found real knowledge of so delicate a point— the new Constitution is regarded merely as what Father Newman would call a 'preservative addition' or a 'necessary development,' essential to the 'chronic continuance' of the Napoleonic system; for the moment the mass of the people wish the President to govern them, but they don't seem to me to care how. The political people, I suppose, hate it, because for some time it will enable him, if not shot, to govern effectually. I say if not shot—for people are habitually recounting under their breath some new story of an attempt at assassination, which the papers suppress. I am inclined to think that these rumours are pure lies; but they show the feeling. You know, according to the Constitution of 1848, the President would now be a mere outlaw, and whoever finds him may slay him if he can. It is true that the elaborate masterpiece of M. Marrast is already fallen into utter oblivion, (it is no more remembered than yesterday's *Times*, or the political institutions of Saxon Mercia); but nevertheless such, according to the antediluvian *régime*, would be the law, and it is possible that a mindful Montagnard may upon occasion recall even so insignificant a circumstance.

I have a word to say on the Prologue of the President. When I first began to talk politics with French people I was much impressed by the fact to which he has there drawn attention. You know that all such conversation, when one of the interlocutors is a foreigner, speaking slowly and but imperfectly the language of the country in which he is residing, is pretty much in the style of that excellent work which was the terror of our childhood—Joyce's 'Scientific Dialogues' —wherein, as you may remember, an accomplished tutor, with a singular gift of scholastic improvisation, instructs a youthful pupil exceedingly given to feeble questions and auscultatory repose. Now when I began in Parisian society thus to enact the *rôle* of 'George' or 'Caroline,' I was, I repeat, much struck with the fact that the Emperor had done everything: to whatever subject my diminutive enquiry related the answer was nearly universally the same—an elegy on Napoleon. Nor is this exactly absurd; for whether or not 'the nephew' is right in calling the uncle the greatest of modern statesmen, he is indisputably the modern statesman who has found the greatest number of existing institutions. In the pride of philosophy and in the madness of an hour, the Constituent Assembly and the Convention swept away not only the monstrous abuses of the old *régime*, but that *régime* itself—its essence and its mechanism, utterly and entirely. They destroyed whatever they could lay their hands on. The consequence was certain—when they tried to construct they found they had no materials. They left a vacuum. No greater benefit could have been conferred on politicians gifted with the creative genius of Napoleon. It was like the fire of London to Sir Christopher Wren. With a fertility of invention and an obstinacy in execution, equalling, if not surpassing, those of Cæsar and Charlemagne, he had before him an open stage, more clear and more vast than in historical times fortune has ever offered to any statesman. He was nearly in the position of the imagined legislator of the Greek legends and the Greek philosophers—he could enact any law, and rescind any question. Accordingly, the educational system, the banking system, the financial system, the municipal system, the administrative system, the civil legislation, the penal legislation, the commercial legislation, (besides all manner of secondary creations—public buildings and public institutions without number), all date from the time, and are more or less deeply inscribed with the genius, the firm will, and unresting energies of Napoleon. And this, which is the great strength of the present President, is the great difficulty—I fear the insurmountable difficulty—in the way of Henry the Fifth. The first revolution is to the French what the deluge is to the rest of mankind; the whole system then underwent an entire change. A French politician will no more cite as authority the domestic policy of Colbert or Louvois than we should think of going for ethics and æsthetics to the bigamy of Lamech, or the musical accomplishments of Tubal Cain. If the Comte de Chambord be (as it is quite on the cards that he may be), within a few years restored, he must govern by the instrumentality of laws and systems, devised by the politicians whom he execrates and denounces, and devised, moreover, often enough, especially to keep out him and his. It is difficult to imagine that a strong government can be composed of materials so inharmonious. Meanwhile, to the popular imagination, 'the Emperor' is the past; the House of Bourbon is as historical as the House of Valois: a peasant is little oftener reminded of the 'third dynasty' than of the long-haired kings.

In discussing any Constitution, there are two ideas to be first got rid of. The first is the idea of our barbarous ancestors—now happily banished from all civilised society, but still prevailing in old manor-houses, in rural parsonages, and other curious repositories of mouldering ignorance, and which in such arid solitudes is thus expressed 'Why can't they have Kings, Lords and Commons *like we have*? What fools foreigners are.' The second pernicious mistake is, like the former, seldom now held upon system, but so many hold it in bits and fragments, and without system, that it is still rather formidable. I allude to the old idea which still here creeps out in conversation, and sometimes in writing,—that politics are simply a subdivision of immutable ethics; that there are certain rights of men in all places and all times, which are the sole and sufficient foundation of all government, and that accordingly a single stereotype government is to make the tour of the world—and you have no more right to deprive a Dyak of his vote in a 'possible' Polynesian parliament, than you have to steal his mat.

Burke first taught the world at large, in opposition to both, and especially to the latter of these notions, that politics are made of time and place—that institutions are shifting things, to be tried by and adjusted to the shifting conditions of a mutable world—that, in fact, politics are but a piece of business—to be determined in every case by the exact exigencies of that case: in plain English—by sense and circumstances.

This was a great step in political philosophy—though it *now* seems the events of 1848 have taught thinking persons (I think) further. They have enabled us to say that of all these circumstances so affecting political problems, by far and out of all question the most important is *national character*. In that year the same experiment—the experiment, as its friends say, of Liberal and Constitutional Government—as its enemies say of Anarchy and Revolution—was tried in every nation of Europe—with what varying futures and differing results! The effect has been to teach men—not only speculatively to know, but practically to feel, that no absurdity is so great as to imagine the same species of institutions suitable or possible for Scotchmen and Sicilians, for Germans and Frenchmen, for the English and the Neapolitans. With a well-balanced national character (we now know) liberty is a stable thing. A really practical people will work in political business, as in private business, almost the absurdest, the feeblest, the most inconsistent set of imaginable regulations. Similarly, or rather reversely, the best institutions will not keep right a nation that *will* go wrong. Paper is but paper, and no virtue is to be discovered in it to retain within due boundaries the undisciplined passions of those who have never set themselves seriously to restrain them. In a word—as people of 'large roundabout common sense' will (as a rule) somehow get on in life—(no matter what their circumstances or their fortunes)—so a nation which applies good judgment, forbearance, a rational and compromising habit to the management of free institutions, will certainly succeed; while the more eminently gifted national character will but be a source and germ of endless and disastrous failure, if, with whatever other eminent qualities, it be deficient in these plain, solid, and essential requisites.

The formation of *this* character is one of the most secret of marvellous mysteries. Why nations have the character we see them to have is, speaking generally, as little explicable to our shallow perspicacity, as why individuals, our friends or our enemies, for good or for evil, have the character which they have; why one man is stupid and another clever—why another volatile and a fourth consistent—this man by instinct generous, that man by instinct niggardly. I am not speaking of actions, you observe, but of tendencies and temptations. These and other similar problems daily crowd on our observation in millions and millions, and only do not puzzle us because we are too familiar with their difficulty to dream of attempting their solution.

Only this much is most certain, all men and all nations have a character, and that character, when once taken, is, I do not say unchangeable —religion modifies it, catastrophe annihilates it—but the least changeable thing in this ever-varying and changeful world. Take the soft mind of the boy, and (strong and exceptional aptitudes and tendencies excepted) you may make him merchant, barrister, butcher, baker, surgeon, or apothecary. But once make him an apothecary, and he will never afterwards bake wholesome bread—make him a butcher, and he will kill too extensively, even for a surgeon—make him a barrister, and he will be dim on double entry, and crass on bills of lading. Once conclusively form him to one thing, and no art and no science will ever twist him to another. Nature, says the philosopher, has no Delphic daggers!—no men or maids of all work—she keeps one being to one pursuit—to each is a single choice afforded, but no more again thereafter for ever. And it is the same with nations. The Jews of to-day are the Jews in face and form of the Egyptian sculptures; in character they are the Jews of Moses—the negro is the negro of a thousand years—the Chinese, by his own account, is the mummy of a million. 'Races and their varieties,' says the historian, 'seem to have been created with an inward *nisus* diminishing with the age of the world.' The people of the South are yet the people of the South, fierce and angry as their summer sun—the people of the North are still cold and stubborn like their own North wind—the people of the East 'mark not, but are still'—the people of the West 'are going through the ends of the earth, and walking up and down in it.' The fact is certain, the cause beyond us. The subtle system of obscure causes, whereby sons and daughters resemble not only their fathers and mothers, but even their great-great-grandfathers and their great-great-grandmothers, may very likely be destined to be very inscrutable. But, as the fact is so, so moreover, in history, nations have one character, one set of talents, one list of temptations, and one duty, to use the one and get the better of the other. There are breeds in the animal man just as in the animal dog. When you hunt with greyhounds and course with beagles, then, and not till then, may you expect the inbred habits of a thousand years to pass away, that Hindoos can be free, or that Englishmen will be slaves.

I need not prove to you that the French *have* a national character. Nor need I try your patience with a likeness of it. I have only to examine whether it be a fit basis for national freedom. I fear you will laugh when I tell you what I conceive to be about the most essential mental quality for a free people, whose liberty is to be progressive, permanent, and on a large scale; it is much *stupidity*. I see you are surprised—you are going to say to me, as Socrates did to Polus, 'My young friend, *of course* you are right; but will you explain what you mean—as yet you are not intelligible.' I will do so as well as I can, or endeavour to make good what I say—not by an *a priori* demonstration of my own, but from the details of the present, and the facts of history. Not to begin by wounding any present susceptibilities, let me take the Roman character—for, with one great exception,—I need not say to whom I allude—they are the great political people of history. Now, is not a certain dullness their most visible characteristic? What is the history of their speculative mind?—a blank. What their literature?— a copy. They have left not a single discovery in any abstract science; not a single perfect or well-formed work of high imagination. The Greeks, the perfection of narrow and accomplished genius, bequeathed to mankind the ideal forms of self-idolising art—the Romans imitated and admired; the Greeks explained the laws of nature—the Romans wondered and despised; the Greeks invented a system of numerals second only to that now in use—the Romans counted to the end of their days with the clumsy apparatus which we still call by their name; the Greeks made a capital and scientific calendar—the Romans began their month when the Pontifex Maximus happened to spy out the new moon. Throughout Latin literature, this is the perpetual puzzle—Why are we free and they slaves? we prætors and they barbers? Why do the stupid people always win, and the clever people always lose? I need not say that, in real sound stupidity, the English are unrivalled. You'll hear more wit, and better wit, in an Irish street row than would keep Westminster Hall in humour for five weeks. Or take Sir Robert Peel—our last great statesman, the greatest member of parliament that ever lived, an absolutely perfect transacter of public business—the type of the nineteenth century Englishman as Sir Robert Walpole was of the eighteenth. Was there ever such a dull man? Can any one, without horror, foresee the reading of his memoirs? A *clairvoyante*, with the book shut, may get on; but who now, in the flesh, will ever endure the open *vision* of endless recapitulation of interminable Hansard. Or take Mr. Tennyson's inimitable description:—

> No little lily-handed baronet he,
> A great broad-shouldered genial Englishman,
> A lord of fat prize oxen and of sheep,

> A raiser of huge melons and of pine
> A patron of some thirty charities
> A pamphleteer on guano and on grain,
> A quarter-sessions chairman, abler none.

Whose company so soporific? His talk is of truisms and bullocks; his head replete with rustic visions of mutton and turnips, and a cerebral edition of Burn's 'Justice!' Notwithstanding, he is the salt of the earth, the best of the English breed. Who is like him for sound sense? But I must restrain my enthusiasm. You don't want me to tell you that a Frenchman—a real Frenchman—can't be stupid; *esprit* is his essence, wit is to him as water, *bons-mots* as *bon-bons*. He reads and he learns by reading; levity and literature are essentially his line. Observe the consequence. The outbreak of 1848 was accepted in every province in France; the decrees of the Parisian mob were received and registered in all the municipalities of a hundred cities; the Revolution ran like the fluid of the telegraph down the *Chemin de fer du Nord*; it stopped at the Belgian frontier. Once brought into contact with the dull phlegm of the stupid Fleming, the poison was powerless. You remember what the Norman butler said to Wilkin Flammock, of the fulling mills, at the castle of the Garde Doloureuse, 'that draught which will but warm your Flemish hearts, will put wildfire into Norman brains; and what may only encourage your countrymen to man the walls, will make ours fly over the battlements.' *Les braves Belges*, I make no doubt, were quite pleased to observe what folly was being exhibited by those very clever French, whose tongue they want to speak, and whose literature they try to imitate. In fact, what we opprobriously call stupidity, though not an enlivening quality in common society, is nature's favourite resource for preserving steadiness of conduct and consistency of opinion. It enforces concentration; people who learn slowly, learn only what they must. The best security for people's doing their duty is that they should not know anything else to do; the best security for fixedness of opinion is that people should be incapable of comprehending what is to be said on the other side. These valuable truths are no discoveries of mine. They are familiar enough to people whose business it is to know them. Hear what a dense and aged attorney says of your peculiarly promising barrister:—'Sharp! oh yes, yes! he's too sharp by half. He is not *safe*; not a minute, isn't that young man.' 'What style sir,' asked of an East India Director some youthful aspirant for literary renown, 'is most to be preferred in the composition of official dispatches?' 'My good fellow,' responded the ruler of Hindostan, 'the style *as we* like is the Humdrum.' I extend this, and advisedly maintain that nations, just as individuals, may be too clever to be practical, and not dull enough to be free.

How far this is true of the French, and how far the gross deficiency I have indicated is modified by their many excellent qualities, I hope at a future time to inquire.

I am, my dear sir, yours truly,

AMICUS.

Letter IV.—On the Aptitude of the French Character for National Self-Government

Paris, January 29, 1852.

My Dear Sir,—There is a simple view of the subject on which I wrote to you last week that I wish to bring under your notice. The experiment (as it is called) of establishing political freedom in France is now sixty years old; and the best that we can say of it is, that it is an experiment still. There have been perhaps half-a-dozen new beginnings—half-a-dozen complete failures. I am aware that each of these failures can be excellently explained—each beginning shown to be quite necessary. But there are certain reasonings which, though outwardly irrefragable, the crude human mind is always most unwilling to accept. Among these are different and subtle explications of several apparently similar facts. Thus, to choose an example suited to the dignity of my subject, when a gentleman from town takes a day's shooting in the country, and should chance (as has happened) at first going off, to miss some six times running, how luminously soever he may 'explain' each failure as it occurs, 'however expanded a view' he may take of the whole series, whatever popular illustrations of projectile philosophy he may propound to the bird-slaying agriculturists—the impression on the crass intelligence of the gamekeeper will quite clearly be 'He beint noo shot homsoever—aint thicker.' Similarly, to compare small things with great, when I myself read in Thiers and the many other philosophic historians of this literary country, various and excellent explanations of their many mischances;—of the failure of the Constitution of 1791—of the Constitution of the year 3—of the Constitution of the year 5—of the *charte*—of the system of 1830—and now we may add, of the second republic—the annotated constitution of M. Dupin,—I can't help feeling a suspicion lingering in my crude and uncultivated intellect—that some common principle is at work in all and each of these several cases—that over and above all odd mischances, so many bankruptcies a little suggest an unfitness

54

for the trade; that besides the ingenious reasons of ingenious gentle-men—there is some lurking quality, or want of a quality, in the national character of the French nation which renders them but poorly adapted for the form of freedom and constitution which they have so often, with such zeal and so vainly, attempted to establish.

In my last letter I suggested that this might be what I ventured to call a 'want of stupidity.' I will now try to describe what I mean in more accurate, though not, perhaps, more intelligible words.

I believe that I am but speaking what is agreed on by competent observers, when I say that the essence of the French character is a certain mobility; that is, as it has been defined, a certain 'excessive sensibility to *present* impressions,' which is sometimes 'levity,'—for it issues in a postponement of seemingly fixed principles to a momentary temptation or a transient whim; sometimes 'impatience'—as leading to an exaggerated sense of existing evils; often 'excitement,'—a total absorption in existing emotion; oftener 'inconsistency'—the sacrifice of old habits to present emergencies; and yet other unfavourable qualities. But it has also its favourable side. The same man who is drawn aside from old principles by small pleasures, who can't bear pain, who forgets his old friends when he ceases to see them, who is liable in time of excitement to be a one-idea-being, with no conception of anything but the one exciting object; yet who nevertheless is apt to have one idea to-day and quite another to-morrow (and this, and more than this, may I fancy be said of the ideal Frenchman) may and will have the subtlest perception of existing niceties, the finest susceptibility to social pleasure, the keenest tact in social polite-ness, the most consummate skilfulness in the details of action and administration,—may in short be the best companion, the neatest man of business, the lightest *homme de salon*, the acutest diplomat of the existing world.

It is curious to observe how this reflects itself in their literature. 'I will believe,' remarks Montaigne, 'in anything rather than in any man's consistency.' What observer of English habits—what person inwardly conscious of our dull and unsusceptible English nature would ever say so. Rather in our country obstinacy is the commonest of the vices, and perseverance the cheapest of the virtues. Again, when they attempt history, the principal peculiarity (a few exceptions being allowed for) is an utter incapacity to describe graphically a long-passed state of society. Take, for instance—assuredly no unfavourable example—M. Guizot. His books, I need not say, are nearly unrivalled for eloquence, for philosophy and knowledge; you read there, how in the middle age there were many 'principles,' the principle of Legitimacy, the principle of Feudalism, the principle of Democracy; and you come to know how one grew, and another declined, and a third crept slowly on; and the mind is immensely edified, when perhaps at the 315th page a proper name occurs, and you mutter, 'Dear me, why if there were not *people* in the time of Charlemagne! Who would have thought that?' But in return for this utter incapacity to describe the people of past times, a Frenchman has the gift of perfectly describing the people of his own. No one knows so well—no one can tell so well —the facts of his own life. The French memoirs, the French letters are, and have been, the admiration of Europe. Is not now Jules Janin unrivalled at pageants and *prima donnas*?

It is the same in poetry. As a recent writer excellently remarks, 'A French Dante, or Michael Angelo, or Cervantes, or Murillo, or Goethe, or Shakespeare, or Milton, we at once perceive to be a mere anomaly; a supposition which may indeed be proposed in terms, but which in reality is inconceivable and impossible.' Yet in requital as it were of this great deficiency, they have a wonderful capacity for expressing and delineating the poetical and voluptuous element of every day life. We know the biography of De Béranger. The young ladies whom he has admired—the wine that he has preferred—the fly that buzzed on the ceiling, and interrupted his delicious and dreaming solitude, are as well-known to us as the recollections of our own lives. As in their common furniture, so in their best poetry. The materials are nothing; reckon up what you have been reading, and it seems a *congeries* of stupid trifles; begin to read,—the skill of the workmanship is so consummate, the art so high and so latent, that while time flows silently on, our fancies are enchanted and our memories indelibly impressed. How often, asks Mr. Thackeray, have we read De Béranger—how often Milton. Certainly, since Horace, there has been no such manual of the philosophy of this world.

I will not say that the quality which I have been trying to delineate is exactly the same thing as 'cleverness.' But I do allege that it is sufficiently near it for the rough purposes of popular writing. For this *quickness* in taking in—so to speak—the present, gives a corresponding celerity of intellectual apprehension, an amazing readiness in catching new ideas and maintaining new theories, a versatility of mind which enters into and comprehends everything as it passes, a concentration in what occurs, so as to use it for every purpose of illustration, and consequently, (if it happen to be combined with the least fancy), quick repartee on the subject of the moment, and *bon-mots* also without stint and without end—and these qualities are rather like what we style cleverness. And what I call a proper stupidity keeps a man from all the defects of this character; it chains the gifted possessor mainly to his old ideas; it takes him seven weeks to comprehend an atom of a new one; it keeps him from being led away by new theories—for there is nothing which bores him so much; it restrains him within his old pursuits, his well-known habits, his tried expedients, his verified conclusions, his traditional beliefs. He is not tempted to 'levity,' or 'impatience,' for he does not see the joke, and is thick-skinned to present evils. Inconsistency puts him out,—'What I says is this here, as I was a saying yesterday,' is his notion of historical eloquence and habitual discretion. He is very slow indeed to be 'excited,'—his passions, his feelings, and his affections are dull and tardy strong things, falling in a certain known direction, fixing on certain known objects, and for the most acting in a moderate degree, and at a sluggish pace. You always know where to find his mind.

Now this is exactly what, in politics at least, you do not know about a Frenchman. I like—I have heard a good judge say—to hear a Frenchman talk. He strikes a light, but what light he will strike it is impossible to predict. I think he doesn't know himself. Now, I know you see at once how this would operate on a parliamentary government, but I give you a gentle illustration. All England knows Mr. Disraeli, the witty orator, the exceedingly clever *littérateur*, the versatile politician; and all England has made up its mind that the stupidest country gentleman would be a better Home Secretary than the accomplished descendant of the 'Caucasian race.' Now suppose, if you only can, a House of Commons all Disraelis, and do you imagine that Parliament would work? It would be what M. Proudhon said of some French assemblies, 'a box of matches.'

The same quality acts in another way, and produces to English ideas a most marvellous puzzle, both in their philosophical literature and their political discussion. I mean their passion for logical deduction. Their habitual mode of argument is to get hold of some large principle or principles; to begin to deduce immediately; and to reason down from them to the most trivial details of common action. *Il faut être conséquent avec soi-même*—is their fundamental maxim; and in a world, the essence of which is compromise, they could not well have a worse. I hold, metaphysically perhaps, that this is a consequence of that same impatience of disposition to which I have before alluded. Nothing is such a bore as looking for your principles—nothing so pleasant as working them out. People who have thought, know that enquiry is suffering. A child a-stumbling timidly in the dark is not more different from the same child playing on a sunny lawn, than is the philosopher groping, hesitating, doubting and blundering about his primitive postulates, from the same philosopher proudly deducing and commenting on the certain consequences of his established convictions. On this account mathematics have been called the paradise of the mind. In Euclid at least, you have your principles, and all that is required is acuteness in working them out. The long annals of science are one continued commentary on this text. Read in Bacon, the beginner of intellectual philosophy in England, and every page of the 'Advancement of Learning' is but a continued warning against the tendency of the human mind to start at once to the last generalities from a few and imperfectly observed particulars. Read in the 'Méditations' of Descartes, the beginner of intellectual philosophy in France, and in every page (once I read five) you will find nothing but the strictest, the best, the most lucid, the most logical deduction of all things actual and possible, from a few principles obtained without evidence, and retained in defiance of probability. Deduction is a game, and induction a grievance. Besides, clever impatient people want not only to learn, but to teach. And instruction expresses at least the alleged possession of knowledge. The obvious way is to shorten the painful, the slow, the tedious, the wearisome process of preliminary inquiry— to assume something pretty—to establish its consequences—discuss their beauty—exemplify their importance—extenuate their absurdities. A little vanity helps all this. Life is short—art is long—truth lies deep —take some side—found your school—open your lecture-rooms— tuition is dignified—learning is low.

I do not know that I can exhibit the way these qualities of the French character operate on their opinions, better than by telling you how the Roman Catholic Church deals with them. I have rather attended to it since I came here; it gives sermons almost an interest, their being in French—and to those curious in intellectual matters it is worth observing. In other times, and even now in out-of-the way

Spain, I suppose it may be true that the Catholic Church was opposed to inquiry and reasoning. But it is not so now, and here. Loudly—from the pens of a hundred writers—from the tongues of a thousand pulpits—in every note of thrilling scorn and exulting derision, she proclaims the contrary. Be she Christ's workman, or Anti-Christ's, she knows her work too well.—'Reason, Reason, Reason'—exclaims she to the philosophers of this world—'Put in practice what you teach, if you would have others believe it; be consistent; do not prate to us of private judgment when you are but yourselves repeating what you heard in the nursery—ill-mumbled remnants of a Catholic tradition. No! exemplify what you command, enquire and make search—seek, though we warn you that ye will never find—yet do as ye will. Shut yourself up in a room—make your mind a blank—go down (as ye speak) into the 'depths of your consciousness'—scrutinise the mental structure—inquire for the elements of belief—spend years, your best years, in the occupation—and at length—when your eyes are dim, and your brain hot, and your hand unsteady—then reckon what you have gained: see if you cannot count on your fingers the certainties you have reached: reflect which of them you doubted yesterday, which you may disbelieve to-morrow; or rather make haste—assume at random some essential *credenda*—write down your inevitable postulates—enumerate your necessary axioms—toil on, toil on—spin your spider's web—adore your own souls—or, if ye prefer it, choose some German nostrum—try the intellectual intuition, or the 'pure reason,' or the 'intelligible' ideas, or the mesmeric *clairvoyance*—and when so or somehow you have attained your results, try them on mankind. Don't go out into the highways and hedges—it's unnecessary. Ring the bell—call in the servants—give them a course of lectures—cite Aristotle—review Descartes—panegyrize Plato—and see if the *bonne* will understand you. It is you that say '*Vox populi—Vox dei;*' but you see the people reject you. Or suppose you succeed—what you call succeeding—your books are read; for three weeks, or even a season, you are the idol of the *salons*; your hard words are on the lips of women; then a change comes—a new actress appears at the Théâtre Français or the Opéra—her charms eclipse your theories; or a great catastrophe occurs—political liberty (it is said) is annihilated—*il faut se faire mouchard* is the observation of scoffers. Anyhow, *you* are forgotten—fifty years may be the gestation of a philosophy, not three its life—before long, before you go to your grave, your six disciples leave you for some newer master, or to set up for themselves. The poorest priest in the remote region of the *Basses Alpes* has more power over men's souls than human cultivation; his ill-mouthed masses move women's souls—can you? Ye scoff at Jupiter. Yet he at least was believed in—you never have; idol for idol the *de*throned is better than the *un*throned. No, if you would reason—if you would teach—if you would speculate, come to us. We have our *premises* ready; years upon years before you were born, intellects whom the best of you delight to magnify, toiled to systematise the creed of ages; years upon years after you are dead, better heads than yours will find new matter there to define, to divide, to arrange. Consider the 100 volumes of Aquinas—which of you desire a higher life than that. To deduce, to subtilise discriminate, systematise, and decide the highest truth, and to be believed. Yet such was his luck, his enjoyment. He was what you would be. No, no—*Credite, credite.* Ours is the life of speculation—the cloister is the home for the student. Philosophy is stationary—Catholicism progressive. You call—we are heard, &c., &c., &c. So speaks each preacher according to his ability. And when the dust and noise of present controversies have passed away, and in the silence of the night, some grave historian writes out the tale of half-forgotten times, let him not forget to observe that profoundly as the mediæval Church subdued the superstitious cravings of a painful and barbarous age—in after years she dealt more discerningly still with the feverish excitement—the feeble vanities—and the dogmatic impatience of an over-intellectual generation.

And as in religion—so in politics: we find the same desire to teach rather than to learn—the same morbid appetite for exhaustive and original theories. It is as necessary for a public writer to have a system as it is for him to have a pen. His course is obvious; he assumes some grand principle—the principle of Legitimacy, or the principle of Equality, or the principle of Fraternity—and thence he reasons down without fear or favour to the details of every-day politics. Events are judged of, not by their relation to simple causes, but by their bearing on a remote axiom. Nor are these speculations mere exercises of philosophic ingenuity. Four months ago, hundreds of able writers were debating with the keenest ability and the most ample array of generalities, whether the country should be governed by a Legitimate Monarchy, or an illegitimate; by a Social, or an old-fashioned Republic, by a two-chambered Constitution, or a one-chambered Constitution;

on 'Revision' or Non-revision; on the claims of Louis Napoleon, or the divine right of the national representation. Can any intellectual food be conceived more dangerous or more stimulating for an over-excitable population? It is the same in parliament. The description of the Church of Corinth may stand for a description of the late Assembly: every one had a psalm, had a doctrine, had a tongue, had a revelation, had an interpretation. Each member of the Mountain had his scheme for the regeneration of mankind; each member of the vaunted majority had his scheme for newly consolidating the government; Orleanist hated Legitimist, Legitimist Orleanist; moderate Republican detested undiluted Republican; scheme was set against scheme, and theory against theory. No two Conservatives would agree what to conserve; no Socialist could practically associate with any other. No deliberative assembly can exist with every member wishing to lead, and no one wishing to follow. Not the meanest Act of Parliament could be carried without more compromise than even the best French statesmen were willing to use on the most important and critical affairs of their country. Rigorous reasoning would not manage a parish-vestry, much less a great nation. In England to carry half your own crotchets, you must be always and everywhere willing to carry half another man's. Practical men must submit as well as rule; concede as well as assume. Popular government has many forms, a thousand good modes of procedure; but no one of those modes can be worked, no one of those forms will endure, unless by the continual application of sensible heads and pliable judgments, to the systematic of stiff axioms, rigid principles, and incarnated propositions.

I am, &c.,

AMICUS.

P.S.—I was in hopes that I should have been able to tell you of the withdrawal of the decree relative to the property of the Orleans family. It was announced in the *Constitutionnel*, of yesterday; but I regret to add was contradicted in the *Patrie* last evening. I need not observe to you that it is an act for which there is no defence, moral or political. It has immensely weakened the government.

The change of Ministry is also a great misfortune to Louis Napoleon. M. de Morny, said to be a son of Queen Hortense (if you believe the people in the *salons*, the President is not the son of his father, and everybody else is the son of his mother), was a statesman of the class best exemplified in England by the late Lord Melbourne,—an acute, witty, fashionable man, acquainted with Parisian persons and things, and a consummate judge of public opinion, M. Persigny was in exile with the President, is said to be much attached to him, to repeat his sentiments and exaggerate his prejudices. I need not point out which of the two is just now the sounder counsellor.

Letter V.—On the Constitution of
the Prince-President

[Undated]

My Dear Sir,—The many failures of the French in the attempt to establish a predominantly parliamentary government, have a strong family likeness. Speaking a little roughly, I shall be right in saying that the constitutions of France have perished, both lately and formerly, either in a street-row or under the violence of a military power, aided and abetted by a diffused dread of impending street-rows, and a painful experience of the effects of past ones. Thus the constitution of 1791 (the first of the old series) perished, on the 10 of August, amid the exultation of the brewer Santerre. The last of the old series fell on the 18th Brumaire, under the hands of Napoleon, when the 5 per cents. were at 12, the whole country in disorder, and all ruinable persons ruined. The Monarchy of 1830 began in the riot of the three days, and ended in the riot of the 24 of February; the Republic of February perished but yesterday, mainly from the terror that Paris might again see such days as the 'days of June.'

I think all sensible Englishmen who review this history (the history of more than sixty years), will not be slow to divine a conclusion peculiarly agreeable to our orderly national habits, viz., that the first want of the French is somebody or something able and willing to keep down street-rows, to repress the frightful elements of revolution and disorder which, every now and then, astonish Europe; capable of maintaining, and desirous to maintain, the order and tranquillity which are (all agree) the essential and primary pre-requisites of industry and civilisation. If any one seriously and calmly doubts this, I am afraid nothing that I can further say will go far in convincing him. But let him read the account of any scene in any French revolution, old or new, or better let him come here and learn how people look back to the time I have mentioned (to June, 1848), when the socialists, —not under speculative philosophers like Proudhon or Louis Blanc, but under practical rascals and energetic murderers, like Sobrier and

Caussidière,—made their last and final stand, and against them, on the other side, the National Guard (mostly solid shopkeepers, three-parts ruined by the events of February) fought (I will not say bravely or valiantly, but) furiously, frantically, savagely, as one reads in old books that half-starved burgesses in beleaguered towns have sometimes fought, for the food of their children; let any sceptic hear of the atrocities of the friends of order, and the atrocities of the advocates of disorder, and he will, I imagine, no longer be sceptical on two points,—he will hope that if he ever have to fight it will not be with a fanatic socialist, nor against a demi-bankrupt, fighting for 'his shop;' and he will admit, that in a country subject to collisions between two such excited and excitable combatants, no earthly blessing is in any degree comparable to a power which will stave off, long delay, or permanently prevent the actual advent and ever-ready apprehension of such bloodshed. I therefore assume that the first condition of good government in this country is a really strong, a reputedly strong, a continually strong, executive power.

Now, on the face of matters, it is certainly true that such a power is perfectly consistent with the most perfect, the most ideal type of parliamentary government. Rather I should say, such and so strong an executive is a certain consequence of the existence of that ideal and rarely found type. If there is among the people, and among their representatives, a strong, a decided, an unflinching preference for particular ministers, or a particular course of policy, that course of policy can be carried out, and will be carried out, as certainly as by the Czar Nicholas, whose ministers can do exactly what they will. There was something very like this in the old days of King George III, of Mr. Pitt and Mr. Perceval. In those times, I have been told, the great treasury official of the day, Mr. George Rose (still known to the readers of Sydney Smith) had a habit of observing, upon occasion of any thing utterly devoid of decent defence, 'Well, well, this *is* a little too bad; we must apply our *majority* to this difficulty.' The effect is very plain; while Mr. George Rose and his betters respected certain prejudices and opinions, then all but universal in parliament, they in all other matters might do precisely what they would; and in all out of the way matters, in anything that Sir John could not understand, on a point of cotton-spinning or dissent, be as absolute as the Emperor Napoleon. But the case is (as we know by experience of what passes under our daily observation) immensely altered, when there is no longer this strong, compact, irrefragable, 'following;' no distinctly divided, definite faction, no regular opposition to be daily beaten, no regular official party to be always victorious—but, instead, a mere aggregate of 'independent members,' each thinking for himself, propounding, as the case may be, his own sense or his own nonsense—one, profound idea applicable to all time; another, something meritorious from the Eton Latin grammar, and a mangled republication of the morning's newspaper; some exceedingly philosophical, others only crotchety; but, what is my point, each acting on his own head, assuming not Mr. Pitt's infallibility, but his own. Again, divide a political [assembly] into three parties, any two of which are greater than the third, and it will be always possible for an adroit and dexterous intriguer (M. Thiers has his type in most assemblies) to combine, three or four times a fortnight, the two opposition parties into a majority on some interesting questions, on some matter of importance. The best government possible under the existing circumstances will be continually, and, in a hazardous state of society, even desperately and fatally weakened. We have had in our own feasible House of Commons—aye, and among the most stupid and sensible portion of it, the country gentlemen, within these few years, a striking example of how far party zeal, the heat of disputation, and a strong desire for a deep revenge, will carry the best intentioned politicians in destroying the executive efficiency of an obnoxious government. I mean the division of the House of Commons on the Irish Army Bill, which ended in the resignation of Sir Robert Peel. You remember on that occasion the country party, under the guidance of Lord George Bentinck, in the teeth of the Irish policy which they had been advocating and supporting all their lives, and which they would advocate and support again now, in the teeth of their previous votes, and (I am not exaggerating the history) almost of their avowed present convictions, defeated a government, not on a question of speculative policy or recondite importance, but upon the precautionary measures necessary (according to every idea that a Tory esquire is capable of entertaining) for preventing a rebellion, the occurrence which they were told (and as the event proved, told truly) might be speedy, hourly, and immediate. Of course I am not giving any opinion of my own about the merits of the question. The Whigs may be right; it may be good to have shown the world how little terrible is the bluster of Irish agitation. But I cite the event as a striking example of an essential evil in a three-sided parliamentary system, as practically showing that a generally well meaning opposition will, in defiance of their own habitual principles, cripple an odious executive, even in a matter of street rows and rebellions. I won't weary you with tediously pointing the moral. If such things are done in the green tree, what may be done in the dry? If party zeal and disputation excitement so hurry men away in our own grave, business-like experienced country—what may we expect from a vain, a volatile, an ever changing race?

Nor am I drawing a French Assembly from mere history, or from my own imagination. In the late chamber, the great subject of the very last *Annual Register*, there were not only three parties but four. There was a perpetually shifting element of 200 members, calling itself the Mountain, which had in its hands the real casting vote between the President's government and the constitutional opposition. In the very last days of the constitution they voted against, and thereby negatived, the proposition of the questors for arming the Assembly; partly because they disliked General Changarnier, and detested General Cavaignac; partly because, being extreme socialists, they would not arm anybody who was likely to use his arms against their friends on the barricades. The same party was preparing to vote for the Bill on the Responsibility of the President, actually, and according to the design of its promoters, in the nature of a bill of indictment against him, because they feared his rigour and efficiency in repressing the anticipated convulsion. The question, the critical question, *Who* shall prevent a new revolution? was thus actually, and owing to the lamentable divisions of the friends of order, in the hands of the parliamentary representatives, of the very men who wished to effect that revolution, was determined, I may say, ultimately, and in the last resort by the party of disorder.

Nor on lesser questions was there any steady majority, any distinctive deciding faction, any administering phalanx, anybody regularly voting with anybody else, often enough, or in number enough, to make the legislative decision regular, consistent, or respectable. Their very debates were unseemly. On anything not pleasing to them, the Mountain (as I said) a yellow and fanatical generation—had (I am told) an engaging knack of rising *en masse* and screaming until they were tired. It will be the same, I do not say in degree, (for the Mountain would certainly lose several votes now, and the numbers of the late Chamber were unreasonably and injudiciously large), but, in a measure, you will be always subject to the same disorder. A fluctuating majority, and a minority, often a ruling minority, favourable to rebellion. The cause, as I believe, is to be sought in the peculiarities of the French character, on which I dwelt, prolixly, I fear, and *ad nauseam*, in my last two letters. If you have to deal with a *mobile*, a clever, a versatile, an intellectual, a dogmatic nation, inevitably, and by necessary consequence, you will have conflicting systems—every man speaking his own words, and always giving his own suffrage to what seems good in his own eyes—many holding to-day what they will regret to-morrow—a crowd of crotchety theories and a heavy percentage of philosophical nonsense—a great opportunity for subtle stratagem, and intriguing selfishness—a miserable division among the friends of tranquillity, and a great power thrown into the hands of those who, though often with the very best intentions, are practically, and in matter of fact, opposed both to society and civilisation. And, moreover, beside minor inconveniences and lesser hardships, you will indisputably have periodically—say three or four times in fifty years—a great crisis; the public mind much excited, the people in the streets swaying to and fro with the breath of every breeze, the discontented *ouvriers* meeting in a hundred knots, discussing their real sufferings and their imagined grievances with lean features and angry gesticulations; the parliament, all the while in permanence, very ably and eloquently expounding the whole subject, one man proposing this scheme, and another that; the opposition expecting to oust the Ministers, and ride in on the popular commotion; the Ministers fearing to take the odium of severe or adequate repressive measures, lest they should lose their salary, their places and their majority: finally, a great crash, a disgusted people, overwhelmed by revolutionary violence, or seeking a precarious, a pernicious, but after all a precious protection from the bayonets of military despotism. Louis Philippe met these dangers and difficulties in a thoroughly characteristic manner. He bought his majority. Being a practical and not over sentimental public functionary, he went into the market and purchased a sufficient number of constituencies and members. Of course the *convenances* were carefully preserved; grossness of any kind is too jarring for French susceptibility; the purchase money was not mere coin, (which indeed the buyers had not to offer,) but a more gentlemanly commodity— the patronage of the government. The electoral colleges were extremely small, the number of public functionaries is enormous; so that a very respectable body of electors could always be expected to have like a four-year old barrister (since the County Courts), an immense prejudice for the existing government. One man hoped to be *Maire*, another wanted his son got into St. Cyr or the Polytechnic School, and this could be got, and was daily got (I am writing what is hardly denied) by voting for the government candidate. In a word, a sufficient proportion of the returns of the electoral colleges resembled the returns from Harwich or Devonport, only that the government was the only bidder; for there are not, I fancy, in any country but England, people able and willing to spend, election after election, great sums of money for procuring the honour of a seat in a representative assembly. In fact, to copy the well known phrase, just as in the time of Burke certain gentlemen had the expressive nickname of the King's friends, so these constituencies may aptly be called the King's constituencies. Of course, on the face of it, this system worked, as far as business went, excellently well. For eighteen years the tranquillity was maintained. France, it may be, has never enjoyed so much calm civilisation, so much private happiness; and yet, after all such and so long blessings, it fell in a mere riot—it fell unregretted. It is a system which no wise man can wish to see restored; it was a system of regulated corruption.

But it does not at all follow, nor I am sure will you be apt so to deduce, that because I imagine that France is unfit for a government in which a House of Commons is, as with us, the sovereign power in the state, I therefore believe that it is fit for no freedom at all. Our own constitutional history is the completest answer to any such idea. For centuries, the House of Commons was habitually, we know, but a third-rate power in the state. First the Crown, then the House of Lords enjoyed the ordinary and supreme dominion; and down almost to our own times the Crown and House of Lords, taken together, were much more than a sufficient match for the people's house; but yet we do not cease to proclaim, daily and hourly, in season and out of season, that the English people never have been slaves. It may, therefore, well be that our own country having been free under a constitution in which the representative element was but third-rate in power and dignity, France and other nations may contrive to enjoy that advantage from institutions in which it is only second-rate.

Now, of this sort is the Constitution of Louis Napoleon. I am not going now, after prefacing so much to discuss its details; indeed, I do not feel competent to do so. What should we say to a Frenchman's notion of a £5 householder, or the 4th and 5th clauses of the New Reform Bill? and I quite admit that a paper building of this sort can hardly be safely criticised till it is carried out on *terra firma*, till we see not only the theoretic ground-plan, but the actual inhabited structure. The life of a constitution is in the spirit and disposition of those who work it; and we can't yet say in the least what that, in this case, will be; but so far as the constitution shows its meaning on the face of it, it clearly belongs to the class which I have named. The *Corps Législa if* is not the administering body, it is not even what perhaps it might with advantage have been, a petitioning and remonstrating body; but it possesses the legislative veto, and the power of stopping *en masse* the supplies. They are not a working, a ruling, or an initiative, or supremely decisive, but an immense checking power. They will be unable to change ministers, or aggravate the course of revolutions, but they could arrest an unpopular war—they could reject an unpopular law—they are, at least in theory, a powerful and important drag-chain. Out of the mouths of its adversaries this system possesses what I have proved, or conjectured, or assumed to be the prime want of the French nation—a strong executive. The objection to it is that the objectors find nothing else in it. We confess there is no doubt now of a power adequate to repress street rows and revolutions.

At the same time, I guard myself against intimating any opinion on the particular minutiæ of this last effort of institutional invention. I do not know enough to form a judgment; I sedulously, at present, confine myself to this one remark, that the new government of France belongs, in theory at least, to the right class of Constitutions—the class that is most exactly suited to French habits, French nature, French social advantages, French social dangers,—the class, I mean, in which the representative body has a consultative, a deliberative, a checking and a minatory; not as with us a supreme, nearly an omnipotent, and exclusively initiatory function.

I am, yours, &c.

AMICUS.

P.S.—You may like five words on a French invasion. I can't myself imagine, and what is more to the point, I do not observe that anybody has here any notion of any such inroad into England as was contemplated and proposed by General Changarnier. No one in the actual conduct of affairs, with actual responsibility of affairs, not, as the event proved, even Ledru Rollin could, according to me, encounter the risk and odium of such a hateful and horribly dangerous attempt. But, I regret to add, there is a contingency which sensible people here (so far as I have had the means of judging) do not seem to regard as at all beyond the limits of rational probability, by which a war between England and France would most likely be superinduced; that is, a French invasion of Belgium. I do not mean to assure you that this week or next the Prince-President will make a razzia in Brussels. But I do mean that it is thought not improbable that somehow or other, on some wolf-and-the-lamb pretext, he may pick a quarrel with King Leopold, and endeavour to restore to the French the 'natural limit' of the Rhine. Now, I have never seen the terms of the guarantee which the shrewd and cautious Leopold exacted from England before he would take the throne of Belgium; but as the only real risk was a French aggression upon that tempting territory, I do not make any doubt that the expressions of that instrument bind us to go to war in defence of the country whose limits and independence we have guaranteed. And in this case an invasion of England would be as admissible a military movement as an invasion of France. I hope, therefore, you will use your best rhetoric to induce people to put our pleasant country in a state of adequate and tolerable defence.

I see by the invaluable *Galignani*, that some excellent people at Manchester are indulging in a little arithmetic. 'Suppose,' say they, 'all the French got safe, and each took away £50, now how much do you fancy it would come to (40,000 men by £50, nought's nought is nought, nought and carry two)—compared to[1] the *existing* burden of the National Debt!! Was there ever such amiable infatuation! It is not what the French could carry off, but what they would leave behind them, which is in the reasonable apprehension of reasonable persons. The funds at 50—broken banks—the *Gazette* telling you who had *not* failed—Downing street *vide* Wales—destitute families, dishonoured daughters, one-legged fathers—the mourning shops utterly sacked—the customers in tears—a pale widow in a green bonnet—the Exchange in ruins—five notches on St. Paul's—and a big hole in the Bank of England:—these though but a few of the certain consequences of a French visit to London, are quite enough to terrify even an adamantine editor, and a rather reckless correspondent.

[1] *The Inquirer* (p. 84) has 'while' for 'compared to'.

Letter VI.—The French Newspaper Press

Paris, February 10.

M Y D E A R S I R,—We learn from an oriental narrative in considerable circulation, that the ancient Athenians were fond of news. Of course they were. It is in the nature of a mass of clever and intellectual people living together to want something to talk about. Old ideas—common ascertained truths—are good things enough to live by, but are very rare, and soon sufficiently discussed. Something else—true or false, rational or nonsensical—is quite essential; and, therefore, in the old literary world men gathered round the travelling sophist, to learn from him some thought, crotchet, or speculation. And what the vagabond speculators were once, that, pretty exactly, is the newspaper now. To it the people of this intellectual capital look for that daily mental bread, which is as essential to them as the less ethereal sustenance of ordinary mortals. With the spread of education this habit travels downward. Not the literary man only, but the *ouvrier* and the *bourgeois*, live and did live on the same food. This day's *Siècle* is discussed not only in gorgeous drawing-rooms, but in humble reading-rooms, and still humbler workshops. According to the printed notions of us journalists, this is a matter of pure rejoicing. The influence of the Press, if you believe writers and printers, is the one sufficient condition of social well-being. Yet there are many considerations which make very much against this idea: I can't go into several of them now, but those that I shall mention are suggested at once by matters before me. First, newspaper people are the only traders that thrive upon convulsion. In quiet times, who cares for the paper? In times of tumult, who does not? Commonly, the *Patrie* (the *Globe* of this country), sells, I think, for three sous: the evening of the *coup d'état*, itinerant ladies were crying under my window, 'Demandez la *Patrie*—Journal du soir—trente sous—Journal du soir;' and I remember witnessing, even in our sober London, in February, '48, how bald fathers of families paid large sums, and encountered bareheaded the unknown inclemencies of the night air, that they might learn the last news of Louis Philippe, and, if possible, be in at the death of the revolutionary Parisians. 'Happy,' says the sage, 'for the people whose annals are vacant;' but 'woe! woe! woe!' he might add, 'to the wretched journalists that have to compose and sell leading articles therein.'

I am constrained to say, that even in England this is not without its unfavourable influence on literary morals. Take in *The Times*, and you will see it assumed that every year ought to be an era. 'The Government does nothing,' is the indignant cry, and simple people in the country don't know that this is merely a civilized *façon de parler* for 'I have nothing to say.' Lord John must alter the suffrage, that we may have something pleasant in our columns.

I am afraid matters are worse here. The leading French journalist is, as you know, the celebrated Emile de Girardin, and, so far as I can learn anything about him, he is one of the most unprincipled politicians in existence. Since I have read the *Presse* regularly, it has veered from every point of the compass, well-nigh to every other,—now for, now against, the revision of the constitution,—now lauding Louis Napoleon to the skies,—now calling him plain M. Bonaparte, and insinuating that he had not two ideas, and was incapable of moral self-government,—now connected with the red party, now praising the majority; but all and each of these veerings and shiftings determined by one most simple and certain principle—to keep up the popular excitement, to maintain the gifted M. de Girardin at the head of it.

Now a man who spends his life in stimulating excitement and convulsion is really an incendiary; and however innocent and laudable his brother exiles may be, the old editor and founder of the *Presse* is, as I believe, now only paying the legitimate penalty of systematic *arson*.

When a foreigner—at least an Englishman—begins to read the French papers, his first idea is 'How well these fellows write? Why, every one of them has a style, and a good style too. Really, how clear, how acute, how clever, how perspicuous; I wish our journalists would learn to write like this;' but a little experience will modify this idea, at least I have found it so. I read for a considerable time in these witty periodicals with pleasure and admiration; after a little while I felt somehow that I took them up with an effort, but I fancied, knowing my disposition, that this was laziness; when on a sudden, in the waste of *Galignani*, I came across an article of the *Morning Herald*.

Now you'll laugh at me, if I tell you that it was a real enjoyment. There was no toil, no sharp theory, no pointed expression, no fatiguing brilliancy, in fact, what the man in Lord Byron desired, 'no nothing,' but a dull creeping satisfactory sensation that now, at least, there was nothing to admire. As long walking in picture galleries makes you appreciate a mere wall, so I felt that I understood for the first time that really dulness had its interest. I found a pure refreshment in coming across what possibly might be latent sense, but was certainly superficial stupidity.

I think there is nothing we English hate like a clever but prolonged controversy. Now this is the life and soul of the Parisian press. Everybody writes against everybody. It is not mere sly hate or solemn invective, nothing like what we occasionally indulge in, about the misdemeanours of a morning contemporary. But they take the other side's article piece by piece, and comment on him, and, as they say in libel cases, *innuendo* him, and satisfactorily show that, according to his arithmetic, two and two make five—useful knowledge that. It is really good for us to know that some fellow (you never heard of him) it rather seems can't add up. But it interests people here—*c'est logique* they tell you, and if you are trustful enough to answer, '*Mon Dieu, c'est ennuyeux, je n'en sais rien*, they look as if you sneered at the Parthenon.

It is out of these controversies that M. de Girardin has attained his power and his fame. His articles (according to me at least) have no facts and no sense. He gives one all pure reasoning—little scrappy syllogisms; as some one said most unjustly of old Hazlitt, he 'writes pimples.' But let an unfortunate writer in the *Assemblée Nationale*, or anywhere else, make a little refreshing blunder in his logic, and next morning small punning sentences (one to each paragraph like an equation) come rattling down on him: it is clear as noonday that somebody said 'something followed,' and it does *not* follow, and it is so agreed in all the million *Cabinets de Lecture* after due gesticulation; and, moreover, that M. de Girardin is the man to expose it, and what clever fellows they are to appreciate him, but what the truth is who cares? The subject is forgotten.

Now all this, in my notion, does great harm. Nothing destroys common-place like the habit of arguing for arguing's sake; nothing is so bad for public matters as that they should be treated, not as the data for the careful formation of a sound judgment, but as a topic or background for displaying the shining qualities of public writers. It is no light thing that. M. de Girardin for many years has gained more power, more reputation, more money, than any of his rivals; not because he shows more knowledge—he shows much less; not because he has a wiser judgment—he has no fixed judgment at all; but because he has a more pointed sharp way of exposing blunders, intrinsically paltry, obvious to all educated men; and does not care enough for any subject to be diverted from this logical trifling by a serious desire to convince anybody of anything.

Don't think I wish to be hard on this accomplished gentleman. I am not going to require of hack-writers to write only on what they understand—if that were the law, what a life for the sub-editor; I should not be writing these letters, and how seldom and how timidly would the morning journals creep into the world. Nor do I expect, though I may still, in sentimental moods, desire,—middle-aged journals often buoyed up by chimerical visions of improving mankind.

You know what our eminent *chef* (by Thackeray profanely called Jupiter Jeames), has been heard to say over his gin and water, in an easy and voluptuous moment: 'Enlightenment be ——, I want the fat fool of a thick-headed reader to say, "Just *my own* views," else he aint pleased, and may be he stops the paper.' I am not going to require supernatural excellence from writers. Yet there are limits. If I were a chemist, I should not mind, I suppose, selling, now and then, a deleterious drug on a due affidavit of rats, then and there filed before me; yet I don't feel as if I could live comfortably on the sale of mere arsenic. I fancy I should like to sell something wholesome occasionally. So, though one might, upon occasion, edge on a riot, or excite to a breach of the peace, I should not like to be every day feeding on revolutionary excitement. Nor should I like to be exclusively selling diminutive acute quibbling leaders (what they call in the Temple special demurrers), certain to occupy people with small fallacies, and lead away their minds from the great questions actually at issue.

Sometimes I might like to feel as if I understood what I wrote on, but of course with me this indulgence must be very rare. You know in France journalism is not only occupation, it is a career. As in far off Newcastle a coalfitter's son looks wistfully to the bar, in the notion that he too may emulate the fame and fortune of Lord Eldon or Lord Stowell, so in fair Provence, a pale young aspirant packs up his little bundle in the hope of rivalling the luck and fame of M. Thiers; he comes to Paris—he begins, like the great historian, by dining for thirty sous in the Palais Royal, in the hope that after long years of labour and jealousy he, too, may end by sleeping amid curtains of white muslin, lined with pink damask. Just consider for a moment what a difference this one fact shows between France and England. Here a man who begins life by writing in the newspapers, has an appreciable chance of arriving to be Minister of Foreign Affairs. The class of public writers is the class from which the representative of Lord Aberdeen, Lord Palmerston, or Lord Granville will most likely be chosen. Well, well, under that *régime* you and I might have been important people; we might have handled a red box, we might have known what it was to have a reception, to dine with the Queen, to be respectfully mystified by the *corps diplomatique*. But angry Jove forbade—of course we can hardly deny that he was wrong—and yet if the revolutions of '48 have clearly brought out any fact, it is the utter failure of newspaper statesmen. Everywhere they have been tried: everywhere they have shown great talents for intrigue, eloquence, and agitation,—how rarely have they shown even fair aptitude for ordinary administration; how frequently have they gained a disreputable renown by a laxity of principle, surpassing the laxity of their aristocratic and courtly adversaries. Such being my imperfect account of my imperfect notions of the French press, I can't altogether sympathise in the extreme despondency of many excellent persons at its temporary silence since the *coup d'état*. I might even rejoice at it, if I thought that the Parisian public could in any manner be broken of their dependence on the morning's article. But I have no such hope; the taste has got down too deep into the habits of the people: some new thing will still be necessary; and every government will find some of its most formidable difficulties in their taste for political disputation and controversial excitement. The ban must sooner or later be taken off; the President sooner or later must submit to censure and ridicule, and whatever laws he may propose about the press, there is none which scores of ingenious men—now animated by the keenest hatred, will not try every hazard to evade. What he may do to avoid this is as yet unknown. One thing, however, I suppose is pretty sure, and I fancy quite wise. The press will be restrained from discussing the principles of the government. Socialists will not be allowed to advocate a democratic republic. Legitimists will not be allowed to advocate the cause of Henri Cinq: nor Orleanists the cause of the

Comte de Paris. Such indulgence might be tolerable in more temperate countries, but experience shows that it is not safe now and here.

A really sensible press, arguing temperately after a clear and satisfactory exposition of the facts, is a great blessing in any country. It would be still more a blessing in a country where, as I tried to explain formerly, the representative element must play (if the public security is to be maintained), a rather secondary part. It would then be a real stimulus to deliberate inquiry and rational judgment upon public affairs; to the formation of common-sense views upon the great outlines of public business; to the cultivation of sound moral opinions and convictions on the internal and international duties of the state. Even the actual press, which we may expect to see here may not be pernicious. It will doubtless stimulate to many factious proceedings, and many interruptions of the public prosperity; it may very likely conduce to drive the President (contrary, if not to his inclination, at least to his personal interest) into foreign hostilities and international aggression; but it may be, notwithstanding, useful in preventing private tyranny, in exposing wanton oppression, in checking long-suffering revenge; it may prevent acts of spoliation like what they call here *le premier vol de l'aigle*—the seizure of the Orleans property;— in a word, being certain to oppose the executive, where the latter is unjust its enemy will be just.

I had hopes that this letter would be the last with which I should tease you; but I find I must ask you to be so kind as to find room for one, and only for one, more.

I am, yours, &c.,

AMICUS.

Letter VII.—Concluding Letter

Paris, February 19, 1852.

MY DEAR SIR,—There is a story of some Swedish Abbé, in the last century, who wrote an elaborate work to prove the then constitution of his country to be immortal and indestructible. While he was correcting the proof sheets, a friend brought him word that—behold! the King had already destroyed the said polity. 'Sir,' replied the gratified author, 'our sovereign, the illustrious Gustavus, may certainly overthrow the constitution, but never *my book*.' I beg to parody this sensible remark; for I wish to observe to you, that even though Louis Napoleon turn out a bad and mischievous ruler, he won't in the least refute these letters.

What I mean is as follows. Above all things, I have designed to prove to you that the French are by character unfit for a solely and predominantly parliamentary government; that so many and so great elements of convulsion here exist, that it will be clearly necessary that a strong, vigorous, anti-barricade executive should, at whatever risk and cost, be established and maintained; that such an Assembly as the last is irreconcilable with this; in a word, that riots and revolutions must, if possible, come to an end, and only such a degree of liberty and democracy be granted to the French nation, as is consistent with the consolidated existence of the order and tranquillity which are equally essential to rational freedom and civilised society.

In order to combine the maintenance of order and tranquillity with the maximum of possible liberty, I hope that it may in the end be found possible to admit into a political system a representative and sufficiently democratic Assembly, without that Assembly assuming and arrogating to itself those nearly omnipotent powers, which in our country it properly and rightfully possesses, but which in the history of the last sixty years, we have, as it seems to me, so many and so cogent illustrations that a French chamber is, by genius and constitution, radically incapable to hold and exercise. I hope that some checking, consultative, petitioning Assembly—some βουλή, in the real sense of the term—some *Council*, some provision by which all grave and deliberate public opinion (I do not speak more definitely, for an elaborate constitution, from a foreigner, must be an absurdity) may organise and express itself—yet at the same time, without utterly hampering and directing—and directing amiss—those more simple elements of national polity, on which we must, after all, rely for the prompt and steady repression of barricade-making and bloodshed.

I earnestly desire to believe that some such system as this may be found in practice possible; for otherwise, unless I quite misread history, and altogether mistake what is under my eyes, after many more calamities, many more changes, many more great Assemblies abounding in Vergniauds and Berryers, the essential deficiencies of debating Girondin statesmen will become manifest, the uncompact, unpractical, over-volatile, over-logical indecisive, ineffectual rule of Gallican parliaments will be unequivocally manifest (it is *now* plain, I imagine, but a truth so humiliating must be written large in letters of blood before those that run will read it), and no medium being held or conceived to be possible, the nation will sink back, not contented but discontented, not trustfully but distrustfully, under the rule of a military despot; and if they yield to this, it will be from no faith, no loyalty, no credulity; it will be from a sense—a hated sense—of unqualified failure, a miserable scepticism in the probable success and the possible advantages of long-tried and ill-tried rebellion.

Now whether the constitution of Louis Napoleon is calculated to realise this ideal and intermediate system is, till we see it at work, doubtful and disputable. It is not the question so much of what it may be at this moment, as of what it may become in a brief period, when things have begun to assume a more normal state, and the public mind be relaxed from its present and painful tension. However, I should be deceiving you, if I did not inform you that the state of men's minds towards the Prince-President is not, so far as I can make it out, what it was the day after the *coup d'état*. The measures taken against the socialists are felt to have been several degrees too severe, the list of exiles too numerous; the confiscation of the Orleans' property could not but be attended with the worst effect; the law announced by the government organs respecting or rather against the Press, is justly (though you know from my last letter I have no partiality for French newspapers) considered to be absurdly severe, and likely to countenance much tyranny and gross injustice; above all, instead of maintaining mere calm and order, the excessive rigour, and sometimes the injustice, of the President's measures, have produced a breathless pause (if I may so speak) in public opinion;—political conversation is a whispered question, what will he do next? Firstly, the government is dull, and the French want to be amused; secondly, it is going to spoil the journals (depreciate newspapers to a Frenchman, disparage nuts to a monkey); thirdly, it is producing (I do not say it has yet produced, but it has made a beginning in producing), a habit of apprehension;— in fact, I believe the French opinion of the Prince-President is near about that of the interesting damsel, in George Sand's comedy, concerning her uninteresting *prétendu* '*Vous l'aimez? n'est-ce pas?*' '*Oui, oui, oui, certainement je l'aime. Oui, oui, mille fois, oui. Je dis que oui. Je vous assure.* AU MOINS *je fais mon possible a l'aimer:*' the first attachment is not extinct, but people have begun—awful symptom—to add the withering and final saving clause. Yet it is, I imagine, a great mistake to suppose that the present constitution, if it work at all, will permanently work as a despotism, or that the *Corps Législatif* will be without a measure of popular influence; the much more helpless *Tribunal* was not so in the much more troublesome times of the Consulate. And the source of such influence, and the manner of its operation may be, I imagine, well enough traced in the nature of the forces whereby Louis Napoleon holds his power.

A truly estimable writer says, I know 'that the legislative body cannot have, by possibility, any analogy with the consultative and petitioning senate of the Plantagenets,' nor can any one deny that the likeness is extremely faint (no illustration ever yet ran on all fours), the practical differences clear and convincing. But yet, according to the light which is given me now, I affirm that for one vital purpose,— the resisting and criticising any highly unpopular acts of a highly unpopular government,—the *corps législatif* of Louis Napoleon must, and will, inevitably possess a power compared with which the forty-day followers of the feudal *noblesse* seem as impotent as a congregation of Quakers; a force the peculiarity of which is that you can't imprison, can't dissolve, can't annihilate it,—I mean, of course, the moral power of civilised opinion. You may put down newspapers, dissolve parliaments, imprison agitators, almost stop conversation, but you can't stop thought. You can't prevent the silent, slow, creeping, stealthy progress of hatred, and scorn, and shame. You can't attenuate easily the stern justice of a retarded retaliation. These influences affect the great reservoir of physical force—they act on the army. A body of men enlisted daily from the people, take to the barracks the notions of the people; in spite of new associations, the first impressions are apt to be retained; you overlay them but they remain. What is believed elsewhere and out of doors gives them weight. Each soldier has relations, friends, a family—he knows what they think. Much more with the officers. These are men moving in Parisian society, accessible to its influences, responsible to its opinion, apt to imbibe its sentiments. Certainly *esprit de corps*—the habit of obedience, the instinct of discipline, are strong, and will carry men far; but certainly, also, they have natural limits. Men won't stand being cut, being ridiculed, being detested, being despised, daily and for ever, and that for measures which their own understandings disapprove of. Remember there is not here any question of barbarous bands overawing a civilised and imperial city; no question of ugly Croats keeping down cultivated Italians; it is but a question of French gentlemen and French peasantry in uniform acting in opposition to other French gentlemen and other French peasants without uniform. Already there has been talk, (I do not say well-founded, but still the matter was named) of breaking a couple or three hundred officers, for speaking against the Orleans decrees. Do you fancy that can be done every day? Do you imagine that a parliament, whatever its nominal functions may be (remember those of the old *régime*), speaking the sense of the people about the question of the day, in a time of convulsion, and in a critical hour, would not be attended to, or at any rate thought of and considered, by an army taken from the people, in a few years to return to the people,— commanded by men selected from and every day mixing with common society and very ordinary mankind. The 2nd of December showed how readily such troops will support a decided and popular President, against an intriguing, divided, impotent chamber. But such hard blows won't bear repetition. Soldiers—French soldiers, I take it especially from their quickness and intelligence, are neither deaf nor blind. If there be truth in history or speculation, national forces can't long be used against the nation; they are unmerciful, and often cruel to feeble minorities; they are ready now for a terrible onslaught on mere socialists, just as of old they turned out cheerfully for awful dragonnades on the ill-starred Protestants; but once let them know and feel that everybody is against them—that they are alone, that their acts are contemned and their persons despised,—and gradually, or all at once, discipline and habit surely fail, men murmur or desert, officers hesitate or disobey, one regiment is dismissed to the Cabyles, another relegated to rural solitudes; at last, most likely in the decisive moment of the whole history, the rulers, who relied only on their troops, are afraid to call them out; they hesitate, send spies and commissioners to inquire, '*Vive le Gouvernement Provisoire!*'—the black and roaring multitude rises and comes on; but two seconds, and the obnoxious institutions are lost in the flood; nothing is heard but the cry of the hour, sounding shrill and angry over the waste of Revolution—'*Vive le Diable!*' With such a force behind them, a French parliament, of whatever nature, with whatever written duties, is, if at the head of the movement, in the critical hour, apt to be stronger than the strongest of the barons.

Nor do I concur with those who censure the President for 'recommending' avowedly the candidates he approves. It is a part of the great question, how is universal suffrage to be worked successfully in such a country as France? The peasant proprietors have but one political idea that they wish the Prince to govern them;—they wish to vote for the candidate most acceptable to him, and they wish nothing else. Why is he wrong in telling them which candidate that is?

Still, no doubt, the reins are now strained a great deal too tight. It is possible, quite possible, that a majority in this parliament may be packed, but what I would impress on you is that it can't always be packed. Sooner or later constituencies who wish to oppose the government will, in spite of *maires* and *préfets*, elect the opposition candidate: it is in the nature of any, even the least vigorous system of popular election, to struggle forwards and progressively attain to some fair and reasonable correspondence with the substantial views and opinions of the constituent people.

I therefore fall back on what I told you before—my essential view or crotchet about the mental aptitudes and deficiencies of the French people. The French, said Napoleon, are *des machines nerveuses*.

The point is, can their excitable, volatile, superficial, over-logical, uncompromising character be managed and manipulated as to fit for entering on a practically uncontrolled system of parliamentary government? Will not any large and omnipotent Assembly resemble the stormy constituent and the late chamber, rather than business-like formal ennui-diffusing parliament to which in our free and dull country we are felicitously accustomed? Can one be so improved as to keep down a riot? I foresee a single and but a single objection. I fancy, indeed I know, that there is a school of political thinkers not yet in possession of any great influence, but, perhaps, a little on the way thereto, which has improved or invented a capital panacea, whereby all nations are, within very moderate limits of time, to be surely and certainly fitted for political freedom; and that no matter how formed— how seemingly stable—how long ago cast and constructed be the type of popular character to which the said remedy is sought to be applied. This panacea is the foundation or restoration of provincial municipalities. Now, I am myself prepared to go a considerable length with the school in question. I do myself think, that a due and regular consideration of the knotty points of paving and lighting, and the deciding in the last resort upon them is a valuable discipline of national character. It exercises people's minds on points they know, in things of which there is a test. Very few people are good judges of a good constitution; but everybody's eyes are excellent judges of good light; every man's feet are profound in the theory of agreeable stones. Yet I can't altogether admit, nevertheless, that municipalities are the sufficient and sole, though they may be very likely an essential prerequisite of political freedom. There is the great instance of Hindostan to the contrary. The whole old and national system of that remarkable country—a system in all probability as ancient as the era of Alexander, is a village system; and one so curious, elaborate, I fancy I might say so profound, that the best European observers—Sir Thomas Munro, and that sort of people, are most strenuous for its being retained unimpaired. According to them the village hardly heard of the imperial government, except for the purpose of imperial taxation. The business of life through that whole vast territory, has always been practically determined by potails[1] and parish-vestries, and yet nevertheless and in spite of this capital and immemorial municipal system, our subjects, the Hindoos, are still slaves and still likely to be slaves; still essentially slavish, and likely, I much fear, very long indeed to remain so. It is therefore quite certain that rural and provincial institutions won't so alter and adapt all national characters, as to fit all nations for a parliamentary constitution; consequently the *onus probandi* is on those who assert that it will so alter and mould the French. Again, I assure you the French do think of paving and lighting; not enough, perhaps, but still they have begun. The country is, as you know, divided into departments, arrondissements, and communes; in each of these there is a council, variously elected, but, in all cases, popularly and from the

---

[1] A Madras word meaning a kind of village mayor.—Ed.

district, which has the sole control over the expenditure of the particular locality for every special and local purpose, and which, if I am rightly informed, have, in theory at least, the sole initiative in every local improvement. The defect, I fancy, is that in the exercise of these, considerable bodies are hampered and controlled by the veto and supervision of the central authority. The rural councils discuss and decide what in their judgment should be then done and what money shall be so spent; the better sort of the agricultural population have much more voice in the latter, than have the corresponding class in England, in the determination and imposition of our own county rate;—but it is the central authority which decides whether such proposals and recommendations shall in fact be carried out. In a word, the provinces have to *ask leave* of the Parisian Ministry of the Interior. Now I admit this is an abuse. I should maintain that elderly gentlemen with bald heads and local influence, ought to feel that they in the final resort, settle and determine all truly local matters. Human nature likes its own road, its own bridge, its own lapidary obstacles, its own deceptive luminosity. But I ask again, can you fancy that these little luxuries, to whatever degree indulged in, alter and modify in any essential particular, the levity and volatility of the French character. How much light to how much logic? How many paving stones, to how much mobility? I can't foresee any such change. And even if so, what in the meantime?

We are left then, I think, to deal with the French character pretty much as we find it. What stealthy, secret, unknown, excellent, forces may, in the wisdom of Providence, be even now modifying this most curious intellectual fabric, neither you nor I can know or tell. Let us hope they may be many. But if we indulge, and from the immense records of revolutionary history, I think, if with due distrust, we may legitimately and even beneficially in system-building and speculation, we must take the *data* which we have, and not those which we desire or imagine. Louis Napoleon has proposed a system: English writers by the thousand (if I was in harness instead of holiday-making I should be most likely among them) proclaim his system an evil one. What then? Do you know what Father Newman says to the religious reformers, rather sharply, but still well, 'make out first of all where you stand—draw up your creed—write down your catechism.' So I answer to the English eloquence, 'State first of all what you would have—draw up your novel system for the French government—

write down your political constitution.' Don't criticise but produce—do not find fault but propose—and when you have proposed upon theory and have created upon paper, let us see whether the system be such an one as will work, in fact, and be accepted by a wilful nation in reality—otherwise your work is nought.

And mind, too, that the system to be sketched out must be fit to protect the hearths and homes of men. It is easy to compose policies if you do but neglect this one essential condition. Four years ago, Europe was in a ferment with the newest ideas, the best theories, the most elaborate, the most artistic constitutions. There was the labour, and toil, and trouble, of a million intellects, as good, taken on the whole, perhaps, as the world is likely to see,—of old statesmen, and literary gentlemen, and youthful enthusiasts, all over Europe, from the Baltic Sea to the Mediterranean, from the frontiers of Russia to the Atlantic Ocean. Well, what have we gained? A parliament in Sardinia! Surely this is a lesson against proposing polities which won't work, convening assemblies that can't legislate, constructing executives that arn't able to keep the peace, founding constitutions inaugurated with tears and eloquence, soon abandoned with tears and shame; beginning a course of fair auguries and liberal hopes, but from whose real dangers and actual sufferings a frightened and terrified people, in the end, flee for a temporary, or may be a permanent, refuge under a military and absolute ruler.

Mazzini sneers at the selfishness of shopkeepers—I am for the shop-keepers against him. There are people who think because they are republican there shall be no more 'cakes and ale.' Aye, verily, but there will though; or else stiffish ginger will be hot in the mouth. Legislative assemblies, leading articles, essay eloquence,—such are good—very good,—useful—very useful. Yet they can be done without. We can want them. Not so with all things. The selling of figs, the cobbling of shoes, the manufacturing of nails,—these are the essence of life. And let whoso frameth a constitution for his country think on these things.

I conclude, as I ought, with my best thanks for the insertion of these letters; otherwise I were so full of the subject that I might have committed what Disraeli calls 'the extreme act of human fatuity,' I might have published a pamphlet: from this your kindness has preserved me, and I am proportionably grateful.

I am, yours,
AMICUS.

The New Mexican Empire[1]

THE selection of the Archduke Maximilian to occupy the throne of
Mexico is one of the most singular events in history, and we are hardly
surprised at the incredulity with which it has, up to this moment, been
received. This generation, though unaccustomed to conquest, is still
familiar with its traditions, and, had the Emperor declared Mexico a
dependency of France, the public of Europe, if annoyed with the
audacity of the proceeding, would still have accepted it as beneficial
to Mexico, and a natural sequence of the previous incidents in the affair.
But the selection of a Hapsburg by a Napoleon, of a German to fill a
'Latin' throne, of an Austrian to rule over a great transatlantic empire,
has baffled all calculation, and left in the minds of observers so exclusive a sensation of surprise that they seem half deterred from any
conclusion whatever. Yet, setting carefully aside all the rumours in
which any great Napoleonic achievement is sure to be shrouded, and
confining the view strictly to the few known and certain facts, it does
not appear very difficult to arrive at a tolerably definite opinion. There
may be, of course, concealed projects dependent upon this election
which would materially affect its policy; Napoleon *may* have made a
bargain with Austria; or a treaty with the Southern Confederacy; or
an arrangement with England about guarantees; or conditions for
territorial cessions with the Archduke; but none of those designs are
as yet in a position to require examination. All that is *known* is that the
French have obtained a military occupation of Mexico, that they have
induced the population to abstain from very desperate resistance, that
they have convoked an assembly of conspicuous Mexicans, and that
they have persuaded those Mexicans to accept the transformation of a
federal republic into an empire, one and indivisible, and to elect an
Austrian Archduke as emperor, and that the Archduke in question
has, under certain conditions, accepted the glittering prize. That policy
is not so satisfactory as a bolder one might have been, but it contains

[1] This article was first published in *The Economist* for August 22 1863, Volume XXI,
pp. 925–6.

nothing with which Englishmen have any reason to quarrel, and is, if not so beneficial as other arrangements might have been made, still in its degree beneficial to France, to Mexico, and to the world.

1. To France this scheme is, perhaps, rather more advantageous than is exactly just. Napoleon has contrived to obtain a splendid position upon the American continent without incurring all the responsibility a colony would have imposed. Whatever the secret conditions of the election, it is quite certain that the Archduke must for some years occupy the position of viceroy of the French Emperor. Even his brother's support could not relieve him from that, for Austria, though she has troops, has no navy which could keep the sea for a week against the inevitable anger of the North. He cannot hope for much aid from England, and he must, therefore, for a time, lean on his great protector and rely on his guarantee. In a few years he may, indeed, so administer Mexico that its conquest by the North would be an enterprise of great difficulty, or even, if the Catholic Germans throng to his standard, an enterprise not to be undertaken. The million of pure whites left may, for example, be so strengthened that an invading force would have to deal with a regular and extremely dangerous army, well-acclimatised, occupying fortresses like Puebla, and supported by clouds of irregular Indian cavalry. The Emperor may, moreover, so change the face of Mexico by unbroken order, by judicious grants of mining and railway concessions, and by reviving the Indian civilisation, that Europe would be extremely unwilling to see the new *régime* overset. But these changes require years, and till they are accomplished, the Mexican Emperor must be dependent upon the favour of France. A letter from Napoleon will, it is certain, have as much weight in Mexico as a letter from Queen Victoria would have in India. It would not be precisely an order, but its views would, nevertheless, have a very appreciable force. This immense power has been obtained without much sacrifice of money, for Mexico can pay the expenses of the expedition and occupation without any unbearable suffering, and without any permanent or unchangeable liability. France must fight, no doubt, as long as the occupation lasts, but she is not responsible for Mexican debts subsequently contracted, and not bound to defend her after the occupation has ceased, and not bound even while it lasts to fight to utter exhaustion, as she must for any colony of her own. She becomes the protecting power in Mexico, without the liabilities involved in its direct administration.

2. The arrangement is not the best for Mexico, for a regular French viceroy could have been changed until the Emperor had secured precisely the right kind of man. But the new government will be in any case infinitely better than the ancient *régime*. Germans often abuse the Archduke as vain and ambitious and impulsive, but they always add that he is an able and intelligent man. The Hapsburgs, with many defects, have a rare talent for holding all they can get; and the 'Emperor Max.'—he will probably call himself Emperor Ferdinand—may prove an admirable administrator, and will certainly prove a better one than any obtainable half-caste or Indian President. He will have the advantage of permanence, of means to retire if necessary from the throne, and of the connection which gradually springs up between any decent sovereign and the people he is called on to govern. His German tendencies will not be much in the way, for he cannot if he would create an aristocracy, and he will certainly endeavour to maintain that social order under which Mexico, with its marvellous natural resources, must inevitably grow rich. He may do as well as a French viceroy, and the oddity involved in his acceptance of the position is his affair, and not that either of America or of Europe. Indeed, he has one recommendation which a French viceroy would not have. His tendency will be as soon as possible to be rid of his French allies, and, therefore, to try to conciliate the subjects among whom he and his house must live. A viceroy retiring after his term of service, and looking for his reward to Parisian rather than local opinion, would have no such inducement.

3. Lastly, the change is beneficial to Europe because it gives Mexico a chance of enjoying a permanent order and stability. It is not so good as the conversion of the country into a colony would have been, because it does not create an impassable barrier to North American ambition. But it does create *a* barrier, which is immensely strong while the French occupation lasts, and which a few years of good government may render almost as strong after that occupation is over. If the Archduke can attract any large immigration, whether of Spaniards or Italians—who settle in thousands at Buenos Ayres—or of Catholic Germans, or of Irishmen, or of freed negroes from the South, or of all of them—and all have certain temptations to select a warm, Catholic, or neighbouring country—he may ultimately form an army which shall render Mexico defensible, and once defensible it is beyond the power of the North to reduce it by mere blockades. Even if he should

THE NEW MEXICAN EMPIRE

fail, he will at least during the French occupation maintain order—
that is, he will restore to the sum of civilised wealth the produce of a
country which is as large as Europe within the Vistula, which will
grow everything from apples to rice—the two most distinctive products of temperate and tropical climates—which is rich in every variety
of mineral wealth, and which there is much reason to believe can yield
a much needed addition to the stock of silver existing in the world.
While the old anarchy continued, all these resources were as much
lost to mankind as if lava were flowing over them; but social order
will at once replace them within our grasp. It is as if a vast new land
had been discovered—an Australia added to the domain of material
civilisation. We regret that the arrangement should not have taken a
more certainly permanent form, and France been pledged like Great
Britain to resist active aggression from the Union; but the advantages
gained are still very considerable.

Nothing has yet transpired in relation to Mexican financial affairs;
but one thing would appear certain. Any civilised ruler of Mexico
must for his own sake make some definite arrangement with respect
to the foreign debt, and when made *adhere to it*. It may not be a very
profitable, or even a very satisfactory, arrangement to the holders of
Mexican bonds, but when made it will be fixed, and uncertainty will
come at all events to an end. The Austrian government is not one of
those which think it wise to repudiate; and it must be remembered
that the only power likely to upset the new *régime* is one which offered
to guarantee Mexican obligations rather than Europe should interfere.

France or England[1]

M. PERSIGNY, in an elaborate discourse, just delivered before the *Cercle des Arts and du Commerce at St Etienne*, raised in its most simple and striking form a political question, perhaps more important to Europe and the world than any other. He maintained not only that the present *régime* in France had conferred incidental benefits on the French people,—not only that it was a *régime* suited to the habits, and agreeable to the feelings, of a vast majority among them; but also that it was intrinsically a better and more perfect form of government than a free government—than such a government as that of England. In the present state of the world it is impossible to overrate the importance of such a proposition when set forth by such a speaker. M. Persigny is not to be confounded with the flatterers who fawn on or the time-servers who obey the present Emperor; they would obey and fawn on any other existing government, whatever it might be. M. Persigny was an adherent of Napoleon when he was thought to be a dreamer if not a madman; M. Persigny has the best right to propound the creed which he held in adversity just when its evident prosperity is most likely to convince mankind. He believes every word he says, and he chooses his time well. Large parts of Europe are changing or seem likely to change their form of government; it will be for them to choose what kind of government they will have; it would be more natural for them to follow the example of France, for its prestige is greater. Is, then, M. Persigny really wrong in advising them to follow this example and not that of England?

It is impossible to deny that the present Government of France has a great number of certain and considerable secondary excellences. It may justly claim to rank high in the short list of intelligent despotisms, even if its advocates are wrong in calling it the most intelligent which has ever existed. It may claim to be judged by results. The material progress of France under its rule has been far greater than the progress of France in any equal period of years before. Louis Napoleon has

[1] This article was first published in *The Economist* for September 5 1863, Volume XXI, pp. 982-3.

developed the railway system, improved the coinage, improved the post office; he has improved the army, he has vastly improved the navy; he has given France the most complete, perfect, and well-placed arsenal in the world; he has maintained, or even extended, the prestige of her influence and her name; he has given her as much of railroad as she has been willing to receive, and he would gladly give her more. Under his rule France has taken one of those sudden and mysterious *starts* which sometimes occur in the history of nations. She has in all economical respects improved so much that the closest and best observers can scarcely account for it; and that after the best explanations have been given, there is an uneasy feeling that the problem is only half solved, and that something remains to be said.

Nor can there be any reasonable question but that *at present* the Empire is a satisfactory and suitable government to a great and over-whelming majority of the French people. If their votes could be taken, not by the ballot—for that has been tried, and we know with what result—but by some magical and searching process that should detect the secret thoughts and wishes of men's hearts, we should certainly find the true and sincere adherents to the Empire to be beyond any comparison more numerous than the true and sincere adherents to the Orleanist Monarchy, or the Legitimist Monarchy, or the Republic, or than the adherents of all these added together. The French people care little for the play and spectacle of parliamentary conflict which the Empire denies them; they care much for the social equality—equality of impotence if you like, but still equality—which the Empire ensures; they care much for that visible *efficiency* both at home and abroad, which is the palpable and certain characteristic. That the French as a nation *do* like and prize the Empire is most certain, what-ever rationale we may give of it, or whatever comment we think fit to make upon it.

But a government may be suitable to the tastes and predilections of a particular people at a particular time, and may confer great benefits on that people at that time, and yet that government may not be intrinsically good or generally desirable. Such a *régime* may have momentary merits and permanent defects: the very qualities which fit it for one nation may unfit it for most others; its sins may be easily transplanted to other countries, and its excellences may not; it may be for other countries rather a warning to be spurned than an example to be copied.

The great majority of cultivated men in Europe believe that the French Government is an instance of this. They acknowledge that it is a very intelligent despotism, but all such governments must observe the fundamental precept which the most ordinary cookery books prescribe for the dressing of a very familiar quadruped. First, *catch* your despot. There is no security that the head of an absolute government should be a superior man, and there are reasons why he should be an inferior man. He is almost necessarily the spoiled child of the world. From his cradle everybody wishes to please him, and scarcely any one has the means to improve him. Most of those around him indulge him, in the hope of improving their own future, and the very few who are tolerably rigorous, commonly make themselves hated without being able to do any good. There is no security that the common elements of a good education should be given to princes, much less admirable culture or real wisdom. From the palace of France, Louis XIV came forth destitute of much elementary knowledge, and remained to the end of his life a very shrewd, but also a very ignorant, man. In the present case Louis Napoleon is a man of remarkable character and of strong mind. But his heir is a child. His wife has no real political tastes, is likely to show no true political ability, and believes in priests if she believes in anything. What possible reason is there for believing that the admitted intelligence of the present French Empire will survive the present Emperor? The despotism may endure; it is easy to take a military master, and hard to get rid of him; but who shall ensure us a continuance of the mind and spirit which have made that despotism endurable and valuable?

Again, it is true, as it is often boasted, that the French Emperor follows the opinions of France, and that therefore, to a not inconsiderable extent, France, notwithstanding appearances, is a free country. But it is also true that the present Government has no organised method of improving the condition of France. A parliamentary government lives by discussion, a free press has its life in argument and dissertation. By the play of these in really free countries, a public opinion is formed, that daily improves, that hourly adapts itself more nicely to the exigencies of the hour, that by continual learning comes to know great principles and understand great questions. The government, which, in such countries as in France, also follows public opinion, is therefore obliged to improve. It follows a progressive and learning guide, and itself therefore is compelled to grow and learn. But in France no such machinery exists. Parliament is even yet a shadow for which the mass of Frenchmen care little, and which influences them very little: the press—the daily newspapers at least—from which most men take their daily politics, cannot speak out. If the newspaper says disagreeable things, it endangers its suppression; it endangers the ruin of its proprietors. Public opinion in France may be and is still potent, but it is at the very best unimproving and stationary.

If we examine the matter closely, we may see reason to think that public opinion in France is likely even to retrograde. France is deprived of effectual daily instruction, and it was by that instruction that her present public opinion was created. Her present Government follows, by admission and profession, the wishes of the people,—that is, of the uninstructed mass, who are influenced by passion rather than argument, whose notions to-day are the *débris* of the educated theories of yesterday, only mistaken and distorted, who have no accurate information, who are incapable of careful thought. The continual following of this low opinion will deteriorate all opinion. There is no motive for the formation of a high and pure judgment, if a low and impure judgment is sure to rule.

A government, moreover, like that of Louis Napoleon, though it may be and is most intelligent, and most suitable to its subjects, is sure to be an *uneasy* government. It prohibits daily and efficient discussion, and the instructed classes, who love discussion, who delight in argument, who love the noble play of mind upon mind, become its irreconcilable enemies. The government may be the chosen representative of the dumb majority, but it is hated by the speaking minority —the few *élite*. But no despotic government can afford to despise the opinion of the instructed classes. They may be a minority in the nation, but they are the most formidable of minorities, for they contain the greater part of its intelligence. Their opinion may before long penetrate the masses, and a government which lives upon the masses is more likely, like the present French Government, to be anxious and nervous about it, than to despise it.

These arguments are sufficient to show that such a government as the French Empire, notwithstanding its subordinate excellences,—is not a really good government, is not a government which a nation with the power of selection should choose. It contains no peculiar good which will probably be permanent, and it contains the certain seeds of much incurable evil. It cannot even be a firm and easy government, because it is always conscious that there is a natural conspiracy plotting against it,—a conspiracy of *mind*.

It is probable that M. Persigny did not at heart feel that his eulogy on the French Empire was in all respects satisfactory, for he has endeavoured to show that at all events the Constitution of England did not present to the French or to most continental nations an available alternative. Following the guidance of the Emperor, M. Persigny does not deny the excellence of our English institutions; he only says that they are insular and cannot be transplanted. He says, in substance, that representation is possible, practicable, and excellent in England, because the English aristocracy remains still so powerful; but that a representative government is neither good nor possible in a country in which a territorial aristocracy does not exist or has lost its social influence. The English Constitution is successful, says M. Persigny, because, in England, the aristocracy choose the Prime Minister in fact, though not in theory; the imitations of the English constitution in France have been and must be unsuccessful, because in them a mere chamber of deputies, unguided by an aristocracy, would choose the Prime Minister. In England the parliamentary ministry is chosen by persons of hereditary property traditionally instructed: in France and other countries imitating England it can only be chosen by a chance assembly not allied to hereditary property, and not taught by any tradition.

Now we should be ready to admit, and indeed we have very often maintained, that the influence of the instructed aristocracy is desirable in this country, and that it beneficially exercises a composing and moderating influence on our polity. It occasionally retards desirable innovation, but it consolidates and preserves whatever good exists, whether it was made yesterday or some centuries since. The hereditary aristocracy is a good subsidiary element. But when it is said that the aristocracy appoint the Prime Minister and rule England, we deny it. We assert that every one who knows England well, well knows that it is the general body of educated Englishmen who rule England, and not the hereditary nobility. We say that the House of Lords is now-a-days a very timid body, conscious that it is acting among stronger powers of an alien nature, and that it is hesitating, anxious, and fearful in the exercise of its legal rights. We say that the opinion of the unaristo-cratic classes in England caused the Crimean war in opposition to the opinion and to the wishes of the aristocracy. We say that it will not be denied by *any* practical English statesman, whether Liberal or Conservative, that the pronounced opinion of the general mass of middle-class Englishmen is as much a law for the nobility as it is for the crown. The aristocracy is a useful counsellor of the nation, but it is not the nation.

In fact, M. Persigny, like many other continental critics of English institutions, confounds two things, both of which we have in England, and both of which usually co-operate, but which are in themselves and their own nature distinct. We have in England an hereditary aristocracy, and we have also a polity based on property, and, through property, upon education and intelligence. The aristocracy might be swept away as a separate body; and though the English polity would lose much that was valuable, much which could not be replaced, much which has often given a beneficial guidance, it would still be *itself*; it would not have lost its vital essence; it would still be a strong, enduring, efficient government, though a less discerning and consistent one. It is not open to the French to have a real hereditary aristocracy, and many continental nations have the same misfortune; but all great nations,—and France as much as any,—possess a great middle class, with intelligence, with property, with education. If it were wished, it would be possible for France and for every other nation to place, not necessarily the whole power, but, as with us, the predominant and supreme power, in the hands of those persons. The *true* British Constitution is adapted to the continent, though the apparent one is not; its simple essence would grow if it were cherished in any country in the same stage of civilisation as, and with analogous economical conditions to, our own.

The evil is that France does not wish to adopt such a constitution. Her *bourgeois* are just now as unpopular as her *noblesse*. Her passion for equality is so great that she will sacrifice everything to it. Free government involves privilege, because it requires that more power should be given to the instructed than to the uninstructed: there is no method by which men can be both free and equal. France has chosen the latter, England the former, nor need either interfere with the other. But when an abstract question is raised as to the general desirability and respective inviolability of the two forms of government, all sound thinkers are bound to prefer, and to say that they prefer, the liberty of England to the equality of France.

The 'Monroe Doctrine' in 1823 and 1863 [1]

MR. EVERETT, the American diplomatist, has published in the American journals a long paper on the English origin of what is called the *Monroe doctrine*,—viz., President Monroe's declaration that 'the American continents, by the free and independent condition which they have assumed and maintain, are henceforth not to be considered as subjects for future colonisation by any European Power.' We have no fault whatever to find with the tone of Mr. Everett's letter. He points out in moderate language that the exclusive doctrine which now sounds so objectionable and arrogant to English ears, is, strictly speaking, of English origin,—that Mr. Canning himself eagerly pressed some such declaration on President Monroe, that its enunciation by President Monroe practically defeated the danger which was then held to be imminent of a European Congress meeting to discuss the fate of the revolted Spanish colonies, that the Monroe doctrine might, therefore, quite as fairly be called the Canning doctrine, and that it was received in Parliament by Mr. Brougham and the Liberal party of that day with shouts of exultation. All this is unquestionably true. Sir James Mackintosh's remark on the occasion is quoted by Mr. Everett. He said that he was delighted to see how completely England and the United States agreed on the matter in question; and added: 'This coincidence of the two great English commonwealths,— for so I delight to call them, and I pray that they may be for ever so united in the cause of justice and liberty,—cannot be contemplated without the utmost pleasure by every enlightened citizen of the earth.' Mr. Canning was in this matter at least the true exponent of the foreign policy of the Liberal party, which sympathised eagerly with the revolted Spanish colonies, looked hopefully to their future, and suspected France of coveting territory in Spanish America, where she would reintroduce the principle of tyrannising from a distance over enslaved

[1] This article was first published in *The Economist* for November 14 1863, Volume XXI, pp. 1263–4.

colonies in the Gulf of Mexico. The experiment of republican institutions for Spanish America was looked upon with great hope. The encroaching policy of the continental despotisms was looked upon with great hatred. Mr. Canning thought that he could not give a greater impulse to the cause of freedom than by warning off all the old Powers, except England, from the American continent;—for no great country in Europe was at that period (1822–3) in any sense free, and even in England such little popular freedom as there was, held up to itself the freedom of the American States as its true type and model.

Things are greatly changed now. Mr. Everett very naturally expresses his heartfelt wish that such words as Sir James Mackintosh's 'were oftener heard in the British Parliament' now. The wish is very natural, and not very important. But it is not very likely to be granted. When Mr. Everett expresses his wonder at England's pleasure in hearing 'that a French invasion, the precise movement which Mr. Canning in 1823 urged the United States to join him in forbidding, has succeeded in trampling in the dust the policy which England then had so much at heart, and to which it is as much her interest now as ever to adhere,'—he merely shows how little he understands the English view of American politics. We wish to express no judgment on either the justice or wisdom of the present French invasion of Mexico. As regards the Mexican population there may be much to urge against it. Even, however, as regards Mexico itself we are forced to view the matter very differently from Mr. Canning. In 1823 people were very hopeful of the experiment of freedom in the Spanish American colonies. In 1863 people are not hopeful of that experiment, and, though they may think the French invasion unjust and unwise. can hardly regard the Mexicans as they regard the Poles or the Italians, The Mexicans have had their chance of freedom and have preferred anarchy. They have had their chance of self-government and preferred pillage. France may have been very wrong in interfering with it, because she may have little power to substitute anything better, but we cannot be expected to feel deeply for the Mexicans. A strong and permanent foreign influence over them would be much better than no government. Even a weak and temporary foreign influence, though it might be bad and add to the discord, could scarcely be conceived as greatly aggravating the mischief. England in 1863 is certainly quite unable to feel the same hope of Spanish American liberty as England in 1823.

But if, as regards considerations for the welfare of Mexico, the liberal view of the danger of European aggression is necessarily greatly changed, as regards considerations for limiting the power of France, and strengthening at once the influence of England and the welfare of the United States, it is still more greatly changed. What the Liberal party of that day feared from the meddling of France in Mexico was some great increase of French strength—an impulse to the power and despotic influence of France on both sides of the Atlantic. What the Liberals now hope from the invasion of Mexico is a great expenditure of French strength—a fresh guarantee against her restlessness on both sides of the Atlantic. We no longer hold the idea that formerly prevailed, that mere extent of territory means substantial increase of power. Probably few English politicians who congratulate themselves on the French adventure in Mexico, look upon it as anything more than a great drain on French resources, which will leave the Emperor a much smaller disposable force for European schemes of 'reconstructions'—as a sort of political seton lowering the physical strength but clearing the brain of France.

But again, English Liberals in 1823 supposed that the greatest danger of the American colonies lay in the ambition of European Powers, which were eager to resist or restrict the natural spread of the free institutions of America. But the experience of forty years has shown us how little of reality there is in this danger, how much reality in a quite different danger then scarcely anticipated. It was the first time that the experiment had been tried of letting a nation of freemen, and of free men in the highest phase of civilisation, grow and expand quite without any resisting or constraining force to limit and compress and mould it into the shapes which a society of nations necessarily imposes. It was supposed that the political life of this people would grow like a forest tree, all the more rich and free and magnificent for not being jostled by a number of competing neighbours. So many of the miseries of Europe had obviously arisen from the fierce competitions and rivalries of nations,—so much freedom had been extinguished simply because it was incompatible with the genius of neighbouring powers, that at that time the idea of a continent over which a single nation might spread and stretch at pleasure, without encountering a single formidable rival, had in it a peculiar attraction for the Liberal party. Here it was thought all the conditions of political freedom were combined in the most perfect harmony. No Liberal politician of really thoughtful intellect, however, is so well satisfied on this head now. Very many—amongst whom we must reckon ourselves—have come to the conclusion that it is with young nations much as it is with young children:—if they are brought up in close association with each other, they will fight much and create the most dreadful disturbances in their youth, and yet they will on the whole grow up into more various, more interesting, and better disciplined forms of mature life than 'only children' educated at home. The constant action and re-action of different tempers, different talents, different tastes, is, on the whole, an advantage, a great advantage, to their originality of character —a great advantage also to their self-knowledge. Liberal politicians, who are far from wishing to see the dull uniformity of American life broken by the successful inauguration of so great a national evil as a slave empire, yet admit freely that the experiment of one nation for one continent has turned out on the whole far from well. The American nation has very much the sort of faults which 'only children' are said to have. It has no correct measure of its own strength. Having never entered into close competition with any other nation, it indulges in that infinite braggadocio which a public school so soon rubs out of a conceited boy. And what is a more serious though a less disagreeable fault, there is inevitably a terrible uniformity about the American national character, a frightful want of play and variety in its political life. We now see clearly that 'undisturbed expansion' for political institutions has at least vast evils to counterbalance the great economy of strife and animosity which it ensures. The sincerest well-wishers to the American people, who look with dismay on secession if it is to give the North a rival only on the basis of slavery, would still see with satisfaction the growth of any specific national peculiarities in different parts of the continent, which would ensure competition and rivalry without that evil peculiarity. There is the sort of feeling amongst all acute observers which Mr. Disraeli expressed about a year ago, that the Northern States are beginning to want a little general political society,—equal competitors in the political race,—not only to sober their pretensions, but to give them the wholesome sense of close foreign observation and the wholesome duty of observing vigilantly in their turn.

Now, of course, this feeling essentially affects our view of the French invasion of Mexico. Without pronouncing on its justice, it is impossible to feel that alarm which Mr. Canning expressed on behalf of the liberal foreign politics of England, and which he successfully instilled into the United States. If the United States could get foreign neighbours of anything like equal political intelligence, without slavery,—neighbours who would keep them under critical, if not hostile, surveillance,—neighbours whom they would have to keep under critical, if not hostile, surveillance,—both the restraint and the variety this would give to their politics would do them a great deal of good. No conviction has grown more steadily on politicians of late years than the conviction that freedom, though the essence of all that is highest in political life, is not sufficient for the development of a high form of political character without also variety, competition, and restraint. Even in the internal political organisations of nations, those political constitutions are the highest which, like those of England and Italy, comprehend the most various elements in harmonious combination. The politics of France and America are inferior just because the number of really distinct social and political elements is much less. But when to this interior uniformity you add complete external isolation, as in the case of America, the evil is, of course, greatly exaggerated. And though we could not expect Mr. Canning to foresee in 1823, the course of events which has brought all this home to us with so much vividness, Mr. Everett must excuse us from accepting that statesman's somewhat obsolete authority for a policy, the danger of which every year since Canning's death has helped to illustrate and increase.

The Emperor of the French[1]

In ruder times, and amid less complicated politics and civilisations than our own, the currents of great events and the destinies of great nations often hung distinctively and solely on the decisions of individual men. Kings, warriors, or ministers determined everything. Peoples had comparatively little to do with the arrangement of their own affairs, and public opinion had not, as it has now, a voice potential in the direction of the national action. One man, of great intellect and resolute will, placed in a lofty position, could habitually and at his own single option decide on peace or war, on progress or stagnation, without his subjects having anything to say in the matter, and even in opposition to all their wishes and interests, so far as they felt the one or understood the other. Monarchs thought, determined, and commanded: nations were only summoned to follow, to suffer, and to obey. In proportion as wealth and freedom have advanced, in proportion as constitutionalism has made good its ground, in proportion as the concerns of different nations have been more closely bound up with each other, in proportion as the issues of political disputes have become more extensive and important,—in just such proportion has the influence of individuals, whether sovereigns or statesmen, dwindled away. In speculating on the probable course of events in critical and menacing conjunctures, we now enquire much more anxiously what are the sentiments and interests of such and such *peoples*, than what are the views and characters of such and such rulers. And though great men still have, and must always have, great influence on the course of political events, on particular occasions and in special circumstances; yet as a rule we do not fear as we used to do the consequences of the personal passions of a prince or the illicit sway which that prince's mistress may hold over his mind. No individual man in any nation is so influential as the aggregate of men.

There is, however, one remarkable exception to this rule; and the

[1] This article was first published in *The Economist* for November 28 1863, Volume XXI, pp. 1322–3.

exception is, in a curious manner, illustrative and confirmatory of the rule. In the very midst of our most complicated system of polity, in an age of preeminently democratic tendencies and temper, in one of the most advanced countries of Europe, and in a stage of civilisation when public opinion has more influence and when national interests are better understood than at any former period, there exists one man whose character and views are studied and investigated as if they were one of the strongest and most determining facts and powers of the political world, and whose words are listened to with as much anxiety and almost as much deference as were of old the utterances of the oracle of Delphi. It is idle to disguise the truth—that on the decisions of the Emperor of the French hang the course of public events and of national fate to a degree usually only true of the decisions of whole nations, or great parliaments, or mighty congresses. He wields, in his own hands, more real power of calming or disturbing the world, of making or upsetting kingdoms, of compelling every state in the world to spend countless millions or permitting it to save them, than any man now living or who has lived for the last half century at least. And, to make good the remarks with which we began, he owes this paramount and dangerous power far less to the largeness or vigour of his intellect, than to the fact that he embodies in himself the characteristics and desires of a great nation, and is the representative and to a considerable extent the sympathising organ of a great party which is spread over all nations. In estimating future probabilities, in endeavouring to ascertain what is likely to be the course of public events and the immediate destinies of Europe, it is of less consequence to comprehend accurately the resources and characteristics of Russia, or Austria, or Prussia, or Italy, or even, perhaps, the sentiments and resolutions of English statesmen and the English people, than thoroughly to master the peculiarities of Napoleon III—the proclivities of his singular nature, and the exigencies of his anomalous position. When we wish to know whether we are to have war or peace, whether Poland is to be rescued from extermination, whether the Kingdom of Italy is to be completed by the annexation of Venetia and the withdrawal of the French troops from Rome, whether and when the Confederate States of America are to be recognised and established, whether our next income tax is to be sixpence or tenpence in the pound,—the element in our calculation which it is most essential to discern and estimate aright is the intentions of the Emperor of the French.

THE EMPEROR OF THE FRENCH

Two points need to be studied—his *character* and his *position*. Sometimes these appear to be antagonistic, sometimes co-operative forces. First, then, he is distinguished by one quality which is almost equally to be deprecated in the sovereign of a military empire and in the finance minister of any state. He is essentially *restless*. He has a busy mind, rather than a prompt and active will. He broods much; and he broods in silence and in darkness. He is ever full of schemes and projects, which from time [to time] he throws out to disturb and dismay Europe. Occasionally he puts them forth in a tentative form, and when they have only reached the nebulous and floating stage in his brain. At other times he waits till he has matured them. It is the *incalculable* nature of his restlessness that renders it so peculiarly pernicious. He is for ever breaking out in a fresh place. You never know what he will do or say next. You only know that he will not be long quiet. He is, and will always be as long as he lives, the volcanic and *rémuant* element in the cauldron of European politics.

But though ever stirring, he is not precisely active. Physically, indeed, and for considerable periods together, he is even what may be called lazy. He is slow in forming his plans. He is slow in coming to a practical decision upon them when matured. He often procrastinates and postpones because he shrinks from *irrevocable* steps, and wishes to keep as many courses as possible open to him, and to keep them open as long as he can. He is a singular mixture of tenacity and hesitation, of daring and timidity. He has often astonished the world as much by the persistence as by the inconsistency of his ideas. He recurs over and over again to projects and notions which every one believed he had abandoned; yet he surrenders them, or appears to surrender them, when met by unforeseen obstacles, or by obstacles unexpectedly strong. He recoils easily before vigorous opposition. He is not usually rash. On the contrary, he takes great pains to make his steps as safe as he can, and to secure as great an amount of support as possible beforehand. He has none of the obstinate wilfulness of the first Napoleon. He is not a man likely to venture on desperate or *very* hazardous attempts. His position is too great a one to be lightly risked. He takes infinite pains to avert all chance of failure. His schemes are vast and daring enough; but he is singularly cautious, deliberate, and patient in carrying them out. He is a person of extraordinary *mental* courage; but of the courage of the sanguine man of action he has comparatively little. In the *coup d'état*, no doubt, he showed daring of both sorts in a sense, though the details even of that event, carefully studied, will go far to confirm our diagnosis; but since that marvellous success his caution, next to his restlessness, has been the quality he has displayed most steadily and most remarkably. We may feel very confident that he will never face Europe, or run any risk of acting in such a fashion as to combine all Europe against him. He would never have engaged in the Crimean war if he had not secured the vigorous co-operation of Great Britain. He would never have gone to Mexico if England and Spain had not joined the expedition. He has twice abandoned, or at least postponed, his design of recognising the Confederates, because Great Britain discouraged and would not support him. He would probably never have ventured on the Italian campaign if he had not felt certain of a mighty power at his back sufficient to *ensure* success, if it was found necessary to call it into action; and he paused half-way in his career of hard-contested victory lest he should have to call it into action. Moreover, in that case he found himself hemmed in between two risks, and he decided to encounter the smallest and the most remote.

He is vain, also, though not to any irrational degree. His vanity is rather a moral fault than a weakness that can be counted upon or played upon. He loves grandeur, he loves power, he loves admiration, and he is desirous on all accounts to fill unceasingly a vast space in the eye of Europe and the world. In this, as in so many other points, policy and personal sentiment combine to indicate his course. To sum up all, he has a restless, scheming, brooding, *cavernous* mind; daring in idea— hesitating when it comes to action; a singular mixture of tenacity and inconsistency; recoiling before the difficult and hazardous; shrinking from the irrevocable; and certain not to venture on the desperate. For the rest, unusually farseeing and forecasting; thoroughly understanding his nation, his day, and his position; and, perhaps, beyond any other statesman in the world, acting with a purpose and on a system.

The Emperor of the French[1]

THE Emperor is the Crowned Democrat of Europe. The position is no doubt one of great elevation and of enormous power, but it is also one full of peril and full of exigencies. 'The Masses,' though an effective, and under many circumstances, an almost resistless servant make a capricious, exacting, and relentless master. Both at home and abroad Napoleon III has a contract with the agencies that have made him what he is and that sustain him where he is, the terms of which contract must be rigidly fulfilled. At home he rules *over* the middle classes, *in defiance* of the educated classes, and *by the support* of the lower classes and the army. In ultimate resort he may be said to reign by the right of numbers and by the instrumentality of bayonets. It is true that he has done much—perhaps as much as lay in his power—to widen the basis of his throne, and to make all classes interested in maintaining him. He has tentatively and modestly allowed the intellectual classes to raise their heads; he has conciliated the *bourgeoisie* by the material prosperity which he has so sagaciously and indefatigably fostered; and he has cancelled or moderated the hostility once felt towards him by the rich and great by convincing them that property was in habitual danger from the *Rouges*, and that his was the only hand that could avert that danger. So that beyond all dispute the number of those who wish to overthrow him has largely diminished, and the number of those who desire to maintain him has largely increased, each year since 1852. Still it remains true that to retain his popularity and prestige with FRANCE—*i.e.*, with the two ultimately governing bodies in France,—he must be sedulous to please, or at all events careful not to offend, the populace, the peasantry, and the army. Now France loves two things above all others—gain and glory. It is difficult to say what it loves most. Both the French peasant and the French bourgeois thirst for wealth with an inordinate longing; yet both are singularly susceptible to what Goëthe calls 'the tyranny

[1] This article was first published in *The Economist* for December 5 1863, Volume XXI, pp. 1348–9.

of ideas.' They are easily carried away by political sympathies and by the cravings of national vanity:—this is true even still more strongly of the populace of the towns. They are delighted with seeing their country so influential, so disturbing, so dictatorial in Europe, and are ready to worship the man who has made her so. Yet at the same time they are little inclined to pay the natural price for so distinguished a position. The peasants will not endure fresh taxation, nor will the middle classes patiently face the interruption to industry and commerce consequent on extensive wars. But such wars as can be carried on by means of loans at high interest raised at home; such wars as can be made to cause an increased demand for native productions or to promise an extension of foreign commerce; such wars as eventuate, or promise to eventuate, in accession of territory; such wars as are not too difficult or dangerous, and hold out hopes of feeding ancient grudges or gratifying long disappointed hopes,—such wars, finally, as bring France grandly before the eyes of the world as the defender of oppressed nations and the champion of crushed democracies,—such wars, and such only, are likely to be undertaken by the Emperor. France demands of him that he shall exhibit her unceasingly in the blended attitude and colours of the peacock and the eagle;—and so long as he does this, she is satisfied to leave him the choice of means— whether he prefer sudden wars, magnificent congresses, or distant naval expeditions. Thus far he has succeeded wonderfully in giving his exacting nation precisely what she wants, and avoiding precisely what she detests and dreads. The wealth and commerce of France under his reign have increased with wholly unexampled rapidity. Both in peace and war he has been a most expensive ruler; but his vast expenditure has been met either by the increased productiveness of the existing taxes, or by open loans which every saving and hoarding peasant has felt as a positive source of affluence. Never, except under his uncle and during a short period of Louis XIV's reign, has France been so influential, or at least so *disturbing* (and that is what Frenchmen really like), as she is now. Then for glory, or what in Gallic eyes passes for such, Louis Napoleon has given her her fill. He has not only humbled and defeated the two great continental monarchies which chiefly brought about his uncle's ruin; he has not only re-established that Imperial dynasty which all Europe once banded together to overthrow, and declared should never reign again in France; he has not only added two much coveted provinces to her territorial limits; but he has created one kingdom, that of Italy, and one empire, that of Mexico; and if England would have sanctioned or encouraged the enterprise, he would probably have added the Southern American Confederacy to the list of republics and Poland to the list of monarchies. To France certainly he has amply fulfilled his obligations.

But he has another master besides France to satisfy,—a power at once his master and his tool—*viz.*, the revolutionary party throughout Europe—the democratic element in continental states—the discontented and oppressed Nationalities—those, in a word, who are fond of describing themselves as the adherents and devotees of 'the Principles of 1789.' With this party Louis Napoleon has strong sympathies; to it he is under great obligations; from it he has great hopes; of it he entertains great fear. He understands thoroughly its strength, its nature, and its designs. His early *Carbonari* connections gave him this knowledge; and it is a knowledge which, being his exclusive possession, confers upon him a notable advantage over all other governments and potentates. Then, too, he not only understands this party, but he believes in it. He is, we apprehend, strongly convinced that the 'Principles of 1789' are those which will finally prevail; that in the perennial contest between democracy and its rivals, the ultimate victory will remain with the former; and that all political progress, as well as all political convulsions, is tending towards the establishment in all lands of the sovereignty of the people, delegated to and embodied in the sovereignty of one man, as the ultimate form which states and governments will assume. Of this tendency he is determined to be the exponent, the patron, and the leader,—as he has contrived to make himself its first, and most illustrious exemplar. This conviction we hold to be the key to nearly all his policy, past and present. He has no more notion than Tocqueville had that any aristocracy or autocracy can in the end make head against the might of the popular masses; he has a rooted distrust and dislike of a parliamentary and constitutional *régime*; he has no faith in the *working* capacity of really republican institutions. His doctrine—his *idée Napoleonienne*—is the administration of one man sustained by the great body of the people, imbued with their sentiments and wishes, but endowed with sagacity to sift them, to guide them, to modify and enlighten them, but also with full power to enforce and establish them. There is vast might, because there is much truth, in this conception of individual will and talent based upon brute force, backed by it and wielding it. But herein also lies the greatest danger of modern civilisation; and it is the devotion of Louis Napoleon to this conception, the clearness with which he apprehends it, and the vigour with which he grasps it, that renders him the most formidable foe that the higher elements of moral and intellectual, as distinguished from material, civilisation ever had.

We dare not entangle ourselves in any detailed or confident predictions as to how a potentate, so endowed and so placed as we have made out the French Emperor to be, will act in reference to the several pressing questions which lie before him. We are not, probably, and never shall be, in possession of *all* the circumstances which will guide his decision, whenever the hour shall arrive at which decision can no longer be postponed. But we may offer a few suggestions on this interesting speculation.

And, *first*, as to America. There can be no doubt that the position of the Emperor in Mexico makes it a matter of prime importance to him that the disruption of the American Republic shall not be healed, and that the Southern Confederacy should make good its independence. In the one case, he will have to maintain his new creation *single-handed* against a mighty power. In the other case, he will have an ally to help him, and a much weaker antagonist to contend with. He has, therefore, a very strong motive for recognising the South, and assisting it in establishing its separate existence. But, on the other hand, he must feel that to engage in a war with the United States would be a very grave and, perhaps, even a hazardous undertaking, unless England would join him in the venture; and he is aware also that such a war would not be popular in France. His rooted tendency and habit, therefore, of making all his steps as *safe* as possible before he takes them, added to his constant disposition to postpone all irrevocable resolutions, will probably combine to make him procrastinate all decisive action in the matter till some opportunity shall offer itself—such as an insult to the French flag from some American cruiser—which shall give him at once the excuse he wishes for, and the stimulus to a positive determination which his slow nature needs. And if no such an occasion presents itself, it is possible enough that he may procrastinate even till the time for safe or profitable action is past; and may prefer to leave the ultimate conflict with the transatlantic Anglo-Saxons to the chances of the day, perhaps a distant one, when it can no longer be averted.

As to the French occupation of Rome, we apprehend he will make no change till he is forced to do so. The position gratifies his love of power. It also flatters French vanity—so strange a thing is that national passion, and such sad garbage can it feed on. On the one hand, the withdrawal of his troops would almost inevitably embroil him with the Catholic or ultramontane party in France. On the other hand, their continued residence in Rome must end in exhausting the patience and exasperating the animosity of the revolutionary party, who will not always be put off with promises and hopes. We conclude, therefore, that he will remain where he is till this party become dangerous and menacing—more dangerous and more menacing than the papist bigots.

As to Poland, the matter is very different. Intervention in that quarter would be popular with nearly all parties in France. It would be popular with the clergy, because the Poles are Catholics. It would be popular with the masses, because the Poles are democrats and revolutionists. It would be popular with the army, because Prussia must be stepped over in order to get to Poland. But here, again, the element of caution, so largely developed in the imperial mind, comes in. A war against Prussia, Austria, and Russia, with England at the least neuter and disapproving, would be too hazardous a course to be *deliberately* adopted by a man who shrinks from all desperate adventures. On the one hand, he cannot afford to allow a nationality imbued with 'the principles of 1789' to be trodden out. On the other hand, he cannot afford to risk defeat and failure on its behalf. It is a subject that probably perplexes him more than any other, and out of the difficulties of which he will trust to the chapter of accidents to extricate him.

In reference to the congress, it is not likely that the Emperor, who always recoils before unforeseen or very serious obstacles, will persevere in defiance of the discouragement his project has received. But, true to his habit, he will hold himself forth to the world as the would-be pacificator of Europe, and throw upon other powers the whole responsibility of their refusal to aid him in his good designs.

As to the Dano-Germanic quarrel, we may predict with tolerable confidence that he will *wait and see*; that he will watch its development and capabilities with the keenest vigilance; and will seize with instinctive sagacity and promptitude any occasion which its various phases may offer for furthering his own objects by a flank movement, for indemnifying himself for his recent discomfiture, and for repaying with interest those who have baffled him.

Cæsareanism as it now exists[1]

THAT the French Emperor should have spare leisure and unoccupied reflection sufficient to write a biography is astonishing, but if he wished to write a biography his choice of a subject is very natural. Julius Cæsar was the first who tried on an imperial scale the characteristic principles of the French Empire,—as the first Napoleon revived them, as the third Napoleon has consolidated them. The notion of a demagogue ruler, both of a fighting demagogue and a talking demagogue, was indeed familiar to the Greek republics, but their size was small, and their history unemphatic. On the big page of universal history, Julius Cæsar is the first instance of a democratic despot. He overthrew an aristocracy—a corrupt and perhaps effete aristocracy it is true, but still an aristocracy—by the help of the people, of the unorganised people. He said to the numerical majority of Roman citizens, 'I am your advocate and your leader: make me supreme, and I will govern for your good and in your name.' This is exactly the principle of the French Empire. No one will ever make an approach to understanding it who does not separate it altogether, and on principle, from the despotisms of feudal origin and legitimate pretensions. The old monarchies claim the obedience of the people upon grounds of duty. They say they have consecrated claims to the loyalty of mankind. They appeal to conscience, and even to religion. But Louis Napoleon is a Benthamite despot. He is for the 'greatest happiness of the greatest number.' He says, 'I am where I am, because I know better than any one else what is good for the French people, and they know that I know better.' He is not the Lord's anointed; he is the people's agent.

We cannot here discuss what the effect of this system was in ancient times. These columns are not the best place for an historical dissertation; but we may set down very briefly the results of some close and recent observation of the system as it now exists, as it is at work in

[1] This article was first published in *The Economist* for March 4 1865, Volume XXIII, pp. 249–50.

France. Part of its effects are well understood in England, but a part of them are, we think, but mistily seen and imperfectly apprehended.

In the first place, the French Empire is really the *best finished* democracy which the world has ever seen. What the many at the moment desire is embodied with a readiness, an efficiency, and a completeness which has no parallel either in past history or present experience. An absolute government with a popular instinct has the unimpeded command of a people renowned for orderly dexterity. A Frenchman will have arranged an administrative organisation really and effectually, while an Englishman is still bungling and a German still reflecting. An American is certainly as rapid, and, in some measure, as efficient, but his speed is a little headlong and his execution is very rough; he tumbles through much, but he only tumbles. A Frenchman will not hurry; he has a deliberate perfection in detail, which may be always relied on, for it is never delayed. The French Emperor knows well how to use these powers. His bureaucracy is not only endurable but pleasant. An idle man who wants his politics done for him, has them done for him. The welfare of the masses—the present good of the present multitude—is felt to be the object of the government and the law of the polity. The Empire gives to the French the full gratification of their main wishes, and the almost artistic culture of an admirable workmanship, of an administration finished as only Frenchman can finish it, and as it never was finished before.

It belongs to such a government to care much for material prosperity, and it does care. It makes the people as comfortable as they will permit. If they are not more comfortable, it is their own fault. The government would give them free trade and consequent diffused comfort if it could.

No former French government has done as much for free trade as this government. No government has striven to promote railways, and roads, and industry, like this government. France is much changed in twelve years. Not exactly by the mere merit of the Empire, for it entered into a great inheritance; it succeeded to the silent work of the free monarchy which revolution had destroyed and impeded. There were fruitful and vigorous germs of improvement ready to be elicited —ready to start forth—but, under an unintelligent government, they would not have started forth; they would have lain idle and dead, but under the adroit culture of the present Government, they have grown so as to amaze Europe and France itself.

If, indeed, as is often laid down, the *present happiness* of the greatest number was the characteristic object of government, it would be difficult to make out that any probable French government would be better, or indeed nearly so good as the present. The intelligence of the Emperor on economical subjects—on the bread and meat of the people —is really better than that of the classes opposed to him. He gives the present race of Frenchmen more that is good than any one else would give them, and he gives it them in their own name. They have as much as they like of all that is good for them. But if not the present happiness of the greatest number but *their future elevation* be, as it is, the true aim and end of government, an estimate of the Empire will be strangely altered. It is an admirable government for present and coarse purposes, but a detestable government for future and refined purposes.

In the first place, it stops the *teaching apparatus*; it stops the effectual inculcation of important thought upon the mass of mankind. All other mental effort but this the Empire not only permits but encourages. The high intellect of Paris is as active, as well represented, as that of London, and it is even more keen. Intellect still gives there, and has always given, a distinctive position. To be a *membre de l'Institut* is a recognised place in France; but in London, it is an ambiguous distinction to be a 'clever fellow.' The higher kinds of thought are perhaps better discussed in Parisian society than in London society, and better argued in the *Revue des deux Mondes* than in any English periodical. The speculative thought of France has not been killed by the Empire. It is as quick, as rigorous, as keen, as ever. But though still alive, it is no longer powerful; it cannot teach the mass. The *Revue* is permitted, but newspapers—effectual newspapers—are forbidden. A real course of free lectures on popular subjects would be impossible in Paris. *Agitation* is forbidden, and it is agitation, and agitation alone, which teaches. The crude mass of men bear easily philosophical treatises, refined articles, elegant literature; there are but two instruments penetrative enough to reach their opaque minds—the newspaper article and the popular speech, and both of these are forbidden.

In London the reverse is true. We may say that only the loudest sort of expression is permitted to attain its due effect. The popular organs of literature so fill men's minds with incomplete thoughts, that deliberate treatment, that careful inquiry, that quiet thoughts have no hearing. People are so deafened with the loud reiteration of many half-truths, that they have neither curiosity nor energy for elaborate investigation. The very word 'elaborate' is become a reproach: it produces something which the mass of men do not like because it is above them,—which is tiresome because it needs industry,—difficult because it wants attention,—complicated because it is true. On the whole, perhaps, English thought has rarely been so unfinished, so piecemeal, so *ragged* as it is now. We have so many little discussions that we get no full discussion; we eat so many sandwiches that we spoil our dinner. And on the Continent, accordingly, the speculative thought of England is despised. It is believed to be meagre, unculti-vated, and immature. We have only a single compensation. Our thought may be poor and rough and fragmentary, but it is effectual. With our newspapers and our speeches—with our clamorous multitudes of indifferent tongues, we beat the ideas of the few into the minds of the many. The head of France is a better head than ours, but it does not move her limbs, the head of England is in comparison a coarse and crude thing, but rules her various frame and regulates her whole life.

France, *as it is*, may be happier because of the Empire, but France *in the future* will be more ignorant because of the Empire. The daily play of the higher mind upon the lower mind is arrested. The present government has given an instalment of free trade, but it could not endure an agitation for free trade. A democratic despotism is like a theocracy: it assumes its own correctness. It says, 'I am the repre-sentative of the people; I am here because I know what they wish, because I know what they should have.' As Cavaignac once said, 'A government which permits its principles to be questioned is a lost government.' All popular discussion whatever which aspires to *teach* the government is radically at issue with the hypothesis of the Empire. It says that the Cæsar, the omniscient representative, is a mistaken representative, that he is not fit to be Cæsar.

The deterioration of the future is one inseparable defect of the imperial organisation, but it is not the only one,—for the moment, it is not the greatest. The greatest is the corruption of the present. A greater burden is imposed by it upon human nature than human nature will bear. Everything requires the support, aid, countenance of the central government, and yet that government is expected to keep itself pure. Concessions of railways, concessions of the privilege of limited liability,—on a hundred subjects, legal permission, administra-tive help are necessary to money-making. You concentrate upon a small body of leading official men the power of making men's fortunes, and it is simple to believe they will not make their own fortunes. The very principle of the system is to concentrate power, and power is money. Sir Robert Walpole used to say, 'No honest man could be a minister;' and in France the temptations would conquer almost all men's honesty. The system requires angels to work it, and perhaps it has not been so fortunate as to find angels. The nod of a minister on the Bourse is a fortune, and somehow or other ministers make fortunes. The Bourse of Paris is still so small that a leading capitalist may produce a great impression on it, and a leading capitalist, working with a great minister, a vast impression. Accordingly, all that goes with sudden wealth; all that follows from the misuse of the *two* temptations of civilisation, money and women, is concentrated round the imperial court. The Emperor would cure much of it if he could, but what can he do? They say he has said 'that he will not change his men. He will not substitute fleas that are hungry for fleas which at least are partially satisfied.' He is right. The defect belongs to the system, to these men; an enormous concentration of power in an industrial system ensures an accumulation of pecuniary temptation.

These are the two main disadvantages which France suffers from her present Government; the greater part of the price which she has to pay for her present happiness. She endures the daily presence of an efficient immorality; she sacrifices the educating apparatus which would elevate Frenchmen yet to be born. But these two disadvantages are not the only ones.

France gains the material present, but she does not gain the material future. All that gives present industry her Government confers, in whatever needs confidence in future she is powerless. *Credit* in France, to an Englishman's eye, has almost to be created. The *country* deposits in the Bank of France are only £1,000,000 sterling; that bank has fifty-nine branches, is immeasurably the greatest country bank in France. All discussions on the currency come back to the *cours forcé*, to the inevitable necessity of making inconvertible notes an irrefusable tender during a revolution. If you propose the simplest operations of credit to a French banker, he says, 'You do not remember 1848; *I* do.' And what is the answer? The present Government avowedly depends, is ostentatiously concentrated, in the existing Cæsar. Its existence depends on the permanent occupation of the Tuileries by an extra-ordinary man. The democratic despot—the representative despot—must have the sagacity to divine the people's will, and the sagacity to execute it. What is the likelihood that these will be hereditary? Can they be expected in the next heirs, a child for Emperor, and a woman for a Regent? The present happiness of France is happiness on a short life lease; it may end with the life of a man who is not young, who has not spared himself, who has always thought, who has always *lived*.

Such are the characteristics of the Empire as it is. Such is the nature of Cæsar's government as we know it at the present. We scarcely expect even the singular ability of Napoleon III will be able to modify, by an historical retrospect, the painful impressions left by actual contact with a living reality.

The Mercantile Evils of Imperialism[1]

THE peculiar sort of despotism, of which France shows the type is undoubtedly growing in the world. Count Bismarck will, if he can, extend it over all Germany. A school of thinkers who have great influence on young Englishmen say, 'Well, if the new Reform Bill does directly or eventually destroy parliamentary government, it won't have done much harm. Parliamentary government is complex, dilatory, and inefficient. An efficient absolutism chosen by the people, and congenial to the people, is far better than this dull talking, which does little, invents nothing, and prevents everything.' Perhaps, therefore, it may not be useless to show how much *at this very moment* Imperialism is destroying wealth and comfort.

The traditional argument against despotism used to be, that it made property insecure. Everything was at the disposal of one man, and that man might at any moment rob the rich if he wanted money for pleasure or for war. And such is really the case under a coarse Asiatic despotism; the monarch does take the property of his subjects when he stands in need of it, and, therefore, all of his subjects try to make out they have none. But the French Emperor does nothing like it, nor does any European despot now. Absolute monarchs are too wise to kill the bird which lays the golden eggs; on the contrary, they foster it with the most sedulous and ostentatious care. A rich man in Paris is as secure as a rich man in London. Even the taxation of a free country is as likely to be heavy as that of a despot, because the despot is often unwilling to impose on the nation burdens so heavy as those which, if of its own will and for its own objects, it will readily undergo. Nor does the despot nowadays wish to impose fetters upon trade as such. The Emperor Napoleon is as good a free trader as there is in France; and, in general, the despotic governments of the continent are economically more instructed than their subjects. They wish to augment wealth, and they know that industrial freedom is the best way to make wealth

[1] This article was first published in *The Economist* for August 31 1867, Volume XXV, p. 983.

grow. And as for the common English notion that such freedom stimulates the demand for political freedom, the governments are aware that very often it does nothing of the kind. On the contrary, whatever makes men richer makes them more timid, and the more men fear revolution and spoliation, the better for a decent government which is in possession and keeps peace in the streets at all events.

But though despotism is favourable to property, it kills *credit*. Just now, every bourse in Europe is trembling to know what the French Emperor and the Austrian Emperor are about to do. The nations they rule leave the most momentous decisions of present politics wholly to them; they can go to war if they choose, and remain at peace if they please. But this brings into politics an incalculable element, and makes it supreme. If the choice rested with free nations ruled by public parliaments, we should have *data* to spell the future. A debating government is a government which rules in the face of day. A free nation assisting daily at its own government often shows its inclinations unmistakably, and can never out of diplomacy disguise them. A person who has lived among them can tell at once what they will think. But no one can pretend to predict with similar accuracy the decisions of single persons, especially of persons who have every means of hiding what they desire, and often the keenest motive to disguise what they intend. Nobody *can* tell what either of these Emperors are going to do: very likely—it is the rule in such cases—they hardly know themselves. Great potentates live from day to day like other people, and often more so, for the great events amid which they are cast are more sudden, more incalculable, and more derange preconcerted designs. As soon as despotism begins foresight ceases, and where foresight ends, all sound business ends too. The whole foreign policy of the Continent is now, and probably for years must be, a confusing element in commerce and in finance, because it depends on secret decisions, which can be foretold by no one, and for a long time after they are made can be known by but a few.

And in the interior of a despotic country the effect is worse than outside. Everybody knows that in France the whole future depends upon the life of one man—of the Emperor. Everybody knows, or imagines he knows, what may happen during his life; but after he dies, anything may soon happen. There may be a republic, a monarchy, or a continuation of the Empire. No one can predict upon real reasons, and the only persons who are confident are those who have a great risk and heavy stake on some event. In consequence, the development of credit in France is contemptible. On every other side, an English traveller sees nothing incalculably inferior to England. Means of communication, trade, agriculture, are all excellent in France, and if some of them are better in some respects than in England, on the other hand, some of them are in other points worse. But the French banking system is childish, or rather looks childish, till you understand the secret dread which dwarfs it. A French banker, in answer to all comments upon his timidity, has a single reply: he says, 'It is all very well for you to talk in England; but *we* in Paris, have revolutions; you were not here in 1848; *I* was.' If you discuss the currency question with a Frenchman, he begins from a fixed point which would never occur to an Englishman. He says, 'There must be in time of revolution a note fit for the *cours forcé*; that is, which you can compel people to take, though they can no longer get gold for it.' The Frenchman's theories begin with references to political confusion, which no Englishman dreams of even taking into consideration. In consequence, Paris is not a great money market, and never can be while this uncertainty lasts. She cannot distribute the savings of France to the *activity* of France as London distributes our savings to our merchants. She is a great place of pleasure,—she is an inferior place of lending business.

The advocates of Imperialism should, therefore, distinctly see what it is which they are advocates of. It is a system which, by concentrating all power in single persons, makes the future incalculable, destroys all reliance upon it, and so prevents those who trade from being able to borrow, and those who save from being able to lend.

Continental Alarms[1]

It cannot be denied that the prevalent uneasiness in Europe, to which we alluded last week, far from subsiding, appears rather to increase. We think little of the agitation and disturbance manifested on the Paris Bourse, nor of the rumours of ministerial changes and diplomatic communications to which that agitation is in a great measure to be attributed; for these things among our neighbours, far more frequently than with us, are artificial effects got up by jobbing speculators for their own sinister ends and to aid mere temporary operations, which the very next week they might find it for their interest to reverse. But the mere prolongation of anxiety and expectation in a case of this sort is of itself an aggravation of the danger, and has a tendency both to realise men's fears, and to render the state of fear by degrees almost more intolerable than the reality would be. The subject of war, and the mutual distrust and irritation which alone make war likely, are kept perpetually before the public mind, and discussed, often with ill-temper and insulting comments, in the journals of the countries more immediately concerned. It is notorious that France and Prussia are both vigorous and incessant in military preparations, so as to be prepared for any emergency; and now the disturbances, local, isolated, and thus far insignificant as they appear to be, which have occurred in Italy in consequence of Garibaldi's mischievous projects and their judicious prevention by his timely arrest, have come to complicate the position and augment the peril. Still, in spite of all these obvious symptoms of excitement and sources of danger, we believe the alarm felt at this moment to be exaggerated, and we regard the probabilities to be in favour of present, and, we would fain hope, of ultimate peace. Almost the most menacing feature of the case in our judgment is the alarm itself; because if that cannot be allayed, commerce will not revive, enterprise must be suspended, industry will languish, employment will decrease; and in all countries, and notably in France, an unemployed

[1] This article was first published in *The Economist* for October 5 1867, Volume XXV, pp. 1121–2.

and suffering population always become dangerous to a government which refuses to occupy their minds and divert their passions by a foreign war. Nevertheless, and giving full weight to all these considerations, we incline to a tolerably hopeful view of the position, for the following reasons:—

First. There is the vagueness of the subject matter of the quarrel. It is difficult even for the French to go to war from mere jealousy of the increasing power and prosperity of a rival nation, which has done them no wrong, which has offered them no insult, which has taken no action whatever in their concerns, which is simply endeavouring with singular consentaneousness of feeling and wonderfully prompt success to carry out those doctrines of nationality which France has always proclaimed as sacred. It is difficult even for the lawless and vicious eloquence of M. Thiers to goad them into an *abstract* war of this sort. If, indeed, there were any distinct demand that had been refused, any specific object to be gained, anything which if conceded would satisfy French greed or ambition, and which if denied would be worth a campaign to take by force, the danger would be far more imminent. If the evacuation of Luxembourg had been resisted; if Sarre Louis had been distinctly claimed, and any decent pretext for the claim could have been made out; or if, at the time, France had formed an alliance with the King of Hanover, and insisted that he should not be despoiled, then, no doubt, hostilities would have been natural, and, probably, inevitable. But now there is literally no ground for a war with Prussia which France can allege to herself, or put into any plain words which would not make its irrationality and immorality self-evident. If she goes to war now, she will do so simply to soothe and indulge her own wounded susceptibilities; to gratify mortified vanity, —vanity mortified not by anything which she has lost, but by something which a neighbour has gained, or is in the way of gaining. Or she will go to war to prevent German states and peoples from doing what they have a perfect right to do if they please, and what they are the best judges whether or not it would be wise to do. And, moreover, it is likely enough that a war undertaken for such aims, and under such auspices, would neither hinder German unification nor gratify French vanity.

Secondly. There is considerable reason to doubt whether any great majority of the French nation do seriously just now desire war with Prussia. Parliamentary orators and Orleanist or Legitimist journalists, whose patriotism is not always pure nor often very enlightened, may desire it. The excitable population of Paris, and some of the great cities of the Empire, who have got a dim and angry notion that French honour has been tarnished, and that French preponderance is threatened, may long for the recurrence of those days of turbulent passion and disorder which constitute the element in which they love to live; and it is possible that ere long, if the present uneasiness continues to paralyse industry and commerce, their ranks may be swelled by hosts of unemployed artisans, in which case the danger would be much increased. But the peasantry, to whom war means a doubled conscription, on whom the chief weight of the conscription falls, and among whom the conscription is of all their burdens the most unpopular, are certainly not anxious for war, and, indeed, seldom can be so, unless under the pressure of actual danger or artificially excited passions. Commercial men, as distinguished from speculators and stock-jobbers, are always averse to hostilities, and they constitute a far more influential class in France than formerly. It is very doubtful, too, from all that we can learn, whether the army itself is very sincerely eager for a struggle with an enemy whose real prowess and resources they feel unable to calculate or measure with any confidence. They hate the Prussians, no doubt, and long to humble them; but we have reason to believe that among the officers of the French army, there is not that conviction of easy and certain superiority in such a conflict which hitherto they have been wont to feel; while among the private soldiers, there prevails a kind of vague alarm at the possible powers of the new weapon which did such wonders at Sadowa, and an unavowed but still widespread feeling of doubt, and almost of discouragement, at the prospect of encountering troops who overthrew in a short campaign and in a series of desperate encounters the adversaries whom they themselves found so hard to beat at Magenta and Solferino.

Thirdly. But it is on the statesmen at the head of the two angry nations that we mainly rely for our hopes that peace will be maintained. The times are changed since eager rulers dragged reluctant peoples into war. Now, it is the people who are ready to fight, and monarchs and ministers who hold them back. We believe that both Count Bismarck and Napoleon are anxious to avoid a rupture, and have good reason to be so, and will do all that can be done to avert it. As for the Prussian statesman, his work of unification is going on, at least as fast as he can desire—perhaps even faster—and a war with France, if it could not prevent it or retard it, would either complicate and perplex, or, at all events, precipitate his schemes. His ultimate success is certain, and that success will be complete and beneficent, probably just in proportion to the gradual and spontaneous manner in which it is wrought out. His great desire now must be to consolidate and fuse the already vastly increased dominions of his master,—not to repeat the policy which Garibaldi in 1860 forced upon the Italian Government. He can have no possible motive to hasten an absolutely certain issue,—still less, to have it precipitated and confused by a foreign war, which, however glorious and successful it might possibly be, would be long, desperate, bloody, costly, and desolating. The Emperor of Austria has even stronger motives to withhold him from allowing France to drag him into a struggle to prevent that German unity which has now become the cherished hope and dream of the entire fatherland. Such a blunder, he must be well aware, would, probably, cost him his German subjects and relegate him to the inferior position of the chief of a mere mass of miscellaneous Sclavonic and Hungarian provinces; while any hope of regaining ascendancy—either in Italy or at home—is obviously futile. But it is on the sagacity and self-interest of the French Emperor that we place our principal reliance. It is calculated that since his accession he has cost Europe on the average forty millions a year, either in actual war, or in preparations to be ready for it, or in efforts to avert it. It is fit that he should now atone in some measure for this enormous infliction, by becoming the chief influence in preserving peace. He has every motive to be so; and he is a man who is usually governed by motives and not by passion. Had his uncle been ruler of France at such a conjuncture, the Continent would have been in a blaze long ere this. Napoleon knows well that a war with Prussia would be a war with all Germany; that it would be a long and desperate war, with a doubtful issue as to military glory, and with scarcely a possibility of success in preventing the ultimate fusion of the German states,—if even it did not assist that hated result. He sees clearly, too, we cannot doubt, that with the Teutonic idea and passion for national grandeur and unity so fiercely aroused as it now is, the prospect of seizing and retaining the cis-Rhenane provinces of Prussia and making the Rhine his boundary is all but hopeless. There may, perhaps, linger in his fancy some idea that he may be able to conquer and annex Belgium, and thus balance the aggrandisement of Prussia by a corresponding aggrandisement of France; but so cool and calculating a brain cannot be slow to discover that if he cannot annex the Rhenish provinces when he has only Prussia to contend against, it is unlikely that he will be able to seize Belgium against the united forces of both Belgium and Germany, with England, Russia, and, most probably, Holland, more or less actively arrayed against him, and with Italy either hostile or impotent to aid him.

Lastly. No one sees more clearly than the sagacious Emperor of the French that, if he can only remain at peace and avoid actual mortification and humiliation (which no power in Europe is foolish enough to *volunteer*), he may reign in tolerable security during his lifetime; while a decided checkmate, an unsuccessful war, or a crushing defeat—all of which are possibilities, if hostilities be once commenced—would be almost inevitably fatal to his dynasty. And no one is more sure to be determined in his policy by considerations of this nature. He will hardly go to war, unless war be forced upon him, or unless victory be highly probable. And neither of these contingencies is very likely.

France and the Money Market[1]

T HE debate upon the Roman question in the French chamber is of very grave moment. That question is in itself most important. Whether the Italian people are reasonable or unreasonable in wishing to possess Rome is not material; they do wish it, and will wish it for many years. Again, whether Catholics are right or are wrong in valuing so much the temporal power of the Pope is not material; they do so value it, and will so value it for many years. To a practical statesman the present intensity and probable endurance of such sentiments are principal facts to be heeded, whatever may be his own idea about their wisdom. But the French debate upon the subject has a far keener interest, and touches upon the most critical problem of present politics; upon *the* European topic which may convulse calculations, and which men of business should necessarily watch.

What men of business want to know is, will there be a general war or will there continue to be a general peace?—and on that subject there has been of late a vast change in a vital element. The position of France in Europe has changed. She is no longer the single predominating power upon the continent as of late years; she has two new nations on either side of her—Germany and Italy. Together these are now more than a match for her, and in a cause which really touched the German nation, Germany by herself would be at least her equal— perhaps more than her equal. What the Congress of Vienna tried in vain to effect by creating and patching together artificial powers, has been effected by the almost simultaneous rise of two national powers. France has become a balanced and counterpoised power, instead of a supreme and predominant power. At least, such is the general opinion of Europe, and for this purpose opinion is almost as important as fact. The French people see that Europe thinks they have descended in rank; that their monopoly of unity (the source of their strength) is gone and lost; that in appearance, at least, they are only one of several great

[1] This article was first published in *The Economist* for December 14 1867, Volume XXV, pp. 1405–6.

states, not the admitted superior of all states. They see, too—and if they did not see of themselves M. Thiers is for ever explaining—that the traditional policy of France—the policy which made it so supreme —is become impossible. France became what she was by dividing her neighbours,—especially by dividing Germany,—by taking care to have alliances when she had wars,—by surrounding herself with needful dependents. But now these dependents have vanished, these divisions are over, and these alliances cannot be reframed. *One* Germany and *one* Italy make the *bits* of Germany and the *bits* of Italy which used to adhere to France impossible.

The immense question inevitably comes—Will France endure this change in peace and silence, or will she try to counteract it by the only means by which she can counteract it,—by war? The problem is pressing, too. France cannot but feel that time is against her. Every year of unity will make both Germany and Italy more united and more powerful. Every sensible politician would say to France, 'If you are wise you will accept what has happened; you will not run counter to the tendencies of the time; you will not try to destroy what nature and providence have made. But if you *will* be unwise, be unwise *now.* Do not let your rivals grow compact and strong before you strike, but strike hard and quick while they are weak.'

The French Emperor might be trusted upon this question. He knows the force of 'nationalities;' he introduced the word into orthodox and conventional politics; he learnt its meaning years ago when he saw the hidden and seething elements of Europe, and was himself an outcast and a conspirator. But exactly because it was his policy which created Germany and helped Italy, he has now less than usual power. When M. Thiers reproaches him with having diminished the effective power of France, and with having raised up to her competitors and counter-weights, he has no real reply, no reply which the French would like to hear or which he would choose to make. He could truly say, 'No doubt the issue of my policy has been bad for France, but it has been good for Europe, and good for the world. It is better that France should be weaker; it is better that other nations should be stronger; a republic of nations is better than an empire with dependencies.' But of all men Louis Napoleon could not say this, and would lose his throne if he tried to say it.

The exact problem, therefore, is not what will the French Government choose to do, but what will France herself—the irritable, interfering French nation—compel it to do? And upon this the late debate gives strong and painful evidence. The Emperor's Roman policy may have been a wise or unwise policy; but it was as his usually are, a tentative and *un*committing policy. He knew he was treading on red hot coals, and he tried to tread as lightly as he could. But the French chamber—seemingly expressing but too clearly the eager feeling of Paris if not France—would not permit a shade of ambiguity. They have compelled the Emperor to say, 'Italy shall not gain Rome; on the contrary, she shall not trench upon the existing Papal territory; France will interfere if Italy tries to become more than she is, or to make the papal power less than it is;' and the language which to please the chamber the imperial ministers have been forced to utter is, if possible, more painful to Italy even than its meaning. That the French people at large care deeply for the Pope is not true. There is an ultra-montane party in France as everywhere which cares much, and now it comes to the surface. But what the French care for is their own prestige. Now, the pro-French and the pro-papal sentiment run together; and, therefore, the latter seems very powerful, but if, as sometimes before, the pride of France had been gratified by humbling the Pope, we should soon see which in France was the more popular passion, an ultramontane zeal or the national vanity.

That the Emperor should be wise in this matter, and wise in vain, is most characteristic of imperialism. In its best form, as now in France, it raises apparently to absolute power a man in some respects very wise; it enables him to do what the nation is not wise enough to wish, and to avoid committing blunders which the nation wants to begin. But it is not a *teaching* government; it does good things for the nation, but it does not show the nation why they are good; it does not state the arguments upon which they rest; it trusts to success for such conviction as it desires. Accordingly, upon a mere turn of the tide, the best imperial measures may become unpopular; though for fifteen years the French Emperor has supported the principle of nationalities, the French nation cares as little, and knows as little about them as when he began.

But the faults of the French form of government are but a sub-ordinate matter now. The vital consideration is the disposition and tendency of the French nation, and upon that the evidence given by the Roman debate is as bad very nearly as it can be. Men of business— even those who commonly care little for continental politics—should carefully watch all future signs which may show how France feels. If she *means* to fight for her old place in Europe,—and at present it looks as if she did mean it,—the life of the present generation will be very different and far sadder than that which we had hoped for it.

If war should break out,—not immediately, for we are not now speaking what is to happen to-morrow or next day, but of what seems impending and to happen sometime,—the value of money will tend to rise through Europe. Capital will be wasted in destruction, which should have aided commerce in distribution and production. And much worse than a mere rise in the rate of interest is that disheartening uncertainty necessarily caused by the unrest and dissatisfaction of a warlike and central nation, which is an impediment in every kind of business, and disinclines all wise merchants to connect themselves with undertakings lasting over a considerable period, and depending for their profit upon a continued peace.

The Gravity and Difficulty of
Affairs in France[1]

WE scarcely think that most Englishmen apprehend the full magnitude—the full importance perhaps for good, and the equal importance otherwise for evil—of the events now occurring in France. We have been so occupied with the Church which is falling across the Irish Channel, that we have not thought enough of the Empire which is falling across the English Channel. For it is not anything less, at least as far as can now be seen. By the 'Empire,' we mean of course the sort of government founded by force in 1852; a government in which the executive power is separate from the legislative; in which the executive is everything and the legislative nothing; in which one single judgment decides everything, and one single will impels everything. In 1852, and for years afterwards, this government was undoubtedly upon the whole popular with a great majority of the French people. It was not and could not be popular with the large towns, whose ideas it stopped: it was not and it could not be popular with literary men whose career it arrested; but it was popular with the peasantry, for it assured them 'peace and property,' which, so went the notion, great cities might assail and literature could not protect. But now this government is become unpopular; a new generation has grown up, which wants something different, and will have something different. Persons who have not attended to the subject can have no notion how vexatious and even how stupid this despotism of necessity was. It was essentially a government of innumerable restrictions enforced by innumerable persons. By its nature it had to follow the detail of men's lives to see that such and such persons did not meet; that so and so did not conspire; that 'this or that' was not printed. And this watching employs many eyes which would mistake what they saw, and many hands which would do just what they ought not. For example,—we mention the thing as an illustration only,—every now and then, four or five

[1] This article was first published in *The Economist* for August 7 1869, Volume XXVII, pp. 926–7.

times a year perhaps, *The Economist* would be stopped. And this means a great deal. If *The Economist* would make a revolution, what would not make a revolution? If Frenchmen of business were so easily to be turned against the Emperor that they could not be trusted to read a paper not generally thought too stirring, written in a foreign language, full of figures, not always opposing the imperial government but often praising it, what then were they to read? What would *not* set them against their government? What did not need looking after? If such surveillance was necessary for grave things in English what extreme care must not be necessary for light things in French? And what illustrates the matter more, the *seizing* clerk could not read English, or at least not read it quickly; so articles favourable to the Empire would be stopped if the title looked odd or suspicious;—at one time any article with 'French despotism' in it was seized, no matter what followed, and though it were laudatory. This is but a specimen of the French administration,—and then comes the dilemma. A government which interferes in such small things, and interferes so foolishly, cannot last; and, on the other hand, unless it interferes, it lets the hostile classes arrayed against it do as they like, and then it cannot last either.

But unfit as this government is to endure, the difficulty of substituting for it a parliamentary government is very great. In the first place, a parliamentary government is of all others the government which most requires to be made gradually, and which can least easily be made suddenly. The essence of it is that the legislative assembly, the elected chamber, chooses the executive government. But who is the chamber to choose? It can only have real confidence in those whom it really knows; and who are these? In this country they are those who have been long in parliament, whose powers have been displayed, whose defects gauged, whose characters are known there. Mr. Gladstone was more than thirty years in parliament before he was premier; Lord Palmerston was fifty. But in a new country, or in a country long without parliamentary government, there cannot be any such well-known persons. The men from whom to choose a cabinet fit to be trusted cannot be looked for in France now,—at least, though they may be there, we cannot hope to know *which* they are;—for the long years of trial, the 'face to face' life of speech and action by which parliament is able to discriminate good statesmen from bad ones, has not existed in France for many years. Parliamentary statesmen are products of slow growth, and in France they have not been planted.

It is true that under a parliamentary constitution in some cases the nation in fact chooses the premier, and not parliament. Such was Cavour's case. In the judgment of Italy he was so above every rival that the Italian parliament did not really select him to be premier; it only ratified the selection the nation had made before. But then Cavour had done great things and headed a great struggle. He had had good means of making his name known; his ability had been tried. But in France of late years the Emperor's has been almost the only mind really felt—the only mind France has tested. M. Thiers, it is true, has an old name, but it is not a respected name. No one trusts his judgment; almost as few have confidence in his character. If an ingenious speech is wanted to split half united parties or to explain the blunders of a faulty minister, M. Thiers can supply it—is better at it probably than any man living, from natural disposition and long practice; but ingenious speeches do not make a great minister. His name has long been known in France, but is connected with no great success. On the contrary, it is connected with the recollection of a great failure. He was one of the ministers of the 'Monarchy of July,' which, whatever its merits or defects, did not please France, and which brought parliaments to an end there. The one thing the new Parliament is said to have fixed is that M. Thiers shall not lead it.

This is the first great danger of France now—that it has to make 'bricks without straw;' it has to begin a parliamentary government without a premier or a cabinet that parliament knows. And there are plainly two others—one that the 'Red' party is very strong, and that the 'Red' party never wins, or, we should say, has never yet won. They have had momentary periods of power, but they have never yet established a coherent parliamentary government. Many of them indeed would despise a success so bounded. They have 'socialist aims,' more or less, and aim at a 'reorganisation of society,' and pending that they scarcely care whether France is ruled by a sovereign or by a parliament. And there is besides a deep incompatibility between the 'Red' character—the sort of character we mean which makes the Red republicans and keeps them so—and parliamentary government. That government lives by compromise; it cannot go on except by a sort of 'give and take,' in which all concede something and all lose something. But the 'Red' character is incapable of compromise, and boasts that it is so. It prides itself on its 'logic'—that is, on its bigoted adherence to a few abstract formulæ (got no one knows where) with all their consequences. Such men would have given up nothing if they had been in the position of the 'Lords' lately, still less if they had been in that of the Commons. They pull, and say they ought to pull, every rope of a constitution till it breaks. In consequence as yet the party has founded nothing, and is likely to found nothing. It has been, as Burke long since said, the 'Vitruvius of ruin,' but its constructions, its edifices, cannot be found.

Even if we forget that many 'Reds' despise parliaments, at best parliamentary government is about to be tried in France by new men and violent men, and it is tried in the face of an enemy. Constitutional monarchy is a government which the ancients would have deemed impossible. They would never have believed that a king would subject himself to an 'invisible strait waistcoat;' to have it said he could do everything and be content to do nothing; to have omnipotence in theory and nullity in practice. We do not yet know that out of England any set of kings will long do so. But if we know anything, we know that Louis Napoleon will not submit if he can help. Through his whole career he has said to the French people—'I will represent you but a parliament shall not represent you.' He and his satellites have proved as they think a thousand times that constitutional monarchy is impossible in France, and that if possible pernicious. At this moment we believe that the Emperor plays the 'waiting game;' he trusts in the 'errors of his enemies;' he believes that after the semblance of a trial parliamentary government will look impossible, and then France may hurry back to him again.

But we may be asked, why are you so anxious, if you only fear the Emperor's coming back again? We *have* the Emperor now, and know that though perhaps not good certainly he is bearable; we can endure him at any rate if there is nothing worse coming. But there may be something worse, for the Empire might be removed for a moment by violence and then riveted by force for years. We might have a revolution and a counter-revolution, with all their blood and all their evils. And of course in that case the Empire would come back worse than it went; it would have wrongs to revenge, and it would be strong as the tide that bore it back. But this is not all, or the worst. A defeat of French Liberals is not their defeat only; it is a defeat of *all* Liberals. Throughout Europe for years free action and free thought were beaten and helpless because of the calamities of 1793 and the calamities of 1848. May Paris do us no such harm now, but rather may she do us much good.

The Emperor's Letter[1]

WE doubt whether a reflective posterity may not find much more to interest it in the character of the remarkable man who now sits on the throne of France than even in that of his more sudden and brilliant and meteoric uncle. To us at all events there seems to be something much more rare and unique in the slow and pondering intellect which has so curiously studied and so perseveringly measured,—almost as it were by the successive tentative instalments and gradual approximations of some mathematical formula,—the political wants and needs of France, than in that of the far swifter and more self-willed genius which flashed with an irregular lustre over Europe and fell through the excess of the very qualities by virtue of which it rose. Louis Napoleon has now been the first man in France for a far longer period than his uncle ever was. Reckoning from the date of his first consulship, the whole of the first Napoleon's career lasted but sixteen years; and reckoning even from the date of the first public success, his military suppression of the revolution in 1795, his career lasted exactly twenty years, one year less than his nephew's has already endured. The triumphs and the collapse of genius such as his, though they make an exciting story, do not to our minds furnish one half so singular and unexampled in history as that of the present Emperor's plodding, painstaking, uphill, intellectual efforts to gauge and adapt himself to both the superficial tastes and permanent demands of the French people, to win them by theatric glitter, to conquer them by a profoundly-meditated display of force far from congenial to his own nature, to rule them by satisfying deliberately both their longing for quiet and prosperity and their desire for a showy international position, to measure surely the returning thirst for freedom, to ladle out in anxiously considered portions just enough and no more than enough at a time to avert any hurricane of popular wrath, to keep the drag fairly on the spirit of revolution as it rolled on in its irresistible course

---

[1] This article was first published in *The Economist* for March 26 1870, Volume XXVIII, pp. 379–80.

to popular liberty, and at last to consummate the whole strange history by the concession of last Monday which virtually gives back, and with the air of spontaneous though half tardy and reluctant generosity, to the people the arbitrary power which he had persuaded the people eighteen years ago to confer upon him. What strikes us as so unique in all this history is its evidently purely intellectual and reflective source. All the Emperor's great strokes,—many of which, like his earliest attempts on the French people, have been failures, failures frankly admitted, and as soon as possible rectified,—have been long prepared for, approached by careful parallels and calculated approximations, and though delivered with an authoritative air at last, yet quite without any of the divination of genius, nay, with a very marked air of a design long resolved upon, and even at the last almost hesitatingly matured. It would seem as if he understood French feeling itself far less by sympathy with it, than by deep meditation on its phenomena. It is precisely this slow and patient intellectual assimilation of the political symptoms of France which has enabled him to survive so many errors, to descend with dignity where another would have fallen with disgrace, and to give back bit by bit with at least apparent disinterestedness, generosity, and something of a grand consistency, the power which he had always claimed to wield only as a trust from the people, the gift of which the people had themselves ratified.

Now for the last four years, compelled partly by the failure of his foreign policy, partly by the stimulus which the growth of popular power and freedom in neighbouring states has given to the desire for it in France, the Emperor has been constantly, though very slowly, and apparently very reluctantly, modifying the constitution in this direction, till at last he has accustomed France so completely to the habit of expecting voluntary Imperial concessions, that there is no shock to his dignity in that final surrender of personal power accorded in Monday's letter. For ten years, though much more rapidly in the last four, he has been steadily descending from the height of personal government on which he once stood, and, as it would seem, the descent has been accomplished much as the first ascent was accomplished, as the result of deliberate conviction, of intellectual necessity, slowly engendered in his mind, and often coldly and almost clumsily expressed. Probably no great ruler, so little scrupulous as Louis Napoleon certainly is, ever so deliberately and inexorably gave judgment as it were *against* himself. Did ever any man before, who had succeeded so well in accumulating power, succeed equally well in surrendering it again? Did ever before a vaulting ambition show as cold a sagacity in leaping down from a height as in scaling it? Does not the present Emperor of the French stand alone amongst rulers who have made their own fortunes, in having given up power, inch by inch, not because he was sick of it, not because it was absolutely wrenched from him, but both against his will and willingly, with conspicuous reluctance as far as his own disposition was concerned, and yet with equally conspicuous determination to forestall necessity and anticipate rather than surrender to popular demands?

It is to us astonishing how little attention has been bestowed in England on this last announcement of the Emperor that the representative power which *the plebiscite* of 1852 conferred upon him, is to be returned to the people, and exercised for the future by the legislative assembly and the senate,—he himself ruling as a purely constitutional monarch,—*i.e.* not ruling it at all except so far as he can influence the minds of his responsible ministers. It is true of course that the senate, which is nominated by the Emperor, will continue to represent his views, and may now and then exercise some little influence, when the popular and elective assembly is undecided, in furthering his wishes. But in point of fact the concession of full co-ordinate legislative authority to the assembly, is equivalent to the utter subordination of the senate which can never exercise even so much power as our own House of Lords. The assembly which chooses and supports the ministry, by whose vote the ministers live or die, must, now that it is to resume the right of an initiative in legislation, become, like our own House of Commons, the whole state. The Emperor knows perfectly well that in conceding it full legislative powers, he is conceding it all but exclusive legislative powers. The senate has no prestige in France such as our House of Lords has in England. If it opposes the will of the nation it will be well understood in France that it is as the nominees of the crown, and not as senators, that its members dare to throw themselves into the breach. Therefore, unless the Emperor intends to court a collision with his people, such as he has uniformly avoided, he will never allow the senate to disappoint any hopes of France, clearly and strongly expressed in the popular chamber. The senate can no longer be anything more now than a mere revising assembly, at least as regards all great measures. The power which the Emperor resigns nominally to the *two* chambers he really resigns wholly to one.

The only conceivable restriction on the Emperor's surrender of power is that he may not even now be prepared to sanction any speedy dissolution of the present chamber of deputies, which is known to be far more favourable to personal government and far more opposed to the development of freedom than any new assembly, elected under the new *régime*, probably would be. The Emperor knows that the deputies are by no means eager to face their constituents, and he may possibly count even on the reluctance of M. Ollivier and his colleagues to hasten an event which might well put a term to their own power. Of course he still retains the power of dissolving in his own hands; and though after his complete adoption of the advice of his ministers he could hardly afford to refuse to act in the matter on their advice, he may have very good reasons to know that their advice will not willingly be tendered in favour of dissolution. But now that events have gone so far as they have done, this is after all a rather small matter. Ministers may be very reluctant to dissolve, as reluctant as they please,—but if France is bent on electing a new parliament, and makes her wishes distinctly heard, they will have no real choice in the matter. They could stave it off a few months beyond the time at which the country would desire to have it; but no constitutional ministry retaining power by favour of the people can afford to lose all favour through a cynical display of distrust. While the legislative body was really far from supreme, a part of the odium of delay might have been thrown on the throne and the senate. Now all France will know that the ministers have the power to go back to the country for an expression of its wishes as soon as they choose to do so. That implies, we take it, a pretty early dissolution, if France really desires a pretty early dissolution. The march of events cannot be long delayed. The power which the Emperor did not venture to keep in his own hands cannot long be monopolised by the nominee of an unpopular assembly against the will of the country at large.

The Emperor's Proclamation[1]

THE plebiscitum is, comparatively speaking, a new and untried power in European politics, and its working deserves to be attentively studied by Liberal politicians. It is a mistake to consider it a shrewd device of the Emperor Napoleon, intended to give a moral basis to an otherwise illegitimate power. It is the extreme form of universal suffrage, and it has therefore a secret charm for almost all democrats; and there is some reason to believe that all democracies tend towards a trial of this tremendous weapon. In America the President of the United States is now elected by direct plebiscitum, the elaborate device by which the framers of the constitution hoped to secure a parliament *ad hoc*—an electoral college of the wisest and best—having broken down so completely that outsiders fancy the popular vote is given directly for the opposing candidates, whereas it is given to certain dummies pledged to elect the popular nominee. In many states of the Union, moreover, important laws, and more especially amendments to the state constitutions, are now 'submitted to the people'—that is, to a plebiscitum; while in Switzerland several cantons have agreed to submit even executive acts, provided they cost money. The device, in its democratic character, its power, and its rapidity of action, attracts the imagination of many republicans, and may spread, and every example of its working, therefore, well deserves analysis. We alluded last week to the extraordinary power which the plebiscitum exercises over opinion, as shown in the dismay which the mere threat of employing it had spread among the Emperor's foes, and this week we have even more complete evidence to offer. It is clear that those who know France best think that the plebiscite will have moral power not only to override the opinion of the legislature, but to reverse the judgment of the people itself as expressed in a less direct and massive form. It is not yet twelve months since the French people elected by universal suffrage a chamber which was instructed to limit 'personal power,'

[1] This article was first published in *The Economist* for April 30 1870, Volume XXVIII, pp. 531–2.

and which as its first act did so limit it—did, for instance, compel the Emperor ostensibly to resign all his 'constituent' prerogatives. Nevertheless the plebiscite is no sooner determined on than the Emperor and his chief Minister think themselves, probably with justice, able to appeal to the people *en masse* to reverse the verdict which the whole people divided into sections had given. The manifesto of the Emperor, published on Sunday, is a request for a vote of confidence, accompanied by a promise that if he obtains it he will preserve the constitution 'Imperial and Democratic,' that is, not parliamentary, and will never cease to labour for the people, that is, will do as he always hitherto has done—make his government popular, but retain most of the power of governing. His Minister, M. Ollivier, is even more explicit. He says in an address to his constituents, the electors of the Var, a vote of Yes will enable him to do more for the people than he has ever yet done, that it will free him from constitutional discussions and interpellations, and enable the Emperor and himself—not the legislature,—to devise measures for benefiting those who have nothing without injuring those who are possessed of property. In other words, the plebiscite will restore the power of the Emperor to the full, and *pro tanto* diminish that of the representatives—that is, will exactly reverse the vote which elected the last chamber.

It seems at first sight almost inexplicable that men like Napoleon and M. Ollivier, men who know France, should think the people likely to vote, when summoned *en masse*, so differently from the way they voted when summoned by districts, but it is evident that they do think so, and they must have some reasons. Those reasons are probably of this kind. A plebiscitum being a very rare and exciting event, preceded by great agitations, and accompanied by direct appeals from the Emperor and his principal advisers, draws out a mass of voters who are usually indifferent to politics, and who from ignorance, indifference, or timidity, are usually prone to vote with rather than against the government. Then the issue stated is so very large, being, M. Ollivier says with some truth, nothing less than 'the Emperor or the Revolution,' that hundreds of thousands who dislike the personal power will vote yes rather than risk a general overturn, with the immense and uncertain changes which would follow in the State, in the Church, and above all, in the security of property. But the main reason is this:—In the usual elections the electors do not give a decree, but elect a man whom they know and more or less trust to give a decree if he thinks it is on the whole safe. They create a power which can moderate itself. In the plebiscitum they give a direct decree. They do not even elect men with power to expel or accept the Emperor, but are compelled to decide for themselves whether they, the men then voting, will expel or retain him. When so pressed, the mass of men, and especially the mass of men possessed of a little realised property, are sure to be more or less conservative, to distrust themselves, and to vote that no great change should be made. It may not be imperialism but only conservatism which guides them, but the effect is to generate a timidity not felt when they were electing members who, though obedient to their wishes, would still have the right and the power to moderate their execution. Even in England and among politicians men will vote against government on a special proposal who will vote for them and for that proposal if it is made a question of confidence, and the plebiscitum is a wider application of the same practice. It may in fact be used to annul the vote of the very people who vote it. The plebiscitum is not only inconsistent with parliamentary government, but is of necessity almost hostile—tends not to confirm but rather to reverse parliamentary decisions.

That is of course no proof in itself that parliamentary government is the wiser system of the two, but the history of this plebiscite supplies strong evidence upon that point also. If there is anything clear in politics it is that the value of almost any measure depends mainly upon details, that to accept or reject a vast multitude of propositions in a single yes or no is very foolish. Yet the people of France are compelled by the wording of this plebiscite to decide whether or no 'they approve the liberal reforms effected in the Constitution since 1860 by the Emperor, and ratify the Senatus Consultum of 20 April 1870.' In other words, they are asked to say whether or no they approve many hundreds of propositions, some of them inconsistent with each other, and most of them so beyond their mental range that they barely comprehend the meaning of the words in which they are embodied. Probably no man in France, not even the Emperor who framed them, approves them all; yet division is impossible, as the nation could not be kept together in its comitia for the completion of such a process. Now this division is precisely what a parliament can do. Being elected it may have to say yes or no to broad principles as electors do in a plebiscitum; but it can make yes or no comparatively innocuous by definitions, limitations, and arrangements of detail, by infusing a tone even into its obedience to its instructions, which will gravely modify the effect of its acts. The nation, which is denied this privilege, is therefore of necessity less qualified for the business of life than the representative body. We say nothing of the filtering process a nation undergoes to produce such a body, for there is at least one representative council in the world which is inferior to the majority of its own electors, but confine ourselves to the patent fact that the nation must, if it acts directly, act too roughly, with too little attention to the refinements needful to meet the complexities of opinion, of society, and of circumstance.

Whether the frankness, not to say the audacity of the imperial request, as explained by the Emperor and his Minister, will injure the chances of an affirmative vote is of course doubtful, but we should say it would not. That frankness makes the issue very broad and simple, and masses of people always prefer broad and simple issues, and usually vote for the man who proposes them. By 8 May the terms of the question will be almost forgotten; each elector will think he is voting for or against revolution, and on that point the peasantry who form a majority of the electors are very clear and decided. They think a republic would impose new taxes, which the Empire does not do, and they will vote against any possibility of taxation. Whether the vote will be large depends on many accidents—among others the state of the weather; but that it will be given for the Emperor we entertain no doubt. That the probabilities should be so visibly on his side, when at the general election his majority was so small, is another proof among many of the divergencies sure to exist between the will of the people taken in plebiscite, and its will when expressed in any other form.

The Lessons of the Plebiscite[1]

IT is not always the wisest acts which yield the most useful lessons, and the plebiscite appears to be one of the foolishest of them. Indeed, the very fact that long-headed men will do such foolish things at times indicates, we suppose, that they extremely need the lesson to be gained from watching the result of their folly,—which, in this way, may be said to be a self-regulating piece of machinery for its own diminution or cure. If the French nation, from its ruler downwards, is inclined to turn the recent escapade, as we may call it, of its chief and itself to good account, it will not be difficult to do so.

In the first place, the Emperor may have learned something from it, though it is not always easy to teach even an able man with an *idée fixe* anything that runs counter to that *idée fixe*. The Emperor of the French has always cherished the idea of democratic autocracies,—in other words, has always favoured the notion that you can strengthen the foundations of a throne by periodically digging them up to see whether they are as sound as ever. This time, at least, we think he may have learned not only that they are not quite so sound as they were, but that the way to make them sounder is not to invite the people to inspect them under very critical circumstances. Who can suppose for a moment that the Emperor is stronger than he was before the plebiscite, or that his son has even as *much* chance of succeeding him as he then had? The Emperor no doubt has got an immense majority. Seven-tenths of the people of France have given him their votes under the moral pressure of the government and the alarm caused by the discovery of the conspiracy to assassinate him and upset the present order of things. But then every one knows that a considerable proportion of these seven-tenths voted with the utmost reluctance, and merely as a mode of averting violence and revolution, and that a great number of them voted for the Emperor because he has shown that he has *a mind*, who have not voted, and would not have dreamt

[1] This article was first published in *The Economist* for May 14 1870, Volume XXVIII, pp. 594–5.

of voting, for his son, had the first question been of his dynasty. Whether plebiscites do or do not strengthen an individual ruler who has personally gained a certain hold on the people, they clearly cannot by any chance strengthen dynasties which are like plants growing out of habit and custom and which are not likely to bear the practice of pulling them up constantly in order to look at their roots. The plebiscite has proved how vast a majority of the country people object to revolution. But it has also proved that in the most populous towns, the centres of all the intellectual activity of France, the feeling is positively hostile to the Emperor. The departments of the Seine (round Paris) and of the Bouches du Rhone (round Marseilles) have returned great majorities against the Emperor. Paris and Marseilles themselves have only headed the great towns in doing the same. Nor is it always the *greatest* towns which have condemned the Emperor by the largest majorities. The hostile majority of Paris was about 182,000 'Noes' against 138,000 'Ayes,' with about 95,000 abstentions, which are very nearly equivalent to 'Noes.' Marseilles gave about 34,000 'Noes' to 18,000 'Ayes,' (the number of abstentions we do not know); but so small a town as Beaune (in Burgundy) gave 1,500 'Noes' to only 130 'Ayes,' or a vote of more than ten to one against the Emperor, and Nîmes gave 8,000 'Noes' to 2,000 'Ayes,' or four to one against the Emperor. Even Grenoble, at one time the most Bona-partist of towns, gave a hostile vote—4,000 'Noes' to 3,000 'Ayes.' So that the Emperor may be assured of this, that the effect of the plebiscite has been to indicate a very great and menacing change of feeling towards him in the towns, and not most in the largest towns where the strongest exciting influences prevail. While the ordinary country districts still fear nothing more than any change of system,— the Gironde, for instance, which is supposed to be radical, having given a vote of 40,000 'Ayes' to only 3,000 'Noes,'—the towns are openly professing their weariness of the Emperor's *régime*, even in the very face of a conspiracy against his life. Nor is this all. It is certain that the army have voted as many as 50,000 'Noes,' and that there have been a very considerable number of abstentions as well. In other words, in spite of the influence of military discipline, there is as much change of feeling in the army as in France itself, and it is openly manifested. All this surely ought to teach the Emperor in how very critical a situation his 'personal' government stands. He has, of course, all the dull conservatism of the peasantry on his side; but in these twenty years of rule he has not gained but rather lost ground with the people. Can he even pretend to think that the vote has made his son more sure of the succession? And all this happens even after what is called reform. Is it not plain that he must be very cautious in his policy, and very liberal; that he must retract nothing he has given, and try to strengthen himself by the counsels of genuinely popular statesmen, if he would not lose ground rapidly in the next few years? The Emperor is far too wise to be in any degree really reassured by the plebiscite. For him it has been a striking and we may hope a wholesome warning. It has been a very remarkable assertion of the disgust with which personal government is viewed in the most intelligent regions of France. And no one knows better than the Emperor that valuable as is the support of timid stupidity, it is as impossible to rely solely upon it for the purposes of government as it is to depend solely upon the *vis inertiæ* for the development of the great constructive and destructive forces by which railways are worked and armies annihilated; you must have the intelligence to use and guide the *vis inertiæ* with you, or you may be brought to grief at any moment. At present the Emperor himself is that intelligence. But he cannot always be on the scene, and even while on the scene he cannot always be at all parts of it. He has received a serious lesson—and we doubt not will not neglect to avail himself of it—on the need for allying himself more closely with the active mind of France.

But the liberals and radicals, who are, we are sorry to say—however much higher their tone,—far less teachable than the Emperor, ought to learn quite as much from the results of this plebiscite as he can do. They ought to learn firstly,—that if they are *true* democrats, they should not again attempt to disturb the existing order at least during the Emperor's life, so long at least as he liberalises, instead of narrows, his political system. Democracy seems to us to consist as often as not in the free use of the people's name *against* the vast majority of the people. Now whatever the republican party may be entitled to say as to the abstract righteousness of their doctrine, they cannot possibly base it for France on *democratic* principles after such a vote as last Sunday's. Admit, if you will, that the intellect of France was one way and its masses the other. Still it is the teaching of democracy that the masses should govern the intellect and not the intellect the masses. The latter is a doctrine which indeed no democratic or republican party in Europe now professes. The stupid must count for as much as the wise, the labouring peasant for as much as the keenest philosopher. If this be so, a vote of seven millions against a million and a half is absolutely decisive of the view taken by the democracy of France on the subject, and all these riots and revolutionary plots must be fairly admitted to be riots and revolutionary plots against the will of the democracy rather than against the Emperor. Grant that a good many votes were given from pure fear of violence and socialism; well, that only means that the voters still regard the Emperor as their chosen instrument for repressing violence and socialism, and therefore that all violence against the Emperor is in fact directed against the moral authority of the voters themselves. There is nothing so intolerable as the acrid enthusiasm of revolutionists who rebel, in the name of the people, against the deliberate will of the people, and insist on saving the people from the people by their own headstrong plans. Surely they ought now to see that rural France is all but unanimous against any interruption of the Empire, at least during the life of the present Emperor. They can sow the seeds of their doctrines, if they please, in the hope that those seeds will bear fruit when once the sceptre devolves on another. But they have heard the masses speak clearly enough for the present their positive will, and everything hostile to that declaration of will is hostile to the democratic principle. The radicals should learn to defer more to the inert masses of their countrymen,—or at least, if they can't do so, to give up talking of the rights of man and democratic ideas as if they favoured their own views. If seven men in any country are against fundamental change for every two or three who are in favour of it in that country the rights of man and democratic ideas are clearly hostile to fundamental change and not favourable to it. What the revolutionary party in France really wish is to give France to the masses so long as the masses wish for a republic, but to deny them power to establish anything else. That may be a tenable creed, but it is not a democratic one. The results of the plebiscite will hardly be of as much use to the revolutionary party as to the Emperor. But these results may perhaps do something towards impressing on the minds of the agitators of France that they have recently been on a wrong tack;—that if they would carry rural France as well as urban France with them, they must ask for a popular and constitutional system in co-operation with the Emperor, and defer all ideas of a republic, at least till the present ruler of France has vanished from the scene.

The Liberals and the Emperor[1]

W E argued last week that the Emperor would doubtless learn much from the result of the plebiscite, and that what he would learn would all be in favour of pursuing his liberal policy,—from which indeed, with such a demonstration of the opinions of the great cities of France, of Algeria, and of an important fraction of the army, against him, it would be the utmost rashness, and a sort of rashness not at all natural to the Emperor, to depart. If it is true, as the French papers tell us, that 'in 17 departments where the number of the uneducated is less than a twentieth, there have been 26 per cent. of Noes, while in 63 departments where the number of the uneducated is from a half to three-quarters, the number of "Noes" was only $11\frac{1}{2}$ per cent.,' the force of this argument will be very much strengthened, and is not at all likely to be overlooked by the Emperor. He well knows that education must go on and must go on rapidly, and that if the Empire is to be regarded favourably only by the uneducated, its cause will soon be doomed; whereas it is not likely to be regarded favourably by the educated unless he makes great concessions to that sense of personal dignity in the people, and that love of freedom, which education is sure to produce. On the other hand, we argued that the liberals, if they were wise, would recognise the vote as decisive at least for the Emperor's life-time, and not attempt to overthrow, on popular principles, the vote of so immense a majority of the people of France. We said at the time that we entertained very much more fear lest the liberals should fail to profit by the results of the *plebiscite* than lest the Emperor should so fail. He has shown throughout his career a steady purpose of studying the signs of the times, and accommodating his conduct as a ruler to the lesson so obtained; and this habit of his, whatever may be the character of its motive, is a tolerably sure index to his action. But the radicals as a party, on the other hand, have been to some extent so intoxicated with the popular *sound* of

---

[1] This article was first published in *The Economist* for May 21 1870, Volume XXVIII, pp. 626–7.

their ideas, that they have always showed too much contempt for that process of verification which tests whether or not their ideas be really popular,—really the ideas of a majority of their countrymen. To be more popular than the people themselves is a not uncommon fault of democratic parties, the general effect being more reaction against the name of democratic principles than the people, if they were *really* consulted by their self-elected spokesmen, would be at all likely to approve.

But whatever the course pursued by the irreconcilables, there is a very considerable party of parliamentary liberals, whose preference of course would be for a parliamentary government without an Empire, but who would be quite willing to act in any manner most likely to secure to France the largest portion of practical freedom. We wish to discuss in this article what course they ought to pursue for the special end they have in view,—the consolidation of free institutions, whether with an Empire or without it. Will they be wiser to give their support to the Emperor, and to try to commit him to genuinely representative principles of government, or to lead a bitter opposition to the Emperor on the ground that by this plebiscite he has virtually assailed the constitutional principles he had seemed to accept, and that he has since acquiesced in an administration devoted to him personally, instead of one which commands the confidence of the genuine liberals in the *Corps Législatif*? We believe that so far as it is possible, so far as support of the Empire does not involve support of personal government either by the Emperor or his creatures, the wisest thing the moderate liberals can do is to make it perfectly clear that they do support the Empire,—that they have no sort of wish for any change of *régime*, for any start *de novo*, so long as the present system is steadily worked in a liberal direction. And for this we believe that we can give very strong reasons.

The real alternative in France is between an empire and a republic; nay more, we sincerely believe that it is an alternative between a Bonapartist empire and a socialist republic. The Bonapartist Empire may, we sincerely believe, be made consistent with a very large amount of practical freedom, with an honestly-worked constitutional system of parliamentary government. The socialist republic, if it were to succeed at all, would no doubt be also worked by parliamentary forms, and it is quite conceivable that a parliamentary form for it might be invented which would be strong enough, however wanting it might be in popularity with the peasantry. But the Empire, as an Empire, has outlived its day of absolutism, and is already aware that if it is to continue it must sober down into constitutionalism. On the other hand, the republic, as a republic, has never yet succeeded in fairly trying the experiment of republicansim; and there is no sort of doubt but that the class with which republican ideas are most popular, the class whose wishes would determine the drift of the republican policy, if it were ever tried, would be in favour of a great socialistic experiment. France is not a country to be governed without some appeal to the imagination. The Empire appeals to the imagination of the peasantry in one way—as a symbol of stability and magnificence. The republic would appeal to the imagination of the operative classes in another way—as a symbol of equality and fraternity. It would be of no use in the world to try either experiment without satisfying the imaginative needs of the classes by whose favour it was to succeed. The Bonapartist Empire, with all its faults, evidently does fairly satisfy the wish of the peasantry of France for a safe and conservative government, and also for a certain unity and splendour in connection with that government. The republic, if it were ever to succeed, could not succeed by the mere help of those who wish for a useful, free, and sober government, without any nonsense in it, such as may be said, perhaps, to have been aimed at, if not to exist, in America. The masses who heartily desire a republic in France do not really wish for a government of this type. On the contrary, they wish for one which should attempt a far more exciting experiment than any empire,— a socialist experiment on a grand scale,—and it would be quite impossible, if once the magic word 'republic' were uttered, to restrain the most ardent supporters of such a scheme from moulding the attempt to their own views. We do not then feel the slightest doubt but that the few rationalist republicans who only wish for a republic from dislike of what may be called the unreality and vulgarity of the Empire, would become utterly powerless so soon as they had answered their purpose as instruments in the hands of the fanatical republicans who are republicans from the socialist point of view. In founding a polity you must look to gain the strong support and attachment of large numbers of the people to your form of government. In France we believe that strong support and attachment can only be obtained from putting forth two quite opposite ideas,—either, the safety of property under a form of constitution which satisfies the vanity of France, or, the attempt to

149

obtain an equal division of property under a form of constitution which satisfies the desires expressed in the formula, 'Liberty, Equality, Fraternity.' To attempt a republic, and yet sternly resist the devotees of that formula, would be a course which would disgust the peasantry, alarm the middle classes, and yet alienate the operatives themselves; in other words, a course holding out no prospect of founding a stable government at all.

Moreover, there is this vast advantage about the utilisation of the Empire as it is, that, as we have already hinted, the fanatical stage of the imperial idea is exhausted and over, while the fanatical stage of the socialist idea is still in reserve. The era of 'personal government' has passed its meridian, has fairly lost its youthful vigour, the people of France very clearly showing that they wish for a very much sobered form of the Empire—a form of it, indeed, quite consistent with *bona fide* parliamentary government in all essentials. Now, rational and wise views of government always have an infinitely better chance when the fundamental fanaticism on which the popular support for any form of government too often depends, is on the wane, than when it is still waxing in popularity. When the unreasoning political emotions subside, the reasoning judgment begins to exercise a sensible sway. The years which followed the *coup d'état* were years of profound darkness for all reasonable and thoughtful politicians; but the blackness of that night is now passed, and the Empire, if it is to be heartily supported, must be liberal and in all important respects parliamentary. Not so with the republican idea, if that should regain its ascendancy. In France it would certainly have to pass through a fanatical stage before it could sober down into such a government as moderate men and sensible economists could for a moment approve. For this reason especially we wish to see the thinking liberals of France avail themselves of the existing Empire rather than seek to bring about any change of constitutional form. A blind popular feeling once fairly on the wane is the best conceivable cement for a political system; and if you can engraft upon it rational and liberal principles, which shall win support by their own intrinsic merit, you come very near the best conceivable form of popular government. That is what we have in England. The liberals of France will do well to avail themselves of the advantages offered by the present situation to secure a similar combination of political advantages for France.

The Declaration of War by France[1]

THE declaration of war by France against Prussia is one of those awful events which bring comment to a stand, and which of themselves make an impression far deeper and greater than anything which can be said about them. This time last week almost all the best judges in Europe would have considered such an event impossible. It was bad enough that France should say that the accession of a very distant relative of the King of Prussia to the throne of Spain would be esteemed by her a *casus belli*; it was worse in her to volunteer this in an offensive way before any occasion required it, and so as if possible to cause a quarrel; it was yet worse in France when Prince Leopold resigned his candidature to 'ask for more,' and want stipulations for the future which were inconsistent with the dignity of Prussia and which were meant to be refused; it was yet worse to make these further offensive demands in an unprecedently offensive manner on the King of Prussia in a public place; but worse than all is the sudden declaration of war which implies a 'foregone conclusion,' and shows that, whatever may be said, the momentary candidature of the Hohenzollern prince was but a pretext, that the Emperor meant from the beginning to fight Prussia, and meant nothing in the least else.

To account for such conduct we have to abandon all recent ideas of the French Emperor, and forget our experience of him as an important statesman and as for years one of the conservators and guardians of the peace of Europe. We must recur to the times following the *coup d'état* when Louis Napoleon was regarded as a gambler and a desperado capable of planning any misdeed and of committing any crime,—as a man who might invade any country without notice, and who would not want even a decent pretext for a war he thought convenient to himself or France. For years we have held other opinions of the French Emperor, and have thought that these old unfavourable ones were fears and fictions. But nothing in them is worse than what

[1] This article was first published in *The Economist* for July 16 1870, Volume XXVIII, pp. 877–8.

he has now done. The most desperate act of a midnight conspirator is not morally worse than a breach of the peace of Europe in this manner on a sudden, and with no object which anyone can state.

When indeed the French proclamation of war reaches us we shall have the decent drapery in which the Emperor clothes his policy. But use what words he may, the momentary pretext can only come to this —that what is called a 'relative' of the King of Prussia, that is, a German prince, who has a common ancestor with the King before the year 1200,—should for a moment have been a candidate for the Spanish crown, and that the King of Prussia will not promise that he never shall be so again. But what two nations are ever to be at peace if shadows like these are to cause war? England or Prussia might have attacked France on the first beginning of a Bonaparte empire, on the ground of the probable injury to European equilibrium and its inconsistency with the Vienna treaties, upon far more plausible reasons. A Bonaparte at the Tuileries was much more of a menace to Europe than a Hohenzollern at Madrid is of a menace to France. And the Hohenzollern is not even at Madrid—on the contrary, says he won't go there; and all the complaint is that Prussia will not say that if he changes his mind he shall not be let go there. A pretext for a great war so little specious and so evanescent was hardly ever seen.

Of course the real reasons are very different. The only rational motives for war are two—one national, and the other personal. It is said (and is we fear true) that war is popular in Paris, because Prussia is grown suddenly great, and because France has less prestige and is less thought of since she had so large a neighbour. But what is more infamous than to declare that the more prosperous and strong another state, the more bound we are to attack it at once? The same sort of doctrine might be urged in England. No doubt the immense growth of the United States does in some degree diminish the exclusive weight of England. The present French Ambassador at Washington says that 'the nations of the past were France and England, but that the nations of the future are America and Germany.' And on that showing, England has as much a right to attack America as France to invade Germany. *We* are glad the United States are great, and similarly France ought to be glad that Prussia is powerful as well as herself.

But perhaps in the obscure mind of the Emperor the personal fate of his dynasty has precedence over the national prosperity of France. Because many soldiers voted against him at the *plebiscite* he may wish to divert them, and to make himself popular by an immense war. The new parliamentary government to which he is bound is not probably very agreeable, and to get rid of it he wishes to turn men's thoughts elsewhere, and nothing so much as war changes the current of all ideas and all thoughts. But this is but saying that the French and the Prussians are to be killed for 'diversion's sake.' We seem not to be speaking of this age or of any civilised age, but of some barbarous period, when we discuss the killing of multitudes to please soldiers or to keep a dynasty upon the throne.

Nothing that can be said is adequate to the meaning of this most awful and painful event, and it is most melancholy that with all our boasts of civilisation, and after so many centuries of Christianity, so great a crime (for it is no less) should be possible in the world.

The Collapse of Cæsarism [1]

THE marvellous failure of the French imperial system to effect that which seemed *most* likely to be within its power, the complete military organisation of France, and the still more marvellous success of the Prussian system in the attainment of that end for Prussia,—a success such as, if you consider the *proportion* between the military strength attained and the wealth and population of the nation which has attained it, is not to be paralleled in the history of the world,—present a very instructive contrast. You can hardly say that in France it is 'personal government' which has failed, without admitting that in some true sense in Germany it is 'personal government' which has succeeded. That Prussia, if it had followed precisely in the steps of parliamentary England, would never have attained one-fourth part of the colossal military power, which for short periods at all events, though at the cost of a great strain to the nation, it can now put forth, is we think so obvious as not to need argument. It has been the 'personal government' of the Prussian Crown in relation to the army— and, we must admit too, a personal government fiercely attacked and till lately extremely unpopular with the representatives of the nation— which has made the Prussian army what it is, and what a strictly parliamentary system, voted freely by the deputies of the people, would never have made it. Indeed, the great object of popular attack, during the struggle between the Crown and Parliament before the Austrian war, was the very military system so strenuously defended by the crown which has turned out so splendid a success. It can then hardly be said that it is personal government which has failed so desperately in France. Had the conditions been the same, it is not too much to say that France might have gained as brilliant a military organisation by personal government as Prussia. But we think we may say safely that it is Cæsarism that has utterly failed in France,— meaning by Cæsarism, that peculiar system of which Louis Napoleon

[1] This article was first published in *The Economist* for August 20 1870, Volume XXVIII, pp. 1028–9.

—still, we suppose, nominally the Emperor of the French—is the great exponent, which tries to win directly from a *plebiscite, i.e.,* the vote of the people, a power for the throne to override the popular will as expressed in regular representative assemblies, and to place in the monarch an indefinite 'responsibility' to the nation, by virtue of which he may hold in severe check the intellectual criticism of the more educated classes and even the votes of the people's own delegates. That is what we really mean by Cæsarism,—the abuse of the confidence reposed by the most ignorant in a great name to hold at bay the reasoned arguments of men who both know the popular wish and also are sufficiently educated to discuss the best means of gratifying those wishes. A virtually irresponsible power obtained by one man from the vague preference of the masses for a particular name,—that is Cæsarism, and that is a system which has undoubtedly undergone a sudden and frightful collapse such as none but the very worst hereditary monarchies in Europe have sustained. The reverse for France is infinitely greater than the reverse of 1866 for Austria. Everyone knew that Austria was a weak, divided, and all but bankrupt State, torn by the internal divisions of populations of the most diverse blood, language, and religion, and behind the world in the application of science to the military arts. With France it was in every respect different. Homogeneous, as few states in Europe are homogeneous—animated by but one spirit in relation to this particular war—if not leading the military science of the day, at least known to be one among the leaders—rich in money—full of credit—high in military pride—there was hardly one element of failure which she had in common with Austria, and yet her reverses have been as signal and all but as complete.

And we do not doubt at all that the explanation is to be found in the very nature of Cæsarism,—*i.e.,* in the absence of all intermediate links of moral responsibility and co-operation, which such a system necessarily leaves between the throne and the people. It is the very object of the plebiscite to give the Emperor an authority which reduces all intermediate powers to comparative insignificance if they come into collision with his own. Consequently everything must depend on him, and if he be not practically omniscient there is no substantial check at all on the creatures whom he sets up to execute his will. This has evidently been the ruin of the great military power of France. The Emperor, unlike the first Napoleon, has had neither genius, nor health, nor perhaps the industry to check or superintend personally any considerable part even of the military organisation of the Empire. He has been compelled to trust implicitly to his own creatures. And his own creatures, suddenly raised from insignificance into positions of high power where they had nothing to fear except the displeasure of the Emperor, were exposed to all sorts of temptations to let all those minor arrangements on which the success of a great organisation must depend fall into disorder rather than incur enmities which might have risked their position, and could hardly have strengthened them. There were no real checks, social or otherwise, over the Emperor's creatures, except the Emperor's own watchfulness, and the Emperor's own watchfulness has evidently been a very insignificant check indeed. The original substitution of new men, imperial partisans, for the old officers of the army, must have gone far to destroy all the *esprit de corps* and the strict conventions of military honour, which are some of the greatest obstacles to laxity and corruption. Still for a time the anxiety of the Emperor about his chief engine of power, the test of frequent use in the Crimea and Italy, and the fears of subordinates who had not had any time to systematise a corrupt system, probably kept the army in decent working order. Certainly no such breakdown in arms, commissariat department, local knowledge—everything—seems to have taken place in 1859 as has taken place now. But, as the Emperor grew older, his health worse, and the army, in Europe at least, had less to test its efficiency, it is obvious that Cæsarism began to bear its natural fruits, and that the creatures of the Emperor served him less and less efficiently every year,—till now at last the collapse has come, and the great physical basis of Cæsarism, the army, which one would have thought it was a matter of life and death to keep in the highest state of efficiency, has broken in his hand as if it were a worthless reed.

In Prussia, though it has been, no doubt, in some sense, 'personal government' which has created so wonderful an instrument of war, yet it has not in any sense been Cæsarism, but indeed a system as strongly contrasted with Cæsarism as our own system of parliamentary omnipotence. The army has been the special object, indeed, of the King's care. His policy has been directed to perfect in every way its organisation. For this he has fought with his people so many of those indeterminate battles, in which a victory might be claimed on either side, but the final end of which has been that when the people saw by the experience of 1866 what he had done in the perfection of the army, they were convinced and gave way. But in spite of the King's special personal care of the army, he has, in fact, *never* been at liberty to do with it what he liked. Nowhere is the respect for military custom and the power of military caste more keenly felt than in Prussia. The King has always officered his army through the nobility, and that alone is a strong guarantee for an *esprit de corps* that no personal power could defy. The danger with an army, officered by nobles, and that has inherited as it were the special protection and anxiety of an hereditary throne, is not either caprice or loose administration, but a rigid martinetism too little elastic for the new ideas of new times. That the Prussian war administration has availed itself of the newest lights of science is highly creditable to the ruling powers; but there never could have been the same danger of the army falling into inefficiency through the inefficiency of any one man, whether at its head or not, that there is under a Cæsarist system. The King of Prussia, in relation to the army, is only the head of a ruling caste, bound by very strict traditions and etiquettes which have grown up in it continuously for many generations, and had he been as incompetent and as negligent as the Emperor of the French seems to have been, there would still have remained a thousand checks against the dishonesty and corruption which seem to have undermined the French military system. The Prussian military system is to the imperial French military system much what a ship built on the cellular system is to an ordinary ship in time of tempest; with the former, if one cell fills with water, the other cells may remain as clear of water as ever, and consequently the leak does not spread. But with the Cæsarist system the Emperor *is* the army. If he fails and has not head or health to look after it, all his creatures are pretty sure to fail also. They have no interest but their own to consult. And they can consult their own interest better by winking at malpractices than by exposing them. Caste may be a bad principle. But no caste is so bad as a caste containing virtually only a single family. The imperial system in France is a caste containing only a single family, which has indefinite *power* but not indefinite *capacity* to make instruments of all beneath it. In the Prussian system the whole military caste is bound together by the loyal ties which reduplicate a hundredfold any real vigour and earnestness at the head, while they put a strong check on recklessness or incapacity at the head. In the Cæsarist system there is no such check on Cæsar except the wishes of the masses of the people, and that is often the source of the greatest weakness. There seems the strongest reason to suppose that Louis Napoleon never had the courage to enforce his newest conscription law, because it was so unpopular, on those masses upon whom he depended for his lease of power and for his plebiscite. We doubt whether the wonderful disproportion between the paper figures of his armies and the numbers he actually brought into the field was not really due to his necessary dependence on the favour of the ignorant peasantry, and his fear of incurring unpopularity by putting the new conscription law in force. An hereditary king, strong in the affection of an aristocracy near his throne, and of a middle class that shows an educated preference for the old dynasty, has no need to fear the displeasure of the lowest among the population. But a Cæsar who is supported *against* the aristocracy and the educated and professional classes by the ignorant peasantry is compelled to limit his measures by their ignorant likes and dislikes. We hold, therefore, that Napoleon has failed, not only through that loneliness of power which has given him no natural allies among the educated people of France, and compelled him to seek the aid of men of little honour or scrupulousness, but that he has failed also exactly in consequence of his abject dependence on that ignorant conservatism of the peasantry to which he has looked for the popularity of his *régime*.

The Emperor Napoleon[1]

THE death of the Emperor Napoleon throws a flood of light upon his later life. It was in 1868 that he first began perceptibly to lose confidence in himself, to shrink from the responsibility of his own power, and to desire if means might be found to transmute his Cæsarism into constitutional monarchy. Observers imagined that he was alarmed by the progress of Prussia, and the foreseen necessity of embarking on a new and a great campaign; and no doubt the success of Prince Bismarck's policy did weigh upon his mind and disturb his judgment, but, as is now perceived, there was another cause. He had been attacked by a malady, which, besides threatening the constitution, exerts a singular power over the mind, frequently depriving it of nervous strength, of energy, and of the capacity of resolution. It was as a victim to incipient stone that the Emperor formed the Ollivier ministry and his new plan of government, and many of his delays, hesitations, and vacillations, together with the febrile irritability with which he pressed forward his idea of a new plebiscite, may be attributed to the growing, though secret, influence of his malady. Under its influence he ceased to be able to examine into details, lost his confidence in old friends, and began to indulge in the despondency which sent him in 1870 to the field a man beaten in advance. He lost the inclination to take the trouble to select new men who had become indispensable, and to bear with men who had independent opinions, or opinions hostile to his own. When during the campaign his exertions increased his complaint, he had no longer the energy to direct; and when at Sedan a tremendous effort might have saved him, he had not the physical power to make it, or even to entertain strongly the idea of making it. His later failures were in fact the results of his physical condition, or at all events so far the results of it, that it is impossible to form a just conception of the degree to which his original powers had been impaired.

[1] This article was first published in *The Economist* for January 11 1873, Volume XXXI, pp. 31–2. Napoleon had died at Chislehurst on January 9.

In spite of his failure, and of the stream of contemporary thought, which is greatly influenced by the misfortunes that failure brought on France, we believe those powers to have been very considerable. Napoleon the Third, though not a great administrator—a function for which he was too indolent—was perhaps the most reflective and *in*-sighted, not farsighted, of the modern statesmen of France. He perceived years before other men the spell which the name of his uncle threw over the Frenchmen who had forgotten the disasters of 1815. He comprehended years before other men that the peasantry were the governing body, and would, if secured in their properties, adhere firmly to any strong executive. He understood the latent power existing in the idea of nationalities years before old diplomatists could see in it anything but a dream. He was aware of the resources which might be developed by a Free-trade policy before a single politician in France had realised the first principles of economic finance. Alone among French politicians he contrived to conciliate the papacy, or rather to master it, without breaking with the republicans, and alone among Frenchmen he ventured to declare that England was the best ally France could have. Whenever his brain could work freely without necessity for previous labour he was a clear-sighted statesman, and it was only when a subject had to be learned up, like the condition of the Northern States of the Union or the organisation of Prussia, that his mental power became useless or even deceptive. We are by no means convinced that had he not gone to war his new constitution would have failed, for it would have given France her freedom, and yet allowed, through the plebiscite, of the occasional revolutions which France from time to time will always demand. A new generation of men would have come forward, and would have exercised the power which the Emperor, pressed by pain, by despondency, and by indolence, no longer desired to wield. He had perceived long before his great adherents that Frenchmen were tired of compression, and the violence of the expansion was due in great measure to his decaying energy and resolution. Up to the day of his death he could still be resolved, but it was only in the passive way—the way possible to a man not required to do anything but sit quietly in an arm-chair and weigh advice. The effect of his bodily health is an argument to the discredit not the credit of personal government, but it must be considered in any just estimate of the Emperor's mental power. We do not expect from M. Thiers the pliability of a young man, nor is it fair to expect from a middle-aged Emperor, tortured with the stone, the serene reflectiveness of a political philosopher.

It is too early yet to discuss frankly the character of the Emperor, but as we have indicated the greatest of his mental powers—cool and broad political insight—we may also indicate the greatest of his mental defects as a politician. He had, we think, an incapability, almost beyond precedent, of securing competent agents. He never discovered a great soldier. He never found out a great statesman. He never secured a great financier. Only two of his agents—M. de Morny and M. Pietri—can be pronounced first-rate men of any kind, and the mass of them could hardly be classed as fourth-rate or fifth-rate men. This was the more remarkable because he himself was not unpleasant to his people, not capricious, not exacting, not disposed to change; and as France is full of able men only too anxious to serve, it must have been due to some want in his own mind—a want which it is by no means easy to understand. Mere want of insight into individual character does not explain the failure, for that would leave promotion open to everybody, and consequently leave to the able all their chances unimpaired. Mere indolence does not explain it, for amidst the 500,000 officials employed in France it does not take very much trouble to pick out a few strong men; and mere carelessness does not explain it, for the Emperor was well aware how badly he was some- times served. It is difficult, considering the wealth of intellect in France, to doubt that the Emperor had the foible of men whose position is slightly uncertain, that he was jealous of very able persons, particularly if they were statesmen; regarded all such as his uncle regarded Moreau —as possible rivals and successors. Such men are usually independent, and he wanted his agents to obey. Such men in France argue well, and the Emperor was not good at debate either in public or private. Such men above all, if Frenchmen, are anxious to make their personality felt, and the Emperor could not bear that any personality should be felt except his own, lest it should attract the regard of a population accustomed to raise its favourites to the top. It was this feeling which induced him twice to accompany his armies, though he knew he was no soldier, and so secure that no general should obtain the suffrages of the army. It was this feeling which made him close up so many political careers, till it became nearly impossible for an able man in France to manifest his ability, and this feeling which induced him to prefer mere red tapists in the war department, where he never but once had a first-rate man, Marshal Niel, who was practically nominated by the army. Above all it was this feeling, greatly exasperated by disease, which induced him to underrate his own position, and doubt whether without victory he could retain his hold on France. There is not a doubt that, if he had remained quiet, the peasantry and the army would have remained true to him; but he could not with his morbid sense of insecurity, irritated to madness by disease, believe the truth, and therefore he fell. We shall, as time goes on and memoirs appear, know much more of Napoleon III than we do now, but we believe, when all is known, the world will decide that his grand merit as a politician was a certain clearness of insight, and that his grand defect was self-distrust, leading to jealous impatience of capacities unlike or superior to his own. To declare him a great man may be impossible in the face of his failures, but to declare him a small one is ridiculous. Small men dying in exile do not leave wide gaps in the European political horizon.

The Imperialist Manifesto [1]

THE intimation put forth from Chislehurst as to the position to be assumed by the Prince Imperial, the son of the ex-Emperor of the French, is modest, and wisely modest. It amounts to this, that the death of the late Emperor has reconciled all the conflicting elements in the party of his adherents, that his heir is to be under the joint guardianship of Prince Jerome and the Empress, and that he will not assume the title of Napoleon IV until that title has been endorsed by the eight millions of the French electorate. It is a favourite proverb, that necessity is the mother of invention; but necessity is not only a stimulant, it is quite as often a sedative, and it has been so in this case. There was really nothing for the Bonapartists just now to do except to lie by. It is of course possible that their turn may come again; odder things have happened; indeed, the fortune which raised Louis Napoleon to the throne may be said to have been stranger than any similar fortune for his son could be, for certainly after the reigns of two Bonapartes there is more of a dynastic tradition—if that be of any value in France—than there was after the reign of a single man of genius of that family, who was so unique that his achievements seemed to stand alone, and scarcely to offer the suggestion of a dynasty. But for the rest the very conception of Napoleonic Imperialism has always included an assumption of the capacity of the Head of the House to represent personally the French people. The centre of the Imperialistic idea is the personal ability of the sovereign who embodies it. Without prestige for him,—without at least a mysterious rumour of his ability and sympathy with the French people,—there can be no Imperialism. And it is obvious therefore that while the hopes of the party are centred on a boy, the party must keep quiet, or only exert themselves to spread impressive whispers of the boy's growing capacity for political administration, and growing susceptibility to weighty political ideas. It may not be necessary for party purposes and

[1] This article was first published in *The Economist* for January 25 1873, Volume XXXI, pp. 93–4.

party chances that the heir of Louis Napoleon should have a real political head and judgment of his own. But it will be necessary that his followers should be able to persuade themselves, or think they persuade themselves, that he has those qualities. It will be necessary that they should at least have a decent excuse for talking of the young Prince as a statesman and a leader, which it is impossible to do of a boy of sixteen. The Imperialist tradition is a tradition of personal qualifications to rule, for which only a popular sanction is to be asked. You cannot even ask a popular sanction for the qualifications of an unformed boy.

Still less can you ask such a sanction for the qualifications of his guardians, especially where those guardians are as little as possible in sympathy with each other, and can only just manage to effect an appearance of reconciliation over the Emperor's grave. To appeal to France to sanction the joint regency of the Empress and Prince Jerome would be a bad joke. Those of the French people who might be favourably inclined to the Empress would certainly be most bitterly hostile to Prince Jerome, and those of them—and they will be very few—who might like to intrust the destinies of France to Prince Jerome would be bitterly hostile to the Empress. You might almost as well propose to put the Viceroyalty of Ireland in commission, and to nominate on the commission Archbishop Cullen and the Fenian Head-Centre Stephens, as ask the French people to intrust the regency jointly to the leader, or perhaps we should say the most distinguished follower, of the *parti-prêtre* in France, and the clever but unscrupulous Voltairian radical who is the only acknowledged Prince of the blood except the young Head of the House himself. The policy of delay is therefore practically *forced* upon the Imperialists in France. The only possible regents are neither of them separately popular in France, and would be impossible together. The real hope of the party is only a hope, and could not by any amount of fanciful exaggeration be made into anything more. Imperialism means something very different indeed from the dynastic claim of the Bourbons. It has always rested on a double qualification—blood and personal ability; and of personal ability in this case there is no room to judge. Reticence and delay are therefore prescribed for the Imperialists by the very conditions of the case. And on reticence and delay they have, not so much wisely as inevitably, determined. If they had taken any other course, and proclaimed Napoleon IV as the mere dynastic heir of the late Emperor, they would have made a double blunder. They would have done for the son what the father, when in exile, took care not to do for himself; and they would have confounded the specific claims of the Prince Imperial with the specific claim of the Count de Chambord,—a claim much stronger on its merely dynastic side than that of the young Napoleon, and, if compared with it solely on that side, certain to outweigh it, but not nearly so strong on the side of popular ideas— the very side on which a premature proclamation of the young Prince would effectually undermine his pretensions.

Perhaps it is the reverse of a misfortune for the Imperialists that they should have so imperious a reason for a policy of reticence and delay. Of course in a country so changeful as France it is but a small chance that this party of unlucky exiles can look forward to in any case. Still it will be no smaller,—perhaps even better, for waiting. It was not even on the cards that the representative of a policy so disastrous to France, and so full of keen and ignominious popular memories as that of the late war, should have had any immediate chance of soon returning to rule there. And yet every year that the late Emperor might have passed in exile would have been a year of diminishing prestige and advancing shadow. The fortunes of the party must always have been compared with its past fortunes so long as the Emperor who had ruled and fallen was alive. But now that the Emperor is gone the party will be again one of expectancy instead of one of regrets. At every change in the fortunes of France the possible restoration of a Napoleon by plebiscite will be at least one of the contingencies to be discussed, nor will the candidate's name be clouded by the associations of a military catastrophe and a partitioned Empire. We do not say, and do not believe, that the Prince Imperial's chances are good. Change is the law of French politics, and the prospects of an enduring republic are at least not less good, and we hope somewhat better, than those of any other single constitutional experiment. But nothing in the world, —certainly not the prolonged life of the late Emperor,—could have made the chances of Imperialism good. If they are to be ever good again, it must be due to the abilities and tact of some younger heir of the Napoleons, and it is just for this that the death of the Emperor, and the policy of patience which must succeed it, open the way. Of all political dreams, dreams of restoration are usually the most futile. Still dreams of restoration are perhaps a little less absurd in the head of a young adventurer of a popular house, than in the head of an exile who has played out his hand and lost. Grant that experience and known capacity,—which the late Emperor certainly had,—go for something. Yet failure, and disastrous failure, in spite of experience and capacity, go for much more; and there is besides that mysterious depression to popular feeling involved in the notion of a worn-out constitution and a played-out hand. For the present at least the political stock of the Imperialist party must be withdrawn from the quotations. It cannot be really brought forward again till there is some sort of excuse for talking of the young Prince as a leader of parts, which can hardly be for another three or four years. In that time the republic will probably be either made or marred. Let us hope that by moderation and administrative skill it will be made, and not marred; at all events, the disappearance of one of the rival candidates for the favour of France is, so far as it goes, favourable to M. Thiers' astute policy of gradually accustoming France to associate order and strength, and a certain limited amount of liberty, with the name and form of a republic.

The Prospects of Bonapartism in France[1]

THE election of a Bonapartist candidate for the *Nièvre*, in opposition to a republican candidate who counted on the victory, and after so many republican victories in other constituencies as to render his reckoning not unreasonable, is an event which deserves very careful consideration. It is the first public confirmation of a deep and diffused impression among persons acquainted with French politics, that the progress of Imperialism in France, though impeded and latent, is nevertheless steady and regular. As in England we find it difficult to understand this, it may be well to reflect why it is so.

To an Englishman, the second Empire seems the greatest of failures. He would say that it suppressed liberty, that it impeded thought, that it depended on the life of a single man, that it is responsible for the most fatal of modern wars, in which it fell without an effort and almost without a friend. And no doubt this is all true; but, as a Frenchman thinks, it is not the whole truth, nor even the most important part of it. There is something to a Frenchman dearer than free thought, much dearer than parliamentary government, dearer even than successful foreign policy, and that is *fixity*. He wants to be sure that he will have the same government to-morrow as to-day, next month as this month, next year as this year. He lives in the constant presence of a revolutionary force; he is always imagining an outbreak of it; he has heard of the terrors of '93, and has seen the losses of the Commune; above all things he desires a sufficient and incessant force which is able to prevent revolutions, and make them impossible. In England we have always had a secure government, and we find it difficult to bring home to our imaginations the evil of wanting it. But if we lost it, no people would suffer half so much. The whole industrial life of England is based in an unexampled degree on credit and confidence, and that credit and confidence the faintest idea of a revolution would at once destroy. It would be worse than a mercantile panic many

[1] This article was first published in *The Economist* for May 30 1874, Volume XXXII, pp. 650–1.

times over. If our system of credit is so delicate as to be shaken by the failure of Overend, Gurney, and Co., it would collapse into ruins at the fall of Queen Victoria. We must imagine Lombard street to be for months in possession of the roughs, and then we shall understand what it is which Frenchmen fear. Against this sort of calamity, at any rate, the French consider that the Empire preserved them. Before it they feared a revolution daily, after it revolution began again; during the Empire they felt safe from its recurrence. Until it is succeeded by some system of equal fixity, the Empire will always be remembered with sadness. Many Frenchmen who do not hope for its return refrain because they think it almost too good a thing to hope for.

Even in this country, accustomed as we have long been to parliamentary government, a *Commune* at the Mansion House, continuing for months and completely despotic, would make us comprehend that other things were more certainly essential to life and industry. And to the French, who have no prized traditions of parliamentary life, to choose a government that lives on discussion in preference to a government which confers security seems absurd. Forms will change and names will alter; but sooner or later the French will set up some government which gives them the sensation of fixity. Perhaps it is not in the temperament of any nation—it certainly is not in theirs—to be satisfied with anything less.

Where, then, at this moment can persons in this temper look for such a government? They certainly cannot expect it from the present Assembly, for the Assembly was never more hopelessly divided against itself. Even in a country used to parliamentary government its dissensions would be serious. It cannot appoint a ministry or an executive whom it will certainly trust for any time; and, therefore, there is no one certain for any time to govern the country. As it is itself unstable, nothing which rests upon or which depends upon it can be stable. An attempt has indeed been made to give the government of Marshal MacMahon an appearance of fixity. But it has been an appearance only: the assembly has never been able to agree what sort of fixity it is to be. It has determined that in some manner the Marshal may rule for seven years if he chooses, but in what manner it has not and cannot determine, for there are endless opinions about it. And whether he will rule at all is not certain, for no one can say whether he will have the means. He can only rule by means of a ministry, and at present he has the greatest difficulty in forming one. He has been unable to find a premier; he has been obliged to 'take the formation of a cabinet' into his own hands. But the necessary result of his making the cabinet is that it becomes his cabinet when it is made. He is identified with it; he resembles no longer the constitutional monarch who receives equally all ministries—who is impartial to all, but who constructs none. He becomes at once a politician of definite type and temper who cannot be disconnected with the ministry which he has made—who must share its fate and its policy, who must succeed if it succeeds, and fail if it fails. No confidence is felt anywhere in France in the stability of this government, and none ought to be felt. Impartial foreigners can see in it only a tottering executive awkwardly attached to a changing assembly.

The obvious remedy for the faults of the present Assembly is to dissolve it and to substitute another assembly. But the present one refuses its consent, and its consent is necessary; it was elected when there was no other power in France, and, therefore, there is no other power which can according to law dissolve it. Mr. Cobden said of English parliaments that he had never been able to find out what time it was which their members thought suitable to dissolution; and the saying has been, and most likely will be, much truer of the present French chamber, because its powers are much greater than those of any English chamber, because there is not, as in England, any certain period at which it must come to an end, whether it wishes or not, and because in no English parliament have so many members sat who owed their former election to singular circumstances of the moment, and who have no chance of being again elected. Any parliament which can only be legally dissolved by itself is likely to be a 'Long Parliament,' and the present in France, unless some illegal event stops it, is likely to be a peculiarly long one.

But supposing it to dissolve itself, is its successor more likely to found a fixed government? We own we doubt it. Such an assembly would no doubt be more consistently republican than the present. The royalists would, at present, lose more than the Imperialists would gain; but the Imperialists would probably gain considerably, and as they are for the most part men of business, used to affairs and practical in combination, they will count in a chamber for much more than an equal number of respectable but stupid legitimists. But this is not the principal danger of the new Assembly. The worst period is the essential function which belongs to it. As it will be republican, it will have to make the republic; and though its members will be agreed that the government shall bear that name, they will, if they resemble present republicans in France, be agreed on little else. Between the republic of M. Thiers and of M. Gambetta, between that of the moderate left and of the extreme left, between that which is desired for socialist and that which is desired for political ends, there are immense differences. Though French republicans are united by the accident of a common name, many of them are much nearer to the partisans of other forms of government than they are to one another. To obtain the consent of an assembly thus divided to any sort of constitution will probably be a work of long time, especially as it will probably be very loquacious and very disorderly, as other French assemblies have been. And when, after long labour, the constitution emerges, what is the chance that it will be a constitution which will work? If, indeed, it were to be worked by Americans, it would not be difficult to make something which will 'pull along' somehow, as they would express it. They are used to political combination, and their tempers easily bear being outvoted. But the new constitution will have to be worked by the *French*—who are unused to republics, who have never been able to combine either for monarchy or republic, who cannot bear compromises, who will not endure being outvoted. A new constitution which is to be worked by such a people ought to be a masterpiece of political skill. The wisest and most considerate of political philosophers would scarcely hope to hit on such a marvel; but, in fact, it will be framed by the casual majorities of an angry assembly, necessarily ignorant of constructive politics, inevitably inflamed by political contention, incapable of seeing how one provision in a constitution is interlaced with another, voting each just as it comes. To expect a good constitution from such a source is, according to rational likelihood, to expect in vain; you might with equal reason hope to make, by parliamentary debate and division, a suit of well-fitting clothes for a restless and strangely-shaped person.

Who can wonder that persons who wish soon to possess a firm and strong government are deterred by such a prospect? who can be surprised that they turn fondly to the memory of the Empire, which, with all its faults, gave them that which they most covet, rather than to the republic, which can hardly give them this, whatever may be its other merits?

Why an English Liberal may look without disapproval on the progress of Imperialism in France[1]

WE last week endeavoured to explain why Imperialism was making much progress in France, and why, in our judgment, it was likely to make very much more. We now wish to explain why we think that this progress is by no means the grave misfortune which many liberals believe it to be, but, on the contrary, is an improvement in the present politics of France, and a thing to be glad of in the present sad state of that country.

The French have a neat mode of explaining this when they say that France is fit for a consultative, but not yet fit for a representative government. The distinction is this: In a consultative government the first power is the person at the head of the executive. The English Constitution was in that state in the Tudor times. The monarch was then the predominant authority in the realm. King Henry or Queen Elizabeth convened a parliament; consulted it; regarded or disregarded its advice, not, of course, entirely, but still very much according to his or her own will and pleasure. There were, doubtless, many things which the king could not do without parliamentary authority; he could not, as we know, impose new taxes or make new laws; but these were rather additional and extraordinary than common and necessary requirements. The ordinary revenue was enough for ordinary times; the old laws did well enough for an age which would hardly have understood, and would certainly have disliked the idea of constantly changing them. In the ordinary business and daily *rule* of the country the monarch was supreme. In a parliamentary government, on the other hand, as we daily see, the case is reversed. The assembly, which in the consultative government is the minor, is here the supreme authority. It is the parliament which settles all the policy of the state,

[1] This article was first published in *The Economist* for June 6 1874, Volume XXXII, pp. 681–3.

which chooses the ministers, which dismisses them, which incessantly watches that they do all which it enjoins, and do nothing which it does not approve. The hereditary sovereign, though in constitutional monarchies he is still permitted to exist, and is still allowed to be first, exists as a relic, and is first only in name and dignity; the ruling influence has passed to other hands.

We are not blind to the defects of parliamentary government; we are constantly experiencing them, and it is difficult at times not to exaggerate them. But, nevertheless, a fair judge will, we are sure, decide that it is a better government than the consultative. A parliamentary government is essentially a government by discussion; by constant speaking and writing a public opinion is formed which decides on all action and all policy. This opinion is by no means always right, it is often very wrong; but on familiar matters it has a great average of correctness; and the effort of forming it at first, and the habit of watching whether it turns out right at last, have been, and are, the best modes of training nations not only in political thought, but in all thought. But in consultative governments there is no similar process—discussion can only suggest, and opinion only advise. It is the supreme, and, perhaps, self-willed monarch, who must determine at last. The nation feels no responsibility, for it does not take the decision; it will learn little from watching whether it turns out well or ill, for it will always think that it would have avoided the error if things go ill, and secured the success if things go well. As it was not consulted, it will always say, and always believe, that if it had been consulted it would have been right.

Parliamentary government also brings to the supremacy of the state an unrivalled average of continued ability. No doubt it excludes the most peculiar and original understandings; a Bismarck or Richelieu will not consent to ask leave for all he does, and often would not get leave if he did ask. Such dominating wills and far-seeing minds are not to be found among parliamentary statesmen; the nature of their trade forbids it. But, on the other hand, parliamentary government keeps out all the fools, for a parliamentary premier works in the face of day, and utter incapacity would be dismissed in an instant; and it secures an unbroken series of capable men, now rising to a Pitt or Peel, now descending to a Liverpool or Perceval, always surpassing ordinary men in ability, and always presentable in great affairs. To this constant supply of equable excellence consultative governments have nothing analogous. The hereditary monarch upon whom all depends is an 'accident.' He may be a sage, or he may be a simpleton or an idiot. All that can be said is that in a restless nation and in stirring times only a man of considerable ability will be able to keep the lead; on the whole, national selection will maintain a high standard; strong kings only will long reign, because weak ones will be unable to cope with insurrection and civil war. But then this is a very costly process. History shows that you will pretty generally get a good ruler if you choose him by a fair fight, but the evils of the conflict are obvious and endless. And as in no other way can consultative government secure an able ruler, it is plainly in that respect far inferior to parliamentary government, even though parliamentary government is not perfect.

It is an excellence which follows from those we have mentioned that a parliamentary government can change its policy and can suit itself to times far better than a consultative. If a particular kind of policy is wanted, you choose a premier suited to that kind. If Lord Aberdeen is too pacific for a war policy, you put in a Palmerston; if a Gladstone government is too innovating for the temper of the time, you turn it out and substitute our present government. But in a consultative government, if the fixed head who at last rules is pacific, the policy of the state is, without appeal, pacific; if his temper is innovating, more or less of innovation there is sure to be. Of the two machines, the parliamentary is the more delicate and serviceable, for it can shift its power whenever it has to change its work.

If, therefore, a nation has a choice between the two forms of government, we are satisfied that it would prefer the parliamentary. But has France really such a choice? We own that we much doubt it. Parliamentary government is not a thing which always succeeds in the world; on the contrary, the lesson of experience is that it often fails, and seldom answers, and this because the necessary combination of elements is rare and complex.

First, parliamentary government requires that a nation should have *nerve* to endure incessant discussion and frequent change of rulers. This discussion is its life, and these changes are its sure result. But much present evidence and much past goes to prove that France does not possess this nerve. She now is, as we showed last week at length, anxious for one thing above all others, and that one is fixity. She wants, above all things, to see *who* is to be her ruler; to see it for certain; and to be able to make sure the rule will last for some time—long enough to support industry and confirm credit. But this is exactly what parliamentary government will not give to her. It puts the choice of rulers in an assembly, and assemblies are in all countries unstable and fickle—in France they are particularly so. Part of the good of parliamentary government is the easy change of rulers, and exactly for that reason France fears it. She does not want an easy change of rulers; on the contrary, she wants to make such changes difficult. To offer her, therefore, this result of parliamentary government—specially good and specially characteristic as it is—is to offer her that which she would, above all things, shun and shrink from.

No doubt, in countries where parliamentary government has been long established, and where it is prized and understood, a change of ministry tries no nerve and needs no courage. In England for the most part it does not change consols an eighth. Especially where, as here, there is a constitutional monarch behind the ministry, to preserve at least an appearance of stability, and to disguise from the many the magnitude of the event, no one need fear its consequences. Human life and industry are sure to continue pretty much unchanged. But in France there is no such tradition of parliament, and no such fixed royal person. To the mind of a common Frenchman a change of ministry is a portentous event; it amounts to much and it threatens more. He, more than anything else, wishes for a stable government, and parliamentary government seems to him more than any other unstable.

Unquestionably also there are races to whom this would not matter so much, and among whom it would be, in comparison, easy to found *de novo* a parliamentary government. But the French are not one of those races; they are naturally excitable, uncontrollable, and sensitive to risk; they have been so used to political misfortune that they now are scared at any shadow. There are generally two simultaneous, but contrary, excitements; one of the revolutionist, who wants to revive the *Commune*: the other of the peasant or the shopkeeper, who fears the *Commune*. And the passion of each tends to intensify the passion of the other. These frenzies—for on both sides they are often little better—work on the most inflammable and least stoical of national characters. There is no soil so unsuitable to parliamentary government.

This difficulty lies in the character of the nation, but there is a second in the character of its parliaments. They have always been—at least, since there was universal suffrage—unruly and excitable past English belief. The chamber is split into parties who often will not hear one another, who never heed one another, who unite only to hate those who would mediate between them. Such assemblies cannot choose a good ministry, and would not keep one if they had chosen it. The parliaments of Louis Philippe, no doubt, belong to a different type, but they were elected by a suffrage now impossible, and cemented by means which could not be revived. The characteristics of a good parliament are a disposition to hear, a willingness to compromise, and a tendency to cohere; and any French parliament in our time is more likely to be remarkable for the absence than for the possession of these qualities.

There is, too, as we last week explained, a third difficulty in the present French circumstances. We have been arguing as if the French had to work a parliamentary government; but it has in fact to do besides something much more difficult, it has to make that government. The first step in the undertaking is the election of a 'constituent' assembly, and it is a step of which France has great experience. There have been many such since 1789, and none have been successful, for the work of all of them has passed away. For a composite chamber of discordant factions to make a free constitution both strong enough and well adjusted enough for such a country as France, would indeed be close on a political miracle.

Such being the difficulty in France of making a parliamentary government, she of necessity falls back on the older modes of governing great nations, in which the monarchial executive is the first and the strongest force, and in which the parliamentary government is the weaker and the inferior. The Empire is plainly the government of this kind which is most likely to be popular in France, and most likely to be strong; perhaps it is the one strong government of this sort or of any sort which is now possible; at any rate, it is the government which, as far as we can at present see, has by far the best prospect of strength. And, therefore, it is we think not unreasonable and not inconsistent with firm allegiance to parliamentary government, where parliamentary government is possible, to look on the rapid revival of Imperialism in France without dismay and even with satisfaction.

Bagehot and the American Civil War

by Michael Churchman [1]

'THE greatest Victorian' is the title which G. M. Young would award to Walter Bagehot.[2] Other historians may challenge the merits of Bagehot's claim, but historians of the American Civil War can only rejoice that this brilliant editor and author succeeded to the editorship of *The Economist* in the autumn of 1860, at exactly the time of Abraham Lincoln's election to the Presidency. As editor, Bagehot wrote continuously on the Civil War, and his articles form a valuable but often neglected compendium of British opinion. Subtler and more philosophical than the writings of any of the public figures overseas, Bagehot's pieces show a clear intelligence which combined a grasp of theoretical principles of government and economics with a sense of realism and an experience of affairs. As contemporary history of the war as it appeared across the Atlantic, Bagehot's articles are almost unmatched in value and interest.

Bagehot's Civil War pieces reflect his own complex personality and versatile mind. He was the unusual combination of both thinker and doer, philosopher and man of action, essayist and rider to hounds. Imbued with a deep sense of the past, he was temperamentally a conservative, but intellectually a convinced liberal. Bagehot himself remarked that he was 'between sizes in politics'. He excelled in analysing the real workings of institutions and in explaining the psychology of the public figures who made them work. He was detached and independent-minded, 'neither a doctrinaire nor an enthusiast, but essentially a man of the centre', as Mr. Norman St John-Stevas says in his biography of Walter Bagehot.[3]

Not only was Bagehot a brilliant editor, he was also through *The Economist* an influential personage. England was the Civil War's most important neutral state, and among *The Economist*'s readers were

[1] Mr. Churchman is headmaster of the Kent School, Denver, Colorado, and is married to a collateral descendant of Walter Bagehot.
[2] G. M. Young, 'The Greatest Victorian', *Today and Yesterday* (London, 1948).
[3] Norman St John-Stevas, *Walter Bagehot* (London, 1958), p. 46.

certainly cabinet ministers, members of Parliament, and leading businessmen, who as members of the Victorian establishment were in a position to act decisively on their views. *The Economist*'s leaders helped to form their opinions, and its files are an important index to the educated thought of the period. Another of Bagehot's recent biographers, Alastair Buchan, quotes the financial historian, Sir John Clapham, as saying that

> *The Economist* has been neglected, just as *The Times* has been overworked, as a general guide to the tenor of opinion in Victorian England. . . . Wilson and Bagehot had access to very good sources of political information . . . and their treatment of news was much more dispassionate than that of, say, *The Times*, under Delane.[4]

II

With this pattern of background and interests it is not surprising that Bagehot's articles on the American Civil War were very wide-ranging. First, as editor of a financial paper, he was concerned with commerce, particularly in cotton; and his free-trade principles, no less than his paper's following in Lancashire, led him to deplore the interruption of the cotton supply. As a banker and merchant he was interested in the fiscal policies of both Northern and Southern governments, and he recognised the value of British trade with the North. Secondly, his anti-slavery sentiments were profound. Buchan says he had 'a hatred of slavery . . . and fewer illusions than some Englishmen about the aristocratic quality of the South, the "deeply ulcerated semblance of civilisation", as he called it'.[5] His third great interest, as befitted the future author of *The English Constitution*, was the functioning of the American Governments and their leaders. As a conservative, he made a careful distinction between liberty and democracy; he criticised Lincoln for infringing the former, and he thought that democracy would mean that politics would lapse into the hands of the 'vulgarer and shallower men of the nation'. He deplored the fact that 'the masses are everywhere omnipotent, and the masses in most parts are as ignorant as those of Europe and far more ruffianly'.[6] He valued a centralised, parliamentary form of government—the English system

---

[4] Alastair Buchan, *The Spare Chancellor* (London), 1959, p. 132. See *The History of The Times: The Tradition Established, 1841–1884* (London, 1939), ch. 18.
[5] Buchan, 155.
[6] *The Economist*, XIX (August 17 1861), pp. 897–8. Quotations from *The Economist* are hereafter indicated by volume, date, and page only.

in short—and disbelieved in the capacity of a federal constitution with balanced powers and fixed elections.

As a fourth theme, he continually decried the wastefulness of war. Indeed he felt that if South Carolina and her sisters were so foolish as to persist in seceding, they should be allowed to go in peace, even though their departure would be a blow to what Bagehot called the sense of 'unrivalled prosperity and power which swelled so flatulently and disturbingly in the breast of every citizen of the Transatlantic Republic'.[7] By inaction the North, besides averting a ruinous and immoral war, would purge their country of the degradation of slavery. In the fifth place it must be noted that Bagehot's interests in the Civil War were coloured by an intense, even smug, Englishness. Along with the racy language and astringent wit, an unmistakable air of English superiority hovers around his writings on America. There is also a consciousness of English national interests—an assured cotton supply, lower tariffs, easier defence of Canada—and a resentment of 'Yankee brag'. Uniting all these elements was a continuous assessment of the Union's chances of victory and a series of speculations on the war's outcome. These speculations run a kind of three-course cycle, and some sense of the substance and direction of Bagehot's outlook may be gained by looking in turn at his articles in each of these phases.

III

In the first phase Bagehot, like most observers domestic and foreign, expressed uncertainty as to whether the war would be prosecuted at all. When it did start in earnest, he began to deal regularly with a whole stream of matters which foreshadowed the themes he was to follow throughout the war—neutral rights and the blockade, cotton, British neutrality, and diplomatic crises. But, most important, he stated flatly throughout this period that the North could not win the war and that it was not desirable that it should.

Among his earliest topics was the career of British shippers which was particularly uncertain, and Bagehot noted that the doctrine of neutral rights now worked against Britain. Privateering was a real menace, and Bagehot lamented that 'the population of certain states in America is largely composed of the outcasts of civilisation—the worst "rowdies", the best-trained scroundrels in the world—and it is those

[7] *Ibid.*

who are to have commissions of license to search our ships'.[8] This was a galling prospect for the Mistress of the Seas. As the coastal blockade became more effective and as the Confederacy took steps to curtail the export of cotton in the hope of forcing British intervention, Bagehot considered the 'threatened famine in cotton'. This theme recurred throughout the war, accompanied by a counterpoint of wishful statistics on the growing cotton production of Egypt and India. The distress in Lancashire was analysed time and again; but, as Buchan notes:

> Bagehot insisted that Britain must respect the Northern blockade even though the Lancashire cotton mills ground to a halt for lack of cotton. . . . Better to face temporary ruin of Britain's large export trade to America and subsidise Lancashire from the Exchequer than to risk war with the North, argued Bagehot.[9]

Though Lincoln had insisted the war was merely a domestic insurrection, the blockade of Southern ports belied his stand, and the Queen's Proclamation of Neutrality, May 13 1861, recognising the belligerent status of the Confederates, was inevitable but highly irritating to the Northern government. On the question whether Palmerston's government should go further and accord full diplomatic recognition to the Confederates, or even—later in the war—intervene, *The Economist*, like *The Times*, supported a policy of strict neutrality.

The first serious diplomatic crisis of the war was the near fatal *Trent* affair. Bagehot's columns reflected the rise and fall of the British national temperature throughout the crisis. While his views were restrained compared with those of *The Times* and other papers of 'rule, Britannia' outlook, he urged firmness and even war if necessary. Two newly appointed Confederate 'Commissioners', James M. Mason and John Slidell, had run the coastal blockade and had reached Havana, whence they departed for Europe and their respective posts at London and Paris on the British packet *Trent*. Captain Charles Wilkes, U.S.N., commander of the Union sloop-of-war *San Jacinto*, intercepted the *Trent* on his own responsibility and carried off Mason and Slidell to Boston, where his rash exploit was greeted with great popular enthusiasm. The *Trent* reached England November 27 1861, where there was great indignation and an outbreak of war fever. Bagehot

[8] XIX (May 18 1861), pp. 534–5.　　　[9] Buchan, p. 156.

called the seizure 'an act contrary to the usage of civilised nations'. The Northerners, 'a half-instructed people whose political passions know no restraint', seemed to be willing to risk any calamity to get at their adversaries. 'Our duty is clear. We must demand, moderately but firmly, apology for the insult' and the release of the 'Confederate gentlemen', and if the United States refused, 'we have no alternative save war. The calamity is great, but the obligation is greater.'[10] Bagehot added the next week that the whole episode reinforced the impression that the American government was 'not only willing but rather anxious to insult us', and that soon Americans will be 'boarding and searching for rebels, envoys, and despatches every packet that plies between Dover and Calais'.[11]

He hoped that peace-loving people on both sides of the Atlantic would urge the American government to apologise and at least to refer the question of 'substantial right and law to the proper legal authorities, to American Prize Courts, of which all the world has long admired the impartiality'.[12] A European war must be fatal to the hopes of the Federals: war with Britain must 'insure the permanent independence of the South. . . . It will entail the loss of the vast *debatable land* upon which the present conflict has in the main been carried on'. The Federal Government had so far failed to recover the South, and a war with England might be Seward's hope of diverting attention from this failure. Ruinous though this would be, 'nothing is impossible to a democracy in revolution'.[13] Seward got the Cabinet to release the 'white elephants', as Lincoln called Mason and Slidell. Bagehot acknowledged that 'we have obtained all which we did ask, all which we could ask, and more than we could venture with any certainty to expect. . . . It is evident', he opined, 'that the out-of-doors multitude in many parts of America are strongly inclined rather to blame the tameness than to praise the wisdom of the government.'[14]

But perhaps the most interesting side of Bagehot's articles in this first phase was their conviction, repeatedly set down in 1861 and the early part of 1862, that Northern hopes of subjugating the South were illusory. In common with most foreign observers—indeed with many American observers—he persisted in this view until the end of the war. Though amply provoked, the North, he felt, could not hope to

[10] XIX (November 30 1861), p. 1317.　　[11] XIX (December 7 1861), p. 1347.
[12] XIX (December 7 1861), p. 1347.　　[13] XIX (December 14 1861), p. 1373.
[14] XIX (December 14 1861), p. 1374.

subjugate the South and should not try. Peaceful separation was the only realistic course.

Now the politician who believes that 5 or 6 millions of resolute and virulent Anglo-Saxons can be forcibly retained as citizens of a Republic from which they are determined to separate, or that they would be desirable or comfortable fellow citizens if so retained, must have some standard for estimating values and probabilities which is utterly unintelligible to us.[15]

The Government, controlled by the ignorant masses of the North, did not possess the fortitude or stamina to win the war, an opinion not contradicted by America's success in the Revolutionary War, when, as Bagehot told it, 'the indescribable imbecility of their enemies was yet more wonderful than their own vigour'. Subsequent American wars were mere raids 'against naked Indians and degenerate and undisciplined Mexicans'.[16] This denigration of American military prowess seemed to be confirmed by Bull Run, after which Bagehot remarked that 'the patriotism of the volunteers seems to bear an inverse ratio to their bluster'.[17] Northern hopes increased after the fall of New Orleans in April 1862, but Bagehot still characterised the aim of preserving the Union as 'utterly hopeless'.

IV

Northern victories on the Mississippi seem to mark the beginning of what may be called Bagehot's second phase in the Civil War pieces. His conviction that the North could not win began to waver slightly, and he now felt more and more the full uncertainties of the struggle, both as to its duration and outcome. The longer and more frightful the war's course appeared to him, the more he urged peace and mediation. Against a background of what he came to regard as the confused and unreadable development of a war which might be indefinitely prolonged, he continued to write on earlier themes and to treat new crises as they came up. Among the topics which interested him were the related questions of mediation and recognition, now complicated by the activities of Napoleon III in Mexico; the Emancipation Proclamation; and the highly charged question of the Laird Rams.

The year 1862 was notable for the threat of British intervention.

[15] XIX (June 8 1861), p. 621.   [16] XIX (August 17 1861), p. 897.
[17] XIX (August 17 1861), p. 897.

The Northern blockade prevented replenishment of Britain's raw cotton inventories, and great suffering followed in Lancashire, with consequent pressure on the British Government to intervene in American affairs. The cotton famine, the desirability from Britain's point of view of having two Americas instead of one as neighbours to Canada, Cabinet sympathy for the aristocratic South, which they looked upon as a gallant underdog, and pressure from Napoleon III for recognition of the Confederacy all contributed to Palmerston's and Russell's mooted plan of mediation in the autumn of 1862. The success of Napoleon III's ventures in Mexico was absolutely dependent on securing an independent and complaisant Confederacy. The French Emperor sent up a trial balloon in June 1862, in the form of an article in the *Constitutionelle*, which suggested European mediation, looking toward recognition of an independent Confederacy. Bagehot, commenting on June 14 1862, discussed the just role of the mediator but concluded that the attempt in this case would be unsuccessful because of interested motives.

After Parliament recessed on August 7 1862 Palmerston and Russell took up the question of mediation with great seriousness. Bagehot urged that because of the apparent military stalemate mediation should be accepted; but he never favoured forcible intervention and recognition of the South. He dwelt on this theme in *The Economist* of August 30 1862, saying that as the war became more desperate so it became more wicked and ferocious, leading to such outrages as General Butler's occupation of New Orleans and the suspension of civil liberties. In a third successive issue, he wrote on the same subject:

> Every utterance on either side implies that passions have reached a pitch at which the parties themselves can neither see plainly, nor think rationally, nor feel decently. . . . It is for bystanders and mutual friends to say to them what they really cannot, from the very bewilderment of mutual fury, say to themselves. Without the good offices of Europe, the prospect of a termination of the strife seems very hopeless.[18]

Gladstone's speech at Newcastle on October 7 1862, in which he asserted that Jefferson Davis had 'made a nation', intimated government intentions of recognition. The press assumed—wrongly, in the event—that Gladstone had acted as a government spokesman, and most papers, including *The Times*, approved this apparent new policy. Bagehot was more cautious: he agreed with Gladstone that the Con-

[18] XX (September 6 1862), p. 982.

federacy was in fact independent and 'that there is not the slightest prospect of their forcible subjugation or forcible re-annexation. . . . We consider that we are entitled to recognise them if we choose . . . still, we are scarcely prepared to recommend immediate recognition'.[19]

Recognition, Bagehot argued, would impair the hopes of European mediation for which he felt the time was then ripe. The distinction between mediation and recognition was in a sense an artificial one, because mediation would have led almost certainly to an independent Southern state which would shortly have been recognised by the mediators. Lincoln and Seward knew this, and they put up a flinty resistance to any intermeddling in the American War.

Palmerston and Russell consulted their colleagues, considered, and drifted. Sensing that a mediation offer would be unwelcome in the North, impressed by the Northern repulse of Lee's forces at Antietam, and faced with the opposition of Sir George Cornewall Lewis, the Duke of Argyll, and others in the Cabinet, they allowed the mediation plan to drop; and, as it happened, it was never revived. Napoleon III again made the suggestion in November that France, Great Britain, and Russia should join to offer their good offices as mediators. Bagehot reiterated his view that such an action would work to the advantage of the South and called it an 'unfriendly offer' which was ill-timed. The lapse of this second proposal ended a serious threat to the Union.

Added to Union anxiety about England's intentions was disappointment at the reception given to Lincoln's Emancipation Proclamation. When the War started there was a generally diffused belief in England that a Northern victory would mean the end of slavery. But Lincoln denied that abolition was a war aim and asserted that the preservation of the Union was the war's sole object. Therefore, when Lincoln did emancipate the rebel's slaves, his Proclamation appeared to be not so much an idealistic goal as a war measure, which, of course, it was in part. The British thought it was well calculated to stir up a servile rebellion. *The Times* conjured up a picture of 'horrible massacres of white women and children, to be followed by the extermination of the Black Race in the South'. Lincoln's name would head the 'catalogue of monsters'.[20] Bagehot expressed a typical criticism of the Emancipation Proclamation:

[19] XX (October 18 1862), p. 1149. The circumstances of Gladstone's speech and his later (1896) reflections on it are described in John Morley, *The Life of Gladstone* (London, 1903), II, pp. 75–83.
[20] *The Times*, October 21 1862.

Both the occasion and the mode are calculated to discredit the motive and impair the effect. . . . The proclamation, so half-hearted and inconsistent, far from commanding the moral support of Europe, will alienate what little sympathy for the northern causes had survived the long series of blunders, boastings, and affronts. . . . The position taken by the President in this decree is so curiously infelicitous, so grotesquely illogical, so transparently *un*-anti-slavery, that we cannot conceive how it could have emanated from a shrewd man and have been countersigned by an educated one.[21]

As no black uprising followed the Proclamation after it went into effect on January 1 1863, this unfavourable estimate abated somewhat, and it gradually came to be accepted that for the Northern Government emancipation was at least partly a moral object as well as a tactic in the strategy of victory.

The crisis of 1863 was the fiery controversy of the Confederate Rams, which their naval agent, Captain James Bulloch, an uncle of President Theodore Roosevelt, had ordered earlier from the Laird brothers' shipyard at Birkenhead. The '290' or *Alabama*, a cruiser constructed for the Confederates, had already been allowed to escape, unarmed and unequipped, from British waters. The guns and equipment of the *Alabama* followed her on two other ships to the Azores, whence, after being fitted out, she proceeded on her notoriously destructive mission of raiding Northern commerce.[22] The Azores rendezvous was a means of circumventing Britain's Foreign Enlistment Act of 1819, which forbade anyone 'to equip, furnish, fit out, or arm' store-ships, transports, or vessels of war 'with intent to commit hostilities against any power with which we are at peace, or to be employed hostilely in the service of any foreign potentate'. The vigilant American minister, Charles Francis Adams, protested vigorously against this clear evasion of at least the spirit of the Act, and Bagehot granted that the American had some justice on his side:

We may fully believe that we were right in our inaction. . . . At the same time we may frankly admit that the Americans may fairly be excused for being angry and that they had a very decent prima facie ground for the energetic and repeated remonstrances which they have addressed to our government on the subject.[23]

[21] XX (October 11 1862), pp. 1121–2. A summary of British reaction to the Emancipation Proclamation is contained in John Hope Franklin, *The Emancipation Proclamation* (New York, 1963), pp. 70–78; 130–135; 145–147.
[22] See Raphael Semmes, *The Confederate Raider Alabama* (New York, 1962).
[23] XXI (January 16 1863), p. 59.

Bagehot acknowledged the 'astonishing amount of injury . . . a surface cruiser or privateer may inflict' and allowed that the British would be mightily angry if they were in the same spot.[24]

Adams renewed his representations so forcefully in April 1863, when a second cruiser, the *Alexandra*, was ready to depart on similar mischief that the Government issued a holding order but lost the subsequent suit at law and were assessed damages.

The powerful iron-clad rams being readied in the Lairds' yard were still a greater threat to Northern shipping. Adams' rain of notes on the ministry culminated in his coldly angry message of September 13 1863, in which he told Russell that if the rams were not detained 'it would be superfluous in me to point out to your Lordship that this is war'. But Russell and Palmerston had already decided to seize the rams. Most papers approved this course, including *The Times* and *The Economist*, in which Bagehot wrote that 'the Government, from motives of policy, are wisely resolved to attempt to exercise the power which the clause in the Foreign Enlistment Act is supposed to give them'.[25] The British Government finally ended the affair by buying the rams for their own navy, thus terminating the last crucial diplomatic issue of the Civil War.

Later that fall Bagehot summed up 'English Opinion as Distinguished from English Action on American Questions', pointing out that the English nation was united in knowing what it was going to do—namely, remain neutral—and felt free therefore to express a wide range of sympathies and opinions. As pro-Northern in outlook Bagehot listed the anti-slavery people, 'most of our merchants', Radical politicians such as Bright, and a 'considerable portion of the Democracy', all of whom ardently hoped for negro emancipation and the triumph of the democratic Republic. Wishing victory for the Confederacy were the 'governing classes as a whole, the conservatives generally, and probably the majority of the middle classes, and most statesmen certainly.'[26] This editorial underlined the fact that British commentary after the summer of 1863 did not portend action. The threat of diplomatic intervention lifted along with the rise in the fortunes of Northern arms.

As already noted, Bagehot's uncertainty about the results of the war appeared throughout this second period, and he had written after

---

[24] XXI (January 16 1863), p. 60.   [25] XXI (September 19 1863), p. 1036.
[26] XXI (October 17 1863), pp. 1153–4.

Gladstone's Newcastle speech that he could not see 'the slightest prospect' of the South's 'subjugation or forcible reannexation'.[27] Early in 1863, writing under the heading, 'The Increased Probability of a Long Duration of the American War', he said that he could see neither end nor victory in the conflict.[28] Noting that summer that the war was 'all action and no go', he argued that the North should try to end the war on a negotiated basis 'as soon as ever they are cool and sagacious enough to see that separation is not only inevitable but as desirable for them as for their foes'.[29] Summarising *The Economist*'s hopes from the beginning of the war, the editor wrote, after the fall of Vicksburg, that the desired results were Southern independence, rather than unwilling reunion; a weak Confederacy from which slavery would soon disappear; and above all an early end to the war. It is 'scarcely possible that the South will be conquered. . . . Moreover, if they are, as we assume and believe, absolutely determined never to yield, they are as yet only in the *first stage* of defensive civil war'.[30]

The same viewpoint, with a note of weariness, continued the next year:

We had come to regard the American War as a painful but chronic calamity. We were surprised when it broke out, and we shall, perhaps, be as much surprised when it ends. . . . There is a tiresome monotony in the events which has killed all our interest. . . . We did not believe when Ft. Sumter was taken, that the North could conquer and retain the whole of the South. We thought they might overrun and ravage it; but the size of the territory and the number of the population seemed to us to forbid all hope of thorough and permanent subjugation. What we said they could not hold, it now appears they cannot take.[31]

This was written while Grant was slugging it out in the Wilderness. As late as February 1865, when there were rumours of peace, Bagehot was writing that there was little warrant 'for the expectation of any sudden or speedy change in the position of affairs'.[32] However, two months later, noting that the fall of Richmond was 'one of the most striking events in modern history', he recognised that the South had spent all its resources, that guerrilla warfare was unthinkable, and that the war was as good as over.[33]

[27] XX (October 18 1862), p. 1194.   [28] XXI (January 17 1863), p. 58.
[29] XXI (June 13 1863), pp. 645–6.   [30] XXI (December 26 1863), p. 1445.
[31] XXII (July 30 1864), p. 954.   [32] XXIII (February 4 1865), p. 127.
[33] XXIII (April 22 1865), p. 461–2.

V

The trend of Bagehot's outlook on the war is nowhere better illustrated than in his treatment of Abraham Lincoln and other leaders North and South. His final editorials on the fall of Richmond and the assassination of Lincoln may be taken as marking the third and concluding phase of his commentary in which he quite simply accepted Union victory and tried to re-evaluate his ideas in its light. His treatment of Lincoln is a kind of microcosm of the whole series of *The Economist* articles.

Jefferson Davis was generally rated as a cultivated gentleman and an experienced leader, and the adherence of such patrician soldiers and statesmen as Robert E. Lee also commended Southern leaders to the favourable notice of such papers as *The Times* and *The Economist*. Lincoln, by contrast, was disregarded as unknown, inexperienced, and of low origins. His emerging qualities of character and leadership were appreciated late, if at all, by contemporaries abroad, *The Times* reluctantly conceding after his death that Lincoln was 'as little of a tyrant as any man who ever lived'.

Bagehot at first was inclined to view Lincoln as a moderate leader, though attributing his election to a shift in the sentiments of the 'lower orders'. In an article of June 1 1861 American difficulties were chalked up to the cumbrous and artificial nature of the Constitution which placed power in the hands of the men least likely to cope with the crisis. Bagehot said of the President in his first year of office that 'Mr. Lincoln is nearly an unknown man' and a 'sectionalist' who was unequipped to forge a sprawling democracy into a fighting nation capable of subduing the South.[34] 'Mr. Lincoln's Two Proclamations', an article in October of the next year, focused on what Bagehot called Lincoln's remarkable lack of statesmanship. The suspension of the right of habeas corpus and the declaration of martial law appeared tyrannical to the editor, who tagged the Emancipation Proclamation as hypocritical and 'more injudicious still'.[35]

Prominent Britishers were nettled in general by the apparent indifference of America's leaders to British opinion, and Bagehot reflected this irritated state of mind when he wrote that

[34] XIX (June 1 1861), p. 591–3.
[35] XX (October 11 1862), pp. 1121–3.

the government of the Federal states has fallen into the hands of the smallest, weakest, and meanest set of men who ever presided over the policy of a great nation at the critical epoch of its affairs. The President means well, but he does nothing else well. . . . The inexplicable caprice of a forgotten caucus selected Mr. Lincoln as a candidate because no one knew much about him, and therefore scarcely anyone could object to him. His ministers are nearly as feeble as he is, without being nearly as good as he is. The whole tradition of Federal politics is a concatenation of paltry arts which their word 'dodge' and no other will describe.[36]

Nor was the President's literary style appreciated: Bagehot remarked on the 'feeble and ungrammatical prolixity of Abraham Lincoln'.[37]

In praising Salmon P. Chase as one of the few able men in Washington, Bagehot wrote that 'if the American war closed now, history could only say that Mr. Lincoln was a vulgar man with some respectability and a little humour, and that Mr. Chase had got much money under great political difficulties and with very little taxation'.[38] Later that year, after Lincoln's re-election, Bagehot said that 'in Europe and merely considering the choice between the candidates, the election of Mr. Lincoln will give general satisfaction'.[39] The regrettable policies of the American Union would continue. Republican rule would extend to 1869 and with it the war and all its hard effects on England's commerce and cotton manufacturing. Wondering on paper how it would end and how British interests would be affected, Bagehot lamented that 'we cannot expect of the American Republic a conscience commensurate with its strength, but we fear from it an immorality proportioned to its size'.[40] This severe observation he justified by the apparent quality of the newly elected leaders:

It is not even contended that Mr. Lincoln is a man of eminent ability. It is only said that he is a man of common honesty, and it seems, this is so rare a virtue at Washington that at their utmost need no other man can be picked out to possess it and true ability also. . . . Mr. Lincoln has been honest, but he has been vulgar; and there is no greater external misfortune . . . than for a great nation to be exclusively represented at a crisis far beyond previous, and perhaps beyond future, example, by a person whose words are mean even when his actions are important.[41]

Considering the congressional leaders of Johnson's administration, perhaps Bagehot was not altogether wrong, but he was shortly to

[36] XXI (April 25 1863), p. 449. [37] XXI (October 17 1863), p. 1153.
[38] XXII (July 23 1864), p. 922. [39] XXII (November 26 1864), p. 1453.
[40] Ibid. [41] Ibid.

revise his opinion of Lincoln. Barely six months later Bagehot confessed his errors in a rare editorial tribute after Lincoln's death was
reported in London.

The murder of Mr. Lincoln is a very great and very lamentable event,
perhaps the greatest and most lamentable which has occurred since the *coup
d'état*, if not since Waterloo. . . . It is not merely that a great man has passed
away, but he has disappeared at the very time when his special greatness
seemed almost essential to the world, when his death would work the widest
conceivable evil, when the chances of replacing him, even partially, approached nearest to zero. . . . Mr. Lincoln, by a rare combination of qualities
—patience, sagacity, and honesty—by a still more rare sympathy, not with
the best of his nation, but with the best average of his nation, and by a
moderation rarest of all, had attained such vast moral authority that he could
make all the hundred wheels of the constitution move in one direction without exerting any physical force. . . . We do not know in history such an
example of the growth of a ruler in wisdom as was exhibited by Mr. Lincoln.
Power and responsibility visibly widened his mind and elevated his character. Difficulties, instead of irritating him as they do most men, only increased
his reliance on patience; opposition, instead of ulcerating, only made him
more tolerant and determined. The very style of his public papers altered,
till the very man who had written in an official despatch about 'Uncle Sam's
web feet', drew up his final inaugural in a style which extorted from critics
so hostile as the *Saturday Reviewers*, a burst of involuntary admiration.[42]

When it finally came, the end of the war seemed to strike all European observers with its suddenness and finality. Bagehot wrote of the
Confederates that by their great efforts they had gained much sympathy in Europe. Likewise, the 'undaunted courage of the Federals,
their refusal to admit, even to their imagination, the possibility of real
failure', won admiration abroad and combined to give the fall of Richmond the 'intense but melancholy interest' of a tragedy.[43] While
saluting the 'vanquished gallantry' of the Confederates, Bagehot said
that 'every Englishman . . . will feel a kind of personal sympathy with
the victory of the Federals', who fought on obstinately, never admitting defeat, until in the end they were able to gather those 'latent
elements of conclusive vigour' which brought victory. The Northerners, he added, 'won as an Englishman would have won, by obstinacy',
which from Bagehot was the ultimate compliment.[44]

[42] XXIII (April 29 1865), p. 495.   [43] XXIII (April 22 1865), p. 461.
[44] XXIII (April 22 1865), p. 462.

VI

In summary, it may be noted that throughout the war Bagehot was consistent in advocating the end of slavery, in opposing armed intervention, and in urging an early end to hostilities. Like most contemporaries, he did not perceive the growing Union sentiment nor the rapidly increasing centralisation of wartime powers with which Lincoln was able to mobilise Northern resources for victory. However imperfectly the complexity of Lincoln's task may have been understood in England, his increasingly effective use of wartime powers was in contrast with the Confederacy's failure to make maximum use of its considerable resources. Many English editors failed to see that in the hands of its Northern supporters the American Constitution—and the tolerated evasions of it—would suffice to meet the challenge of secession. Another element, imperfectly understood by most observers across the Atlantic, was the 'difficult task Lincoln faced in holding the border states loyal to the Union'.[45] That Bagehot with his excellent 'book' knowledge of America and his experience of centralised parliamentary government did not foresee the sustaining power of Lincoln's administration is not perhaps surprising. No other reputable foreign journal foresaw Northern victory either, and *The Economist* did better than most in keeping a perspective on the war.

Bagehot's pieces reflect above all the enormous complexity of the events of the Civil War as they appeared to writers overseas who were trying to interpret the cascade of transatlantic reports for their readers. He had the advantage of writing for a weekly paper which allowed him a space of time, not permitted to editors of dailies, to reflect on events and to take a longer and more reasoned view. As a journalist and social scientist he was able to give unusual depth and clarity of analysis to his pieces. Alastair Buchan regrets in his biography that Bagehot had not travelled in America and come to know firsthand the country's spirit and institutions. But perhaps Bagehot's point of view, informed and intelligent as it was and redolent of the insularity of the English educated classes, is a more useful guide as it is—in the form of week-by-week reactions uncontaminated with the sympathy and experienced knowledge which American connections might have

---

[45] Arnold Whitridge, 'British Liberals and the American Civil War', *History Today*, XII (October 1962), p. 695.

created. His pieces are better than typical, filled with insight and catchy phrases that give them an air of just having been written. Drawn as they were from the resources of one of the best minds of the nineteenth century, Bagehot's articles stand high as a source for the Civil War historian.

The Political Crisis in America[1]

THE conflict which is now going on in the United States is full of the gravest and most painful significance for all thinking men. In no other quarter of the world are good and evil so distinctly in conflict as is just now the case in America; and yet in no quarter of the world does the magnitude and the solemnity of the crisis seem to be so little understood. The Italians are perfectly aware that the future of their country turns almost entirely upon their firmness and patience in the present year. But in America a vastly deeper and profounder question is now in one of the most critical phases of its history than even the question of constitutional liberty in Italy,—the question whether or not the permanent existence of a servile class is to be incorporated with the essence of modern civilisation in one of the greatest nations of the earth. Yet we affirm, with profound regret, that the American politicians on both sides seem to be intellectually unconscious of the vastness of the issue. Passion, spite, petty personality, small wit, the spirit of compromise, and, as the best and highest of all, the spirit of short-sighted, unstatesmanlike anger against the slave states, mark the tone of the debates in Congress. On neither side is there any feeling that that great question, the false solution of which tended more than anything to dissolve the ancient civilisations of Greece and Rome, is again raised. There seems to be no slavery advocate who, like Lord Strafford in relation to despotism, can grasp the whole question in its breadth and boldly say, 'Evil, be thou my good.' There is, we almost fear, scarcely any anti-slavery statesman in the Congress who can, like Pym or Cromwell in relation to English freedom, clear the question of all personalities, and bring home to the conscience of his nation the tremendous nature of the issue before it.

Let us glance briefly at the situation, to our eyes most sad and gloomy, of the slavery question in America. In the South, all parties, from the highest to the lowest,—from the oldest families in Virginia

[1] This article was first published in *The Economist* for January 21 1860, Volume XVIII, pp. 58–9.

to the 'mean whites' of Maryland,—are stirred up to acts of the most shocking and shameless insolence. The lives even of immigrants from this country who may happen to hint that respect for labour is inconsistent with the axioms of slavery are no longer safe, as is shown by the case of Power in South Carolina, who is said to have recently been judicially punished, and then all but murdered, for a mere accidental allusion to what is the universal faith of this country. The legislature of one Southern state has instructed its representatives to urge the Senate of the United States to insist on such a modification of the criminal justice treaty with England, as shall oblige England and her colonies (Canada of course being the one aimed at) to restore not only 'fugitives from justice,' but 'fugitives from labour.' The House of Representatives of another state (Maryland) has just adopted a resolution 'that John Sherman (the Republican candidate for the speaker's chair in the House of Representatives at Washington) 'or any other black Republican should not be elected speaker, and that if any member from this state (Maryland) voted for him, or any such exceptionable candidate, he would forfeit the respect and confidence of the people of the state.' The white citizens of the state (Maryland) meanwhile have adopted an address to the state legislature, urging strenuously upon its members to abolish 'free Negroism' for ever in that state, on the express ground that government is primarily intended for the benefit of the white population alone, and that the competition of free Negroes is hurtful to white interests. They deliberately ask the legislature to pass an act dividing the free coloured population amongst the white citizens of the state, and adjudging them to permanent slavery, granting, however, as a generous concession, that they shall be 'exempted from sale under execution for debt.' In a word, the Southern states are to the last degree furious and threatening. It is believed that a demand will be made upon the Northern states for the extradition for trial of many of the anti-slavery leaders suspected of being parties to the Harper's Ferry plot, or otherwise conspirators against the peace of the South,—and it is certain that in every way the South are now prepared to push matters to the verge of civil war.

In the North, and in the Federal legislature at Washington, there is little sign of that determined and united front, that clear inflexible principle on the part of the free-soilers which could alone hope to withstand effectually the furious and united onset which is preparing. It is true that the Republican candidate for the Speaker's chair in the

Washington House of Representatives, Mr. Sherman, of Pennsylvania, though hitherto unsuccessful, seems to unite many more votes than any candidate of the Democratic or any other party. But it also seems unfortunately certain that the Republicans are not of one mind,—that their common name embraces many shades of disposition to compromise matters with the South. For example, there is Mr. Stanton, one of the members for Ohio, whom one of his democratic colleagues describes with the highly-coloured, but to European ears not perhaps very lucid epithets, as 'a mahogany Whig slightly varnished with Republicanism.' This unfortunate specimen of complicated political tattooing, although denominated Republican, and apparently a supporter of Mr. Sherman's, is clearly not one who can in the least be depended on for a firm and high-principled resistance to the Southern aggression. He tells the House of Representatives, with some emphasis, that he should not offer any opposition to a 'proper' fugitive slave law. He only opposes the law of 1850 because it is liable to abuse,—because it is turned into an instrument of enslaving, on false pretences, the free coloured population, instead of merely recovering the escaped slaves. Limit the law so as to give good guarantees against its 'abuse' to entrap the free,—and Mr. Stanton, of Ohio, would not oppose it. And Mr. Stanton, of Ohio, is not an exceptional member of the Republican party, a large section of whom are for the old and fatal policy of concessions of all kinds to the South 'to save the Union.' The ultra-Southerners are comparatively few, but violent, desperate, united men. The Republican party is far more numerous, but is neither hot nor cold,—does not know its own principles,—indeed, cannot, as a whole, take up the dignified ground of high principle at all, since its ranks are swelled by men who wail over the tendency to extremes, and sigh weakly for that peace which, in such cases, could only be enduring when gained as the fruit of strife and victory.

Nor is the free North even so much as divided between a wavering and a staunch anti-slavery party. There is there an exceedingly important party of Northern Democrats, who are up to a certain point, purely Southern in their desire for the subordination of the Negro race, though, being free from the self-interested motives of the South, they have not yet reached the Southern extremes of insolence and wickedness. 'Indiana,' we are told, for instance, by one of its representatives in Congress, though a free state, 'would not under any circumstances tolerate any measure designed to elevate Negroes to political equality with the whites. Its whole history and legislation go to confirm this opinion.' Nor is Indiana an exceptional specimen of a Northern state.

What is the cause of a state of opinion so lamentable? The violence and insolence of the abolitionist party, says *The Times*, who have driven states which were getting weary and disgusted with slavery into antagonistic insolence. We fear this is one of those cases of conveniently attributing great and solemn results to inadequate and petty causes, which is itself a sign of complete inability to see the depth and significance of the strife. We do not wish to palliate a single word of injustice, a single proposition of wild and reckless character, which the abolitionists may have put forth. We are fully aware that every such injustice does more injury to the party who are guilty of it than to the party against whom it is aimed. But we confess ourselves wholly unable to believe that the only party who have shown any sense of the awful magnitude of the question at issue, however much they may have sometimes lost self-control from the very excess of their own feeling, have been the main cause of the hard and shameless effrontery of the Southern states. When honourable members of Congress speak in the Senate House of a very calm and respectable, if somewhat heavy writer on the social evil of slavery, as '*that North Carolina thief and renegade, Helper,*' we may surely suspect some deeper and worse root of the pro-slavery passion than just resentment against the exaggerations of abolitionists. We have another senator expressly testifying that no abolitionist exaggerations have driven them to their present attitude. Hear Mr. Mason, one of the senators of Virginia. 'Because of the aggression committed by the servile states, commonly called the free states, upon the condition of the African bondage of the South, the mind of the South has been much turned towards it. By reason of that further consideration, and pondering more deeply on the relations subsisting between the African race of this country and the white race, I believe that the opinion once entertained, certainly in my state, by able and distinguished men, that the condition of African slavery was one more to be deplored than fostered, has undergone a change; and that the uniform,—universal I might say,—sentiment in my state is, that it is a blessing to both races, one to be encouraged, cherished, and fostered.' This is a state of opinion deliberate enough for a statesmanlike defence of the slavery view, if there were any man of sufficiently statesmanlike intellect to adopt it. The only excuse for the men who do adopt it is, that they appear to be men of narrow minds and small passions, who prefer challenging or caning an antagonist to overcoming him in debate. A really great mind fitted to lead the South at the present moment must have something of the diabolic in its disposition,—something of preference for evil,—or it could not fail to see that the whole constitution of society in America must be wrecked and shattered on this rock, before it can be reconstituted in any durable form, if the danger is not grappled with at once.

England can merely look on at this terrible,—we might even say tragic contest, were not the representative leaders in it in general formed on so petty a scale, so unconscious of their parts. But there is one case in which she can and ought to do more. If there be any of our own citizens (not yet naturalised in America) who are subjected to such brutal treatment as Tate in North Carolina or Power in South Carolina, England must firmly demand, and even compel, reparation;—for the outrages of Chinese braves and Mantchou Tartar militia are innocent and even praiseworthy, compared with the acts of these unjust Carolina judges, and the infamous mobs by which they are backed.

The Bearings of American Disunion[1]

THE tidings from what we can no longer call the United States bid fair, for some time to come, to surpass all others in interest and importance. The relations of this country with America, commercial and political, are so intimate, that every transaction on the other side of the Atlantic has its echo and vibration here. Nothing that passes beyond our own shores can affect us so powerfully or concern us so much as the proceedings and condition of the great federal republic; with its prosperity our own is inextricably interwoven in bonds that are painfully close and tight; and what is passing there now demands the most vigilant observation, and the calmest and most thorough appreciation. Commercial panics and trade perplexities we have encountered often from the same quarter, but so formidable a *political* crisis as the present has not hitherto been seen:—and it is not the less serious or startling because it has been long preparing and has for some years been clearly unavoidable. The passions of the native Americans on both sides are so fearfully excited that we cannot gain much assistance in our comprehension of the conjuncture from their writings or their speeches, and those who are resident in this country seem as bewildered as ourselves;—so, in our estimate of what is occurring and what is likely to occur, we must trust pretty much to our own judgment, and will be as judicial as we can.

We shall not pretend to discuss those questions as to which the best qualified and most deeply interested parties seem themselves unable to decide. It is not for us to pronounce whether South Carolina has or has not a right to secede from the Union; whether, if she has not, the Congress has the right to prevent her secession by force; whether the Congress could do so if it tried; and whether it is likely to venture on the trial. These are points for the Americans to settle; and our opinions on the subject would be simply impertinent. Thus much, however, seems certain:—that South Carolina cannot practic-

---

[1] This article was first published in *The Economist* for January 12 1861, Volume XIX, pp. 29–32.

ally and permanently secede *alone*. Either she will find herself isolated, and will resume her place in the Union on such terms as she can obtain; or she will be joined by all or most of the other slaveholding states, in which case a Southern federation will be formed, as extensive and not much less populous than the Northern one. A new state will be added to the commonwealth of nations, with which we shall have to enter into formal political relations. Let us consider, therefore, more calmly and impartially than the Americans themselves seem at this moment capable of doing, what are the real grounds for desiring and for deprecating a severance of the Union; what would be its probable consequences, if consummated; and in what manner it could affect Great Britain.

The first thing that strikes an Englishman is that this tremendous excitement and this formal disruption appear to be caused chiefly by the issue of a contested election, such as occurs and has always occurred every four years. For a long period the Southern states, though somewhat inferior in population and enormously inferior in wealth, have succeeded in electing a President of their own way of thinking;—and now, having been beaten for the first time in a fair constitutional struggle, they are unable to accept their defeat as a national decision; and without waiting to see whether any, and what, practical consequences may follow from this decision, they at once break up a Union which has lasted for three quarters of a century, though they still retain, and would have retained for many months longer, an equality in one House of Congress and a decided majority in the other—in fact, the virtual command of all legislative action. Besides all this, they hold—not only in their newspapers and platform harangues, but in state documents and parliamentary speeches— language towards the North breathing the fiercest animosity and an almost insane degree of virulent excitement. The Carolinians speak of the politicians and people of New York and Massachusetts as even Frenchmen scarcely ever spoke of Englishmen except in the very crisis of warlike irritation—much in fact as Meagher and Mitchell used to speak of Great Britain in the wildest days of the Repeal fever. To such an extent has this gone—so completely has passion superseded both decency and prudence in the minds of many Southern citizens—that many voices have been heard clamouring for secession as an excuse for repudiating the debts, private and commercial as well as public, which they owe to the wealthier classes of the North.

The second point we remark is that the cry for secession is the loudest in those quarters which to all appearances would suffer most from it and have the greatest reason to dread it; while, on the other hand, those who most deprecate disunion and appear most desirous to make questionable compromises in order to avert it, are the states to which of late years it has brought only embarrassment, discredit, and enforced subordination. The Northern states, especially the Atlantic ones, which are comparatively wealthy, populous, and powerful, and which for a quarter of a century have been dragged through every species of moral and political mire by their slaveholding associates,—to whom at first sight it would seem as if severance would be liberation from a galling and dishonouring servitude,—are temperate, conciliating, and rational, and would fain dissipate the danger, if they could see their way to doing so. The Southern states—impoverished as far as money matters go, with no monetary centre, with a slave, and therefore a hostile, population in the midst of them (amounting to more than one-third of the whites, and in many districts far outnumbering them), and with three-fourths of their white citizens sunk into a state of social and moral degradation such as probably no civilised nation ever yet beheld—insist upon separation from a nation their connection with which has long supplied their principal security and their chief resource. Of these states, too, whose most ostensible grievance is the alleged non-execution of the fugitive slave law, the frontier states who suffer most from the escape of slaves are the most moderate and tranquil; while South Carolina, with two states at least and five degrees of latitude between her and freedom, is the soul and leader of the severance scheme, which will throw her on her own unaided strength.

The third point to notice, which affords perhaps some explanation of the two previous facts, is that this secession movement is not a perfectly simple and honest one. South Carolina's passionate determination to secede does not proceed solely from a sense of injustice or from indignation at the alleged interference of the North with her 'domestic institution,' or from fear of further interferences in the same direction. It is complicated with other aims and motives. She is not merely furious because the free states do not surrender fugitive slaves as promptly and as easily as she desires, and because she believes, now Mr. Lincoln is elected, that slavery will be prohibited in the 'territories';—she resents, and with some reason, the protective tariff adopted by

Congress with a view of assisting the manufactures of the Union, which are carried on principally in the North. She knows that, if the Federal customs duties were abolished, she would be able to import British manufactures more cheaply than at present; and she fancies also that Charleston would then become a sort of New York for the South, the future capital and the centre of its commercial operations. She desires, moreover, and has openly avowed it on more than one occasion, to reopen the African slave trade; she believes that her own future prosperity and that of the planting states generally depends on this step; and she is well aware that it will be impossible to carry her designs into effect as long as the Union continues. The Northern states will bear much, but they will not bear *that*.

On this side of the Atlantic we feel considerable difficulty in understanding the views and proceedings of different sections of the federated states, except on the supposition that violent passions and unavowed motives are in operation to complicate the case and to cloud the usually shrewd sagacity of the Americans. There may be said to be four district divisions of the nation in reference to this subject. We can understand that the North-Western states, Ohio, Illinois, Michigan, Indiana, and Wisconsin, should be averse to a severance of the Union; because, in the first place, they grow a considerable amount of the provisions which are consumed in the slave states, and fear a disturbance of their market;—and in the second place, as a glance at the map will show, the formation of a Southern federation would place the command of their great outlet, the Mississippi, in the hands of a foreign state. All the great rivers which drain the North and West, without exception, join in one and flow by New Orleans into the Gulf of Mexico. If this outlet were closed to them, either by hostilities or heavy transit dues, their only water access to the rest of the world would be the costly and precarious one of the lakes and the St. Lawrence.—We can understand also that the frontier slave states, Virginia more especially, should be perplexed and divided on the question. As a slave state, the passions of the Virginians naturally lead them to sympathise with South Carolina and her fellow secessionists; as a slave-breeding state, drawing nearly all her wealth from the negroes which she yearly sells to the South, her interests are closely bound up with its prosperity;—though every year free labour is advancing further and further into the Northern portion of the state, and the sentiments of many of the citizens are undergoing gradual change. On the other hand, the more sagacious and far-seeing of her politicians may well doubt whether the safety and prosperity of the South, and by consequence her power of purchasing and paying high for Virginian negroes, will not be imperilled by separation; whether, in short, a depreciation in the value of slave property from black insurrection and a servile war is not more probable than an enhancement of it by the unlimited extension of slavery in a Southern direction. She may well also have another misgiving (which is fast becoming a well-defined and imminent danger),—viz., whether a severance of the Union would not be almost certainly followed by such a reopening of the African slave trade as would reduce the price of home-bred negroes one-half or two-thirds, and thus bring Virginia slave-breeders to beggary. A revival of the slave trade by the Southern federation would almost compel Virginia to become a free state, when her remaining in a slave union would of course be impossible. Her position, therefore, in the present crisis is peculiarly embarrassing and anomalous.

But though we can understand the sentiments of Ohio on the one side, and of Virginia on the other, in reference to a disruption of the Union, we confess it is difficult on a sober estimate of consequences (and putting irritated passions and ambitious pride apart) to understand why the North should deprecate it so earnestly, or why the South should urge it so eagerly. For a long period, the Northern states have been compelled to submit to a species of subordination and chronic discomfiture mortifying in the highest degree to a proud and a moral people. They felt that they were vastly superior to the Southern states in intelligence, in wealth, in enterprise, in population; that their energies were greater, that their reputation was higher, that their cause was nobler;—and yet in every political contest they were compelled to succumb, or to avoid obvious defeat by some compromise galling alike to their sense of dignity and their sense of right. They must have felt that the semi-barbarism of the South was infecting and degrading their manners, that the terrible social blot of the South was their ceaseless opprobrium in the eyes of the civilised world, and that the violence and cupidity of the South was for ever marring their policy and disturbing their peace. We should naturally have fancied that they would, in consideration of these things, have been anxious to shake off such an incubus and to purify themselves from such a stain; and have looked forward with sanguine enthusiasm to the noble and splendid career of progress which lay before them when relieved from such a moral weight and social fetter. There is, however, little of this feeling—so little that the chief danger appears to be lest the Republicans should compromise too readily and yield too much in the hope of preventing separation—yield even to the extent of impolicy, injustice, and discredit. The explanation is probably threefold. The Northern states, besides dreading the near neighbourhood of an independent and exasperated nation, are perhaps right in anticipating that one of the first ways in which hostile sentiment will show itself may be in imposing an export duty on cotton, and a discriminating import duty on Northern manufactures,—or at all events such an abolition or reduction of all import duties on manufactured goods as would practically operate in favour of England and against the free states. If so, their uneasiness is probably exaggerated; for an export duty on cotton would not tell against them more than against Europe, and their manufactures—their cotton manufactures at least—are not very far inferior to English fabrics either in quality or cost.—In the second place, the industry of the slave states is, to a very great extent, carried on by the aid of Northern capital, and their commercial transactions with Europe are mainly conducted through the monetary centre of New York:—the result is that the Southern states are largely indebted to the Northern for funds advanced on mortgage or on bill security, or on no security at all. This enormous amount of 'indebtedness' there has been much loose talk of repudiating in case of a hostile severance;—and though such repudiation would be too infamous and suicidal a measure even to be contemplated except in the wildest moments of fury, there can be no doubt that an angry rupture, either with or without repudiation, would cause such a commercial and monetary derangement as may well alarm a community so sensitive as the mercantile one must always be. The Northern merchants and monied men, too, see another analogous danger in the distance— and it may be in the not remote distance. There is always the possibility—some consider it an immediate probability—of a general negro insurrection, and a consequent interruption of production, more or less complete, more or less prolonged;—and, as the wealth of the South consists exclusively in its slaves and in the articles they raise,— the security possessed by the North for the debts owing to them would be, in that case, enormously endangered, without anticipating any dishonesty on the side of the planters.

But the cause which is, we believe, more powerful and more general than either of the above considerations in rendering the disruption of the Union supremely unwelcome to the Northerners, is to be found in a nearly universal but not very well-defined conviction that the greatness of the American Republic is bound up with the continuance of the Federation. They have long been accustomed to boast to the world and to themselves of the mighty strength, the unexampled prosperity, the marvellous progress, and the surpassing grandeur of their vigorous young nation. They have flung themselves and their institutions insultingly and bombastically in the face of Europe, requiring every one to avow that no nation of the old world could match their power, or rival their constitution, or hold a candle to them as regarded the well-being, the capability for self-government, and the political wisdom of their people. They have dreamed of omnipotence and immortality; and they feel, with angry disappointment and bitter humiliation, that such a disruption as now seems almost consummated is a deplorable end to all these ambitious hopes and all this measureless self-glorification. We can well imagine that the prospect must be mortifying in the extreme both to their patriotism and their pride;—but here, as in the two former considerations, we think they exaggerate the truth. We incline to believe that, morally, socially, and politically, they will be gainers by the change. It is true there will be two Americas on the continent in place of one; but we believe they will be stronger, because more homogeneous for the compression. It is true their Republic will be less vast, but it will be their own fault if it be less great. Their national life will be purer, more consistent, less incessantly lowered and stained by disreputable compromises. They may be less feared by Europe, but assuredly they will be more respected. They will still be owners of a nearly illimitable territory, not a fourth of which is yet peopled, reaching from the Atlantic to the Pacific, and abounding in every species of mineral and agricultural wealth. They will still ere long be—or may be if they please—the most wealthy, powerful, and populous nation on the globe; and the recent catastrophe may have revealed the weak place in their institutions, and have taught them how to mend it.

The anxiety of the South for secession from a connection which has so long brought it safety, wealth, power, and reputation, appears to us explicable only on the supposition that excited passion has obscured for a time in the minds of its citizens all perception of their real interests, and all sober estimates of probable results. They will gain cheaper manufactures; they may gain possibly more unfettered political action—though in this respect it is not easy to see what they have ever had to complain of. But what else they can hope to gain, we are at a loss to discover, while the sacrifice and the danger are obvious at a glance. They will lose power—for, after all, power must always lie where there is a preponderance of money, population, harmony, and homogeneousness;—and all these the North has and the South has not. They cannot hope to seize on Cuba by their own strength, since it was an achievement scarcely within their reach when backed by all the might of the unbroken Federation. They can scarcely hope to be permitted in their severed condition to renew the African slave trade, in defiance of the general outcry of the civilised world, and the active, persistent, because morally-based and almost fanatic opposition both of England and of the Northern Federation. They can scarcely expect that Great Britain will acknowledge their separate sovereignty or enter into any close alliance with them, except on condition of their acceptance and renewal of those anti-slave-trade treaties to which they, as well as the North, have hitherto been parties. They may hope indeed to keep down their slaves, as Austria keeps down Venice, by incessant vigilance, by increased severity, by organising a large and permanent armed force of whites,—for they are nearly three-times as numerous as the blacks, and are armed and ready. But they can no longer hope, in the event of a servile war, to be backed by either the moral or physical strength of the free states;—and for at least partial and frequent insurrections they must assuredly lay their account. Nor can they fancy that by severance they can protect themselves more effectually than at present from the spread of abolitionist doctrines and stimulants among their coloured population; for no law and no practice can shut these out, if the existing Lynch law and Lynch practice have not succeeded in doing so. On the other hand, they cannot flatter themselves that so strong and so public a step as separation, with its alleged reasons and all the ferocious and alarmist language which has been held by Southerners upon the subject, can be unnoticed by the blacks, or can fail to excite in their minds the most disturbing sentiments, the most exaggerated hopes, and probably, on disappointment, the wildest schemes and the most desperate attempts. It will be impossible to conceal from them the fact that the North and the South have separated, and that the slave question in some form or other has been the ground of separation. That the negro insurrections will be put down we do not affect to doubt;—for the whites are in many districts preponderant in numbers and in most superior in strength; but human nature actually shudders to contemplate the horrors that may first ensue,—the barbarous vengeance of those who have been long so cruelly oppressed—the still more barbarous retaliation which the terrified and infuriated victors will be certain to inflict. Whichever way we view it, the prospect is literally appalling.

In conclusion,—and this is perhaps the most fearful feature of the whole,—what will be the moral and social condition of the Southern states, when liberated from even that faint control over their barbarising and deteriorating tendencies which their connection with Northern freedom and Northern humanity has hitherto held over them;—when the violent and tyrannical passions which the long habit of unchecked brutality towards negroes has generated among the Southern whites (of which we have seen of late such signal proofs and listened to such sickening descriptions) shall have been still further whetted by augmented danger, exasperated fear, and further deadly conflicts in which life and property have been every hour at stake?

We will not pursue this line of speculation: it is needless, and would be too painful. Our intended remarks on the possible reaction of the existing state of affairs and that which is immediately in prospect on England and on English interests, we must postpone till another week.

The Disruption of the Union, as it would affect England[1]

WE last week promised our readers that we would take the earliest opportunity of considering the bearing of the dissolution of the American Republic on the interests of our country, both political and commercial. We will suppose that matters will go on as they have begun; that the other slave states will join South Carolina, and that a Southern slave-holding Confederation will be formed as an independent nation, prepared to enter into relations with other states.

The first question that arises, is, 'Will England recognise the independence and sovereignty of the new state?' The natural and spontaneous answer is, of course, in the affirmative. Our principle is, and has long been, to recognise, and enter into amicable relations with, all *de facto* states and governments. The moment the severance is complete and admitted, we have no concern either with antecedent causes or proceedings. But here a difficulty arises:—What *is* our actual relation to the new Republic? Is the whole Union dissolved, or has there merely been a separation of a portion of it? Are our treaties and engagements with *both* sections of the Union dissolved, by the dissolution of the Union itself?—or do they still hold with the North, as with the original body with which they were made? Do the Southern states, in seceding, still remain bound by the engagements entered into by the confederation of which they formed a part at the date of those engagements? Or will they hold themselves liberated from all foreign contracts by the same act which has severed them from their domestic connection.

These are somewhat difficult questions for international jurists to decide. Probably as far as regards the Northern states, they will continue to call and consider themselves as still THE UNITED STATES, and as holding their former position and treaties,—none the less that they have lost a portion of their territory. The real, immediate, *practical*

[1] This article was first published in *The Economist* for January 19 1861, Volume XIX, pp. 57–61.

problem that lies across our path is this:—'Will the Southern confederated states consider themselves bound by those mutual engagements as to abstinence from and suppression of the slave trade,
entered into and still subsisting between the United States and Great
Britain?'—Probably not—since one of their chief motives for seceding
is to be able to renew the slave trade. If they hold themselves freed,
we do not know how we can bind them, or make themselves regard
themselves as bound. But supposing our diplomacy were able to
obtain this point, the only consequence would be that they would
give us formal notice of their intention to abrogate those treaties and
engagements after a certain date. We might remonstrate; we might
negotiate; but we do not know that we could refuse to accept such
notice. The practical shape, therefore, in which the question will
come before us is this:—'Shall we recognise their independent
sovereignty, without requiring as a condition that they shall renew
and observe the anti-slave-trade treaties which subsist with their
Northern brethren, '—or even accept more stringent ones?' Doubtless
we shall endeavour, and in consistency and as a matter of duty ought
to endeavour, to make this condition; since we cannot shut our eyes
to their notorious and avowed design of reviving the abominable
traffic, and to pretend to do so would be to surrender the most passionately and pertinaciously pursued object of our national policy. We
shall urge upon them that the trade is prohibited by international
agreement and by municipal law in every civilised nation in the world,
and that we can recognise and treat with no nation as civilised which
persists in upholding it. They will, of course, refuse to accept such
a condition, as it would defeat one of their principal purposes; and
will insist on *unconditional* recognition. What are we to do then? It
might seem that we are simply helpless in the matter. Three courses
are open to us—none of them entirely satisfactory.

We may recognise their independence at once, in accordance with
our usual practice; and, when we have done so, may proceed to make
the best terms that we can as to the anti-slave-trade treaties. But this
course, though the simplest and easiest, would be very painful to our
feelings of humanity,—for we cannot disguise from ourselves that it
would be nearly equivalent to unconditional surrender.—Or, secondly,
we may formally refuse to recognise them, and abstain from all
diplomatic intercourse with them, unless or until they shall consent
to abstain from and prohibit the slave-trade;—but it is scarcely likely

that this negative proceeding would bring them to terms, as it would not prevent commercial intercourse, and would at most inflict some trifling inconveniences which might be felt as much on one side as on the other. If we chose slightly to vary our course and to ignore the fact of their separation and continue to regard and treat them as still part of the United States (which would be rather a childish mode of action), all that we could gain would be the right of forwarding formal remonstrances, as against a violation of existing engagements, in case of any of their citizens being discovered to be engaged in the slave trade—remonstrances which they would of course disregard, and which the treaties give us no right of following up by any active measures.—Or, again, we may take up the matter in a high-handed way, and, while refusing our recognition of their independent national existence, treat any of their citizens whom we detect in carrying slaves as pirates, sailing under no known flag, and protected by the nationality of no known state. As to the advisability of so decided a proceeding, we will not as yet offer an opinion.—But there is a fourth and a preferable alternative,—viz., a *cordial* agreement between ourselves and the Northern Federation to prevent the renewal of the traffic at all hazards and by all means. Such cordial agreement *may* now be attainable, but even with it we must bring our forcible interference within the limits of international morality and usage, by procuring from all other civilised nations a consentaneous declaration rendering the slave-trade, like piracy, a crime against humanity and the world's law, and, as such, punishable by any witness and pursuer.

Apart from this perplexing question, we see no reason for anticipating that a severance of the Union, *once affected* peaceably and without catastrophe, will be in any way injurious to Great Britain. On the contrary, we are not sure that it may not indirectly be rather beneficial than otherwise. In the first place, we may expect that America will be somewhat less aggressive, less insolent, and less irritable than she has been. Instead of *one* vast state, acting on every foreign question *cum toto corpore regni*, we shall have *two*, with different objects and interests, and by no means always disposed to act in concert or in cordiality. Instead of *one*, showing an encroaching and somewhat bullying front to the rest of the world, we shall have *two*, showing something of the same front to each other. Each will be more occupied with its immediate neighbour, and therefore less inclined to pick quarrels with more distant nations. Then, too, for some time at least, that inordinate, though most natural sense of unrivalled prosperity and power, which swelled so flatulently and disturbingly in the breast of every citizen of the great transatlantic Republic, will receive a salutary check. Their demeanour is likely to become somewhat humbler and more rational, and it will, therefore, be easier to maintain amicable and *tranquil* relations with them than it has been. In place, too, of Europe being obliged to watch and thwart their annexing tendencies, the two federations will probably exercise this sort of moral police over each other. Neither of them will look with much complacence on the annexation of states or territories which will add power and dominion to the other, and so disturb their relative equilibrium. Unprincipled and reckless Southerners, like Mr. Buchanan, may talk of seizing on Mexico, Nicaragua, and Cuba; unprincipled and inflated Northerners, like Mr. Seward, may talk of seizing on Canada;—but there will be some hope that we may leave them to each others' mutual control, and smile at the villainous cupidities of both. With the Northern Federation, too, we may look to maintaining more cordial relations than we have often heretofore been able to do:—not only will the embarrassing question of slavery, which has caused so much righteous indignation on our side, and so much bitter resentment and irritation on theirs, be for ever removed from between us;—but the immediate and marked improvement which we may look for in the tone and working, if not in the form of the institutions, of the North, when Southern Democracy, complicated as it has been with slavery, shall have ceased to poison and degrade them, can scarcely fail to bring them more into harmony with English feeling, because to command more of English confidence and respect. The more they *civilise* (they must pardon us the word, for assuredly they are getting rid of a barbarising element), the more friendly and cordial shall we inevitably grow.

But what will be the consequences to Great Britain, in a commercial point of view, of the disruption of the Union, if that disruption should be accompanied by war, and should be followed (as in that case would be not improbable) by such a general insurrection of the slave population as would interrupt for a longer or shorter period the growth of cotton in the Southern states. This catastrophe would be so terrible, its accompaniments so shocking, and its results everywhere and in every way so deplorable, that we most earnestly pray it may be averted:—but the danger of it, if a civil conflict does break out, is so obvious and so imminent that it would be simple folly to shut our eyes to so possible a contingency. How, then, would it affect this country?

It is not easy to overestimate the extent or gravity of the consequences to Great Britain of a cessation, or even of any large or sudden diminution, of the supply of cotton from the United States. But even in facing a danger of such vast and admitted magnitude, it is important to be exact as to our facts and reasonings, and to avoid all exaggerated terrors. Let us recall to our readers' minds the precise bearing of the case. The cotton manufacture, from the first manipulation of the raw material to the last finish bestowed upon it, constitutes the employment and furnishes the sustenance of the largest portion of the population of Lancashire, North Cheshire, and Lanarkshire, of a considerable number in Derbyshire, Leicestershire, Nottinghamshire, and Yorkshire, and of scattered individuals in several other parts of England, Scotland, and Ireland. The actual number of hands directly employed was stated by M'Culloch in 1854 to be rather more than half a million: there can be no doubt that it now greatly exceeds this figure;—and if we take into account the subsidiary trades and occupations, coal mines, machine-works, &c., and add the unemployed families of the workmen, we may safely assume that nearer four than three millions are dependent for their daily bread on this branch of our industry.

The total aggregate value of British produce and manufactures exported in 1859 was £130,440,000;—of this sum cotton goods and yarn constituted £48,200,000, or more than one-third. Of this sum the United States took £4,635,000.

Let us now see to what extent we are dependent on the United States for our supply of the raw material for all this enormous production. Many countries contribute to our consumption, but none so largely as North America. In ordinary years she supplies us with about *three-fourths* of our consumption; and we take off more than *half* her production. During the last four years of which we have full accounts, 1857–1860, our consumption was, of all sorts, 9,062,700; of the United States' cotton, 7,140,000 bales, or rather more than 77 per cent.

But although we usually receive 75 per cent. of our supplies from North America, we must not confound this with being actually *dependent* upon that country for this amount. The practical question,—

if we wish to measure the precise degree of dearth to which we should be subjected in case of the Americans supply being interrupted,—is, what proportion of our supply *could* we, under the pressure of high prices and stimulated mercantile enterprise, obtain from other quarters? To answer this question we must look back for exceptional years. It is true that the West Indies send us little, and send us all they grow. Brazil and Egypt might send us somewhat increased supplies, especially by sending less to the Continent. India can send us a very much larger amount than she usually does, because vast quantities are always *grown*, and they are shipped here or consumed at home according to the ruling prices of the year. Now we find that in one year (1857) when the crop in the United States fell short, India sent us 680,000 bales, and other quarters 255,000;* while America supplied only 1,482,000 bales. It will, therefore, we think, be fair and moderate to assume that under such extraordinary pressure and inducements as would be presented by a cessation of the American supply, we should be able to obtain from India, Egypt, Brazil, and miscellaneous quarters, at least *one-third* more than we did in 1857,—or a total supply of about 1,200,000 bales. Now, in 1859 our actual *consumption* (after deducting re-exports) was 2,300,000 bales; and in 1860 (an extraordinary year) 2,630,000 bales. The *extreme* effect, therefore, of an *entire* cessation of the production of cotton in America, would appear to be this:—that all our mills would have to work about half time, as long as the dearth lasted in full intensity. What would be the effect on wages and on profits—whether the manufacturers would gain half-profits, or no profits at all, and whether the workpeople would still earn half wages, or less or more than half—would of course depend upon the question whether the scarcity of the manufactured article raised its price in the same or in a greater or a smaller ratio than the scarcity of the raw material raised *its* price;—a matter as to which conjecture would be simply idle. The result upon our exports it is equally impossible to predict. Very possibly the home market might take off a larger *proportion* of the total production than heretofore; if it did not and if we exported half the *quantity* we usually do, the probability is that the price of this quantity would be so largely enhanced as to leave the aggregate *value* of our cotton exports not far short of its present

---

* It is true that a considerable part of this was re-exported; but we have assumed as the most probable result, that, in such a peremptory demand as the case supposes, we should retain *all* we import, our necessities being more imperious than those of any other country.

amount. The influence on the shipping trade would of course be great:—freights will necessarily fall.

We have stated what in our judgment—and apart from the possible effects of panic—will be the *extreme* effect of the worst that can ensue (viz., an entire stoppage of cotton cultivation in America) on our chief branch of national industry. It is serious enough, no doubt, and may well cause grave uneasiness to all concerned—and who is not directly or indirectly implicated?—in the prosperity of the cotton manufacture. But we may anticipate that the effects we have described will in actual operation be mitigated by degrees in various ways. In the first place, a great stimulus will be given to the already awakened activity of our merchants in procuring supplies of the raw material from quarters that are only now just beginning to be thought of, but from whence, under sufficient pressure, considerable quantities might ere long be procured. Thus, we know by experiment that excellent cotton of the Sea Island description can be grown in Australia. The small shipments of the article that have from time to time been forwarded to this country from Port Natal resemble in quality the production of the United States much more closely than do those from either Egypt, India, or South America. The same observation will apply to the sample bales which have been received from the west coast of Africa. From both these quarters there is reason to believe that, under the stimulus of high prices, considerable quantities might be procured as soon as a regular traffic could be set on foot and means of transport be procured. It has lately become known that cotton is largely grown in the interior, and is even manufactured there; and adequate inducements would no doubt persuade the natives not only to grow more for our use, but to sell instead of manufacturing much of what is already grown. In a few years, too, considerable quantities might again be procured from Asia Minor, as was the case formerly. 'Smyrna cotton' was once well known in the trade, and some is still imported.

In the second place, a considerable economy in the consumption of the raw material would be at once effected, under the influence of a high rate of prices, by a general tendency among manufacturers towards the production of the finer fabrics. Most mills have a range of potential production (without any alteration in their machinery) of at least 30 per cent.—often more. Manufacturers who now use weekly 100 bales could easily, by turning to finer fabrics, reduce their consumption to 70 or 75 bales. Those articles into which the raw material enters most largely would of course be those which relatively would be most enhanced in price, and for which, therefore, the demand would be most curtailed. 'Domestics,' as they are called, or strong cotton cloths and shirtings, and coarse yarns would be discouraged; and, as their price approached more nearly to that of linen and woollen fabrics, would be to a considerable extent superseded by them. This would cause an increase in the production of these latter articles, and a consequent increased demand for work-people; and by this process a considerable number of the hands thrown out of work in the cotton trade would be absorbed, and the suffering to the operatives, though not the loss to the masters, would be greatly mitigated.

These palliatives would no doubt be a work of time; but they would *begin* to operate immediately; and, in conclusion, it must be remembered that, though we have preferred to consider the case in reference to a *total* cessation of cotton production in North America, yet such a total cessation, even in the event of negro insurrection and a servile war, is scarcely to be apprehended. In Texas, already a considerable amount of cotton is grown by free labour, and on many isolated plantations production would most probably continue—at all events for a time.

As to the consequences of the severance of the Union on our trade with North America, in case the severance is peaceably effected and no extensive slave insurrection ensue,—we do not apprehend that any material change will be felt, so soon as the monetary derangement shall have subsided, and the existing organisation of drafts and payments shall have been modified as far as is necessary to meet the altered circumstances. We shall of course continue to receive from the planting states all the cotton that we wish to buy and that they have to sell. Our exports will not probably be much, if at all, affected. It is probable that the Northern states will raise their tariff as much as the Southern states lower theirs:—we shall send more manufactures to New Orleans, and less to New York than we do now. What would be the consequences to our aggregate commerce with America of a general negro insurrection, or of negro emancipation, it is idle to speculate, and impossible to estimate.

Dissolution of the Union as regards America[1]

ALTHOUGH the latest accounts from America still speak of compromise, and although numerous suggestions continue to be made in Congress as to the terms on which such compromise might be effected, yet we confess we have little expectation that they will prove successful. The march of events has been too rapid for the effective intervention of the wiser and soberer politicians; and the insolence of the South is beginning to arouse a corresponding temper in the North. It is true that we have indications that the prompt and passionate steps taken in Carolina to consummate the act of secession have been forced on by the least wealthy, the least really influential, and the most democratic classes of the population; and that the great proprietors and the more respectable public men deprecate those acts which have made retrogression all but impossible. It is true that the danger attendant on the process of severance begins to be seen much more clearly than at first, and that, amidst all their bluster, the South Carolinians are growing very anxious that their secession should be a peaceful and amicable one, as was shown by the speech of Mr. Benjamin in the Senate. But the phrenzy and enthusiasm of the mob have been so violently excited and have now become so general, that it is too late for the warnings of self-interest or of alarm to avert the crisis; shots have already been fired against a Federal vessel in Charleston harbour; and at least three other states have followed the example of Carolina. It is true, certainly, that the proposals for compromise and reconciliation so profusely made even by Northern and Free-soil politicians show an extraordinary eagerness to prevent a dissolution of the Union if it be possible; but the very nature of these proposals indicate also a general conviction that the South can only be conciliated and recovered by concessions which would be equivalent to renouncing

[1] This article was first published in *The Economist* for January 26 1861, Volume XIX, pp. 86–8.

the entire fruits of the victory of which Mr. Lincoln's election was the proof and seal, and which would be simply unprincipled, inconsistent, and dishonouring to the whole Republican party;—and it is pretty certain, too, that these terms of compromise, though discussed by the leaders of that party, are not likely to be ratified by their followers, and could scarcely, with any decency or self-respect, be accepted by the new President. We believe, therefore, that they will come to nothing, and that the Union will be, or is already, dissolved. Whether the disruption will be peaceably effected, is beginning, however, to be more doubtful.

Some people seem to fancy that the Southern states will secede, but only with the intention of making better terms with the Northern ones, and of re-entering the Federation on their own conditions. We see no ground for entertaining such a notion. For, in the first place, it is evident enough that the North will yield more to prevent a severance of their cherished Union than to patch it up again when once dissolved. It is evident that at this moment the victorious Republicans are willing to concede everything short of actual surrender, base compliance, and cowardly departure from the ground of principle and justice which alone enabled them to conquer in the recent presidential election. It is clear that any *re*-admission of the seceding states, except on the inconceivable ground of *their* acknowledgment of error and defeat would be equivalent to an acceptance by the North henceforth of a position of subordination and humiliating helplessness; which proud, powerful, and wealthy states, *who feel themselves to be in the right*, could never submit to. It is clear, finally, that the South can never again obtain such favourable terms from the incoming President and the next Congress as from the authorities now in power. The secession of the slave states, therefore, if it shall take place, will, we conceive, be final and irrevocable.

The most conclusive consideration to our minds, however, is this. The dissolution is consummated already, and by 'the inexorable logic of facts,' as the French Emperor says,—not by the hand of man or the decisions of politicians and popular assemblies. The discrepancy of character, interests, objects and feelings between the free and the slave states has year by year been growing wider, and has now become complete and incurable. When the Federation was formed there were slaves in every state except Maine and Massachusetts, but the total number scarcely exceeded 500,000, and every state looked upon slavery as an institution to be regretted, and as one that ere long was certain to die out, and therefore needed not to be violently extinguished. At that time there were fewer slaves in the United States than in the West Indian Islands, and the extinction of the slave trade after a specified date was provided for. Now, all the North-Western and Atlantic states, with the single exception of Maryland, have ceased to hold slaves, yet the slaves in the entire Union have increased from *half a million* to *four millions*. But the change of feeling is even greater than the change of social condition. While the detestation of slavery has been growing and spreading in the North under the threefold consideration of its guilt in a moral point of view, of its mischief in an economic point of view, and of its confounding and dishonouring influence in a political and social point of view,—the South has clung to it as the source of their wealth, the necessity of their existence, the basis of their agricultural and domestic life; till at last they have reached a point at which (at least in words) they boast of it as a distinction and proclaim it to be a beneficence, a blessing, and a virtue. Thus what one-half of the Union have grown to regard as an evil and a stain, the other half, in the same period, have taught themselves to regard as a merit and a good. While the North could fancy that the damaging and disreputable 'institution' was temporary only, and in process of mitigation and extinction, it might put up with the inconvenience and hope for some solution; but with a slave population of four millions and an entire system of cultivation and society based upon the 'institution,'—and moreover with its entire policy coloured and guided by the 'institution'—it has to consider how far co-existence is compatible with a dark and fearful permanence like *that*. How a people who think slavery bad and wrong, can continue to form part of the same nation with a people who think slavery right and beneficial, when slavery has reached such vast dimensions and such a hopeless and unmanageable magnitude,—we confess ourselves unable to imagine. The moral dissolution of the Union is complete: the political dissolution is only an expression of this foregone fact, and a question simply of time and mode. We do not see how the gulf *can* be bridged over, how the connection can be kept together, how any union worth the name or worth the trouble can be patched up even for a time, unless the South will consent to a plan of gradual abolition, or the North make up its mind to the continuance and illimitable spread of slavery—both of which appear to be morally and equally impossible. Even if the present crisis could, by any contrivance, be got over, we should not expect any advantage from the result:—the same inevitable issue would still hang like a black cloud over the Federation—the same insoluble question, the same radical and incurable discrepancy, would still lie between the partners to poison and sever the unnatural bond.

We, therefore, agree with Mr. Benjamin that the efforts of all patriotic politicians in America should be exerted not to prevent the severance of the Union, but to effect it in as peaceable a mode and in as amicable a spirit as possible. If done by deliberate and tranquil arrangements, the frightful folly of civil bloodshed will be averted, and the danger of wide-spread negro insurrections greatly diminished. If war once broke out, the slaves in many parts would probably rise, with greater or less unanimity and a greater or less degree of organisation; and the planters are well aware, notwithstanding their boastful words, that they could not possibly make head at once against the forces of the free states and the outbreak of their own slaves. On the other hand, both the Northern states and the general government (even when it passes into firmer hands than Mr. Buchanan's) will probably shrink from shedding the blood even of insurgent brethren (unless absolutely forced to do so), even if it should be ruled that constitutional right is on their side;—it is doubtful, too, whether the navy would act against South Carolina; and it is nearly certain that the frontier states would refuse a passage to the Federal troops. We assume, therefore, that the disruption will take place by arrangement, and without any serious fighting. Our object is to inquire how such peaceably arranged disruption will affect the two new republics—the slaveholding and the free?

We need not trouble ourselves much with the prospects of the Northern states. The same energy and enterprise which have made them so great in spite of the difficulties of a slave connection will carry them on still faster and further when liberated from this hampering incubus. We know how commerce contrives to hold on its wonted course in defiance even of actual war, how soon it can modify its action to meet altered circumstances, how soon it can find out fresh channels or new contrivances. It will very speedily adapt itself to the fact of two federations instead of one. The North will soon renew in one form or another its old transactions with the South. It will still supply the Southerners with ships; it will still advance them money; it will still discount their bills,—more cautiously no doubt, at perhaps higher interest, with perhaps stricter security. It will still send them provisions, and receive their cotton in return. It will continue to be their bankers and their carriers, for the slaveholders have few ships and little cash. So long as there is mercantile honesty and productive industry, there will be mercantile transactions and brisk interchange.

But what will be the condition and future of the Southern states? Their trade, as we have said, will, after brief confusion perhaps, go on much as before. British vessels and New York vessels will still carry their corn and tobacco; British mills or Massachusetts mills will clothe their negroes. But what will henceforth be the relation of the planting interest to the 'mean whites'? and what that of the slave-holders to their slaves? The former question we can only answer conjecturally. We have not yet received the census of 1860, so must take our figures from that of 1850. The white population of the slave states was then in round numbers 6,300,000, of which slaveowners and their families could scarcely amount to more than 1,250,000—or one-fifth. (The actual *possessors* of slaves were, and we believe still are, only 350,000.) The slaveowners, the men of wealth and realised property, are, therefore, only a small minority of the free population, and the institutions of the states being all democratic, the political power, potentially or actually, is in consequence in the hands of the 'poor whites'—perhaps the most degraded, ignorant, brutal, drunken, and violent class that ever swarmed in a civilised country. The ultimate issue of such a state of affairs we see at once must be most terrible and sad. But we cannot pursue this part of the subject here. We must pass on to consider the result of the dissolution of the Union on the planters and their slaves.

The first thing that seems inevitable is, that 'the underground railway,' as it is called, will work faster than ever. The fugitive slave law will fall with the Union, and the Northern republic, we apprehend, will repeal or nullify it at once. This, which has long been the sorest point between the two sections of the Union, cannot survive their severance. The South, which complained so furiously of the imperfect execution of this obnoxious law, must now lay its account to have no such law at all. But this is by no means all—nor the worst. Not only will slaves find it far easier to escape than formerly, and be far safer from recapture; but it is next to impossible that the exasperated fears of the masters and the excited hopes of the slaves, consequent upon the severance, should not lead to more frequent insurrections on the one side and to more merciless severities on the other. Probably large bodies of the 'mean whites' will be organised into irregular troops, half soldiers, half police, in order to control and suppress the negro population; and the condition of restless fear, barbarism, and intestine hostility, already bad enough, will grow yearly worse, more shocking and more intolerable. The following table, taken from the census of 1850, will show the relative proportions of white men and slaves in the several states which will probably compose the Southern federation. We leave out the *free* coloured population altogether. We may observe that since 1850 about 700,000 have been added to the total of the slave population. What the increase of the whites has been we have no means of knowing accurately:—

	Whites.	Slaves.
Virginia	894,800	472,500
North Carolina	553,000	288,500
SOUTH CAROLINA . .	274,500	385,000
Georgia	521,500	381,700
Florida	47,200	39,300
Alabama	426,500	342,900
MISSISSIPPI	295,700	309,900
Louisiana	255,500	244,800
Texas	154,000	58,100
Arkansas	162,200	47,100
Tennessee	756,700	239,500
Kentucky	761,400	211,000
Missouri	592,000	87,500

It will be seen that in five of these thirteen states there are only about *two* white men to one slave; in three of the states, the numbers are about equal; while in two (South Carolina and Mississippi) the slaves outnumber the ruling race. At the present moment we may calculate there are about 4,000,000 of slaves to 8,000,000 of whites. That is to say, *two-thirds* of the population live amidst a subjugated and hostile proportion of *one-third*, and keep those down by force for the benefit of 350,000 families only;—for no one pretends that any one except slaveowners profits by slavery.

These relative numbers disclose a state of matters evil and perilous enough. But they do not adequately represent either the evil or the peril. In many portions of these states, on the majority of cotton plantations, in a great number of isolated districts, the slaves outnumber the whites enormously—sometimes twenty, thirty, fifty even, to one,—and are kept down by terror and daily violence alone. We state the case mildly. If any one doubt it, let him read Mr. Olmsted's book. Now, how can such a state of society continue, and how must it terminate? There is no progress towards improvement, either in feeling or condition: on the contrary, the hostility and fear between the two races are daily growing worse. Permanence in such a state seems impossible. Issue out of it seems equally so. Extension will not help it. A renewal of the African slave trade will manifestly make it worse. Perpetual and cruel suppression of perpetually recurring insurrections will do no good;—for who believes that the slaves, yearly becoming more disproportionately numerous, and treated as they are and must be on plantations, will ever conclusively acquiesce in tame and hopeless submission? We confess we see no daylight through this appalling picture. When the dissolution of the Union is consummated without provision being made for ultimate emancipation and abandonment of slavery, we greatly fear that security for life and property must be henceforth at an end for the South. Repeated victories—repeated ever so often, and always felt to be certainties, will avail nothing. And who will advance money on the security of estates, valuable only by slave labour, and cultivated by slaves always on the verge of insurrection?

Progress of American Disunion[1]

THE great drama of disruption is surely and not very slowly evolving in the United States. There are still some features in the case which foreigners cannot well understand, and which seem not perfectly clear even to Americans themselves. But two or three points are becoming plainer day by day. It now appears that secession has not been an act hastily forced upon the seceding states by Mr. Lincoln's election, or by any *bonâ fide* fears brought home to them by that event of fresh aggressions upon their 'peculiar institution'; but that it is an occurrence which has not only been long foreseen and prepared for, but resolutely determined upon. It is obvious that the South were ready to remain in the Union, so long as they could unreservedly dictate its policy and nominate to all places of power and trust, but not one hour longer;— that they had for some time perceived symptoms that this supremacy was about to be wrested from them:—and that Mr. Lincoln's election merely indicated to them that it was gone, and that the expected moment for action had, therefore, arrived. From that date there has been neither hesitation nor delay; they never attempted to make terms; they never proposed any real scheme of arrangement; they never showed the slightest desire or intention of remaining in the Union; but, on the contrary, pushed forward their proceedings with a reckless and indecent haste, as if they dreaded nothing so much as a compromise which would stop the secession movement at the outset. While the border states have been concocting schemes of adjustment, while the Northern politicians have been bringing forward project after project for what is called 'conciliation,' but which in fact is nothing less than ignominious capitulation, the seceding states have not given one moment's attention to any of these countless propositions, but have rushed at once upon action, in a manner which betrays three things as clearly as the sun at noonday. *First,* a violence and intemperate haste which augur ill for the future wisdom and decency of their

---

[1] This article was first published in *The Economist* for March 2 1861, Volume XIX, pp. 226–7.

government; *secondly*, a resolution that *nothing* now shall baulk them of their purpose; and *thirdly*, the absolute certainty that their plans have been laid for months if not for years, and at least the *first* steps consequent upon separation carefully determined on beforehand. They at once seized, where they could, upon the Federal fortresses and stores; they fired on Federal ships; they obstructed the entrances to their harbours; they summoned conventions to meet without an hour's delay; and—while Virginia is still offering her mediation, while senators at Washington are still discussing terms of accommodation, while the obnoxious Lincoln is still uninstalled and powerless—they have already chosen the style and title of their new republic, and nominated Mr. Jefferson Davis President of the SOUTHERN CONFEDERATION. Nay, more, it seems highly *probable*—for without further proof we are unwilling to speak with anything like positive conviction—that at least three members of Mr. Buchanan's Cabinet, in fact all his chief ministers have been for some time traitorously and fraudulently using their positions to facilitate separation, and to make the North comparatively powerless to resist it when it came. There is reason to believe—indeed, there is something amounting to official proof—that the late Secretary at War, the Secretary of the Treasury, and the Secretary of the Interior have combined with each other to manipulate the army appointments and the public chest, with the purpose of impoverishing and disarming the North, and enriching and organising the South in the immediate view of the secession crisis. It is not easy either, as far as appearances at present go, to acquit Mr. Buchanan himself of a guilty knowledge and tolerance of their proceedings—at all events to some extent.

With such promptitude, too, have the secessionists acted, and so resolute do they seem not to lose a single hour, that they have framed their new constitution without a single attempt to improve it in any one of the particulars in which experience had shown it to be defective. They have, in fact, merely re-enacted the old Federal institutions and the old Federal laws. The truth is—and we do not wonder at it— their imaginations have been so fired and their cupidity so excited at the prospect of a vast slave empire, with uncontrolled dominion and almost illimitable territory, stretching over all the magnificent lands which lie between Virginia on the North and the isthmus of Panama on the South, that they are actually intoxicated by the dream; and are resolved, cost what it may, to shake off the incubus of the Northern states, whose citizens they both despise and detest as pedantic and shopkeeping quill-drivers, and envy as being at once more numerous, more wealthy, and more clever than themselves. There is perhaps scarcely a Southerner now who does not fancy himself a member of the ruling class in a republic exercising absolute sway over Central America, Cuba, the Antilles, and the whole of the Gulf of Mexico, as well as over the largest portion of the old Union itself. The Southerners are a very excitable race, and usually very ignorant of their relative power and position in the world: they see no difficulties, and make light of all dangers; they seem actually to have no scruples, and their morality on all points seems to have been strangely warped by slavery.

There are already indications, however, that in their reckless violence and haste they have somewhat overshot their mark. The border states, whose cause is not identical, whose real interests in the strife are far from clear or simple, and who would have protected the seceders against Northern coercion, are by no means all inclined to join or encourage them, now that their policy is so obviously one of aggression. Though the Southerners have introduced into the laws of their new Confederation an absolute prohibition of the African slave trade—with a view to *bribe* the border states, and a contingent prohibition of the internal slave trade from non-seceding states—with a view to *alarm* them,—neither Kentucky, Tennessee, Virginia, nor Maryland, has given in its adhesion to the separation:—on the contrary, they are all pronouncing more and more distinctly in favour of the maintenance of the old Union. We do not for a moment fancy that any line of action adopted by these states can now prevent the consummation of the severance, but their adherence to the North will materially affect both the terms of separation, and the relative prospects of the two republics.

Meanwhile the intentions of the Northern politicians seem to be undetermined, or far from unanimous. They are by no means either as clear or as resolute as their antagonists. They still talk hopefully of the maintenance of the Union. They still go on discussing proposals of compromise and adjustment. They say, with perfect truth, as Mr. Lincoln has well put it in one of his recent speeches, that the crisis is 'artificial'; that there are no new grounds for disunion, and that, if time be given for angry passions and unreasoning panic to die away, the danger will blow over, and the South will return to its allegiance. It is difficult to know how far they believe this in their hearts. Some are for coercion, some are for conciliation, some are for a policy of 'masterly inaction.' The President-elect seems to be of the number of these last. To our thinking, though of course we speak with diffidence, they are all wrong. Coercion we hold to be nearly if not wholly impossible; but whether possible or not, we are sure it would be very foolish. What would they gain by *compelling* eight millions of men to remain members of the Union against their will? How could such compulsion be permanently continued in a republican nation? How could the government at Washington be carried on in the face of such a virulent and hostile minority of representatives as the coerced states would send up? No—depend upon it, it is not for Americans to take a leaf out of the book of Austria. Mr. Lincoln says that retaking by force the Federal fortresses and property from the states which have so lawlessly seized them, would not be coercion or invasion. This may be very true; but where would be the use of retaking them? The moment the separation is effected and acknowledged, the fortresses would necessarily be surrendered, or sold to the Southern Confederation, or to the separate states composing it. *Half* the property in them belongs to the South, if a peaceable and equitable division of territory and property is effected; and it would be simply idle to make South Carolina purchase Fort Sumter, and then return her half the purchase money, and then perform a counterbalancing operation on one of the Northern forts, and pay half the price of that to the Southern Confederation. If the secession be consummated by agreement, of course all the strong places in the seceding states will be given up to them; if consummated by connivance and reluctant acquiescence (which it will be, if no coercion is to be used), then why be at all the pains of retaking what no one would dream of *permanently* holding as a menace and an irritating sore?

Again, why endeavour to retain the reluctant Southerners by compromise which *must* be humiliating and an admission of defeat, and yet could only for a short period postpone the evil day? Does any one in his heart believe that the fiery and ambitious citizens of the slave states will submit to remain in the Union—the power of which, by the inevitable operation of the existing constitution, must yearly be handed over more and more completely to the increasing population of the North—unless they can do so on their own terms? or that these terms will or can be anything short of virtual and secure supremacy? If they remain in the Union, they see clearly enough, they must do so *as a minority*—and a minority which every year becomes more decided;—and how can a minority hope permanently to govern under democratic institutions? Let them go then, since they can only be retained at the price of servility and dishonour.

The policy of 'inaction' might have much to say for it, if the South were really in a panic or merely in a passion, and were likely to come round if time were allowed it. But, as we have said, there is ample evidence that this is not the case. The seceding states have long since determined to be free. Moreover, the position of affairs is growing too serious in the commercial world to permit the continuance of uncertainty. Politicians might live for a while in a provisional condition and wait for the natural development of the crisis; but merchants cannot do so. Already great difficulty and uneasiness is felt, and this must increase day by day till a final settlement is effected. Property is decreasing rapidly in saleable value; cautious men are curtailing their transactions; loans can scarcely be negotiated, because no one knows what positive security can be offered; and, what is still more embarrassing, debtors in the South are withholding payment from their Northern creditors (even where they are not infamous enough openly to speak of repudiation); and merchants at New York, deprived of their remittances on account of the planters of Alabama, Carolina, and Mississippi, are beginning to feel anxious about their power of meeting their own engagements. A continuance of this uncertainty for three months longer, would in all likelihood bring about a more widespread commercial ruin than has been seen for many years. On any account, therefore, an immediate termination of the crisis has become imperatively needed;—and we confess we cannot see any termination that would be at once desirable, possible, and permanent, except *a separation by acquiescence and negotiation.* We are sure that a peaceable severance on such terms as would induce the border states to adhere to the Northern confederation (which sooner or later they must ultimately join), every friend of humanity ought to hail with joy.

The True Issue between
North and South[1]

W E are waiting with deep anxiety the next news from America, which will probably decide the question as to peaceable severance or hopeless civil war. It is idle to speculate now, and the best-informed people both here and there seem in complete uncertainty as to the result. For ourselves—menacing as was the aspect of affairs at the date of the last accounts—we adhere to the opinion we formed at the outset, *viz.*, that there will be no re-union and no fighting; and we hold this view because we believe that no really practical ground for compromise exists, and that the Americans are too sensible to shed each others' blood without a clear reason and an adequate object. The only ostensible and sufficient justification for an attempt at coercion would lie in the knowledge that re-union was desired by a large and respectable minority in the South, who were intimidated, silenced, and overborne by mere numbers. But of any such fact there seems no indication.

Meanwhile, do not let us deceive ourselves by permitting the controversy between the old Federation and the seceding states to be placed, even in our own minds, upon false issues. As the matter at present stands, both parties seem wedded to a grievous economic error and to a sad social injustice and moral wrong. The North is bent upon a protective commercial policy which will injure themselves and wrong the Western states; and the South is bent upon perpetuating and extending slavery, which will be fatal to their future prosperity, and is a shameful iniquity against the African race. We do not mean for one moment to put the two follies and the two wrongs *on a level* as regards either their social gravity or their moral heinousness,— especially as the one must soon be abandoned, while the other may be persisted in for generations. But, in the lines they have respectively taken, each of the two confederations, while conciliating one of our predilections, have done grievous violence to another. The Northern

[1] This article was first published in *The Economist* for April 13 1861, Volume XIX, pp. 395–6.

states are free-soilers and protectionists: the Southern states are slave-holders and free-traders. We can, therefore, contemplate their relative position with some degree of calm impartiality. Do not, then, let us mistake their several aims and principles, and give our sympathies under mistaken pleas. If, indeed, the Northern Federation were pre-pared heartily, resolutely, and unanimously—as no doubt a few of their citizens are—to take their stand on the solemn principle of prohibiting and preventing the extension of slavery to any states and and territories where it does not now exist, then such a ground might be well worth an obstinate struggle and even a long civil war, if there were any reasonable prospect of ultimate success; because if slavery were strictly and for ever confined within its present limits there is every hope that it must ultimately die out. An object like this, if attainable, would be worth fighting for, and might perhaps justify even civil war:—but what ground is there for assuming that any such distinct and noble aim is in the heart of Mr. Lincoln's Government when they speak of coercion? Mr. Lincoln, indeed, contends for the right of congress to make laws for all unannexed, unsettled, and un-admitted territories:—he has never, so far as we are aware, taken up the high ground of saying that slavery *shall not* be introduced into any new districts. This is the ground of the abolitionists; but it is not the ground of the Republican party as a whole; still less is it the ground of the mass of the people in the Northern and Western states. On the contrary, nearly every compromise yet proposed—and *all the proposed compromises have come from the North or from the border states*—has stipulated that slavery shall only be prohibited *North of a certain line* (North of which slavery cannot profitably exist, and consequently need not be prohibited);—but that South of this line, its introduction shall be left to the decision of the inhabitants themselves. Some of the suggested compromises, indeed, have contained a proviso that no new territory shall be acquired without the consent of the majority of all the states, both slave and free. But we can scarcely regard this as likely to be at all effective in *really* limiting the area of slavery, when we consider, first, the enormous space *already acquired* and peculiarly adapted for Negro cultivation; and, secondly, that even the North and North-Western states have never yet, as a whole, shown the slightest reluctance to the extension of the dominion of the republic in any direction or by any means. Do not, therefore, let us give our sym-pathies to those Northerners who would appear to be preparing to maintain the old Union by force, on the erroneous impression that they are about to fight on the grand, intelligible, and worthy ground of confining slavery for ever within its present area. If it were so, and there were a fair prospect of success, we could almost wish them God speed, though a terrible civil war was the only means to their cherished end. But, alas! it is not so. Abhorrence of negro-slavery, as we feel it here, and determination at all hazards to clear their nation's fame and future from so foul a blot, are sentiments confined to but a small minority of the citizens of the Northern Federation. What *all* these are anxious for—and what some are meditating war in order to ensure— is that the vast and rich territories which are still unsettled or which may in future be acquired (and which chiefly lie to the South of lat. 36.30), shall not fall into the hands of slave-holders and planters, and thus give them a preponderance in the senate and control over the policy of the Union. And this object we believe can scarcely be secured by war, and would not be worth a war even if it could.

The real issue between the North and South, then, is not the abolition or the extension of slavery, but the decision whether a free-labour or a slave-holding republic shall henceforth hold the reins and direct the policy of the great American Federation, or the chief part of it— a vast question, no doubt, and a momentous one, but not rising to the moral magnitude of the other. And if it shall really appear that the future of the Negro race is not at issue in this controversy, then there is much in the position and conduct of the seceding states to add strength to our hope and desire that no attempts at forcible re-union shall be hazarded, but that they shall be allowed to separate and to reorganise themselves without interference. They have evidently some sagacious heads as well as some resolute wills among them; and they seem scarcely more intemperate and much more wise than their Northern brethren. In the framing of their new constitution they have laid their finger on nearly every blot of the old one, and seem resolved to profit by experience. They give their President a longer term of office and forbid his re-election. They provide, in a great measure, for the irremoveability and independence of the judges, which had become so fatally impaired. They restore dignity and security to the civil service, by declaring virtually that all except the highest *employés* shall be considered to hold office for life, or during good behaviour. And they empower the ministers (who have hitherto been excluded from Congress) to sit and speak there—but without votes. By these enactments they go far to rectify what were felt by all observers to have become most dangerous and spreading evils under the old system. They have adopted a moderate tariff, which will at least discourage smuggling, and bring some considerable and reliable revenue into their coffers; and, as they have not yet—any more than the Northerners—the nerve or the virtue to establish an onerous scheme of direct taxation, and yet *must have* funds, we are by no means sure that the plan of an export duty upon cotton is not open to as few objections as any other. Certainly, it is not deserving of the unmeasured condemnation which has been passed upon it. If the states were the *only* cotton-producing country in the world, then such a tax would obviously be the right one to impose: it would be analogous to the case of saltpetre in India, which the sagacity of Mr. Wilson at once fixed upon as fit to bear an export duty. America is not the only cotton-producing country, but it is the principal one; and so long as the duty is moderate and the demand brisk, it is not probable that it will perceptibly check exports, though it may prospectively encourage rivals. Of course, as the American cotton thus burdened will have to meet Indian and Egyptian cotton in the markets of the world, the duty will to a great extent come out of the pockets of the American producer;—but then, if ten millions of dollars are wanted and *must be got*, how could they be extracted out of those buttoned pockets at once less noxiously and less vexatiously? It is as if the planter surrendered (say) every tenth bale to the state, to be sold and exported for the public benefit. We by no means say that it is a good financial measure, but if a property tax will not be endured, we do not know that any better could be substituted.

The American News and its Lessons[1]

THERE is a painful sense of imbecility produced by all public criticism on a tide of events apparently so irresistible, and yet so uncertain in direction, as those which are rushing forwards in the United States. Even the American journals feel this: they comment on the stream of events without any hope of influencing it, and with little hope even of divining its immediate tendency. The truth is, that the time for criticism is past; and until some final act of the competing administrations either precipitates the country into civil war, or opens a definite prospect of peace, there is little to do but to bear the political suspense with as much patience as possible. The next mail may, it is feared, bring news of the disaster which we have so long feared yet hoped to see averted—a collision between the seceding and non-seceding states. It was feared at the date of the last advices that such a collision had already taken place at Pensacola, as no telegraphic despatches had been received for several days from Fort Pickens; and three United States frigates were on the point of sailing under sealed orders, whether to succour Fort Pickens or to put down the Spanish filibustering attack on St. Domingo was not known. Another mail must probably clear up the question of peace or war,—and it is only too probable in the worst way.

If we could look forward to even a civil war as decisive,—as likely to end soon, and without ulterior evil consequences, in the triumph either of union or of disunion, we should not shrink even from that terrible remedy for a terrible malady. Unfortunately, we fear it would only result in the further disintegration of what remains of the Union, and in a new and grievous exacerbation of the hatreds and rivalries between the various fragments. At present, the six Northern slave states that have not seceded,—Arkansas, Tennessee, North Carolina, Kentucky, and Virginia,—are waiting with suspended judgments to watch the steps of the rival administrations. On the course of these

[1] This article was first published in *The Economist* for April 20 1861, Volume XIX, pp. 424–5.

border slave states almost everything depends. Their free population is double that of the seceded states, and far more adapted to military purposes. Should they ultimately join the South, the Confederated states would have a *free* population more than one-third of that of the Northern Union, and a government probably much more compact and formidable. But the chances are that the border states will never join the South, though a civil war would in all probability ensure their recoil from the North. Their interests are in many respects different from those both of North and South. To a very large extent they are of course identified with slavery;—but they are not for the most part cotton states, they have very large districts in which free labour would be more effective than slave; and they are warmly interested in preventing any renewal of the slave trade. The result, therefore, of any fresh impulse of disgust towards the North would probably be to cement them into a new Union of their own. And a still worse result of civil war would of course be the growth of that intense jealousy and mutual hatred of which American states seem but too susceptible.

While awaiting the result, it is impossible for Englishmen not to observe that the whole mischief has been, not *caused* but painfully exasperated by the unfortunate mixture of flexibility and inflexibility in the United States Constitution. It is the peculiarity of that constitution to have a prime minister elected periodically by the mass of the people, and yet, during his reign, almost independent of the confidence of the people's representatives. The first effect is that the choice of a president being a much less remediable transaction than the choice of an English prime minister, it has more tendency to induce acts of popular resistance such as we have recently seen. It may be doubted whether the Southern states would have acted so violently, and it is nearly certain that they would not have acted with so much unanimity, if a congressional defeat could at any moment have relieved them, as a parliamentary defeat does in England, of their unwelcome master. They would have hoped, whether justly or not, that the first audacious step would so modify the views of the doubtful supporters of government, as to turn victory into defeat,—and they would have strained all their energies to secure such a defeat rather than to organise a rebellion. No doubt the issue might have been some rapid succession of governments such as we see in our democratic colonies in Australia, which is doubtless a grave evil. Still it is not an evil so great as that which results from rendering the executive independent of the people's representatives. Rapid changes of administration disgust the people, and in the end cure themselves. In the meantime a great change of policy comes gradually though certainly on, and the force of the change is broken to the minority by little successes which modify its influence. But in the American Union the changes of presidents carry a certain exasperating hopelessness with them. The presidents are almost free from congressional influence, and they are in for four years at least. *This* evil at least will be aggravated by the extension of time adopted in the Southern Confederation, though others may be diminished.

Another bad effect of the American form of constitution is that the President, when once he has announced his policy, is far more personally responsible for it, far less able to modify it with credit from time to time as occasion seems to require, than the English prime minister. He does not in the same manner *share* his responsibility with his parliament,—nor his parliament with him. He sometimes tries, indeed, as Mr. Buchanan did, to cast the whole responsibility on Congress; but the only effect is that Congress, being a quite unfit body for executive resolves, does nothing, and finally leaves everything to the President. But what is really wanted for the effective administration of a free country in times of excitement, is that the government should be in such connection with the people as to direct the national policy in harmony with their gradually forming convictions. For this purpose, the ruler must himself belong to the representative body—must fit himself for the guidance of the country by guiding the opinion of that body—must, in short, try his power both of influencing and yielding on the ruling assembly first, as his best aid in trying it on the nation. There is no provision for this in the American Constitution. The Government is in almost as little direct contact with the people as the Russian Government, and yet it has to guide itself by the wishes of the people, which the Russian Government does not pretend to do. If anything has been made manifest by the recent American discussions in Congress, it is this, that it was a fatal mistake to suppose that the administration of a popular government could be strengthened by being raised above the direct influence of parliament. On the contrary, it is seriously weakened. To carry popular opinion with them is, in fact, a necessity of both the American and English Governments; but the English Government, by its immediate dependence on parliament, has a powerful *aid* for this purpose, which the American Government wants. The mutual influence of the Cabinet on the House, and the

House on the Cabinet, keeps the country in a vital connection with the ministry which does not exist in America. If Mr. Lincoln, in making up his mind as to his policy, had felt that the first necessity was to carry Congress with him—that his power was limited by the support of Congress,—he would have first applied himself to testing his influence over Congress. In the course of this process he would in all probability have modified his own view in some measure, as well as that of the body he had to lead, and so have brought the two into distinct and practical harmony. But as it is, nothing of this kind takes place. Now and then, indeed, he sends a message to the Houses; but there is no closer connection between him and them. His policy is formed in the Cabinet, and there is no channel by which he can exert on Congress, or Congress on him, those multiplied influences which connect an English premier and an English parliament. His responsibility is far more exclusively his own. And the result is, that he has neither done anything to persuade Congress that coercion is necessary, nor Congress to persuade him that coercion is dangerous. We fear that he is going to attempt a policy in which Congress will never support him powerfully enough to give any chance of success,—and yet from which it will not attempt to withhold him. A more fatal relation between the Government and the people can scarcely be conceived. The popular power is strong enough to weaken the Government without overthrowing it.

Civil War in America and the attitude of England[1]

THE fall of Fort Sumter must soon, we fear, if we may rely at all on the drift of the recent news, issue in civil war. The rumour that the Southern Confederation intends to anticipate an attack by moving upon Washington is scarcely likely to be true, for President Davis is too sagacious a man to take a step which would so enrage the North as to induce it to enter heart and soul into an internecine contest with the South. If he were wise, indeed, he would not have ventured any active collision at all, such as has taken place at Charleston. It would have been better to trust exclusively to blockade for the reduction of the Federal garrisons in the revolted states. The moral shock of any collision is most dangerous, as the accounts of the frantic excitement in Washington on the arrival of the news of the collision at Fort Sumter and the surrender of Major Anderson, sufficiently prove. It is true that American rage even at its highest pitch usually manages to stop short where policy would direct, and that we in England are exceedingly liable to be deceived by its effervescent symptoms. Still there is now the gravest reason to apprehend a serious civil war; indeed all the free states seem already to have intimated to the President, through the telegraph, their readiness to support a war policy; and, if it is prevented at all, it will only be by the unwillingness of the Northern statesmen to risk the adhesion of the border states by an actual invasion. But if the Southern states should, as is rumoured, be so foolish as to take the initiative by invading Washington, they would play directly into the hands of the extreme party in the North. All compunction would immediately be at an end, and in all probability the border states would themselves be induced by such a step to fight with the North. The situation is very similar to the attitude of Austria and Sardinia. The neutrals will inevitably throw their influence into the scale of the party attacked. Mr. Lincoln, as far as his own popularity

[1] This article was first published in *The Economist* for April 27 1861, Volume XIX, pp. 450-1.

and political position is concerned, can wish for nothing better than to be relieved by his antagonist of the responsibility of a decision. His difficulty has hitherto been, that the great power and wealth of the North has been passive, and reluctant to foment a fratricidal strife. But let once the slave states take the guilt upon themselves, as in some degree they have already done, and Mr. Lincoln would find his hands strengthened and his cause enthusiastically supported by a power such as does not exist in the Southern states at all. We do not believe, then, in the reported invasion of Washington. A course so blind and insane is utterly inconsistent with the general ability shown by the Southern Government. But we do fear that the strife and defeat at Charleston will render it very difficult for Mr. Lincoln, in the attitude in which he now stands, to evade some attempt at reprisal, and that thus a regular war may soon break out.

Under these grave circumstances it is that Mr. Gregory proposes to ask the House of Commons on Tuesday next to affirm the expediency of an immediate recognition of the Southern Confederation. We can imagine no course more disgraceful to England, or less likely to command the assent of the popular body appealed to. Not that we desire to see a civil war in America, even though the North should be completely triumphant. We have often said that unless there were a Union party in the Southern states considerable enough to make some head even without external assistance, the defeat of the newly-confederated states by the North could scarcely lead to any good result. It would be mere military conquest; and a power like the American Union cannot hope to hold together its territory by military force. And seeing that there is, unhappily, but little trace of a powerful Unionist minority among the seceded states, we cannot wish to see a fratricidal strife which would multiply indefinitely the mutual hatreds of North and South without solving the ultimate difficulty. But this is not the question for us to consider. It has been England's universal rule to acknowledge a *de facto* revolutionary government whenever it has established its practical independence by incontrovertible proofs, —then and not sooner. Whatever be the wisdom or folly of the war which there is but too much reason to believe is now declared between the Federal Government at Washington and the revolted states,—it is not yet begun, or is only just beginning. There can be no question whatever of the constitutional right of President Lincoln to treat the hostile Confederation as a treasonable rebellion, which, so far as it trenches on Federal property and laws, he may resist by force. This is his present attitude. He hopes, however little we may hope, to suppress the rebellion. He thinks, however little we may think, that he shall be able to enforce the laws enacted at Washington, and to redeem the United States property from the hands of the seceders. This may be sanguine; nay, it may even be a mere hallucination. With that we have nothing to do. We profess always to abstain from judging the rights of a quarrel between a people and its rulers, and to guide our conduct by the plain results of political fact. We are now on the eve of seeing what these results will be. Either war or compromise seems now inevitable. If it be compromise, we shall know how to act. If it be war, we are bound to await the results of that war. A premature recognition of the Southern Confederation would be a departure from the recognised course of England, and could not but therefore express a political *bias* in favour of the seceders.

Now, is it even *decent* to ask an English House of Commons to express such a bias in favour of such a power as that which has its seat of government at Montgomery—a power which is based on slavery as the very principle of its individual existence, and which, though it professes for the moment to have abolished the slave trade, is worked by men many of whom have openly assailed the laws against that traffic as a gross violation of the rights of the South. The head of the commission appointed to negotiate with the European powers for the recognition of the Southern Federation, the Hon. W. L. Yancey, of Alabama, has devoted a great portion of his public life to denouncing the obsolete views of Washington and the other great American statesmen of the last century on this subject. The men and the journalists who chiefly instigated secession were most of them deeply pledged to a repeal of the slave trade laws. It is true that when secession was achieved, they found it necessary as a political measure to put forward more moderate men,—men like Mr. Stephen, of Georgia, who had done his best to arrest the secession movement—and to acquiesce in their counsels. But it remains certain that such papers as the *Charleston Mercury* and such statesmen as Mr. Yancey were the motive power of the secession movement, and will again become the motive power of a slavery extension policy (which in its turn will require the slave trade as its legitimate result), so soon as the ends of compromise have been answered by securing the recognition of the new power in Europe, and if it may be so, the adhesion of some of the wavering states. Under these circumstances, we earnestly rejoice to see that Mr. W. E. Forster has given notice of an amendment to Mr. Gregory's motion to the effect that 'the House does not at present desire to express any opinion in favour of such recognition, and trusts that the government will at no time make it without obtaining due security against the renewal of the African slave trade.' Such an amendment will come with the greatest weight from the representative of Bradford,—a town which, though identified more with the worsted than the cotton trade, still represents fairly the public spirit of our Northern manufacturing interests. The determination of England not to let interested motives interfere with the high principle which she has always shown on the questions of slavery and the slave trade, could not be expressed more fittingly than by the member for Bradford.

The Evil and the Good in the American Civil War[1]

THE war which has at length broken out in America, in spite of the truly legal caution and forbearance of the President, through the presumptuous aggression of the seceders, will no doubt be fierce and bloody. No one can think of it without dismay; no one can even venture to predict what may be its results and where it will end. The Southern leaders have unquestionably the whole responsibility of this fatal step. The blood which has at length begun to flow must be upon them and on their children. They originated the quarrel by their passionate desire to extend the shameful institution of which they are so proud. At every fresh turn of the dispute they have been the aggressors. They not only declined to submit to a constitutional defeat, but their statesmen had prepared by years of secret treason for the rebellion of last November. When they had consummated their purpose, and found the Northern states still long-suffering, still reluctant to precipitate the unhallowed strife, and yet intent on holding their ground in the Federal property still remaining to them,—they profited by the delay which the intercession of the border states secured, only to mature their aggressive measures, and then did not hesitate to break the truce and plunge the country into civil war. Their plans are well conceived and ably executed. They are directed by a man of prompter mind and more vigorous decision than President Lincoln, and for a time they will probably be successful. The border states, after causing a delay long enough to serve the purposes of Mr. Jefferson Davis, are now going off with rapid explosions to the enemy. Virginia has seceded, and on the attempt of her troops to seize the Federal arsenal at Harper's Ferry, it was blown up and abandoned by the officer in command. North Carolina has again seized the Federal forts. Even Maryland is fiercely divided. The war feeling is strong in Tennessee. Kentucky, alone, appears still to incline to

[1] This article was first published in *The Economist* for May 4 1861, Volume XIX, pp. 478–9.

the Northern side. A march on Washington was apprehended; and the Northern states, at length aroused to the true character of the position, were slowly sending in their succours to the President, while the Southern army was said to be completely organised. Blood had been already shed by the secessionists both at Baltimore and Harper's Ferry, and every hope of compromise was at an end.

Such news seems pure evil. And that it is the herald of frightful calamities, no thoughtful man can deny. Still it is not in our estimation evil quite unmixed and unfathomable. Black as the storm is, we believe there is promise of light through it. Let us take the worst feature first; —and the worst feature about the war undoubtedly is that the eventual victory of the North can scarcely carry with it eventual success. We speak of the Northern victory as ultimately certain, because a wealthy and free population of twenty millions cannot but conquer in the long run in a contest with a poor free population of the same race, numbering at most seven millions even if we give the South the whole of the border states. That the North may be beaten at first, we regard as exceedingly probable. But that a defeat will only animate the Northern states to greater and greater exertion, we consider absolutely certain. And in the long run no doubt wealth and numbers must decide this fatal strife. But suppose the war ended, and ended by the defeat of the Southern Confederation, will victory mean success? We think not. It may bring back one or two doubtful districts or even doubtful states within the Union. It may restore Western Virginia, Missouri, and Kentucky,—possibly even North Carolina to the United States; but in the Gulf states at least victory would be conquest, and conquest only. No one doubts that in these states the secessionist party has always had an enormous majority, which is likely to be increased by civil war into a feeling of ferocious unanimity. Those states may be conquered, may be held in military possession, but they can scarcely again be expected to take a voluntary part in the political institutions of the United States. Unless the issue of civil war were a slave insurrection which should put an end to the institution of slavery altogether as the result of a train of events which it is utterly impossible to measure or foreshadow,—the Gulf states can never again be reasonably expected to act in political concert with the North. Whatever result, therefore, a Northern victory might have,—it could not be a political recovery of the Gulf states. It seems as certain as any human event can be, that by them at least the step taken can never be retraced. It follows, therefore, that the war, bloody and perhaps long as it may be, will be in this respect a fruitless war. The blood of Americans will be poured out by Americans, without any hope of achieving the end which is apparently the only legitimate end of such a war. After the conflict is over, the rival parties will be politically just where they were when it began,—except that mutual animosities will be deeper, both parties will be poorer, and both parties more vindictive than at the outset. The North will beat the South in the end, but when it has done so, we do not see what the Government can do, except leave the South to follow its own devices at the last as it might do at this moment. Surely nothing can well be blacker than a prospect of a war at once vindictive, bloody, and fruitless.

This is the dark side of the prospect, and a very dark side indeed it seems. There is, however, not a little to be said on the other side. And the main consideration appears to us to be that the war will draw together the Northern states as they have never been drawn together yet,—will teach them the all-important character of the slavery issue, —will sweep the political horizon of those petty political controversies which have long frittered away the attention of statesmen and diverted them from the really great issues which were slowly maturing beneath the surface of society,—and finally will impress them with the absolute necessity of a closer union, a stronger central power, a suppression of those repulsive forces which keep state and state jealous and apart,— in one word, with the duty of turning the Federal Government into a really supreme power. Such, we think, may, and most probably will be, one result of the disastrous conflict in which the United States are now engaged.

As a secondary and casual advantage, the struggle will liberate from the authority of the border states all those sections which are already prepared and anxious to extinguish slavery. This would be difficult to effect without war. While the state organisation is still perfect, the stronger party will carry the state. For example, in Virginia the state has declared for the South, but Western Virginia is almost entirely in sympathy with the North. Again, in Kentucky there seems to be a very large Northern party and the same is true of Tennessee. Nothing but war probably could dissolve those state-chains which bind the reluctant freeman to the corrupt and corrupting domestic institution in such cases as these. But war will enable these fragmentary states, chafing under their hateful connection with districts of quite different political tendencies, to achieve their liberty and seek the protection of the Union. This would be in itself no small gain. But the one gain which alone can compensate the North for the horrors of civil war is the growth of genuine Republican conviction to which it will probably give rise;—the learning of the great lesson that there can be no hearty political alliance between freedom and slavery, and no genuine freedom without a strong central government and the surrender of those atomic political privileges which minister to local jealousies and general anarchy.

For the South we see no possibility of a good issue for the war which its statesmen have provoked and commenced. The greater their temporary success, the greater must be their ultimate humiliation. Their policy seems to us able and masterly, but utterly short-sighted. To rouse by gratuitous insult the mettle of a nation three times as numerous and far more than three times as powerful, to force them by aggressive steps into a struggle in which the sympathy of every free and civilised nation will be with the North, seems like the madness of men whose eyes are blinded and hearts hardened by the evil cause they defend. Had they been wise, they would have trusted all to delay and their own obstinate purpose. As it is, they rush on a war which, whether it end in their mere exhaustion or in the horrors of a servile insurrection, cannot but end in humiliating disasters, which will excite no pity, because they have been positively courted by the Southern leaders.

The Legal Relation of England and of Individual Englishmen to the Civil Struggle in the United States[1]

NOTHING is more desirable than that we ourselves should have, and that the rest of the world should have, accurate notions of our precise position with respect to the civil conflict which is in progress between the now disunited states of America; and, at the same time, not many things are more difficult. The case is so new that it is difficult to realise its true features and to apprehend distinctly its proper relations either to recognised principles or to our own interests. Curiously, too, we in England have generally been the belligerent and America the neutral nation; and, now that the position is reversed, in some not unimportant points our former tenets are the more agreeable to them, and their former tenets are more agreeable to us. In these circumstances our duty is a duty of caution. We should be wary in acting, and almost as wary in speaking: we should be very slow to do any act which would embroil us in a discord from which neither of the combatants can hope for anything but disaster; and we should be slow, too, in committing ourselves to any international *formulæ* which might in the rapid course of events, from the unforeseen effect of some omitted consideration, commit us to the very course of conduct we wished to avoid, and immerse us in the dangers we had hoped to shun.

Some important conclusions, however, can be laid down very easily and very clearly. In the first place, we should on no account as yet recognise the Southern states as a new nation. Such an act would be wholly uncalled for, either by precedent, by reason, or by natural feeling. We cannot, with our ethical maxims, be over-ready to favour a federation of which slavery is not the accident but the principle:

---

[1] This article was first published in *The Economist* for May 11 1861, Volume XIX, pp. 505–6.

reason tells us that we should be slow to offend a government with which we are in amity by recognising any seceders from it: the established precedents of international law tell us that we have our choice, and that there is no call upon us to recognise the Southern states of America unless we like it.

On the other hand, we are bound by all sound principle and by precedent to recognise the Southern states as belligerents. Common sense tells us that when two great sections of a nation are contending, whether the cause of strife be mastery on the one hand or independence on the other, or any other cause whatever, it would not only be absurd but wicked to treat either of the combatants as a herd of rioters or casual breakers of the peace. The two parties themselves are obliged to treat each other more or less according to the international law of belligerent relations, and lookers-on must do so also. We adopted this course in the case of Greece and Turkey; and though in no other respect are the Northern states of the Union at all like the empire of Turkey, they are like it in being the state from which the secession is in progress. Both are, to use a phrase familiar to all Scotchmen, the *residuary* states; and the entire difference of collateral circumstances must not withdraw our attention from the single material consideration. It is scarcely necessary to point out what would be our position if we did not recognise the South as having the usual rights of belligerents. We should then be constant and close spectators of a maritime conflict in which we gave one party all the rights of civilisation, and the other party none of the rights; in which we recognised one party as regular combatants, and treated the other as tumultuous rebels; in which we, though constantly professing neutrality, should be in fact taking by distinct policy a definite side. It will be very difficult for England as it is to stand clear of all collision in the complicated naval war which seems to be close at hand. Though the force of privateers and other ships that the South can raise will be petty in comparison with European ideas, it is nevertheless considerable, and may come into collision with us at very many points, and therefore it is our clear interest as well as our great duty to steer clear of the conflict by maintaining an *absolute* neutrality.

This absolute neutrality would in one respect be very favourable to the North. It would compel us to deal with a blockade of the Southern ports as if it were an ordinary blockade between hostile nations. It has been questioned whether a nation could blockade its own ports, and it would be a serious question whether a government would be justified in using such an extreme expedient to quell a mere local disturbance, or a riot in a town, or some series of acts by a municipality which it did not recognise. But when the ordinary rules of real war are by admission to regulate the conflict, the right of blockade must be accepted as one of the inseparable peculiarities of the adopted code.

It is possible that the American navy may at present be too dispersed to make such a blockade effective for the present, and it is also possible that now that the cotton crop of this year has been shipped, the Southern states will not much care for it for the present; but still it is one of the not improbable incidents of a not very distant future, and therefore it is important to observe that the admission of the South to the *status* of a belligerent will then be as advantageous to the North, as for the moment it is advantageous to the South itself.

These considerations are the most important of any at the present juncture as to the conduct of England as a state. It remains to consider the conduct of individual Englishmen, and on this point the English law is tolerably clear. The Foreign Enlistment Act, which is held to be only declaratory of the common law, is express on the one most essential point. It has been thought that letters of marque could be issued to Englishmen, and that British ships could be fitted out as privateers in London or in Canada, but such acts are as plainly illegal as any words can make them. The Act says:—'That if any person, within any part of the United Kingdom, or in any part of His Majesty's dominions beyond the seas, shall, without the leave and licence of His Majesty for that purpose first had and obtained as aforesaid, equip, furnish, fit out, or arm, or attempt or endeavour to *equip, furnish, fit out, or arm*, or procure to be equipped, furnished, fitted out, or armed, or shall knowingly aid, assist, or be concerned in the equipping, furnishing, fitting out or arming of any ship or vessel, with intent or in order that such ship or vessel shall be employed in the service of any foreign Prince, State, or Potentate, or of any foreign colony, province, or part of any province or people, or of any person or persons exercising or assuming to exercise any powers of government in or over any foreign state, colony, province, or part of any province or people, as a transport or store ship, or with intent *to cruise or commit hostilities against any Prince, State, or Potentate*, or against the subjects or citizens of any Prince, State, or Potentate, or against the persons exercising or assuming to exercise the powers of government in any colony, province, or part of any province or country, or against the inhabitants of any foreign colony, province, or part of any province or country, with whom His Majesty shall not then be at war;' shall be guilty of a misdemeanour and be punishable personally by fine and imprisonment while the ship so equipped is to be forfeited with its stores and ammunition.

It is happily therefore clear that we should not be tempted to embroil ourselves with either party in this disastrous conflict by permitting individuals to fit out privateers to aid and assist the other. It would have been very dangerous to England if our law had by any inadvertence allowed any unauthorised acts of individual intervention. We might then have been drawn into the conflict at any moment by some thoughtless act of some reckless individual, or the overbearing passion of either of two most passionate combatants.

This would have been aggravated if the North should persevere in their unwise declaration to treat the Southern privateers as simple pirates, and to visit them with the appropriate penalties. If, indeed, the United States had been wise enough to abolish privateering when requested to do so by the Congress of Paris, they would have had a clear right to act in the manner proposed. But now they have claimed the right of fitting out privateers for themselves, and are bound to afford to their *brethren* of the South the same advantage of those rules of warfare which they claim for themselves. They are bound in duty to carry on a civil war by the rules which *they* admit to be binding for all other war.

On the whole, therefore, it may be said that the duty of England and of Englishmen is for the moment plain and simple, though painful as in such terrible events any duty must be. It is to stand steadily apart from a course of events in which our participation would help no one who should be helped, and aid no cause which ought to be aided. As nations and as individuals, it is our evident interest and an incumbent obligation on us to take no part, by word or deed, with either party,— unaffected either by the Free Trade enthusiasm on the one hand, or the anti-slavery enthusiasm on the other.

The Mercantile Difficulties of the American Civil War[1]

I⊤ is very important that thinking men of business should comprehend the exact difficulties to which our commerce with America is exposed at the present juncture. But many practised men of business do not find it very easy to understand them. There seems to be a puzzle in the subject, and not unnaturally, for its precise state is the result of very ancient controversies, and is hardly intelligible without a reference to very ancient doctrines.

There are in the nature of things two questions which inevitably arise out of every naval war. First, What is to be done with neutral goods on board the ships of belligerents and enemies? Secondly, What is to be done with enemies' goods on board the ships of neutral nations? And with respect to these there are two old jurisprudential theories, and a third modern theory, less logical perhaps than either of them, but more favourable than either to the interests of commerce, and therefore more beneficial than either to the increase of civilisation and the progress of mankind.

The first of these old theories is the rigid English theory. We looked under our old law, and irrespective of what was agreed on quite recently at Paris, exclusively to the *ownership* or property in all goods and merchandise. Whatever belonged to the nation with which we were at war we took *wherever* we could find it; and whatever did not belong to our enemies we did *not* take, wherever it might be. Accordingly, when we found enemies' goods on board neutral vessels we took them undeviatingly and upon principle: when, on the other hand, we found the property of neutrals on board an enemy's ship, we uniformly restored it to its true owners, though we took the ship as lawful prize.

The second of the old theories is the continental theory, which has been advocated by many able jurists, and which has played a very great part in history. Upon this theory the flag of the vessel is an

[1] This article was first published in *The Economist* for May 25 1861, Volume XIX, pp. 561–2.

undeniable and irresistible presumption of the ownership of the goods it is carrying as cargo. You are not at liberty to inquire into the facts; whatever is indicated by the selected presumption, that you are to assume. Whatever goods you find on board a ship *bonâ fide* entitled to carry a neutral flag, those goods are, by an infallible presumption, the property of neutrals. On the other hand, whatever goods you find on board an enemy's ship, these are, in like manner, to be incontrovertibly regarded as enemies' goods.

It will strike any one who reads these two series of precisely conflicting statements, that neither of them are the international rules which the interests of commerce at all times demand, and which in later ages, when the world is complicated, and when war is always either impending or actual, those interests imperatively require. For the good of commerce it is desirable that the greatest possible facility should be given to trading operations at all times, by all persons, and under all circumstances. Accordingly, it would be desirable that *cargoes* should be free wherever they should be found; that, in conformity with the old English theory which looks to facts only, neutral goods should never be touched on board enemies' ships; that, in conformity with the continental theory which regards only an artificial presumption, all goods whatever should be unmolested and free that are found on board a ship that is truly and really neutral. This is the principle recognised by the Congress of Paris. According to the declarations we quoted last week:—

'2. The neutral flag covers enemies' goods, with the exception of contraband of war.

'3. Neutral goods, with the exception of contraband of war, are not liable to capture under the enemy's flag.'

As we, in the interests of commerce, have on former occasions urged, it is most desirable that these rules should be carried further, and that trading ships should not be interfered with, exceptional cases being disregarded, even when belonging to actual belligerents. But we need not complicate an intricate topic just now with any speculative suggestions. *As a fact*, the rule laid down by the Congress of Paris was, so to speak, a compilation from the two opposed codes of naval war which divided the European world; from the one it selected the doctrine 'that free ships make free goods,' and from the other the doctrine that only enemies' goods are to be seized on board any vessel of any country.

As is well known, however, the American Government never
recognised the decisions of the Congress of Paris: it was invited to
accede to those decisions, but it did not. The present American law
is, therefore, exactly what our own old law was before the Congress
of Paris; it exactly embodies what we have called the rigid English
theory. Its terms are concisely laid down by perhaps its greatest
authority:—'The two distinct propositions that enemy's goods found
on board a neutral ship may be lawfully seized as prize of war, and
that the goods of a neutral found on board of an enemy's vessel were
to be restored, have been explicitly incorporated into the jurisprudence
of the United States, and declared by the Supreme Court to be founded
in the law of nations.'

*What, then, is the consequence of the present state of the American
law?* It is this:—That English cargoes will be free on board any ship
whatever; but that English ships will be searched by vessels of war
and by privateers for American cargoes, without check, without control, and without appeal.

Moreover, as we last week pointed out, the Americans have exempted other nations from the necessity of this search. The ships of
several other countries (cases of blockade excepted) will be able to
carry goods from New Orleans to Liverpool without fear of molesta-
tion and under the cover of express compacts, though English ships
will be stopped, examined, and not improbably (considering what sort
of persons are likely to fit out many of the privateers) maltreated and
robbed, while going side by side to the same destination.

As we showed on the occasion just referred to, such an anomaly
must not continue. English ships must at once be placed on an even
footing with the ships of the most favoured nation. According to the
most recent, though we as yet fear uncertain intelligence, the Confederate states are willing to recognise the rule that 'free ships make
free goods,' and as their old jurisprudence recognises that the goods
of neutrals are never to be seized, this (if it should be hereafter confirmed) is all which it is most important to us to ask from them. They
will still, it is true, be continuing the barbarous and degrading practice
of privateering, which all Europe has renounced and which the entire
morality of civilisation forbids; but we shall not suffer from it much.
The declaration just made, if it only have been made, will sufficiently
protect us. But as respects the North—the United States—we are
still in a most unsatisfactory position; our ships may still be stopped,

searched, and scrutinised by any ship of war of theirs or any privateer which they may authorise.

Such is the general law as respects commerce with America. But there is also a special branch of the subject which will practically be important—the law of blockade. The reason upon which this law is rested by jurists and was founded in fact, is very different from the reasons we have just been considering. We have been hitherto concerned with the conditions under which commerce may be carried on during a war with one of the belligerents; we have now to consider the case when no commerce is permitted at all. A siege is one of the oldest incidents of warfare, and entails of necessity peculiar consequences.

In a siege—and what is called a blockade is only a siege by sea—it is a principal object to distress the besieged by cutting off their trading connections with the external world. It is advisable, as far as possible, to prevent their obtaining subsistence by a commerce of import, and to prevent their earning a livelihood by a commerce of export. Neither the belligerent nor the neutral is to be permitted to carry on any trade by sea with the blockaded place.

To a valid blockade two conditions are necessary:—*First*, that there should be an efficient blockading force. Attempts have at various times been made by various nations to throw whole countries under a commercial interdict by decree. Notice has been given that the whole coast is not to be approached by the ships of neutral countries. But such decrees are contrary to the accepted law of nations and to common sense. There is no real siege, the ordinary trade of the coast in its own vessels is going on as usual, and it is pure commercial evil for commercial evil's sake to ruin the commerce carried on in the ships of neutrals. The legitimate object of a blockade is to distress the enemy by cutting off the entire trading communication, and less than this is of no use in a military sense at all.

And, secondly, a blockade must not only exist in fact and reality, and not on paper only, but it must be made known to those whose commerce is to be interdicted. The most common and proper way of effecting such an object is an authentic communication to the executive governments of neutral countries. But such a notification is not absolutely necessary. If the captain of the ship can be proved in matter of fact to know of the existence of the blockade, the vessel is not permitted to escape the ordinary penalties through any formal deficiencies in the technical communication.

The penalty of a breach of blockade is the simple confiscation of ship, and, in most cases, of the *cargo*. If, therefore, the cotton ports of the Southern states of America are blockaded by the Northern states, we trade with them at our peril. Neutral ships which are shut up in the blockaded port at the beginning of the blockade may indeed, by the courtesy of nations, be permitted to come out. But there is no other exception. If the avowed intention of the Northern President should be strictly carried out, no ship, of whatever nation, will be able to bring a bale of cotton from New Orleans, Charleston, or Savannah.

It is deeply to be wished that it may be only merchants and men of business who need think of these considerations. But it is very possible that they may exact the attention before long of the whole nation. A squabble at sea is the most likely cause of war to a maritime nation; and the present juncture is unfortunately very likely to be prolific in such squabbles. We have to do with the privateers of the South— the worst privateers, probably, that the world has ever seen; we have to do with the ships, perhaps with the privateers also, of the North— in the days of their prosperity the most punctilious, overbearing, and contentious government which the world has ever seen, and now, in the bitterness of adversity and the false shame of humiliated pride, perhaps likely to be more overbearing and contentious than ever.

Is the Success of the North possible?[1]

THE virulent and utterly unwarranted and unexplained irritation against England manifested by the United States (or, as we must now call them, the Federalists) is the astonishment of all beholders. It is not confined to one party or to one class. It seems to be felt equally by the people, by the press, by the Government, by the diplomatists, and (strange to say) even by the English correspondents of London newspapers. It is expressed by official persons in most unofficial language, and by ordinary men in wholly unmeasured terms. This is the more singular, as no specific offence is assigned as the cause of all this boiling indignation—no assignable offence of any sort, in fact, having been committed. We have, on the contrary, most scrupulously and anxiously abstained from doing or saying any thing which it was possible to avoid doing or saying. We have, with remarkable delicacy and forbearance, declined discussing American affairs in Parliament. We have given utterance to a nearly unanimous sentiment of regret at the quarrel between parties towards both of whom we entertain much friendly feeling, and with both of whom we have always endeavoured to maintain friendly relations. Beyond this we have literally done and said nothing, except publicly announcing that we should recognise the exercise of the usual belligerent rights by the seceding states—a recognition which even the Federal Government do not argue that we could have refused to eight millions of organised and self-governed citizens, and which that Government, now that the war has actually commenced, finds itself practically obliged to recognise also. The irritation, however, though quite unwarranted, is not unnatural; and, though never yet explained by the Americans themselves, is in truth explicable enough. It is caused by their secret conviction that most Englishmen in their hearts believe that secession cannot be prevented, and that the dissolution of the Union is an inevitable and accomplished fact. The Americans really believe this too—but they

---

[1] This article was first published in *The Economist* for June 29 1861, Volume XIX, pp. 702–3.

cannot bear that we should believe it. The thing is so unwelcome to them, even in idea, that they are furious with all who so much as see it or speak of it. They regard it as a calamity so great, a humiliation so profound, that they cannot forgive us for admitting it to be possible. This is the true explanation of their unreasonable anger. They can give no other, and they shrink from putting anything so futile and pettish into plain words.

Now, though they have not the faintest right or reason to be angry with us for entertaining the conviction they attribute to us, they are quite correct in supposing that we do entertain it. We *do* believe the secession of the slave states to be a *fait accompli*—a completed and irreversible transaction. We believe it to be impossible now for the North to lure back the South into the Union by any compromise, or to compel them back by any force. If to hold this conviction be an offence, it is one which we cannot help committing, and which we must proceed to justify.

If the South had any real or specific grievances to allege against the North, and had seceded on the ground of a refusal to redress those grievances, it might be possible enough to effect a compromise and to negotiate a reconciliation. But the known facts of the case and the conduct of the Southerners from the very outset have negatived any supposition of the kind. Every act and word—their own most deliberate avowals—their public and official proceedings—all prove in the plainest manner that secession was a foregone conclusion the moment Mr. Lincoln's election was certain; that it had been resolved upon and prepared long beforehand, and that their defeat in the presidential contest merely determined the *time*, and not the deed itself. The North, before its passions were aroused, offered every conceivable variety of terms, short of actual surrender at discretion, in order to avert the menaced disruption. The free states proposed plan after plan of compromise, involving every possible concession—except the giving up that fair share of control over the policy of the Union to which they were strictly entitled, and which they had just so hardly won. *Every proposal, every set of terms, was scornfully rejected* by the secessionists. Their answer was uniform—and uniformly insolent and impatient. It was virtually:—'We want severance, not reconciliation —-we want decided preponderance, not fair participation.' They went on their own way, disdaining even to listen to the almost suppliant remonstrances and propositions of the North. Is it probable, is it possible, now, when the passions of both sides have been raised to the highest pitch by mutual invective and by actual bloodshed, that the Southerners will listen to the terms they scouted a few months ago,— or that the Northerners will offer any terms half as liberal? People will do many things to avert a breach which they would never dream of doing to repair one—especially when the repair could only be so imperfect and so transient as it would be in the present case.

But the Federalists themselves admit that the time for compromise is gone by. They are now as little inclined for it as their antagonists. They say they are going to subdue the South—so completely to defeat them as to force them back into the Union—and to keep them in it by compulsion and restraint. This achievement, which in March their own chiefs all disclaimed as wild and unattemptable, they have now worked themselves up to the delusion of believing practicable and within easy reach. To such a point has fury blinded their naturally shrewd intelligence.—This, then, is the project the feasibility of which we have to consider. We appeal to the *map*: we remind our readers of the *race*.

The seceding states extend, from the North of Virginia to the South of Florida and Texas, over 15 degrees of latitude, and from Missouri to North Carolina, over 20 degrees of longitude. This enormous space is inhabited by a rough, scanty, and widely-scattered population, and contains few large towns. A traveller marches for days, and meets only occasional shanties and log-houses. Flying columns might march for days and meet no foe, and no shelter. The largest army would be a mere speck in such a desert. The best appointed army, with the most skilfully organised commissariat, might be in despair at such roads, such rivers, such forests, and such distances. Cleverly managed guerilla bands might harass an army of any size and any quality into speedy ruin. What, then, would become of such a militia as the United States army consists and must consist of—nearly all ill-disciplined volunteers, and scantily provided with the *materiel* of war? It is obvious that anything like a conquest by land of such a country it is mere idleness to speak of. The Confederate troops might, possibly enough, be defeated on the plains of Virginia; but when they retired South, what general would venture to pursue them?

Probably the more rational among the Federalists will admit all this. But they will say:—'That is not our plan, nor our expectation. We believe that the secessionist forces are inferior to ours; that they cannot be extensively recruited; that they will disperse, especially after disaster, more speedily and more certainly than our volunteers; and in fact will soon become sick of the contest. Moreover, we trust mainly to our blockade. By shutting up all the ports, we shall ruin the planters —prevent them effectually from buying what they need and from selling what they must sell in order to raise the purchase money—and in six months compel them to surrender at discretion.'

Well: we will suppose them to be as successful in dispersing Southern forces and in blockading Southern ports as they expect to be. We will for the moment put aside the two possibilities of the blockade being evaded by a fair proportion of enterprising merchantmen, or raised by Confederate privateers and cruisers,—even if no other contingencies should interfere. Is it so certain that mere defeat in the field added to all the inconveniences and privations consequent on an interrupted commerce *will* induce the Southerners to confess themselves vanquished, and submit to accept terms at the dictation of the conqueror? Does any one acquainted with the temper of the Southerner—who unites all the fiery pride of a Frenchman with all the stubborn pride of an Englishman—believe that defeat and privation will do more than envenom and exasperate the strife? Has it not been apparent from the very beginning of the dispute that fanatical passion and not calculating sense has guided the whole people; and that now their cause has become elevated in their eyes into something that is quite patriotism and almost religion? And can we really believe that such men (who are to be counted by millions), because they can only sell their cotton and buy wine and tea and clothing by driblets, will be persuaded to re-enter that Union as suppliant and defeated rebels, in which they refused to remain unless they could wield its whole power and monopolise its whole emoluments? The superior might of the North we do not for one moment question: they have a vast preponderance in wealth, in numbers, in ships, in education; they are as brave, more intelligent, and may possess or create as able leaders;— and all these resources will tell enormously in the long run. Certainly at last—possibly even from the first—victory and success will incline to their side. But victory is not conquest; success will not necessarily entail the enemy's submission. And they are fighting, not with savage Indians, nor with feeble Mexicans, but with Anglo-Saxons as fierce, as obstinate, and as untameable as themselves. Therefore, granting the utmost that can be alleged as to the difficulties and the poverty of the

South, and the numbers and resources of the North, we conceive that though the Federalists may be victorious in the strife, they cannot be successful in their aim. For this last object, they must compel eight millions of free men—trained to self-government and accustomed to regard themselves as not only politically independent but politically supreme—to *sue for peace*,—and to sue to men whom they have habituated themselves to look down upon as snobs and vulgar tradesmen, whom of late they have begun to hate with a *familiar* bitterness, and whom they will detest with tenfold animosity when the humiliation of defeat rankles in their bosoms. Is this a rational anticipation?

There is another and very serious set of considerations connected with this subject, which we must defer till next week.

Cotton and Civil War[1]

THE true mercantile instinct interpreted with true mercantile promptitude the practical meaning of the disastrous defeat of the Federal
troops with which the news of this week opened. The tidings only
reached Liverpool on Sunday afternoon, and on Monday a large
business was transacted in cotton at an advance of $\frac{1}{4}$d a lb. Commercial
sagacity, well trained in the faculty of discerning the bearings of
political events on the price of commodities, concluded with singular
unanimity that the first and most certain issue of the battle at Manassas
Junction must be to postpone all chance of compromise and to prolong
and exacerbate the war. We have no doubt the inference is a correct
one. The South, whose tone has all along been so lofty and whose
demands have all along been so peremptory, will assuredly have their
pretensions confirmed and their confidence restored by a victory which
has certainly surpassed in completeness the expectations even of the
most sanguine. They have always been resolute and hopeful, determined to be content with nothing short of absolute independence, and
confident of ultimate success; but at the same time prepared, especially
of late, to anticipate a long and terrible struggle and severe sacrifices
and privation. But though they entertained no doubt of being able
to hold their own, they did not venture to count on so early and
decisive a victory. Their tone is consequently higher and more im-
perative than ever; and they are prepared, rather too boastfully, to
count on a series of similar successes. The North, on the other hand,
conscious of vast superiority of resource, furious at an unexpected
check, and sore to a not unnatural degree at a defeat which in its
details is so like humiliation, are burning to avenge their losses and to
redeem their military reputation, and are bound by every motive of
interest, of passion, and of pride to make the most vigorous efforts to
prosecute the war and to wipe out the memory of their disaster. It
would be simply *impossible* for them now to listen to any terms of

[1] This article was first published in *The Economist* for August 10 1861, Volume XIX,
pp. 869-71.

compromise or accommodation—even were their antagonists in the mood to offer such. The controversy *must* now be fought out; and the result of the first battle clearly intimates that this 'fighting out' will be a somewhat long business.

At the same time this signal victory, won at the very outset by that party which was believed and is still generally admitted to be the weakest, will we expect do much towards determining the ultimate issue of the contest. It was not needed to confirm those convictions which we on this side of the Atlantic have expressed from the beginning, that the disruption of the Union must be the inevitable result and was in fact already consummated; but it will probably tend materially to infuse something of the same conviction into the minds of the Northerners. Their expectations of being able to subdue and reincorporate the South—so far as they were genuine and rational at all —were based upon two assumptions:—*first*, that they were so incomparably the stronger, as well as the richer and more numerous party, that their victory would be very speedy and very thorough,— that, in short, defeat in the field and blockade of the ports would make short work of their antagonists;—and *secondly*, that there was a large 'Union' party in the slave states, which, if not a majority, was at least a very powerful minority, and which, as soon as any decided reverse sustained by the secession army made it safe to show itself, would rise to the surface and overpower those who now suppressed them. Both these assumptions must have been rudely shaken, if not entirely dissipated, by the late disaster. The Northerners must now admit that their antagonists have, to say the least, been far better handled than their own troops and have shown superior military aptitudes, and are not men to be easily or speedily crushed;—and the moment anything like an equality of strength between the combatants is admitted or is made obvious, the project of subduing the South becomes simply insane, and must ere long be tacitly abandoned or avowedly renounced. It is clear, too, that even if there be, or has been, such an 'anti-secession' party in the South as the Federalists believe, such a victory as that at Manassas Junction will not only diminish their number, but will crush their hopes and dissipate their courage; that, if they have been cowed and silenced hitherto, still more will they be cowed and silenced now. On the whole, therefore,—and in this we only give expression to the sentiments of all the more dispassionate and well-informed of the mercantile community,—the effect of the opening event of the campaign will be at once to make the final issue of the contest more certain, and to prevent that issue from being reached so soon as sanguine men hoped a week ago.

The influence of these conclusions on the cotton market and on our cotton prospects is apparent at a glance. Since the war must continue till the North has, in the first place, wiped out the humiliation of its late defeat, and convinced itself, in the second place, of the capacity of the South to hold its own and to make good its position; and since one of its principal instruments of warfare, and that from which it looks for the greatest results, is the strict blockade of the Southern ports,—it is obvious that our chances of receiving within any moderate time any considerable proportion of the growing crop are greatly diminished. The controversy cannot now be speedily settled. At least six months, probably twelve months, must elapse according to all seeming before the Southern ports will be again open to free intercourse with Europe. If the blockade is really made effective—and the Federal Government, we may be sure, will spare no exertion to make it so—then our usual supply of cotton from the states must be wholly or mainly foregone. We shall have to depend for the next year chiefly upon our present stock and upon our Indian resources. Under the operation of this conviction, prices which have hitherto advanced but slowly and inadequately will take a decided upward tendency, and orders to India will be sent out with much greater confidence than heretofore, and at much more liberal limits. Unusually large quantities are already on the way from that country, and from first to last we shall perhaps receive a million of bales.

Meanwhile, the pressure has as yet been little felt in our manufacturing districts. The spinners, as a rule, are unusually well stocked with the raw material—many people say as far forward as October. The expectation of an advance in price, which was certain to be considerable and might be enormous, has induced purchasers to supply themselves freely with goods and yarn; and as producers were determined not to allow their produce to accumulate, they have met the demand readily. And as they could, generally, at existing prices 'cover themselves' (as the phrase is)—that is, escape actual loss—they have gone on producing nearly at their ordinary rate. Now, however, there is the commencement of a lull in the demand; and as manufacturers are determined not to 'stock,' they will produce only as much as they can sell, and we shall soon see short time resorted to as a general measure.

Already a few mills are working only four days a week. There is no panic and little speculation: caution is the order of the day: people are resolved to 'feel their way'; and in the prevalence of this temper merchants will probably find an escape from ruinous losses and operatives a security against utter destitution and non-employment.

We must now add a few words on a subject which we have more than once considered in this journal, and on which we have been at considerable pains to arrive at all the light that is attainable—viz. the probability and the means of any material proportion of the American crop reaching us by illegitimate or circuitous channels. We are disposed to think that our prospect is rather better than it at first appeared. In the *first* place, the wild notion originally entertained by the Confederate states—that the dearth of cotton would entail such horrible suffering and ruin on the industrial populations of Europe that France and England would interfere to break the blockade, and under the influence of which they were inclined to second the Federalists in preventing its exportation—is fast giving way to saner expectations; and we are satisfied from inquiry in the quarters most concerned, that the planters and the planting states are now quite as willing and anxious to send us their cotton as we are to receive it. The sole question, therefore, now is, what is the extent and the completeness of the impediments which a hostile force can place between eager sellers and eager buyers? The United States will of course, especially since their defeat by land, proceed to render their blockading squadron as ample and efficient as they can; and they either have now or will soon have vessels enough for the purpose. But there is much inevitable *leakage* even in the strictest blockade where a large extent of coast has to be watched,—where the weather is sometimes very boisterous (especially in autumn),—and where harbours of refuge are few and not near at hand, as is the case in the Gulf of Mexico. Vessels will lie ready laden at their safe anchorage within harbour, waiting to take advantage of any favourable opportunity, which keen-eyed watchers and handy telegraphs will instantly announce to them. Storms arise, and the blockading squadron is blown off shore and obliged to run out to sea for shelter; or fogs sweep over the coast and obscure everything for miles around:—these are incidents which we have all read of in the history of every naval blockade. The merchant-ships with their valuable cargoes will seize the critical moment, and in twelve hours will be far beyond the grasp of the blockaders. Many, no doubt, will escape in this way. It is not a week since a vessel arrived in Liverpool, with the Confederate flag flying, from one of the blockaded ports (Wilmington, we believe). She had put out to sea on an evening when the Federal cruiser had left her ground on some casual errand, and had traversed the Atlantic without any interruption. That we have not already had many such instances is probably much less owing to the vigilance and efficiency of the blockading ships, than to the fact that there are scarcely any vessels in the Southern harbours (and they must go in before they can come out), and that we have already received all the cargoes they have to send us. There are now only 50 bales of cotton at sea, it is said. The whole of last year's crop has come forward, and this year's crop is not yet picked.

Again. Though the large harbours of the South are few and easily guarded, the navigable creeks are many, and very difficult to watch. Small craft, of a few hundred tons burden, can without much danger steal in and out, and run with their cargoes to Havana or some other neighbouring and neutral port, in about 30 or 40 hours;—and once there, are safe. Cuba will thus, in all likelihood, become the depôt for American cotton, which will soon find its way to England in British or Spanish or even American bottoms. The extent to which, in dark nights and in hazy weather, this contrivance may be practised with success, it is of course impossible at present to predict; but well-informed men, who know the facilities for the purpose afforded by the planting states, anticipate a considerable supply from this source. We may observe, too, in passing, that the same contrivance will do much to mitigate the expected severity of the *internal* blockade. It is almost as easy, on a long line of coast, to effect ingress as egress; and the same swift-sailing cutters which carry out cotton, will bring in wine, spirits, and coffee (which are much less bulky and more valuable articles), and, to a certain extent, clothing likewise. So that, after all, the Southern deprivation of luxuries may not be so complete as their enemies had flattered themselves they could make it, and one of their chief inducements to submission will be removed.

Thirdly. We do not anticipate any *corrupt* connivance on the part of the Federal cruisers, which would allow cotton vessels to slip through the blockade; but we do anticipate a *cunning* connivance of this sort— and on a very extensive scale. It must never be forgotten that the North want cotton even more imperiously than we do. By preventing any cotton being exported, the Northern cruisers are stopping the

mills and ruining the trade of their own manufacturers: they are cutting
their own throats. They will soon begin to reflect that they will injure
and impoverish their antagonists quite as effectually by capturing their
cotton at sea as by preventing it from putting to sea at all,—while
they will benefit themselves incomparably more. By winking or hiding
away while the valuable cargo steals out of port and then pursuing
and confiscating it, they effect three objects at once: they rob the
secessionists; they supply the Massachusetts spinners; and they put
prize-money into their own pockets. They have the fun of the chase;
they spoil the Egyptians; and they enrich the Israelites. If they were
certain of being able to capture the escaping vessels, of course it would
be far the wisest plan to allow them to run out;—if they have a very
high *probability* of capturing them, it might still on the whole be a
'smart' dodge and a profitable speculation;—and we may be very sure
that their self-confidence will go far in their minds to represent a
chance as a certainty. We cannot but think there will be much done in
this way. Some will be captured: some will escape:—in any case, our
market will be relieved and supplied. What escapes will come to
Liverpool; what is taken will go to Boston or New York; but all will
be available for the consumption of the world.

Lastly. We share to a considerable extent the instinctive conviction
of the Lancashire merchants and manufacturers, that an article grown
by an eager seller and consumed by an eager buyer *will* find its way
from the one to the other, in spite of all hostile barriers and prohibi-
tions. The question is after all one of degree—and of price. We must
remember that the same cause—the blockade—which raises cotton so
much in Liverpool and Havre, lowers it as much in New Orleans and
Mobile. The export being prevented and there being no buyers, cotton
becomes 'a drug' in the planting states, at the very moment when it is
becoming as precious as gold in England;—and when the same article
is worth *twelve pence* on one side of the water, and *six cents* on the
other, while the freight is not *two cents*, the loss of every other cargo
to the adventurous merchant who determined to run the gauntlet
through the blockading squadron would still leave him a handsome
profit on the entire transaction. With such a prospect before him,—to
say nothing of the allurement of the gambling character of such a trade
to the speculative man,—we may be perfectly sure that the venture
will be made, and made on a large scale;—and before long the insur-
ance offices will begin to take cognisance of such transactions.

What *may* be in America[1]

IT is especially important for merchants, the success or failure of whose commercial enterprises so much depends on the correctness of the estimate they form of future contingencies, to consider and be prepared for *any* contingency which is not absolutely improbable. Now, in such a case as America presents to us at this moment, no result that is not impossible can be said to be improbable. There, perhaps, never was a conjuncture of such magnitude in which it was so hopeless to predict the direction which events are likely to take. The materials on which to form a rational guess are extraordinarily scanty and uncertain. It is not so much that *we* do not know the Americans, as that the Americans do not know themselves. From first to last in this matter, they have been singularly at fault in their conjectures and prophecies: we, on this side of the water, have, hitherto at least, been much nearer the truth in the expectations which we entertained.

There is nothing that should surprise us in this uncertainty, when we give the matter a little dispassionate consideration. The fact is, the Americans are *a wholly untried people*;—and till people have been tried, no one can pretend to say what they are, or what under any given circumstances they will do. They have never been *tested* by any great difficulty, any great danger, any great calamity: they have never been called upon for any sustained effort, any serious sacrifices, any prolonged endurance. They do not know, therefore,—nor do we— the possible reach of their virtues and their powers, nor the possible range of their vices and their weaknesses. They have never yet faced a really formidable foe. It will astonish and disgust them to be told this; but it is the simple truth. No one who reads the details of the revolution by which they won their independence, while full of admiration for their pluck and energy, fails to be utterly amazed at their success. The indescribable imbecility of their enemies was yet more wonderful than their own vigour. Against any English army and any English

[1] This article was first published in *The Economist* for August 17 1861, Volume XIX, pp. 897–8.

ministry that have existed since the days of Lord North, they would not have had the shadow of a chance—as every one except themselves is now perfectly aware. And, moreover (be it said in passing), they are not what they were then; both their institutions and their men have degenerated frightfully; their *morale* has gone down almost as fast and as far as their power and prosperity have increased. In the short war of 1812, they fought bravely—behind walls and at sea; but the great feat of Andrew Jackson—for which they made him a hero and a president—was defending a walled city, made almost impregnable by cotton bags and riflemen, against an inadequately-provided invading force lodged in an unhealthy swamp. All their other contests have been against naked Indians and degenerate and undisciplined Mexicans: these were *raids* rather than wars, and though accompanied by individual risk, never involved any serious danger of discomfiture. Therefore we are undoubtedly warranted in saying—and we say it without wishing to throw the slightest slur on American prowess and courage—that till now neither Northerners nor Southerners have ever encountered a capable enemy or a real peril; and how they will behave in the face of such no man can foresee. They have gained their ends hitherto not by fighting but by bullying; they have bullied every nation in turn;—and their success in this sort of warfare has not only enormously enhanced their own conceptions of their military prowess, but has entirely blinded them as to the flimsy and *unproved* foundation upon which these conceptions rest. No one doubts that a regular army of Americans, well disciplined and well officered, would fight as bravely and as skilfully as any in the world; but how American volunteers will fight, hastily got together, utterly unaccustomed to obedience, without experience, and without confidence either in their officers or in each other, no one can venture to predict;—and the panic at Manassas Gap, and the subsequent behaviour of the defeated troops, warrant the very worst and most disrespectful misgivings on this head.

We are in equal uncertainty as to American statesmen and American institutions. They have never been tried in a storm before, and no one can tell how they will stand the strain. The leaders in Washington's time were gentlemen and men of education. The institutions in Washington's time were free, but not democratic. Since that the time country has gone through a course of unexampled and uninterrupted prosperity—demoralising assuredly, though not enervating. Laws and manners have changed to a degree which few persons have yet fully realised. The constitution has become an almost unmitigated *ochlocracy*. The masses are everywhere omnipotent; and the masses in most parts are only half educated, and in many parts are as ignorant as those of Europe and far more ruffianly. The men of thoughtful minds and lofty purpose, the men of noble sentiments and stainless honour, have retired from public life; and, naturally enough, as the work of politics became dirtier and rougher, have left it to dirtier and rougher men. The consequence, as every one is too well aware, and as even Americans themselves have repeated *usque ad nauseam*, has been that the rulers and legislators of the United States are, almost without exception, either the vulgarer and shallower men of the nation who share the popular faults and passions, or cleverer minds who flatter and obey them without sharing them—unworthy in the one case intellectually, unworthier still, in the other, from voluntary moral degradation. Now, how can such men be expected to meet a crisis like the present—a crisis which might try the ablest and the noblest spirits that ever directed the fortunes of a great country? How can men who have risen to power by low means be expected to use power for lofty purposes? How can men who are where they are because they have truckled and temporised and cajoled and cringed and fawned upon the mob, now coerce that mob to its duty, or overawe it into obedience and order? Or how can men who are corrupt, or are believed to be so—or both— preach patriotism and purity and patient endurance and the noble spirit of self-sacrifice to a sneering and unbelieving crowd?—or expect a hearing if they do? Moral courage is more needed at Washington now than any other political virtue—the moral courage to speak unpopular truths, to face popular rage, and to resist popular delusions;—and when was such courage the common virtue of democracies?—and where, in this wide world, has this virtue, rare everywhere, been so utterly trampled out as in America?

Lastly, we know the real qualities of the American people as imperfectly as those of their army and their statesmen. That is, we do not know how they will come out under trial. There is plenty of sterling stuff in them, we may be sure, for they come of a good stock; but, on the other hand, their career has not been of a nature to develop the virtues most needed on an occasion like the present,—*viz.*, fortitude under reverses, submission to needful discipline, and loyal trust in the men who are to lead them; and their whole history as well as their recent conduct has displayed the very opposite characteristics. It would be idle to deny that the behaviour of the people on the occasion of the defeat at Manassas Junction, and since that discreditable occurrence, has given a great shock to the confidence of those who had formed high expectations of Northern capacity and vigour. There has been apparently an entire absence of all sense of shame and mortification, which is absolutely incomprehensible,—a sort of perverse pride in the very magnitude of their disaster and disgrace, combined with the usual and very ominous disposition to lay all the blame on their chiefs and their officers, and to take none upon themselves. The patriotism of the volunteers seems to bear an inverse ratio to their bluster. Without in any way wishing to detract from the extraordinary faculty which the Northern Americans have always shown for recovering and retrieving misfortune, for prompt and energetic organisation, and for ready lavishing of their immense resources,—the events of the last few weeks have begot a fear that the rottenness of the country in all that relates to administration and to political virtue has spread deeper and wider than has yet been believed. So much so that a doubt is beginning to be generally expressed whether there is confidence enough left in the heart of the people to induce them to trust sufficient power in the hands of any public man or of any administration;—whether even in the gravest crisis a dictator could be found, or would be appointed, or would be obeyed if appointed;—whether the political corruption of which every one is conscious in himself, and which every one attributes to his neighbour, has not utterly destroyed the very sources of that mutual faith and loyalty without which the vastest resources are unavailing because no one will be suffered to wield them; and finally, whether the habit of what is there called self-government, but what we should call Lynch law, mob interference, lawless wilfulness, and reckless self-assertion, has not incapacitated the people for that generous, rational, legitimate obedience which is the saving virtue of armies and of nations in the hour of crisis.

Considering all these things, we are strongly impressed with the conviction that there is no degree of incapacity, confusion, feebleness, mismanagement, and thorough imbecility on the part of the Government at Washington, which is not *upon the cards*. We do not say it is probable. We should deeply grieve, for the honour of our common ancestry, to see it. But it would not surprise us; and we think that all men practically concerned ought to be prepared for it as one of the not improbable eventualities of the conjuncture. It is nearly certain that if the secessionist general had known how complete was the demoralisation of the Federal army after their disaster, and had pressed on to Washington, he might have seized the capital (and perhaps the cabinet as well), and ended the war at a stroke. Almost equally certain it is that a second victory as complete, and following soon enough upon the first, will so disgust and dishearten the shouters for the Union that the contest will be abandoned on the instant. The people will then refuse to give any more supplies to a government which they charge with incompetency or with treachery. The army will refuse to fight under generals whose every movement they will denounce and whose heads they will demand. The party adverse to the war—always far more numerous in the North than the Unionist party in the South—will raise their voices and insist upon terms of accommodation;—and some day, with scarcely any notice, we may receive tidings that an armistice has been agreed upon and preliminaries of peace have been signed.

Observe: we do not say that so speedy and so ignominious a result to all the magnificent boasts and all the ferocious bluster of the Federalists is *probable*; but no one can say that it is impossible. No one, moreover, can fail to see the causes which, unless powerfully counteracted, may any moment bring it about. The last accounts from America, public and private, contain two indications of the unsoundness of the state of things which are by no means without significance. One of the most respectable of the Republican journals has a paragraph —bold enough, when we consider the conjuncture at which it appeared —affirming in plain terms that the war clamour in the North is greatly swelled and strengthened by the *contractors*, jobbing politicians and others, who are realising enormous plunder (as such men always can at such times) out of the sudden demands of the executive for stores and works,—an assertion too probable in itself to need any confirmation. At the same time, we learn from a source which we can fully trust, that at New York a petition was being got up and was in process of signature by some of the most influential inhabitants, urging on the Government at Washington more pacific and conciliatory courses. *The police* heard of it:—entered the office where the sheets were lying for signature, and *destroyed them all*! When to these facts we add others equally certain, and more generally known; *viz.*, that the merchants and manufacturers of the North are suffering severely—far more than has been publicly admitted—from the lack both of their raw material and of their usual customers;—that the moneyed men of New York are beginning to feel uneasy at the enormous and wasteful demands upon their coffers;—that the more sober and dispassionate thinkers—few perhaps, and silent amid the uproar, but neither extinguished nor uninfluential—are beginning to reflect and to remind others that after all the South are only fighting for that right to choose their own government and their own co-mates which consistent democrats can deny to no people, and which despots could not withhold from eight millions;—and, lastly, that all are now conscious that no really noble or soul-stirring cause is in any way at issue, since the abolition sentiment has nothing to do with the quarrel, and the protection tariff a great deal, and the mere lust of dominion and of empire more than either;—when we sum up all these considerations, we have influences enough in operation to render a sudden collapse of the Washington Government and the Federal war a very possible and a not very improbable event.

In any case, only one thing can, it appears to us, either effectually restore the fortunes or redeem the reputation of the North;—and that is such a general estimate, such a pervading and overwhelming conviction, of the gravity of the crisis and the greatness of the stake, as shall at once induce the best men of the country to offer themselves as chiefs, and the people to accept them and to trust them, to endow them with the necessary powers and to obey them with unswerving devotion. But the signs of any such saving and redeeming sentiment are yet to seek.

To be added to these considerations is the not improbable contingency of a financial scarcity. The treasury notes are already at a discount—the Western states do not seem ready to pay taxes—the propositions respecting the tariff are a mass of confusion—the proposed income tax bill is as yet indefinite and conjectural—the financial prospects of the Northern states in Europe are indefinitely impaired by the battle at Manassas Junction and by its possible consequences. It seems impossible that such a pecuniary [weakness?] should not aggravate such a political position.

The Practical Operation of the American Constitution at the Present Extreme Crisis [1]

THE civil war between what were once the United States of America has excited an interest, not merely in England, but also throughout the civilised world, which has not been approached since the close of the great struggle of the revolted colonies with their mother country. The sudden outbreak of latent hatreds, the astounding rapidity of important events, were sure to excite earnest and attentive observation.

But sufficient attention has not been paid to the peculiar working of the American Constitution at the critical instant of the whole federal history. Every student of that remarkable document has been impressed with its extreme elaboration. Its primitive principle is the simple one of pure democracy, but in its details there is a singular accumulation of structural refinement and artificial combination. It has always been doubted whether the union of such a violent principle to such delicate machinery would be fitted for the exciting scenes and shifting requirements of a great crisis. The crisis has come, and what has been the result?

We fear it must be said that the result has been an unfavourable one. We do not speak now of the ultimate ending of the present struggle. We are never anxious to be prophets: we know too well the difficulty and complexity even in affairs reputed simple, and we certainly will not prophesy the issue of unprecedented and unexpected events. We are simply analysing the past. We only say that at the crisis of American history the peculiarities of the American Constitution have not corresponded to the hopes and wishes of its wise and well-meaning framers, but have for the most part been purely pernicious.

The decisive test of real excellence in a political constitution at a great crisis is its tendency to place in power the statesmen of the

---

[1] This article was first published in *The Economist* for June 1 1861, Volume XIX, pp. 591–3.

country best fitted to meet it, and its further tendency to give them every possible help and attainable aid in the arduous enterprise of meeting it. Has the American Constitution done this? It would be hardly too much to say that it has done the very contrary; that it has placed in power the very men least fitted to cope with the present emergency; and that it has encumbered them with great accessory difficulties while they were coping with it.

At the very outset of the quarrel the Constitution occasioned a needless danger. The South threatened to secede because Mr. Lincoln had been elected President. Under almost any other free Constitution which has ever existed, and certainly under very good free Constitution, the executive authority whose function it was to oppose secession would have been placed exclusively in the hands of those who were desirous so to oppose it. At an instant of violent irritation the dissentient minority were anxious to break loose from the control of the majority. The majority were at that time, whatever may be the case now, by no means fanatical or irritated or overbearing. They wished to preserve the Union, and under a well-framed Constitution that would have had the power of using the force of the state to preserve the state. But not so under the American Constitution as practically worked. An artificial arrangement prolongs the reign of each president many months after the election of his successor. In consequence the executive authority was, during a considerable and critical interval, in the hands of those who by birth, habit, and sympathy were leagued with the dissentient minority. Mr. Buchanan and his ministers had always been attached to the party of the South, and were the last persons to act decisively against it. It is the opinion of many well-informed persons that there was a sufficient Unionist party in several of the seceding states to have prevented the present movement there if the Federal Government had acted with vigour and celerity. And, whether this be so or not, it remains a singular defect in the working of the American Constitution that it gave power at the decisive moment to those least likely to use that power well,—that just when a revolt was impending, it placed the whole executive influence and the whole military force in the unfettered hands of the political associates of the revolters.

Nor does the accession of Mr. Lincoln place the executive power precisely where we should wish to see it. At a crisis such as America has never before seen, and as it is not, perhaps, probable she will see again, the executive authority should be in the hands of one of the most tried, trusted, and experienced statesmen of the nation. Mr. Lincoln is a nearly unknown man—who has been but little heard of—who has had little experience—who may have nerve and judgment, or may not have them—whose character, both moral and intellectual, is an unknown quantity—who must, from his previous life and defective education, be wanting in the liberal acquirements and mental training which are principal elements of an enlarged statesmanship. Nor is it true to say that the American *people* are to blame for this—that they chose Mr. Lincoln, and must endure the pernicious results. The *Constitution* is as much to blame as the people, probably even more so. The framers were wisely and warmly attached to the principles of liberty, and, like all such persons, were extremely anxious to guard against momentary gusts of popular opinion. They were especially desirous that the President to whom they were intrusting vast power should be the representative, not of a small section of the community, but of a really predominant part of it. Accordingly, they not only established a system of double election, in the hope that the 'electoral college' (of which the electors were chosen in certain proportions by each state) would exercise a real discretion in the choice of president, and be some check on popular ignorance and low violence, but they likewise provided that an absolute majority of that 'electoral college' (a majority, that is, greater than one-half of the whole) should give their votes for the elected candidate. In any other event the election was to be void, and the right of choice lapsed in a peculiar and complicated way. The effect has been painfully different from the design. In reality, the 'electoral college' exercises no choice: every member of it is selected by the primitive constituency *because* he will vote for a certain presidential candidate (for Mr. Lincoln or Mr. Douglas, and so on), and he does nothing but vote accordingly. The provision requiring the consent of an absolute majority has had a still worse effect; it has not been futile, for it has been pernicious. It has made it very difficult to secure *any* election. A nation tends to split into many sections, and each section has its leader; each section has some one whom it would desire more than any one else to see at the head of the state when the great prize of that high place is put up for immediate competition. Still more, every section has its peculiar enmities and jealousies; every man of the least mark is sure to say something or to do something which will offend some large class; if he has had a long public life, probably he will have alienated many. In consequence it is only by a long previous deliberation and consultation that any presidential election can ever be secured. If every one stood who pleased, and every one voted for whom he pleased, there would be no election at all. In practice each party selects at a preliminary caucus the most unexceptionable member whom they can find; they place various names in a complicated and successive 'ballot,' and it is not until some one of them gains a commanding majority that the party candidate is selected. Naturally this very unexceptionable person is one of the most obscure members of the whole party: a very commonplace, ordinary person. He is almost always one of the lowest, the least known member of the party; and out of the party candidates so nominated the President is chosen. If the wit of man had devised a system specially adapted to bring to the head of affairs an incompetent man at a pressing crisis, it could not have devised one more fit; it would not probably have devised one as fit.

And when Mr. Lincoln was elected, the practical working of the American Constitution prevented him from giving due attention to the arduous difficulties of the terrible position in which he was placed,—the most terrible position in which an inexperienced politician ever has been placed,—and compelled him to occupy himself with petty details of patronage, which in ordinary times would have been tedious, and which under a good Constitution would have been unnecessary. The effect of the periodical election of the President has been to make everything turn upon that election. Everything is regarded with a view to that:—great questions, public duties, political efficiency, are secondary to that. The whole patronage of the country is turned into one great bribe. After each election at which a new party is victorious, every political office, large and small, changes hands: the President who comes in turns out all the friends of his predecessor, and brings in all the friends he has secured by previous hopes and previous promises. The labour of this change of offices is immense. Mr. Lincoln is described by eye-witnesses as having been overwhelmed and bowed down by the million minute difficulties which such a system inevitably causes, by the detestable necessity of deciding on the respective fitness of five thousand men for five hundred postmasters' places, by the nauseous accumulation of low detail with which he was burdened just when the very existence of the state was tottering.

Even now the Constitution of the United States is producing great evil. A president, especially a new, an untried, and comparatively untrained politician like Mr. Lincoln, ought to be able to call to his aid a popular assembly, animated by all the feelings which a great crisis calls forth in a great people, and containing all the wisdom which the whole nation can collect to meet that crisis. Mr. Lincoln has no such power. He can, it is true, convene an extraordinary session of the existing Congress; but that Congress was elected years since, when no such crisis as the present was ever thought of, when any one who dreamed of it would have been considered to be mad, when other hopes, other fears, and other thoughts absorbed the public mind. Such a Congress would be worse than useless as a counsellor, and might even be very dangerous as a restraint or as an opponent. Mr. Lincoln is doubtless right in naming a distant day for its session. But what a commentary is it on the working of a political Constitution, that it compels an inferior, unknown, untried, and tired man to decide upon the national difficulties without aid and without control.

The moral is a plain one. The Constitution of the United States was framed upon a vicious principle. The framers were anxious to resist the force of democracy—to control its fury and restrain its outbursts. They either could not or did not take the one effectual means of so doing; they did not place the substantial power in the hands of men of education and of property. They hoped to control the democracy by paper checks and constitutional devices. The history we have sketched evinces the result; it shows that these checks have produced unanticipated, incalculable, and fatal evil, but have not attained the beneficial end for which they were selected. They may have ruined the Union, but they have not controlled the democracy.

The American Constitution at the Present Crisis[1]

IT is not at first easy for an ordinary Englishman to appreciate adequately the favourite arguments which the most cultivated and best American writers use at the present juncture. It seems to him that they are arguments befitting lawyers, not arguments befitting statesmen. They appear only to prove that a certain written document, called the Constitution of the United States, expressly forbids the conduct which the Southern states are consistently pursuing, and that therefore such conduct is culpable as well as illegal. Very few Englishmen will deny either the premiss or the conclusion considered in themselves. It is certain that the Constitution does forbid what the slave states are doing; it is equally certain, that their policy is as mean, as unjustifiable, and every way as discreditable, as was ever pursued by any public bodies equally powerful and equally cultivated. But nevertheless an argument from the mere letter of a written constitution will hardly convince any Englishman. He knows that all written documents must be very meagre; that the best of them must often be unsatisfactory; that most of them contain many errors; that the best of them are remarkable for strange omissions; that all of them will fail utterly when applied to a state of things different from any which its authors ever imagined. The complexity of politics is thoroughly comprehended by every Englishman—the complexity of our history has engraved it on our mind; the complexity of our polity is a daily memento of it—and no one in England will be much impressed by any arguments which tacitly assume that the limited clauses of an old state-paper can provide for all coming cases, and for ever regulate the future.

It is worth while, however, to examine the American Constitution at the present juncture. No remarkable aspect of the great events which are occurring among our nearest national kindred and our most important trading connexions in our own times, can be wisely

[1] 'Causes of the Civil War in America,' by J. Lothrop Motley Manwaring. This essay was first published in the *National Review* for October 1861, Volume XIII, pp. 465–93.

neglected; and it will be easy to show that the Constitution of the United States is now failing from the necessary consequence of an inherent ineradicable defect; that more than one of its thoughtful framers perceived that it must fail under similar circumstances; and that the irremediable results of this latent defect have been aggravated partly by the corruptions which the Constitution has contracted in the progress of time, and yet more by certain elaborate provisions which were believed to be the best attainable safeguards against analogous dangers and difficulties.

Like most of the great products of the Anglo-Saxon race, the American Constitution was the result of a pressing necessity, and was a compromise between two extreme plans for meeting that necessity. It was framed in a time of gloom and confusion. The 'revolted colonies,' as Englishmen then called them, had been successful in their revolt; but they had been successful in nothing else. They had thrown off the yoke of the English Government; but they had founded no efficient or solid government of their own. They had been united by a temporary common sentiment—by a common antipathy to the interference of the mother country; but the binding efficacy of that feeling ceased when their independence of the mother country had been definitely recognised. Nor was there any other strong bond of union which could supply its place. The American colonies had been founded by very different kinds of persons, at very different periods of English history. They had respectively taken the impress of the class of Englishmen who had framed them: Virginia had the mark of the aristocratic class; Massachusetts of the Puritan; Pennsylvania of the Quakers. The modern colonies of England are of a single type; they are founded by a single class, from a single motive. Those who now leave England are, with some exceptions, but still for the most part and as a rule, a rough and energetic race, who feel that they cannot earn as much money as they wish in England, and who hope and believe that they will be able to earn that money elsewhere. They are driven from home by the want of a satisfactory subsistence, and that subsistence is all they care or seek to find elsewhere. To every other class but this, England is too pleasant a residence for them to dream of leaving it for the antipodes. With our early colonies it was otherwise. When they were founded, England was a very unpleasant place for very many people. As long as the now-balanced structure of our composite society was in the process of formation, one class obtained a temporary ascendency at one time, and another class at another time. At each period they made England an uncomfortable place of residence for all who did not coincide in their notions of politics, and who would not subscribe to their tenets of religion. At such periods the dissident class threw off a swarm to settle in America; and thus our old colonies were first formed.

No one can be surprised that communities with such a beginning should have acquired strong antipathies to one another. Even at the present day, the antipathy of the inhabitants of South Carolina to the people of Boston, the dislike of Kentuckians to New Yorkers, has surprised attentive observers. But when their independence was first recognised, such feelings were infinitely more intense. The original founders of the colonies had hated one another at home. Those colonies were near neighbours in a rude country, and the occasional collision of petty interests had kept alive the original antipathy of each class to its antagonistic class, of each sect to its antagonistic sect. M. de Tocqueville remarked, that even in his time there was no national patriotism in America, but only a state patriotism; and though, in 1833, this remark was perhaps exaggerated, it would have been, fifty years before, only the literal expression of an indisputable fact. The name 'American' had scarcely as yet any political signification—it was a 'geographical expression'.

Grave practical difficulties of detail, too, oppressed the new community. The war with England had been commenced by a body calling itself a Congress, but very different from the elaborate and composite body which we now know by that name. It was a simple committee of delegates from the different states, which could recommend to those states whatever military measures it thought advisable, but had no greater power or function whatever. It was in no sense a government. It had no coercive jurisdiction, could compel nothing, and enforce nothing. It was an advising council, which had no resources of its own, and could only rely on its dignified position, and the obvious necessity of united opposition to the common enemy. But, as might be anticipated, so frail an organisation was entirely inadequate to the rough purposes of revolutionary warfare. It could not meet a pressing difficulty; and it did not meet it. It worked well when it was not wanted—when all the states were unanimous; but it was insufficient when the states began to disagree—at the very moment for which it was required.

The responsible leaders of the revolutionary struggle felt the necessity of a closer bond; and in March, 1781, nearly five years after the Declaration of Independence, the first real American Government was formed. It was called the Confederation, and was very simple in its structure. There was no complicated apparatus of President and Vice-president, such as we are now familiar with; no Supreme Court, no House of Representatives. The Confederation rather resembled what existed previously than what exists at present. There was, as before, a committee of delegates from the different states, and there was nothing else: this was the whole government; but this was not as before, simply a committee with powers of recommendation. It could by its own authority make peace and war, establish armies, contract debts, coin money, issue a paper currency, and send ambassadors to foreign nations. It could in theory, and according to its letter, perform all the ordinary acts and functions of sovereignty. It did, in fact, perform the greatest act of sovereignty, as a lawyer would reckon it, that could be conceived. By signing a peace with England, it secured its own existence. Being a loose aggregate of revolted colonies, it obtained a recognition by the mother country against which these colonies had revolted. In the face of Europe, and in the face of England more especially, it maintained the appearance of an organised, regular, and adequate government.

It really was, however, very inadequate. Some one has said that the true way to test the practical operation of any constitution is to ask, 'How do you get money under it?' This is certainly an American mode of testing a polity, and according to this criterion the 'perpetual Confederation' was an egregious failure. 'You could not get dollars by means of it at all.' The national Congress could incur liabilities, but it could not impose taxation. It could, as we have explained, raise an army, contract a debt, issue a credit currency; but it could not of itself, and by its own authority, levy a penny. The states had retained in their own hands the exclusive power of imposing taxes. Congress could only require the several states to find certain quotas of money, and in the event of their not finding them could go to war with them. As a theorist would anticipate, the simplest alternative happened. The states did not find the money, and the Congress did not go to war with them. The debts of the Union were undischarged; the soldiers, even the French soldiers, who had achieved its independence, were unpaid; and the financial conditions of the treaty of independence with England were unfulfilled. Congress could do nothing, and the states would do nothing. Other smaller difficulties, too, were accumulating. The large unoccupied territory of the American continent required care; England was irritated at the non-completion or the infraction of several of the articles of peace; petty quarrels between the states on vexing minutiæ were constantly beginning, and were rarely ending. The impotence of Congress was becoming proverbial, and the entire country was discouraged. In the correspondence of Washington and those around him it is evident that they asked themselves with doubt and despondency, 'After all, will America be a nation?'

Two schemes floated in the public mind for remedying these evils. It was the opinion of some of the wisest American statesmen, and especially, of Hamilton, the greatest political philosopher among them, that it would be better to establish an omnipotent federal government, which should be to America what the English government was to England, which should have the full legislative, the full executive, the full judicial power which a sovereign government possesses in ordinary states.*

* As Hamilton's plan is not easily accessible in this country, and may have some interest at the present moment, when some persons, at least, are desirous of attempting a similar experiment, we give it at length.

'The following paper was read by Colonel Hamilton, as containing his ideas of a suitable plan of government for the United States.

'1. The supreme legislative power of the United States of America to be vested in two distinct bodies of men, the one to be called the assembly, the other the senate, who, together, shall form the legislature of the United States, with power to pass all laws whatsoever, subject to the negative hereafter mentioned.

'2. The assembly to consist of persons elected by the people, to serve for three years.

'3. The senate to consist of persons elected to serve during good behaviour; their election to be made by electors chosen for that purpose by the people. In order to do this, the states to be divided into election districts. On the death, removal, or resignation of any senator, his place to be filled out of the district from which he came.

'4. The supreme executive authority of the United States to be vested in a governor, to be elected to serve during good behaviour. His election to be made by electors chosen by electors, chosen by the people, in the election districts aforesaid. His authorities and functions to be as follows:—

'To have a negative upon all laws about to be passed, and the execution of all laws passed; to have the entire direction of war, when authorised, or begun; to have, with the advice and approbation of the senate, the power of making all treaties; to have the sole appointment of the heads or chief officers of the departments of finance, war, and foreign affairs; to have the nomination of all other officers (ambassadors to foreign nations included) subject to the approbation or rejection of the senate; to have the power of pardoning all offences, except treason, which he shall not pardon without the approbation of the senate.

'5. On the death, resignation, or removal of the governor, his authorities to be exercised by the president of the senate, until a successor be appointed.

'6. The senate to have the sole power of declaring war; the power of advising and approving all treaties; the power of approving or rejecting all appointments of officers, except the heads or chiefs of the departments of finance, war, and foreign affairs.

Hamilton proposed that the 'supreme legislative power of the United States should be vested in two distinct bodies of men,' who should have power to pass all laws whatever, subject to a veto in a governor or first magistrate. For the choice of the members of these bodies, he would have divided the country into electoral districts, and no state as such would have elected a single representative to the united legislature, or have been capable of any function or voice in the Constitution of the Union. 'All laws of the particular states contrary to the Constitution of the Union or laws of the United States were to be utterly void.' And 'the better to prevent such laws being passed, the governor or president of each state' was to be appointed by the general government, was to have a negative upon all laws 'about to be passed therein'. No state was to have any forces, land or naval; and the militia of all the states were to be under the exclusive direction of the general government of the United States, which alone was to appoint and commission their officers. In practice this scheme would have reduced the existing states to the condition of mere municipalities; they would have retained extensive powers of interior regulation, but they would have lost all the higher functions of government, all control over any matters not exclusively their own; they would have continued to be, so to say, county boards for county matters, but they would have had no share in the sovereign direction of general affairs. They would have been as restricted, as isolated as the corporations of Liverpool and Bristol are under the Constitution of England.

'7. The supreme judicial authority of the United States to be vested in judges, to hold their offices during good behaviour, with adequate and permanent salaries. This court to have original jurisdiction in all causes of capture, and an appellative jurisdiction in all causes in which the revenues of the general government, or the citizens of foreign nations, are concerned.

'8. The legislature of the United States to have power to institute courts in each state, for the determination of all matters of general concern.

'9. The governors, senators, and all officers of the United States to be liable to impeachment for mal and corrupt conduct; and, upon conviction, to be removed from office, and disqualified from holding any place of trust or profit. All impeachments to be tried by a court to consist of the chief, or senior judge of the superior court of law in each state; provided that such judge hold his place during good behaviour, and have a permanent salary.

'10. All laws of the particular states contrary to the constitution or laws of the United States to be utterly void. And the better to prevent such laws being passed, the governor or president of each state shall be appointed by the general government, and shall have a negative upon the laws about to be passed in the state of which he is governor, or president.

'11. No state to have any forces, land or naval; and the militia of all the states to be under the sole and exclusive direction of the United States; the officers of which to be appointed and commissioned by them.'

A theorist would perhaps be inclined to regret that some such plan as that of Hamilton was not eventually chosen. At the present moment political speculators in England are singularly inclined to schemes of political unity. The striking example of Italy has given a natural stimulus to them. We have seen a great nation which had long been divided combine into what, we hope, will be a permanent state at the bidding of a few able and active men, and, as it seems to the many, by a kind of political enchantment. The change, when regarded from a distance, has appeared so easy, that we underrate its real difficulties, and are inclined to erect one of the most exceptional events in history into an ordinary precedent and example. But the state of America eighty years since may easily show us why such events have been rare in history; why locality has been called an instinct in the human mind; why large states have almost always been produced by the constraining vigour of some single conquering power. Each of the states of North America was a little commonwealth, with a vigorous political life. Each one of them had its ministry, its opposition, its elections, its local questions; each had its own political atmosphere, each its peculiar ambitions. Even if the different states had been well disposed to one another, it would have been difficult to induce all of them—especially to induce the smaller among them—to give up this local political animation. The Italian states seem to have relinquished it; but, in truth, they had little to relinquish. They were despotically governed. None of them had within their own boundaries that vast accumulation of ideas and sentiments and hopes, of love and hatred, which we call a 'political life'. The best men in Tuscany were not sacrificing a cherished career or an accustomed existence in favouring the expulsion of the Grand Duke; for so long as he remained they had no influence. After his expulsion the question of national unity or of local division could be considered fairly and impartially. It was not so in America: there were in every one of the states men who must have relinquished evident power, attainable proximate ambition—the dearest of ambitions, the power of governing the persons whom they had known all their lives, and with whom they had all their lives been in actual political competition—for the sake of an unknown 'general government'; which was an abstraction which could have excited no living attachment, in which but a very few could take a prominent or gratifying share. Nor, as we have explained, were the different states mutually well disposed. The differences of their origin still embittered, and long seemed likely to embitter, the local squabbles of years. The saying of the Swiss antifederalist, 'My shirt is dearer to me than my coat!' was the animating spirit of nine-tenths of North America. The little state of Delaware refused even to consider the abolition of the fifth article of the Confederation, which preserved the separate existence of the primitive equality of the separate states by enacting that each should have one vote only. The plan of Hamilton could not be carried, and he was too wise a statesman to regard it as much better than a tempting dream.

The second extreme suggestion for amending the 'perpetual Confederation' would have been equivalent in practice to a continuance of that Confederation very much as it was. Its theoretical letter proposed indeed to give additional powers to the central Congress, but the states were to be still the component elements in the constitution. The Congress was still to have no other power than that of requiring from these states what money it needed. It would still be compelled to declare war against them if that money was in arrear. It would still have been in the condition graphically delineated by a contemporary statesman: 'By this political compact the United States in congress have exclusive power for the following purposes without being able to execute one of them. They may make and conclude treaties; but can only recommend the observance of them. They may appoint ambassadors; but cannot defray even the expenses of their tables. They may borrow money in their own name on the faith of the Union; but cannot pay a dollar. They may coin money; but they cannot purchase an ounce of bullion. They may make war, and determine what number of troops are necessary, but cannot raise a single soldier. In short, they may declare everything, but do nothing.' Thus the second suggestion for remedying the pressing evils of America was as inefficient as the first had been impracticable.

The selected Constitution was a mean between the two. As the state governments could not be abolished, and could not be entirely divested of their sovereign rights, a new government was created, superior to them in certain specified matters, and having independent means of action with reference to those matters, but in all other things leaving their previous functions unrestricted, and their actual authority unimpaired. By the active Constitution the central Congress has the right of imposing certain specified revenues, and the power of collecting them throughout each state by officers of its exclusive appointment.

It has, as under the Confederation, the power of making peace and proclaiming war—of engaging soldiers and contracting debts; but it now has likewise a power of collecting a revenue to remunerate those soldiers, and to pay those debts by its own authority, and without the consent of any subordinate body. It has not now to require obedience from the states in their corporate capacity, but to compel the obedience of individuals throughout those states in their natural isolation, and according to the ordinary custom of governments.

We can now understand the answer of an American architect who was asked the difference between a federation and union. 'Why,' he said, 'a federation is a union with a top to it.' There is, in the United States, not simply an assemblage of individual sovereign states, but also a super-sovereign state, which has its officers side by side with theirs, its revenue side by side with theirs, its law-courts side by side with theirs, its authority on a limited number of enumerated points superior even to theirs. No political invention has been more praised than this one. It has been truly described as the most valuable addition to the resources of political philosophy ever made by professed constitution-makers. Greater things have grown up among great nations; studious thinkers have speculated on better devices; but nothing so remarkable was perhaps ever struck out on the impulse of the moment by persons actually charged with the practical duty of making a constitution. American writers are naturally proud of it; and it would be easy to collect from European writers of eminence an imposing series of encomiums upon its excellence.

Yet now that we have before us the pointed illustration of recent events, it is not difficult to see that such an institution is only adapted to circumstances exceptionally favourable, and that under a very probable train of circumstances it must fail from inherent defect. It is essentially a collection of *imperia in imperio*. It rather displays than conceals the grave disadvantages which have made that name so very unpopular. Each state is a subordinate republic, and yet the entire Union is but a single republic. Each state is in some sense a centre of disunion. Each state attracts to itself a share of political attachment, has separate interests, real or supposed, has a separate set of public men anxious to increase its importance—upon which their own depends,—anxious to weaken the power of the united government, by which theirs is overshadowed. At every critical period the sinister influence of the *imperium in imperio* will be felt; at every such period the cry of each subordinate aggregate will be, 'Our interest are threatened, our authority diminished, our rights attacked.'

A presidential election is the very event of all others to excite these dangerous sentiments. It places the entire policy of the Union upon a single hazard. A particular moment is selected when the ruler for a term of years is to be chosen. That ruler has very substantial power of various kinds; he has immense patronage, a legislative veto, great executive authority, and, what is yet more to the present purpose, he has a supreme position in society, which indefinitely attracts his popular choice, and indefinitely aggravates the intensity of the canvass. A homogeneous and simple state, with no subordinate rivals within its frontiers, might well fear to encounter such a struggle. What, then, must be the certain result in a federal union whenever a large minority of the states should consider their rights and their interests to be identified with the election or with the rejection of any one presidential candidate? What can we anticipate when the greatest dividing force, the overt choice of a supreme ruler, after canvass and struggle and controversy, is applied to the most separable of political communities, —to a disjointed aggregate of states, whose local importance has been legally fostered, whose separate existence has been heedfully cherished, whose political vitality is older and more powerful than the bond of constitutional union? Surely, according to every canon of probability, we must confidently anticipate a separation whenever the sinister interest of a large and unconquerable section of the states shall be attacked, or be conceived to be attacked, by the selection of a supreme head for the whole nation. Independently of matters of detail, independently of the actual power which every supreme magistrate possesses, it is too much to expect that a considerable number of vigorous and active communities will, if they can help it, be governed by a person who is the symbol of the doctrine that they must hate and fear, and who is just elected by their special foes precisely because he is that symbol.

More than one of the most discerning of the framers of the American Constitution seems not only to have perceived the inherent defects of the work in which he had participated, but to have had a prevision of the real source from which ultimate danger was to be foreboded. Most of the controversies in the convention which framed the Constitution had turned, in several forms, on the various consequences of the very different magnitude of the states which were about to join.

The large states were anxious to be strong; the small states were fearful of being weak. But Mr. Madison, one of the most judicious men of that time, clearly perceived that, though this was naturally the principal difficulty in securing the voluntary adoption by the several states of any proposed Constitution, it would not be an equally menacing danger to the continuance of the Union when that Constitution was once established. The small states shrank from binding themselves to a union, exactly because they felt that they must remain in it if they entered. If they once contracted to combine with stronger countries, the superior power of those countries would enforce an adherence to the bargain. The really formidable danger which threatened the American Union was the possibility of a difference of opinion between classes of states of which no one was immeasurably stronger than the other. This Madison saw. He observed:

'I would always exclude inconsistent principles in framing a system of government. The difficulty of getting its defects amended are great, and sometimes insurmountable. The Virginia state government was the first which was made, and though its defects are evident to every person, we cannot get it amended. The Dutch have made four several attempts to amend their system without success. The few alterations made in it were by tumult and faction, and for the worse. If there was real danger, I would give the smaller states the defensive weapons; but there is none from that quarter. The great danger to our general government is the great Southern and Northern interests of the continent being opposed to each other. Look to the votes in Congress, and most of them stand divided by the geography of the country, not according to the size of the states.'

It was not, indeed, very difficult for the eye of a practised politician to discern the great diversity between the Northern and Southern societies. It was even then conspicuous to the eye of the least gifted observer. An accomplished French writer, whose essay was written before the perceptions of all of us were sharpened by recent events, has thus described it: 'Au Sud, le sol appartenait à de grands propriétaires entourés d'esclaves et de petits cultivateurs. Les substitutions et le droit d'aînesse perpétuaient les richesses et le pouvoir dans une aristocratie qui occupait presque toutes les fonctions publiques. Le culte anglican était celui de l'État. Le société et l'Eglise étaient constituées d'une façon hiérarchique. Au Nord, au contraire, l'esprit d'égalité dans la société comme dans l'Eglise: "Je crains beaucoup les effets de cette diversité de mœurs et d'institutions," écrivait John Adams à Joseph Hawley, le 25 novembre 1775; "elle deviendra fatale si de part et d'autre on ne met beaucoup de prudence, de tolérance, de condescendance. Des changements dans les constitutions du Sud seront nécessaires si la guerre continue; ils pourront seuls rapprocher toutes les parties du continent." ' Probably, however, no one in those times anticipated the rapidity with which those differences would develop, for no one apprehended the practical working of slavery. Many persons unquestionably understood the immediate benefit with which it buys an insidious admission into uncultivated countries; but perhaps no one understood at how great price of ultimate evil that benefit would probably be purchased. No one could be expected to perceive that both the temporary benefit and the ultimate disadvantages resembled one another in being opposed to the continuance of the newly-formed Union; for even at the present day, and after a very painful experience, it is not steadily perceived by all of us.

Slavery is the one institution which effectually counteracts the assimilative force to which all new countries are subject,—that force which makes all men alike there, and which stamps upon the communities themselves so many common features. In such countries men are struggling with the wilderness; they are in daily conflict with the rough powers of nature, and from them they acquire a hardness and a roughness somewhat like their own. They cannot cultivate the luxuries of leisure, for they have no leisure. They must be mending their fences, or cooking their victuals, or mending their clothes. They cannot be expected to excel in the graces of refinement, for these require fastidious meditation and access to great examples, and neither of these are possible to hard-worked men at the end of the earth. A certain democracy in such circumstances rises like a natural growth of the soil. An even equality in mind and manners, if not in political institutions, is inevitably forced upon those whose character is pressed upon by the same rude forces, who have substantially the same difficulties, who lead in all material points the same life. All are struggling with the primitive difficulties of uncivilised existence, and all are retarded by that struggle at the same low level of instruction and refinement.

Slavery breaks this dead level, and it is the only available device that does so. The owner of a few slaves, partly employed in the service of his house and partly in the cultivation of his land, has a good deal of leisure, and is not exposed to any very brutalising temptation. It is his interest to treat his slaves well, and in ordinary circumstances he does treat them well. They give him the means of refinement, and the opportunities of culture: they receive from him good clothing, a protective surveillance, and some little moral improvement. Washington was such a slave-owner, and it is probable that at Mount Vernon what may be called the temptation of slavery presented itself in its strongest and most attractive form. At all events, it is certain that, by the irresistible influence of superior leisure and superior culture, the Virginian slave-owner acquired a singular pre-eminence in the revolutionary struggle, moved the bitter jealousy of all his contemporaries, and bestowed an indefinite benefit upon posterity. But even this beneficial effect of slavery, momentary as it was, was not beneficial to the Union as such: it did not strengthen, but weakened the uniting bond; it introduced an element of difference between state and state, which stimulated bitter envy, and suggested constant division. In the correspondence of the first race of Northern statesmen, a dangerous jealousy of the superior political abilities of the South is frequently to be traced.

The immense price, however, which has been paid for the short-lived benefit of slavery has been immeasurably more dangerous to the Union than the benefit itself. As we all perceive, it is tearing it in two. In the progress of time slave-owning becomes an investment of mercantile capital, and slaves are regarded, not as personal dependents, but as impersonal things. The necessities of modern manufacture require an immense production of raw material, and in certain circumstances slaves can be beneficially employed on a large scale to raise that material. The evils of slavery are developed at once. The owner of a few slaves whom he sees every day will commonly treat them kindly enough; but the owner of several gangs, on several different plantations, has no similar motive. His good feelings are not much appealed to in their favour; he does not know them by name, he does not know them by sight; they are to him instruments of production, which he bought at such and such a price, which cost so many dollars, which must be made to yield so many dollars. He is often brutalised by working them cruelly; he is still oftener brutalised in other ways by the infinite temptations which a large mass of subject men and subject women inevitably offer to tyranny and to lust. Nor in such a state of society does slavery monopolise the charm which at first attracted men to it. When large capitals have been accumulated, there will be without it sufficient opportunities for moderate leisure and for reasonable refinement. Slavery buys its admission with the attractions of Mount Vernon; it develops its awful consequences in lonely plantations on the banks of the Mississippi, whose owner wants cotton, and wants only cotton; where he himself, or some manager whom he pays, employs himself in brutalities to black men, and enjoys himself in brutalities to black women. The events of this year exhibit the result. The probable disunion of the South and the North is but the inevitable consequence of the existing moral contrast. It is not possible to retain in voluntary combination such a community as Massachusetts and communities whose ruling element is such a slavery as that we have described.

We see, therefore, from this brief survey, that we have no cause to wonder even at the almost magical consequences of Mr. Lincoln's election. It was the sort of event which was most likely to produce such consequences. A republic of united states which put up the first magistracy to periodical popular election, was most likely to part asunder when fundamental contrasts in character, ideas, and habits had long been growing rapidly between two very large classes of states, and when one of these classes persisted in electing to the first place in the republic the very person who embodied the aim and tendencies most odious to the other class. It is evident, too, that the Northern and Southern states cannot hope to continue united under the present Constitution, or to form parts of the same federal republic under any Constitution whatever. No free state can rule an unwilling dependency of large size, except by excluding that dependency from all share in its own freedom. If Ireland unanimously wished to withdraw from the government of England, we could not rule it without excluding its representatives from Parliament. We know what the Irish members are now: we know that they are not very convenient; we know that they seem invented to give trouble, but who can imagine a House of Commons in which one hundred eager Irish members were united by a consistent intention to make an English government impossible? who can imagine the parliamentary consequences of so great a voting power, used not for the purposes of construction, but exclusively for those of destruction? who can suppose that during a series of years we could keep any firm administration at all with so powerful a force ever ready to combine with every one who desired to pull down, and never ready to combine with any one who wished to set up? Yet this is a faint example of what the American Congress would be with a regularly organised Southern opposition retained within the Union by force, but desirous to leave it, anxious to destroy it; never voting for any thing except with this object; never voting against anything save on that account. And such would be the inevitable result of the victory of the North. The Southern States are sure to preserve an intense local feeling for many years. History shows that they have always had it; the occupations and the habits of such bodies insure their having it. Even if the North were to conquer them now, their whole political force for many years would unquestionably be devoted to the attainment of the disunion. Who can doubt that they would eventually obtain it by rendering all government impossible upon any lesser conditions? A free union is essentially voluntary. Sir Creswell Creswell may decree the restitution of matrimonial rights; but even he would not venture to decree the enforcement on an unwilling state of a promise to combine with another into a parliamentary union.

Some of the framers of the American Constitution, as we have seen, foresaw its principal danger, and they did all which they could to provide against it. They erected a Supreme Court, a pre-eminent judicial tribunal, which is empowered to decide causes between state and state, and between any state and the Federal Government. And on many small, and on some important, matters, this Court has worked very well; it has given able if not always satisfactory, judgments on various points of state controversy; it has provided a tolerably fair umpire, and has thus prevented many small *quæstiunculæ* from growing into grave questions. It was excellent upon minor points; it has been useless upon the greatest. When, as recently, great passions have been aroused, great interests at stake, great issues clearly drawn out, a reference to the Supreme Court has not even been contemplated. No judicial establishment could, indeed, be useful in an extra-judicial matter; no law decide what is beyond the competence of law; no supplementary provision, however ingenious, cure the essential and inseparable defects of a federal union.

The steadily augmenting power of the lower orders in America has naturally augmented the dangers of their federal union. In almost all the states there was, at the time the Constitution of the Union was originally framed, a property qualification, in some states a high one, requisite for the possession of the most popular form of suffrage. Almost all these qualifications have now been swept away, and a dead level of universal suffrage runs, more or less, over the whole length of the United States. The external consequences, as we all know, have not been beneficial: the foreign policy of the Union has been a perplexing difficulty to European nations, and especially to England, for many years. Nor have the internal consequences been better. The most enthusiastic advocates of a democratic government will admit that it is both an impulsive and a contentious government. Its special characteristic is, that it places the entire control over the political action of the whole state in the hands of the common labourers, who are of all classes the least instructed—of all the most aggressive—of all the most likely to be influenced by local animosity—of all the most likely to exaggerate every momentary sentiment—of all the least likely to be capable of a considerable toleration for the constant oppositions of opinion, the not unfrequent differences of interests, and the occasional unreasonableness of other states. In democracies, local feuds are commonly more lasting and more bitter than in states of other kinds; and those enmities commonly become more bitter in proportion to the greater nearness of relation, the greater closeness of political connexion, and the greater contrast of disposition, temper, and internal circumstances. What intensity of bitterness was then to be anticipated in a so-called Union, in which two distinct sets of democracies—the Southern and the Northern, the slaveholding and the non-slaveholding —have been for many years augmenting in contrast to, and increasing in antipathy to, one another! The existing crisis is only the natural consequence, the inevitable development, of a long antagonism between these two species of republics, in both of which the most intolerant members are absolute rulers, and each of which presented characteristics which the hidden instincts of the other, even more than its conscious opinion, regarded first as irritating and then as dangerous. The progress of democracy has affected not only the state government, but the Federal Government. The House of Representatives in the latter is elected by the same persons whose choose the most popular branch of the legislature in the former. As the state governments have become more democratic, the Federal Government has inevitably become more so likewise. To this gradual corruption of the American democracy it is principally owing that Europe at large, and England especially, have not grieved much at the close proximity of its probable fall, but perhaps rejoiced at the prospect of some marked change from a policy which was so inconvenient to its neighbours, which must be attended

THE AMERICAN CONSTITUTION AT THE PRESENT CRISIS

to because its range was so wide, and the physical force under its direction was so large, but of which the events were mean, the actors base, and the working inexplicable. A low vulgarity, indefinable but undeniable, has deeply displeased the cultivated mind of Europe; and the American Union will fall, if it does fall, little regretted even by those whose race is akin, whose language is identical, whose weightiest opinions are on most subjects the same as theirs. The unpleasantness of mob government has never before been exemplified so conspicuously, for it never before has worked upon so large a scene.

These latter truths are very familiar. The evils of democracy and the dangers of democracy are great commonplaces in our speculation, though also formidable perils in our practice. But it is not commonplace to observe, that the existing crisis in America has been intensified almost as much by the precautions which the original founders of the Constitution took to ward off what they well knew to be the characteristic evils of democracy, as by those evils themselves. We have been so much accustomed to hear the 'United States' extolled as the special land of democratic liberty, to hear their Constitution praised as the unmixed embodiment of uncontrolled popular power, that we have forgotten how many restrictive provisions that Constitution contains, and how anxiously its framers endeavoured to provide against the special defects of a purely popular polity.

It is not too much to say that a valuable addition to the accumulations of conservative oratory might be extracted from the debates of the Convention which framed the American revolution. The two objects which its most intelligent framers were mainly bent on attaining were, security against the momentary caprice of a purely numerical majority, and some effective provision for the maintenance of a strong executive. What would Mr. Bright say to the following speech of Mr. Morris, not by any means the most conservative member of the Convention?—

'The two branches, so equally poised, cannot have their due weight. It is confessed, on all hands, that the second branch ought to be a check on the first; for without its having this effect it is perfectly useless. The first branch, originating from the people, will ever be subject to precipitancy, changeability, and excess. Experience evinces the truth of this remark, without having recourse to reading. This can only be checked by ability and virtue in the second branch. On your present system, can you suppose that one branch will possess it more than the other? The second branch ought to be composed of men of great and established property—an aristocracy; men who from pride will support consistency and permanency; and to make them completely independent, they must be chosen for life, or they will be a useless body. Such an aristocratic body will keep down the turbulency of democracy. But if you elect them for a shorter period, they will be only a name, and we had better be without them. Thus constituted, I hope they will show us the weight of aristocracy.

'History proves, I admit, that the men of large property will uniformly endeavour to establish tyranny. How, then, shall we ward off this evil? Give them the second branch, and you secure their weight for the public good. They become responsible for their conduct, and this lust of power will ever be checked by the democratic branch, and thus form a stability in your Government. But if we continue changing our measures by the breath of democracy, who will confide in our engagements? who will trust us? Ask any person whether he reposes any confidence in the government of Congress, or that of the state of Pennsylvania; he will readily answer you, no. Ask him the reason; and he will tell you it is because he has no confidence in their stability.

'You intend also that the second branch shall be incapable of holding any office in the general government. It is a dangerous expedient. They ought to have every inducement to be interested in your government. Deprive them of this right, and they will become inattentive to your welfare. The wealthy will ever exist; and you never can be safe unless you gratify them as a body, in the pursuit of honour and profit. Prevent them by positive institutions, and they will proceed in some left-handed way. A son may want a place—you mean to prevent him from promotion. They are not to be paid for their services —they will in some way pay themselves; nor is it in your power to prevent it. It is good policy that men of property be collected in one body, to give them one common influence in your government. Let vacancies be filled up, as they happen, by the executive. Besides it is of little consequence, on this plan, whether the states are equally represented or not. If the state governments have the division of many of the loaves and fishes, and the general government few, it cannot exist. This senate would be one of the baubles of the general government. If you choose them for seven years, whether chosen by the people or the states,—whether by equal suffrage or in any other proportion,—how will they be a check? They will still have local and state prejudices. A government by compact is no government at all. You may as well go back to your Congressional Federal government, where, in the character of ambassadors, they may form treaties for each state. I avow myself the advocate of a strong government.'

This speech, striking as it is, is only a single specimen, and not, in several respects, the most striking of many which might be cited. The predominant feeling of the predominant party in the Convention is clearly expressed in the singularly complicated provisions of the Constitution which they framed. Almost every clause of it bears witness to the anxiety of its composers for an efficient executive, and for an adequate guard against momentary popular feeling.

Unfortunately they either had not at their disposal, or did not avail themselves of, the only effectual instruments for either purpose. There is but one sufficient expedient against the tyranny of the lower orders, and that is to place the predominant (though not necessarily the exclusive) power in the hands of the higher orders. There must be some effectual sovereign authority in every government. In England, for example, the sovereign authority is the diffused respectable higher middle-class, which, on the whole, is predominant in the House of Commons, and in the constituencies which return it. Whatever this class emphatically wills, is immediately enacted. It hears representations from the great mass of the orders which are below, it hears other and better expressed representations from the higher classes, which are above it. But it uses these only as materials by which to form a better judgment. If the House of Commons distinctly expresses an emphatic opinion, no other body or person or functionary hopes to oppose it, or dreams of doing so. Our security against tyranny is the reasonableness, the respectable cultivation, the business-like moderation of this governing class itself; if that class did not possess those qualities, the rest of the community would be always in danger, and frequently be oppressed.

The framers of the American Constitution chose a very different expedient. They placed the predominant power in the hands of the numerical majority of the population, and hoped to restrain and balance it by paper checks and constitutional stratagems. At the present time, almost every one of their ingenious devices has aggravated the calamities of their descendants.

The mode in which the President of the United States is chosen is the most complicated which could well be imagined. A reader of the Constitution, uninformed as to the circumstances of its origin and the intentions of its framers, would imagine that complexity had sometimes been chosen as such, and for its own sake. Each, however, of these singular details was introduced with a very definite object.

'Each state,' it is provided, 'shall appoint, in such manner as the legislature thereof may direct, a number of electors equal to the whole number of senators and representatives to which the state may be entitled in the Congress; but no senator or representative, or person holding an office of trust or profit under the United States, shall be appointed an elector.

'The electors shall meet in their respective states, and vote by ballot for two persons, of whom one at least shall not be an inhabitant of the same state with themselves. And they shall make a list of all the persons voted for, and of the number of votes for each: which list they shall sign and certify, and transmit, sealed, to the seat of the government of the United States, directed to the President of the Senate. The President of the Senate shall, in the presence of the Senate and House of Representatives, open all the certificates; and the votes shall then be counted. The person having the greatest number of votes shall be the President, if such number be a majority of the whole number of electors appointed; and if there be more than one who have such majority, and have an equal number of votes, then the House of Representatives shall immediately choose by ballot one of them for President; and if no person have a majority, then, from the five highest on the list, the said House shall in like manner choose the President. But in choosing the President the votes shall be taken by states, the representation from each state having one vote; a quorum for this purpose shall consist of a member or members from two-thirds of the states, and a majority of all the states shall be necessary to a choice. In every case, after the choice of the President, the person having the greatest number of votes of the electors shall be the Vice-President. But if there should remain two or more who have equal votes, the senate shall choose from them by ballot the Vice-President.

'The Congress may determine the time of choosing the electors, and the day on which they shall give their votes: which day shall be the same throughout the United States.'

'In pursuance of the authority given by the latter clause,' says Mr. Justice Story, 'Congress in 1792 passed an act, declaring that the electors shall be appointed in each state within thirty-four days preceding the first Wednesday in December, in every fourth year succeeding the last election of the President, according to the apportionment of representatives and senators then existing. The electors chosen are required to meet and give their votes on the first said Wednesday of December, in every fourth year succeeding the last election of president, according to the apportionment of representatives and senators then existing. The electors chosen are required to meet and give their votes on the said first Wednesday of December, at such place in each state as shall be directed by the legislature thereof. They are then to make and sign three certificates of all the votes by them given, and to seal up the same, certifying on each that a list of the votes of such state for President and Vice-President is contained therein; and shall appoint a person to take charge of and deliver one of the same certificates to the President of the Senate at the seat of government, before the first Wednesday of January then next ensuing; another of the certificates is to be forwarded forthwith by the post-office to the President of the Senate at the seat of government; and the third is to be delivered to the judge of the district in which the electors assembled. Other auxiliary provisions are made by the same act for the due transmission and preservation of the electoral votes, and authenticating the appointment of the electors. The President's term of office is also declared to commence on the fourth day of March next succeeding the day on which the votes of the electors shall be given.'

The details of these arrangements are involved, but their purpose was simple. The framers wished the President to be chosen, not by the primary electors, but by a body of secondary electors, whom the primary were to choose, because they thought that these chosen choosers would presumably be persons especially likely to make a good choice. They likewise intended that an absolute majority (a majority, that is, of more than one-half of the total number) should be requisite for a valid election; and if such majority could not be procured, that the House of Representatives, voting by states, should make the choice (in which case an absolute majority of all the states was likewise to be necessary); and lastly, they wished that an interval of many months—from November in one year to March in the next—should be secured for the safe transaction of the entire election.

Every part of this well-studied arrangement has produced most unanticipated results, and none more so than the last part. Nothing could be more reasonable than the regulation that a long interval should be provided for the whole complicated election; since, if the choice unexpectedly lapsed to the House of Representatives, much delay and consideration would obviously be necessary. But the consequences have been disastrous.

'At the outset of the quarrel,' observes a recent writer, 'the Constitution occasioned a needless danger. The South threatened to secede because Mr. Lincoln had been elected President. Under almost any other free Constitution which has ever existed, and certainly under every good one, the executive authority, whose function it was to oppose secession, would have been placed exclusively in the hands of those who were desirous so to oppose it. At an instant of violent irritation, the dissentient minority were anxious to break loose from the control of the majority. The majority were at that time, whatever may be the case now, by no means fanatical, or irritated, or overbearing. They wished to preserve the Union, and under a well-framed constitution they would have had the power of using the force of the state to preserve the state. But not so under the American. An artificial arrangement prolongs the reign of each President many months after the election of his successor. In consequence, the executive authority was, during a considerable and critical interval, in the hands of those who by birth, habit, and sympathy were leagued with the dissentient minority. Mr. Buchanan and his ministers had always been attached to the party of the South, and were the last persons to act decisively against it. It is the opinion of many well-informed persons that there was a sufficient Unionist party in several of the seceding states to have prevented the present movement there, if the Federal Government had acted with vigour and celerity. And, whether this be so or not, it remains a singular defect in the working of the American Constitution, that it gave power at the decisive moment to those least likely to use that power well—that just when a revolt was impending, it placed the whole executive influence and the whole military force in the unfettered hands of the political associates of the revolters.'

It is now known that the Southern officials, purposely distributed the fleet of the Union in distant countries, placed stores of artillery where Southern rebels could easily take them, purposely disorganised the Federal army. Nothing else could be anticipated from an arrangement which placed the preparations for maintaining the Union in the exclusive control of the persons desirous to break the Union.

The scheme, too, of a double election has failed of its intended effect; but has produced grave effects which were not intended. The same writer observes:

'Nor does the accession of Mr. Lincoln place the executive power precisely where we should wish to see it. At a crisis such as America has never before seen, and as it is not, perhaps, probable she will see again, the executive authority should be in the hands of one of the most tried, trusted, and experienced statesmen of the nation. Mr. Lincoln is a nearly unknown man, who has been but little heard of, who has had little experience, who may have nerve and judgment, or may not have them, whose character, both moral and intellectual, is an unknown quantity, who must, from his previous life and defective education, be wanting in the liberal acquirements and mental training which are principal elements of an enlarged statesmanship. Nor is it true to say that the American people are to blame for this— that they chose Mr. Lincoln, and must endure the pernicious results. The Constitution is as much to blame as the people, probably even more so. The framers were wisely and warmly attached to the principles of liberty, and, like all such persons, were extremely anxious to guard against momentary gusts of popular opinion. They were especially desirous that the President to whom they were intrusting vast power should be the representative, not of a small section of the community, but of a really predominant part of it. They not only established a system of double election, in the hope that the "electoral college" (of which the electors were chosen by the primary electors in each state) would exercise a real discretion in the choice of President, and be some check on popular ignorance and low violence, but they likewise provided that an absolute majority of that "electoral college" (a majority, that is, greater than one-half of the whole) should give their votes for the elected candidate. The effect has been painfully different from the design. In reality, the "electoral college" exercises no choice; every member of it is selected by the primitive constituency because he will vote for a certain presidential candidate (for Mr. Lincoln or Mr. Douglas, and so on), and he does nothing but vote accordingly. The provision requiring the consent of an absolute majority has had a still worse effect; it has not been futile, for it has been pernicious. It has made it very difficult to secure any election.'[2]

If every candidate stood who wished, and every elector voted for

[2] *The Economist*, June 1 1861.

whom he pleased, there would be no election at all. Each little faction would vote for its own particular favourite, and no one would obtain the votes of half the whole nation. A very complicated apparatus of preliminary meetings, called caucuses, is therefore resorted to, and the working of these is singularly disastrous.

Every man of any mark in the whole nation has many enemies, some private, some public; he is probably the head of some section or minor party, and that minor party has its own antagonists, its special opponents, who would dislike more than anything else that its head should on a sudden become the head of the state. Every statesman who has been long tried in public life must have had to alienate many friends, to irritate many applicants by necessary refusals, to say many things which are rankling in many bosoms. Every great man creates his own opposition; and no great man, therefore, will ever be President of the United States except in the rarest and most exceptional cases. The object of 'president makers' is to find a candidate who will conciliate the greatest number, not the person for whom there is most to be said, but the person against whom there is least to be said. In the English State, there is no great office filled in at all the same way; but in the English Church there is. 'Depend on it,' said a shrewd banker, not remarkable for theological zeal or scholastic learning, 'I would have been Archbishop of Canterbury, if I had been in the Church. Some quiet, tame sort of man is always chosen; and I never give offence to any one.' If he did not, he might have been President of the United States. The mode in which all conspicuous merit is gradually eliminated from the list of candidates was well illustrated at the election of Mr. Pierce.

'The candidates on the Democratic side were no less than eight: General Cass, Mr. Buchanan, Mr. Douglas, Mr. Marcy, Mr. Butler, Mr. Houston, Mr. Lane, and Mr. Dickenson; all men "prominently known to their party," and the three first supported with great enthusiasm by large sections of that party throughout the Union.

'The Convention appointed by the democratic party in each state to decide which among these various candidates should be recommended for their votes at the election, assembled at Baltimore for their first meeting on the 1st of June, 1852. On that day General Cass obtained the greatest number of votes at the first ballot, namely 116, out of the total of 288; but a number far below the requisite majority. A few specimens of the manner in which the votes fluctuated will not be without interest. On the ninth ballot the votes were—Cass, 112; Buchanan, 87; Douglas, 39; Marcy, 28; Butler, 1; Houston, 8; Lane, 13; Dickenson, 1. On the twenty-second ballot—Cass, 33; Douglas, 80; Butler, 24; Lane, 11; Buchanan, 101; Marcy, 25; Houston, 10; Dickenson, 1. On the twenty-ninth ballot—Cass, 27. On the thirty-fifth ballot—Cass, 131; Douglas, 52; Buchanan, 32.

'On this, the sixth day of the meeting (the proceedings of and the scenes in which were fully and somewhat graphically described by the public press of both parties), a new name appeared for the first time upon the lists—that of Mr. Pierce, of New Hampshire, a gentleman well known to his friends as a lawyer of ability; also as having creditably fulfilled the duties of a member of the House of Representatives, and of the Senate of the United States; better known, however, as having joined the army as a volunteer on the breaking out of the Mexican War, and as having commanded with distinction a brigade in that war, with the rank of General. It will, nevertheless, imply no disrespect towards Mr. Pierce, if I repeat what was the universal expression, according to the public prints, throughout the Union, that no individual in the United States could have been more surprised at Mr. Pierce's nomination for the exalted and responsible office of chief magistrate of the Republic than Mr. Pierce himself. On the thirty-fifth ballot, the first in which Mr. Pierce's name appeared, he received 15 votes. On the forty-eighth, he received only 55 votes; but on the forty-ninth, the numbers voting for him were 283, out of the total of 288—a vote which five more would have made unanimous.

'Mr. Pierce was accordingly recommended to the Democratic constituencies throughout the Union, and was elected by a considerable majority over his Whig opponent; the numbers being, for Mr. Pierce 1,504,471, and for General Scott 1,283,174.'

What worse mode of electing a ruler could by possibility have been selected? If the wit of man had been set to devise a system specially calculated to bring to the head of affairs an incompetent man at a pressing crisis, it could not have devised one more fit; probably it would not have devised one as fit. It almost secures the rejection of tried and trained genius, and almost insures the selection of untrained and unknown mediocrity.

Nor is this the only mode, or even the chief mode, in which the carefully considered provisions of the American Constitution have, in fact, deprived the American people of the guidance and government of great statesmen, just when these were most required. It is not too much to say that, under the American Constitution, there was no opportunity for a great statesman. As we have seen, he had no chance of being chosen President, the artificial clauses of the Constitution, and the natural principles of human nature, have combined to prevent that. Nor is it worth a great man's while to be a President's minister. This is not because such a minister would be in apparent subordination to the President, who would probably be an inferior man to him— for able men are continually ready to fill subordinate posts under constitutional monarchs, who are usually very inferior men, and even under colonial governors, who are rather inferior men—but because a President's minister has no parliamentary career. As we know, the first member of the Crown is with us the first man in Parliament, and is the ruler of the English nation. In those English colonies which possess popular constitutions, the first minister is the most powerful man in the state—far more powerful than the so-called governor. He is so because he is the accepted leader of the colonial parliament. In consequence, whenever the English nation, or a free English colony, is in peril, the first man in England, or in the colony, at least the most trusted man is raised at once to the most powerful place in the nation. On the continent of Europe, the advantage of this insensible machinery is just beginning to be understood. Count Cavour well knew and thoroughly showed how far the power of a parliamentary premier, supported by a willing and confiding parliament, is superior to all other political powers, whether in despotic governments or in free. The American Constitution, however, expressly prohibits the possibility of such a position. It enacts, 'That no person holding any office under the United States shall be a member of either House during his continuance in office.' In consequence, the position of a great parliamentary member who is responsible more or less for the due performance of his own administrative functions, and also of all lesser ones, is in America an illegal one. If a politician has executive authority, he cannot enter Parliament; if he is in Parliament, he cannot possess executive authority. No man of great talents and high ambition has therefore under the Constitution of the United States a proper sphere for those talents, or a suitable vista for that ambition. He cannot hope to be President, for the President is *ex officio* a poor creature; he cannot hope to be, *mutatis mutandis*, an English premier, to be a Sir Robert

Peel, or a Count Cavour, for the American law has declared that in the United States there shall be no similar person.

It appears that the constitution-makers of North America were not unnaturally misled by the political philosophy of their day. It was laid down first that the legislative authority and the executive authority ought to be perfectly distinct; and secondly that in the English Constitution those authorities were so distinct. Both dogmas had slid into accepted axioms, and no one was bold enough to contest them. At that time no speculative politician perfectly comprehended that the essence of the English Constitution resided in the English Cabinet; that so far from the executive power being entirely distinct from the legislative power, the primary motive force, the supreme regulator of every thing, was precisely the same in both. A select committee of the legislature chosen by the legislature is the highest administrative body, and exercises all the powers of the sovereign executive that are tolerated by the law. The advantage of this arrangement, though contrary to a very old philosophical theory, is very great. The whole state will never work in harmony and in vigour while by possibility its two great powers—the power of legislating and the power of acting—can be declared in opposition to one another; and if they are independent, they will very often be in open antagonism, and be always in dread of it when they are not so. No government, it may be safely said, can be so strong as it should be when the enacting legislature and the acting executive are not subjected to a single effectual control.

The framers of the American Constitution did not perceive this cardinal maxim. The admitted theory of that day was that the English Constitution was one of 'checks and balances'; and the Americans, who were very willing to take it as their model (the monarchial part excepted), hoped to balance their strong independent legislature by a strong independent executive. They hoped, too, to prevent the introduction into America of that parliamentary corruption—that bribery of popular representatives by money and patronage, which filled so large a space in the thoughts of politicians of the last century, and so large a space in the lives of some of them. But though their intentions were excellent and their reasons plausible, the effect of their regulations has been pernicious. By keeping the two careers of legislation and of administration distinct, they have rendered the life of a high politician, of a great statesman, aspiring to improve the laws and to regulate the policy of a great country, with them an impossibility. They have divided the greatest department of practical life into two halves, and neither of them is worth a man's having.

We see the effect. There is no body of respected statesmen in America at this moment of their extreme need. It is not a fault that they have no great genius at their head. The few marvellous statesmen of the world are of necessity rare, and are not manufactured to order even by the bidding of an awful crisis. But it is a fault that they have not one or more possible parliamentary cabinets—several sets of trained men, with considerable abilities and known character, whose policy is decided, whose worth is tried, who have cast in their lot for years with certain ideas, whose names are respected in every household through Europe. In consequence of the unfortunate caution of their constitution-makers, America has no such men; and Italy has them or will soon have them; but after a political experience of seventy years the United States have none. They have existed during two generations as a democracy without ideals; and are likely to die now a democracy without champions.

It is, however, only fair to observe, that the American Constitution has one great excellence at this moment, not indeed, as compared with the English Constitution, but as compared with that degraded imitation of it which exists, for example, in our Australian colonies. In those governments the parliament is wholly unfit to choose an executive; it has not patriotism enough to give a decent stability to the government; there are 'ministerial crises' once a week, and actual changes of administration once a month. The suffrage has been lowered to such a point among the refuse population of the gold colonies, that representative government is there a very dubious blessing, if not a certain and absolute curse. If such a parliament had met in such a crisis as the American Congress lately had to face, it is both possible and probable that no stable administration would have been formed at all. Every possible ministry would have been tried in succession; and everyone would have been rejected in succession. We might have witnessed debates as aimless, as absurd, as unpractical, in their tenor, as those of certain French parliaments, without the culture and refinement which made the latter more tolerable, though it could not make them more wise.

The American Constitution has at least the merit of preventing this last extreme of political degradation. Having placed Mr. Lincoln, an unknown man, in power, it has at least prevented his being superseded, or its being proposed that he should be superseded by some other equally unknown man. The American Constitution necessitated the choice for the first position at an awful crisis; it has at least settled once for all who he should be; it has compelled a conclusive choice, which an Australian Constitution would not have done.

But with this single item the aid which the American Constitution has given to Mr. Lincoln in his presidency begins and ends. It has put him there, and it has kept him there; but it has done no more. He has had to carry on the government with new subordinates; for at every change of the American President, all the officials, from the cabinet minister to the petty postmaster, are changed. So far from giving him any special powers suitable to a civil war, it authoritatively declares that the right of the people to keep and bear arms shall not be infringed; that it shall be illegal 'to abridge the freedom of speech or of the press, or the right of the people peaceably to assemble or to petition for a redress of grievance'. It does not permit the punishment of any person, or the confiscation of his property, except after satisfactory proof before a civil tribunal. Even now, at this early state of the civil contest, martial law has been declared in Missouri and *habeas corpus* suspended in Baltimore; the property (slave-property, certainly, but still legal property in America) of secessionists has been confiscated; the liberty of speech is almost at an end; the liberty of the press has ceased to exist. These last are indeed infractions of the law, not by the administration, but by the mob; it is they, and not Mr. Lincoln, who have burnt printers' offices and proscribed dissentient individuals. But Mr. Lincoln and his ministers have broken, and have been obliged to break, the law on almost innumerable occasions, because that law provided no suitable procedure for the extreme contingency of a great civil war. The framers of the Constitution shrank naturally, and perhaps not unwisely, from providing against such an incalculable peril. They may have not unreasonably feared that they might augment the probability of such a calamity by recognising its possibility, even in order to provide against it. But their omission must have been grievously lamented by those who have had now to violate the law, for it may hereafter expose them to imminent danger. The English Parliament, in such an emergency, could and would condone every well-intentioned and beneficial irregularity by an act of indemnity. But the American Congress cannot do so. Its powers are limited powers, defined by the letter of a document; and in that document there is nothing to authorise a bill of indemnity—nor, indeed, could there be consistently with the very nature of it. By its fundamental conception, the states should relinquish certain special powers to the Federal Government, and those powers only; if the Federal Government could pass a bill of indemnity for infractions of the law, it would have absolute power; it would be a generally sovereign body, like the King, Lords, and Commons of England; it would have over the states of America, and over their people, not a defined and limited superiority, but an uncontrolled and unlimited one. Mr. Lincoln is, therefore, in peril from the inseparable accidents of the office he holds; he is a President under a Constitution which could give him only defined powers, and he is in a position requiring indefinite powers; he has therefore had to take his life in his hand, and violate the law. At present, popular opinion approves of what he has done; but the Republican party, of which he is the head, has many bitter enemies. If his announced aim should be successful, and he should re-establish the Union, those enemies will be reinforced by the whole constitutional power of the whole South, bitterly hostile to their vanquisher, bitterly aggrieved at the means by which they have been vanquished. Against such a coalition of enemies it will be difficult to defend the illegal, the arbitrary, the impeachable acts (for such, in the eye of American law, they are) of which Mr. Lincoln has been guilty. We doubt much whether he can succeed in compelling the South to return to the Union; but if he should, he will have succeeded at his peril.

It is easy to sum up the results of this long discussion. We cannot regard the American Constitution with the deference and the admiration with which all Americans used to regard it, and with which many Northern Americans still regard it. We admit that it has been beneficial to the American Republic as a bond of union; it has prevented war, it has fostered commerce, it has made them a nation to be counted with. But it always contained the seeds of disunion. There is no chance of saving such a polity when many states wish to separate from it, for the simple reason that its whole action essentially depends on the voluntary union of all, or of nearly all, the states. So far from its being wonderful that the present rupture has happened now, it is rather wonderful that it did not happen long since. It is rather surprising that a Government, which in practice, though not in theory, is dependent on the precarious consent of many distinct bodies, should have lasted so long, than that it should break asunder now. We see, too, that the American Constitution was, in its very essence, framed upon an erroneous principle. Its wise founders wished to guard against the characteristic evils of democracy; but they relied for this purpose upon ingenious devices and superficial subtilties. They left the essence of the government unchanged; they left the sovereign people, sovereign still. As has been shown in detail, the effect has been calamitous. Their ingenuities have produced painful evils, and aggravated great dangers; but they have failed of their intended purpose—they have neither refined the polity, nor restrained the people.

American Complaints against England[1]

TIME and reflection might have been expected to bring the Northern Americans to a fairer and more reasonable tone of feeling in relation to the conduct of Great Britain, but they do not appear to have done so. It was not unnatural that in the first moments of irritation and alarm, some disappointment and even anger should be felt when it was found by the excited Unionists that we in this country, however deeply and anxiously interested in the strange events which were taking place, did not share their somewhat exaggerated sentiments. Therefore, when American journals raved, and American abolitionists whined, and American senators menaced, and even American diplomatists blustered in public in a fashion which covered them with shame, we contented ourselves with quietly explaining our proceedings, and awaited without indignation and in patient confidence the return of reason and of temper,—satisfied that justice would be done to us at last. But when day after day the old charges are reiterated, and the strongest proofs are given that the old soreness still remains; and when a lady of the reputation of the author of 'Uncle Tom's Cabin' writes a formal letter of reproach and accusation to an English Earl; and when a politician of the standing of Lord Shaftesbury sends Mrs. Beecher Stowe's letter to the newspapers,—it is high time to endeavour to place facts and principles in their true light,—to point out what we really feel and what we have really done,—and to show how utterly unjust and irrational are obloquy showered upon us alike for our action and our inaction, for our speech and for our silence. We feel the more called upon to say a few words on this score, because one or two very respectable English journals have been led away by their strong anti-slavery predilections to indorse some of the reproaches and to connive at much of the injustice.

It is not easy to make out with any great definiteness in what our offence consists. Neither Mrs. Stowe nor her British echoes con-

[1] This article was first published in *The Economist* for September 14 1861, Volume XIX, pp. 1010–12.

descend to specify anything in particular which we have done wrong. We did, indeed, at the outset announce that we should acknowledge in both parties equally the usual rights of belligerents; but it is now admitted that we could not decorously have done otherwise,—not indeed have done otherwise at all without a virtual violation of neutrality; and the Federal Government has found itself obliged to do a few months later what the British Government only did a few months earlier. Every Confederate prisoner whom the United States have omitted to hang as a rebel, every privateer seaman whom they have failed to hang as a pirate, is an additional confession on their part of the correctness of the course adopted by this country. This clause of the indictment, therefore, is not now repeated; yet the concession alluded to is in reality the only overt act we have committed. All that we have actually *done*, then, is confessedly unimpugnable. But Mrs. Beecher Stowe says that our *sympathies* are astray, and the *Spectator* alleges that we are *meditating* wrong. As far as we can extract any distinct charges from the long letter of the American lady, she declares that we have been false to our anti-slavery antecedents; that we have encouraged and wished success to the rebels; and that we have acted thus out of a mean regard to our own pecuniary interests;—in truth, that we wish success to the South because we are anxious about our supply of cotton, and prize this above all higher considerations. That a transatlantic abolitionist should transmit such reproaches is natural enough. That an English journal should adopt and repeat them is less explicable and less excusable.

In the first place—and the misrepresentation has so much in it that is mischievous, not to say malignant, that it is high time to speak out upon the subject—the assumption that the quarrel between the North and South is a quarrel between negro freedom on the one side and negro slavery on the other, is as impudent as it is untrue. The conflict may reach this issue, may assume this form; but it did not originate in this; it has not even now reached this;—and if ever it does do so, it will be without the design and against the most strenuous endeavours of those who inaugurated the strife and of those who have hitherto conducted it. Can we forget, and does Mrs. Stowe suppose we have forgotten, that abolitionists have habitually been as ferociously persecuted and maltreated in the North and West as in the South? Can it be denied that the testiness and half-heartedness, not to say insincerity of the Government at Washington have for years supplied the chief impediment which has thwarted our efforts for the effectual suppression of the slave trade on the coast of Africa; while a vast proportion of the clippers actually engaged in that trade have been built with Northern capital, owned by Northern merchants, and manned by Northern seamen? Is it not notorious that the detestation and oppression of the coloured race in the free states have been quite as bitter and almost as unmeasured as in the slave states, and have been manifested in a manner perhaps even more revolting to English sentiments of decency and justice? Why, it is only yesterday, when the secession movement first gained serious head, on the first announcement of Mr. Lincoln's election, that the Northerners offered to the South, if they would remain in the Union, every conceivable security for the permanence and inviolability of the obnoxious institution,—that they disavowed in the most solemn manner all intention of interfering with it,—that their leaders proposed compromise after compromise in Congress *all based upon the concession that slavery should not be meddled with*, and that the 'Personal Liberty Laws,' which were supposed to neutralise the action of the Fugitive Slave Law, should be reconsidered with a view to their modification or repeal. Since then—since the war has been actually commenced—generals and other constituted authorities have distinctly announced that they had no idea of liberating slaves or of interfering with the rights of negro ownership; and they have felt the disposal of the slaves who flocked to their camp to be one of the most obnoxious and embarrassing questions which could have been forced upon them. The very last arrival from America brings a curious comment on these philanthropic pretensions in the announcement that in Missouri the slaves *of rebels only* were to be emancipated, while those of loyal subjects were to be retained in servitude!* In the face of all these facts, it surely argues something more than zeal and something less pardonable than blindness on the part of Mrs. Stowe to draw up an indictment against England because she did not at once regard and treat the struggle as an anti-slavery one, and side enthusiastically with the Northerners as emancipationists in the mass,—because she did not, intuitively and resolutely, put an interpretation upon the civil war which its authors and leaders anxiously laboured to guard against,—and which (we may add) nothing in their antecedents would have warranted us in fixing upon them. It is

* We understand, however, that other versions speak of the proclamation as applying to ALL slaves. Probably all or nearly all the slaveholders in Missouri are secessionists.

true enough that it was the aim of the Republican party which elected Mr. Lincoln to prevent slavery from spreading into the unsettled territories, unless by the deliberate resolve of those territories when erected into states. It may be true that the success of the North, if complete and unconditional, would enable them to confine slavery within the 15 states which have already adopted it, and *might* thus lead to its eventual extinction,—though this is rather probable than certain. It is no doubt honourable to Mrs. Stowe, and to that earnest and devoted abolition sect of which she has in Europe been the stirring mouthpiece,—that they are determined to make the present disastrous civil struggle an anti-slavery conflict, and to convert what was a war for political supremacy into a war for negro emancipation. If they can do so—if they can thus educe good out of evil, without resorting to means which look very like doing evil that good may come—we shall rejoice most earnestly at the beneficial result. But it is to say the least something premature to require that we should from the outset have recognised in the contest a character which, even up to the present hour, *they have failed to imprint upon it.* Unprejudiced spectators have repeatedly deplored as the inherent weak point of their cause that there was no distinct or noble moral purpose stamped upon it. We have heard abundance of misty declaration about patriotism and freedom on both sides,—and not more definite on one side than on the other; but it has been impossible to say what great principle was in reality at stake. And there is really something staggering in the audacity which now demands our sympathy for the Northerners on the ground of that very moral grandeur in their cause, *the absence of which* has prevented our sympathy from being enlisted on their side. Let the conflict once become avowedly and honestly and irretrievably a war for the extinction of slavery, and we suspect the enthusiasm and excitement of Great Britain would rival that of the Americans themselves.

This, therefore, *not* being a war for the emancipation of the negro race, but on the contrary being waged on the part of the North by men who, in an overwhelming proportion, have hitherto dreaded and deprecated such emancipation as involving the probable ruin of their Southern customers and debtors,—on what other ground can we be fairly called upon to sympathise so warmly with the Federal cause? *Apart from the slave question* we really do not see what ground can be alleged. It is true that the conduct of those Southern politicians who, while holding high office under the United States Government, employed their official position to prepare the success of the secession movement by arming the South and denuding the North was simply villainous and base, and their violence and intemperance at the commencement of the movement blameable in the extreme. And no one can say that the unanimous opinion of Great Britain on these transactions was not expressed in the plainest and most indignant language. But what is there, what has there been, in either the recent or the habitual conduct of the United States Government or people that should entitle them to *command* our sympathies or our wishes for their triumph, or to complain, in the tone of men who have been hurt or wronged, because those sympathies and good wishes are lukewarm or undecided, or even altogether withheld? They have themselves, and themselves only, to thank if Great Britain looks on somewhat calmly on their difficulties. Never did a nation, not avowedly inimical, labour so hard to alienate all friendly feeling. They have habitually treated England in a way which England would have borne from no other country. How did they behave to our consuls and ambassadors during the height of our Crimean difficulties? With what vulgar insolence and thoroughly unkind feeling did too many among them take the opportunity to express their sympathy with our antagonist? Not a year has elapsed since a senator from the North, well acquainted with this country, and recently received here with every kindness and attention, and now holding the responsible position of Secretary of State under Mr. Lincoln, openly avowed his wish that the seizure of Canada should be made to compensate for the secession of the South. In the height of the strife, New York papers and New York politicians were not wanting who exhorted the combatants, now that they had large armies in the field, to employ them, not against each other, but against Great Britain—to compromise their internal quarrel (*the slave question included*) and invade the British territory without notice and with overwhelming force. And, even if these exhortations might be passed over as the ravings of mere individual ill-feeling,—what is to be said with reference to the avowed and virulently expressed animosity of the three *accredited* ambassadors of the Northern Federation, who not long since astounded the diplomatic world of Paris by their indecent harangues,—and not one of whom has been recalled, or (so far as we know) even reprimanded for the discreditable exhibition? Lastly, and not to extend needlessly the list of grievances, is the Morrill tariff a title to our gratitude and our sympathy? or is the certainty that, in case of Northern triumph, that tariff will be extended over the whole Republic a reason why we ought to be clamorously anxious for their success?

But putting aside—as perhaps we ought to do—all natural resentment, and all merely English considerations, why should we desire such a complete triumph and conquest on the part of the North as could not fail both to confirm all their national defects, and to stimulate their insatiable ambition? With their warlike spirit whetted by a war, and their habitual arrogance augmented by so signal a success, what chance of peace and comfort would there be for any other state that was unfortunate enough to have any relation with them? Ought we to sympathise with them (as they plead) as being the special champions and the choicest specimens of freedom? They claim this character, we know; but we entirely demur to the admission of their claim. For a long time the true liberty of individual citizens has been as little regarded and as ruthlessly trampled down in the United States as in Austria or in France—and in Washington and New York as in Charleston or Louisiana. The oppression has been exercised in a different name and by a different despot—that is all. The violent suppression of unpopular opinions, the ostracising of the more moderate and wise of the public men, the Lynching of the few courageous citizens who stood up for their conscience and their civil rights, have not been confined to the wild West or the slavery-stained South. Real liberty, as *we* understand it,—liberty to act and think and speak as each man chooses,—we have no scruple in saying, did not exist in the United States before the disruption, and does not exist there now;—would have no chance of raising its head if the triumph of the North were to be signal and complete; and is far more likely to be promoted by their defeat than by their victory. This language will, we are too well aware, be unwelcome to Americans and to the admirers of American institutions; but its deplorable truth cannot be gainsaid. What candid man will say that there is personal and moral freedom in the free states now, or that there is likely to be when all opposition shall have been put down by the sword?

This article has already extended to an undesigned length, but we must add a few words in reference to the charge that our want of sympathy with the North is to be attributed to our interest in an undisturbed supply of cotton; that we are backing up the South because we want their crop more than we disapprove their institutions;

in a word that, as one of our contemporaries indicates, we have stopped our ears with cotton wool against the cries of the maltreated slaves. The accusation on the part of Mrs. Stowe might have been passed over as a natural ebullition of irritated disappointment; but it ought not to have been reiterated and supported by a journal like the *Spectator*, so respectable for its moral earnestness, so distinguished by its marked ability. Nothing in the language or conduct of this country since the beginning of the contest has given warrant for the sneer; on the contrary, everything has tended to manifest its singular baselessness and injustice.—The blockade threatens to deprive us of what is nearly as necessary to us as food, to throw some millions of our people out of work, and to inflict unexampled loss and misery upon our most populous industrial districts. The gravity of the case might almost have excused some interference on our part. But what have we done? At the very outset, our Government announced its intention to respect the blockade, however injurious to ourselves, provided only it was carried on in conformity to the recognised law of nations. They showed also, to say the least, no disposition to facilitate the depredations and reprisals meditated by the South on the commerce of the North, when they prohibited privateers from bringing their prizes into British ports. Our merchants and manufacturers, far from urging the Government to break the blockade or to insist on its abandonment, have not, we believe, raised a single voice in support of such a pretension. On the contrary, they have submitted without a murmur to the warnings and occasional detentions inflicted on their ships by the United States cruisers; and instead of preparing to disregard or violate the blockade, have taken the matter with wonderful calmness, and set themselves vigorously to work to investigate their means of procuring supplies of cotton from other quarters. No doubt, our partial dependence on America for the chief raw material of our manufactures renders us very desirous that the civil war should cease, but we do not know that it need induce us to wish for one issue to it more than for another: —the effectual discomfiture of *either* party would answer our purpose equally well;—and we are quite sure that it is simply untrue and unfounded to allege that our political sympathies have in this case been warped by our mercantile interests. They might be supposed to have been so; but our conduct and language from the first have negatived the supposition. Our *interest* as cotton consumers, we repeat it, is in favour of a termination of the war, but it is not more in favour of a Southern than of a Northern victory—unless in as far as the protective tariff of the foolish Federalists has made it so.

We trust that we shall hear no more of these unworthy and unwarrantable accusations. We fully admit that we, in common with the majority of Englishmen, do not believe that the Northern states will be able to reconquer the Southern ones. For many reasons, which we have stated on several occasions, we do not greatly desire that they should;—but both our belief and our desire are wholly independent alike of any attributed indifference to slave-emancipation, and of any selfish anxiety about slave-cotton.

English Feeling towards America[1]

THOUGH we persist in and reiterate our denial of the charge, liberally made on both sides of the water, of unfriendly feeling towards the United States and discreditable selfishness in the English views of the present civil conflict in America, we fully admit that those views and that feeling require careful watching and distinct analysis and explanation. We believe we may safely affirm that, hitherto at least, neither the British Government nor the British people nor British journalists have done or said anything to warrant the acccusation that they have embraced the cause of the South or are actuated by any hostile sentiments towards the North,—still less that, in their estimate of the matter at issue between the two sections and their expressed opinions as to the result, they have allowed selfish interests to outweigh moral considerations. At the same time we are fully aware that an unfavourable interpretation may, by unfriendly critics, be placed upon much that is said and felt—an interpretation which, though we cannot admit it to be just, is yet by no means unnatural. The failures and shortcomings of the Federalists have no doubt been freely and provokingly commented upon: the boasts and insults of several of their newspapers and of some of their politicians in reference to Great Britain may have been sharply and contemptuously answered; and the improbability of final success in the enterprise they have taken in hand may have been boldly and perhaps coarsely predicted. No great care has been taken, we admit, to spare sensitive tempers or to soothe irritated minds; and this is to be regretted. But in this respect we can only plead that the example set us has been very bad, and that we have only followed it partially and at a distance.

On one point, however, we frankly avow that the Northerners have a right to complain; and on one point also we are bound to be more upon our guard than perhaps we have uniformly been. Our leading journals have been too ready to quote and to resent as embodying

[1] This article was first published in *The Economist* for September 28 1861, Volume XX, pp. 1065–7.

the sentiments and representing the position of the United States, newspapers notorious at all times for their disreputable character and feeble influence, and now more than suspected of being secessionists at heart, of sailing under false colours, and professing extreme Northern opinions while writing in the interests and probably in the pay of the South. Few Englishmen can, for example with any decent fairness, pretend to regard the *New York Herald* as representing either the character or the views of the Northern section of the Republic. Again: we ought to be very careful lest our just criticisms on the Unionists should degenerate by insensible gradation into approval and defence of the secessionists. The tendency in all ordinary minds to *partisanship* is very strong: most men feel an irresistible though unconscious tendency to side with one party or other in a dispute; and when we are obliged to blame one side strongly, we are very apt to extenuate the faults and embrace the views of the other. Now, however warmly we may resent much of the conduct and language of the North; however we may feel satisfied that the prosecution of the war is on their side a blunder, and must issue in certain loss and in probable disaster; however inclined we may be to laugh at their mismanagement, and to look with some complacency on the mortifying and deplorable fulfilment of our own predictions,—we must never forget that the secession of the South was forced on with designs and inaugurated with proceedings which have our heartiest and most rooted disapprobation. We, of course, must condemn the protective tariff of the Union as an oppressive and benighted folly—silly and suicidal in itself, iniquitous towards the West, and hostile as regards ourselves. Of course we reciprocate the wish of the South for low duties and unfettered trade. Of course we are anxious that the prosperity of states which produce so much raw material and need so many manufactured goods should suffer no interruption or reverse. Most of us are of opinion also, that they were entitled to secede, if so it seemed good to them; and that the claim of ten millions of republicans to frame their own unions and to select their own fellow-citizens could not logically be resisted by brother republicans, though numbering twenty millions. We saw, therefore, no reason why they should be hindered from seceding if they chose, and we saw some reason why we should be glad if their secession was successful.

But, at the same time, it is impossible for us to lose sight of the indisputable fact that the real aim and ultimate motive of secession was—*not* to defend their right to hold slaves on their own territories (which the Northerners were just as ready to concede as they to claim) —but to extend slavery over a vast undefined district, hitherto free from that curse, but into which the planters fancied they might hereafter wish to spread. This object we have always regarded as unwise, unrighteous, and abhorrent. The state of society induced in the Southern states by the institution of domestic servitude, appears to English minds more and more detestable and deplorable the more they know of it. And the Southerners should be made aware that no pecuniary or commercial advantage which this country might be supposed to derive from the extended cultivation of the virgin soils of the planting states and the new territories which they claim, will ever in the slightest degree modify our views on these points, or interfere with the expression of these views, or warp or hamper our action whenever action shall become obligatory or fitting. So far as we sympathise with them in the present conflict rather than with their antagonists (which is only to a very partial extent), it is not that we regard slavery or slave extension with one whit less disfavour than the strongest abolitionists of the North; but that we do not consider the 'domestic institution' as lying at the bottom or directly involved in the issue of the strife,— since, if secession had been averted, it would have been averted only by the most solemn confirmation of that institution by the people and Government of the Federation, and if the Union were now to be restored, it would be restored, we well know, only on the basis of such a solemn confirmation. We sympathise with the South (so far as we sympathise with it all), not because we are slaves to our necessity for cotton, or because we fear that emancipation would ultimately cut off the supply,—but because we think that, politically, the Southern states had a right to leave the Federation without hindrance and without coercion; because their behaviour towards England has been more decent and courteous than that of their antagonists; and because they were desirous to admit our goods at 10 per cent. duty, while their enemies imposed 40 per cent. But, if our relations with the Southern Confederacy when its independence is established, are to be comfortable, amicable, and enduring, it is to the last degree important that they should from the outset be based upon the clearest understanding of our feelings and our principles. We, therefore, pray them to believe that slavery, so long as it exists, must always create more or less of a moral barrier between us,—and that even tacit approval is as far from our thoughts as the impertinence of open interference;—that Lancashire is not England, and, for the honour and spirit of our manufacturing population be it said also, that even if it were, 'Cotton would NOT be King.' There are other sources of supply besides the negro plantations of America; but even were there none, our sentiments in reference to slavery would undergo no change. England and Lancashire are ready to purchase cotton, if need be, at a cost of a shilling a lb,—but never at the cost of one iota of consistency or principle.

And now we must add a few words in answer to the charge of *selfishness* so thoughtlessly brought against the views and sentiments entertained by England in reference to the American crisis. We admit that we do regard the disruption of the Union as a matter rather for rejoicing than for regret; and we maintain that we do this without laying ourselves open to the just imputation of any one mean, narrow, or ungenerous feeling. We avow the sentiment, and we are prepared to justify it as at once natural, statesmanlike, and righteous. If, indeed, the choice lay—as some of our contemporaries both here and there so unwarrantably assume—between the preservation of the Union and the perpetuation of slavery; if 'Union' meant negro emancipation as surely as 'secession' means negro servitude,—then, indeed, we should be called upon to take a very different view of the subject. But since we have had every reason to see, and since any one is scarcely daring enough to deny, that if the Union had been preserved, it would have been preserved on terms which would have sanctioned and riveted that perilous and wicked institution, and that if it is now restored, it will be restored on condition of the most solemn guarantee which can be given to the sacredness and inviolability of that institution;—since, moreover, the dissolution of the Union means the confinement of slavery within the limits of the seceding portion, and the liberation of the Northern states with their preponderant wealth and population from the guilt and the complication and the impolitic and immoral exigencies of that abominable system;—and since, finally, we see in the vigilant and jealous antagonism of the free and exonerated North, and in the establishment of a strong and anti-African government in Mexico (which we earnestly hope for and begin dimly to discern as a reasonable probability), an immeasurably better prospect for the immediate compression and ultimate extinction of negro slavery than any which could be offered by a continued connection with the time-serving politicians of the old Republic,—on all these grounds we entirely repudiate and cast aside the false colour which it has been attempted to fix upon the contest. And having done this, we do not see why we should hesitate to declare our belief that the dissolution of the Union will prove a good to the world, to Great Britain, and probably in the end to America herself. The great Republic of the West had grown in population, in prosperity, and in power at a rate and in a way which was not well either for her neighbours or herself. Her course had been so triumphant, so unparalleled, so free from difficulties, so unchequered by disaster or reverse, that the national sense and the national morality had both suffered in the process. A boundless territory, an exhaustless soil, a commerce almost unequalled, mineral wealth quite unfathomed and apparently unlimited, a people rapidly increasing in numbers and endowed with most of those qualities which ensure empire and predominance to their possessors,—had fairly, and not unnaturally, turned the heads of the whole nation. They believed that no other nation could stand up against them, that none had a claim to interfere with them or thwart them, that the rest of the world had no rights which could for a moment be suffered to stand in the way of their interests or their designs. They were so rough, so encroaching, and so overbearing, that all other governments felt as if some new associate, untrained to the amenities of civilised life, and insensible alike to the demands of justice and of courtesy, had forced its way into the areopagus of nations;—yet at the same time they were so reckless and so indisputably powerful, that nearly every one was disposed to bear with them and defer to them, rather than oppose a democracy so ready to quarrel and so capable of combat. The result was, as might be expected, an increase of arrogance and a stretch of pretensions which made it clear that, sooner or later, all who did not wish to be habitually trampled on and insulted must prepare to fight. At the same time, it became painfully obvious that this very unrebuked exercise of increasing power was demoralising the inmost nature of the people, blinding their eyes alike to what was just in their relations to others and to what was worthy and noble in the true objects of national ambition. This being so—and who can gainsay it?—with what colour or consistency of reason can we be charged with selfishness or want of generosity, because we rejoice that an excess of power which was menacing to others and noxious to themselves has been curtailed and curbed; that we are spared the painful alternative of ceaseless squabbles and ceaseless endurances or of a desperate and decisive conflict; that pride which was fast becoming a disease has met with a salutary check; that the weak places and the radical faults in those democratic institutions which they were accustomed to worship with a blind idolatry have been laid bare in time; and that in future they will have to share the common lot of European nations, and to develop their resources and pursue their progress under the wholesome restraints of powerful neighbours and rival forms of polity? We rejoice that they are weakened, not because we derive gratification from their mortification or desire to take advantage of their misfortunes, but because they both over-estimated and abused their strength, and because this over-estimate and this abuse were bad for them as well as disturbing to us; and our sentiments have in them no alloy for which we need to blush; for if originally prompted by a paramount consideration for the welfare of England, they are perfectly in unison with the most Christian and amicable feelings towards America.

If, indeed, there were any rational ground for the apprehension which some appear to entertain, that with the dissolution of the Union, the real greatness and prosperity of America are at an end,—that the several states will separate and split into so many independent and insignificant republics, without union and without power, jealous, quarrelsome, and mutually destructive, like the feeble and anarchic provinces of the southern continent,—then there would be reason for reconsidering our views. But we do not do the Northerners the discredit to fear so ignominious a termination to their dreams of honourable grandeur. We believe that Anglo-Saxon sense and Anglo-Saxon principles will preserve them from the fate of Mexican and Spanish impulsiveness and imbecility. We are confident that, as soon as the danger shall become apparent and imminent, measures will be taken to avert it; and that the very self-control, mutual forbearance, reciprocal consideration, and fair terms of arrangement and of compromise, which the perilous crisis will necessitate and call forth, will afford the best conceivable discipline for the American character, and will cultivate political and moral excellences which had no chance for growth so long as they had a whole world to bully and a whole continent to overrun. Even if the vast territory belonging to the old Republic, and stretching from Canada to Mexico, were to be severed into four independent states, each of them might be wider in extent, richer in resources, and ultimately more populous and powerful, than the mightiest monarchies of Europe.

Our Duty[1]

THE forcible seizure of certain Confederate gentlemen on board a regular English packet by a Federal man-of-war is an act contrary to the usage of civilised nations, which the Federal Government must be called on to disavow,—and is, if it be not promptly apologised for and disowned, a *casus belli* that a stern duty will not permit us to disregard. The subject may be easily perplexed by needless verbiage; but the essential considerations may be simply stated, and in few words.

The duty of self-exculpation, at the outset, lies with the Federal Government. An armed vessel of theirs has taken from an unarmed vessel of ours, under irritating circumstances, certain passengers whom our ship had received on board at the port of a neutral nation, in the usual course of business, and with no fraudulent intent. Those passengers claimed our protection, and appealed to the inviolable sanctity of the British flag. They claimed the right of asylum which we have boasted that we offer on our ships and our soil to the weaker party of all countries; they asked no aid and no favour from us; they simply sought the ordinary safeguard of our laws and the common assurance of our hospitality. It is no light matter that a foreign government should presume to touch with the tip of a finger men in such circumstances. The honour of England is tarnished by the ill-treatment of our guests; the security of our commerce is impaired by the violation of our vessel. The Americans *may* be able to justify their conduct; but they have done an act of very serious consequences, and needing very conclusive exculpation.

What, then, are their reasons? Their real and true reason very likely was that they wished to apprehend certain persons whom they call, and who are in the eye of their law, rebels. The passion—the fury— of a great civil conflict among a half-instructed people whose political passions know no restraint, has become so intense and eager that for

---

[1] This article was first published in *The Economist* for November 30 1861, Volume XIX, pp. 1317–18.

the sake of capturing their adversaries the Federalists were ready to brave every consequence and risk every danger. But this true and real ground they cannot avow. It is precisely because of the intensity of the evil passions incident to civil war that the right of asylum upon neutral soil is so invaluable to political refugees all over the world, and it is this safe asylum which England has ever and will ever afford them without exception and without distinction. As we should not permit the Austrian Government to take Mazzini from the packet between Dover and Calais—as we should not permit the French Emperor to harm Louis Blanc between Dublin and Holyhead,—so we must protect those so-called American rebels *on our ship* between St Thomas and the Havana.

As the vital reason cannot be alleged, the Federal Government will have to advance legal and technical defences, which may be variously amplified and worded, but which are reducible in substance to these two.

First, it will be alleged that the captured persons were 'contraband of war.' This barbarous term is properly applicable to any munitions or implements of war; to any soldiers or sailors on active service; to any despatches from the belligerent government to its subordinates; and implies that these men and articles are liable to seizure for contravening the peculiar laws of war, just as smuggled goods are likewise liable to it for contravening the common laws of commerce. The ground of this doctrine is the ground of necessity. It is said to be the right and the duty of every belligerent to finish the war in which he is engaged as promptly as he can. For this purpose, therefore, it is his duty to preclude his enemy from obtaining supplies of men and ammunition, from writing letters which might aid him in obtaining them, from the import of arms and men, and from the export of such documents and despatches as may strengthen him and may prolong the war.

The limit of this right is the limit of its reason. It is bounded by its necessity. Neutral nations, and the Americans above all, have been active and anxious for many years to enclose it within rigid bounds. If it were not stringently confined, all trade might be stopped; for all trade strengthens the trader, and the more commerce any belligerent enjoys, the longer he will be able to protract the war. Defined regulations have, therefore, been agreed on by the mutual consent of nations, and we have only to ask whether the act of the captain of the San Jacinto be within those rules.

Beyond all question it is not. The captain of a man-of-war has no power to adjudicate on such questions as the present. Naval officers on remote stations, with passions and without books, are not fit to adjudicate on important and anxious questions. The worst rule regularly adjudicated upon by a competent court of law would be better than the best administered by a sea-captain. It is certain that the act of the Federal commander was one which *he* at all events had no right to do.

And if the case had been brought before a regular prize court, even an American prize court, it would have been doubtless decided that the act now done was illegal. When the news first arrived, it was argued that as the Federals would have a right to intercept a despatch of the Confederates, they would also have a right to intercept an envoy, who was only an 'animated despatch.' But this ingenious suggestion fails for two reasons. First, the American Government would have no right to seize a despatch which was addressed to a neutral. The design of the rule which allows the capture of despatches is the prevention of the military measures of one belligerent by another. This design is presumably promoted by the capture of despatches from the belligerent government to its subordinates, or from those subordinates to the belligerent government, for these probably relate more or less to the conduct of the war. But it is not presumably promoted by the capture of a despatch from a belligerent to a neutral. 'The presumption,' says Kent, the first American, perhaps the first existing, authority on the subject, 'is, that the neutral preserves its integrity.' 'The neutral country has a right to preserve its relations with the enemy, and it does not necessarily follow that the communications are of a hostile nature.' If England were at war by any unfortunate chance with Holland, what insignificant proportion of the despatches of the English Government to other nations would have a material bearing on the fortunes of the war? We should not be asking their aid, nor would they be requesting us to accept of it.

The whole foundation of the alleged analogy of the envoy to the despatch therefore fails; for the Federal Government would in this case, on the authority of their own lawyers, have possessed no right to intercept a despatch. But even supposing it had, there is a material difference between a man and a document. The document proves its own contents; you can say by reading it whether it was or was not designed to facilitate the success of the war in progress. *But the errand*

331

of a man is the secret of his brain. In some sense, political refugees have always treason in their hearts. Mazzini might be said to be a professional envoy, and if that were a ground for seizing him, he might be seized anywhere or at any time. In the present case, it has not been proved, and very likely is not true, that the Confederate envoys were authorised to solicit military aid from Europe. They were probably commissioned to procure, if possible, from France or England, a recognition of the national independence; but that recognition would have given them no military advantage, and the arrival or non-arrival of particular envoys has very little tendency to accelerate or retard events of that kind and magnitude.

On this ground, no judge has ever decided that an envoy could be seized, even in circumstances where written despatches might be intercepted. The object of the man is almost always, as here, uncertain —that of the letters manifest; and it is too much, therefore, for the Americans to contend that they could arrest an envoy where they could not even seize a despatch.

If this first technical ground of justification fail the Americans, the second is yet more shadowy and unsubstantial. We have, at various times, claimed to impress our *own* seamen on board foreign vessels, on the ground that we had a right to claim the military aid of all our subjects whenever or wherever they may be found by us. But it would be a monstrous insult to common sense to say that these envoys were impressed by the Federal captain to serve in the Northern fleet against their countrymen in the South. They are infinitely more likely to be hanged as rebels than to be trusted as auxiliaries. The defence, too, would be inconsistent with the entire bearing of the Federal captain, who throughout acted as if he were apprehending rebels, not as if he were impressing seamen.

These are the only two technical justifications of the American outrage, and, as they both fail, it is left without excuse and without defence. It appears that the Americans seized certain foreigners claiming English protection and in an English asylum; and we should be shrinking from the sacred duties of hospitality, and abandoning one of the highest privileges of a great nation, if we permitted such an act.

Why the Americans have so acted, it is impossible to say. At times we acknowledge we have inclined to the belief that there was a deliberate intention to insult this country. We remembered the antecedents of Mr. Seward; his language as to Canada; his circular to the several states, requesting them to fortify themselves on the North, and, there-fore, against England; we thought of the many recent occasions in which a studious distinction has been drawn between the French and ourselves, in which they have been treated with studious respect, and we *at least* with rudeness; we called to mind the ignorance, not so much of the conspicuous American politicians as of the low 'president-makers' and pot-house patrons on whom they depend; we fancied that some vague scheme of remedying shame *within*, by insult *without* might float in turbid minds. But we will hope not. The highest authori-ties in this country we understand hope not. They believe that this insane outrage was caused rather by enmity to the South than by insolence to us.

Our duty is clear. We must demand moderately, but firmly, apology for the insult, and reparation to the injured. We must require that the gentlemen who have been seized should be at once set at liberty, and that regret should be expressed for the dishonour of our national flag and for the violation of the sacred right of asylum;—and we must intimate that if they refuse we have no alternative save *war*. The calamity is great, but the obligation is greater.

The Unwillingness of Reflecting Men to admit the Probability of an American War[1]

IT cannot be denied that the mercantile classes and the more reflecting and sensible part of the English people at large are very loath to credit the imminent danger of an American war. The utter absurdity of supposing that a nation so hard pushed as the United States can desire to offend, or be unwilling to propitiate, a new combatant so powerful as Great Britain, bewilders the imagination and staggers the judgment of reflecting Englishmen engaged in common avocations. On the other hand, official persons, especially those most closely engaged in warlike preparations, undoubtedly believe an immediate war to be a most probable calamity and peace to be an improbable blessing. Which of these opposed opinions rests upon the better grounds?

Unquestionably our men of business are right in thinking that it would be inexpedient, absurd, and almost mad in the Federal states to force a war upon us now. They are engaged in a difficult civil struggle which they commenced with unnecessary arrogance, which they continue with revolting virulence, in which they have had no conspicuous success, in which they have incurred disgraceful disasters. We were told by Mr. Clay and by other Northerners, 'Conquer the South? *Of course* we can. We can march two columns through their country, overcoming all we meet, and subjugating as we go.' The result has been entirely different. As yet there has been more fear that the Southern army may occupy Washington than well-grounded hope of a permanent subjugation of the Gulf states. History, indeed, does not record a more conspicuous *break down* than we see in the military system, in the administrative system, in the whole efficiency of the United States. Anything wilder than a war with a great European nation under such circumstances it is impossible for a reasoning being

[1] This article was first published in *The Economist* for December 14 1861, Volume XIX, pp. 1373–4.

to imagine. It must ensure the permanent independence of the South:
—that probably is not so much, for it is sure already; but it must
entail the loss of the vast *debateable land* upon which the present
conflict has in the main been carried on. It must secure a frontier line
drawn not as they would have it, but as the South have dreamed of it.

It seems absurd to think that a nation so placed would incur such
risks as these, and an ordinary nation would never dream of it. But
America is a very extraordinary nation; and the time is a very extraordinary time. *Nothing is impossible to a democracy in revolution.* The
President is unequal to the situation in which he is placed. He has
received the training of a rural attorney, and a fortuitous concurrence
of electioneering elements have placed him at the head of a nation. His
ministers are divided; his generals are divided. The policy of the
Government even on the vital question of slavery is at variance with
itself; it is one thing in one place, and altogether different in another
place. Even the most sanguine Americans admit that there is no *head*
at Washington.

How much can we then clearly discern through this misty turbulence? We can see many elements of danger, and but few elements of
hope. We see that the two principal forces at present in American
politics—the mob and the politicians now in power—are very likely
to be inclined to a war with this country. The vast mass of Americans
think they can inflict vital injury on this country. Even travellers here,
acquainted with the relative resources of the two nations, still boast of
what they could do, and of how little they have to fear. They fancy
that they could create a vast though miscellaneous fleet *impromptu*;
they think that they could send forth privateers infinite in number and
invincible in excellence. They dream of acquiring Canada. We know
how false these illusions are, but the decision is to be determined by
their opinions and notions, and not by ours.

The leading politicians of the Republican party, Mr. Seward and
his associates, have a very considerable temptation to commence a
war with Great Britain. They have promised the subjugation of the
South, and it is as evident as the existence of America that the system
they have created, and the measures they have authorised, will not
subjugate the South. They are in the luckless position of prophets
who desire an excuse for the falsification of their prophecy. A war
with England is the best possible excuse which they could have or
hope to have. If a rupture should intervene, they could say and would

say, 'We should have conquered the rebel states; but England, which in former times wished to tyrannise over us, now wishes to destroy the Union which was formed in opposition to her, by which she has been thwarted—which she feels a shame and an obstacle to her glory.' All this would be folly, for England has no such thoughts, but it would be adequate to its purpose. Mr. Seward would *creep out.* He would evade the destruction which awaits false prophets by throwing the blame upon the universal culprit—upon the ever-sufficient scapegoat—upon England. The selfish interest of the present foreign minister—the ablest, most potent, and most unscrupulous politician in the existing Government—the most influential of the public men belonging to the party of which Mr. Lincoln is the nominal representative and the *roi fainéant,*—is as favourable to war as the bitter passion of the New York mob.

Nor is the problem which Lord Russell's despatch will present to Mr. Seward one of which a pacific solution can be easy. The American Government have not formally accepted the act of Captain Wilkes, but they have not repudiated it, and their organs have unanimously accepted and applauded it. If they wished for peace, it would have been more dignified to give up the commissioners before they were asked than to wait till afterwards. No question has been raised even as to the possibility of submitting them to an adjudication—to the decision of a court of admiralty. The violent act of a naval officer has been accepted as adequate to determine the *status* of two persons under British protection.

England cannot so far humiliate herself, and will not do so. If *bonâ fide* proposals of sincere reconciliation should emanate from a government in which we had confidence, we might think it right to pause and hesitate. But for a long time past Mr. Seward and his coadjutors have uniformly, at least in the opinion of those best qualified to judge, acted as if they desired a war with England, and it is not possible to suppose, *if that be so,* that they will forego the present opportunity.

The scene is doubtless a shifting one. Congress is meeting, and may have an influence for good or for evil. An army lies near Washington whose dispositions and whose general may have to be counted with. The President, who is honest though weak, may lapse into right feeling. But we are not prophets to decipher the unseen and all-important future; we can only count up the probabilities of the hour. As far as these go, the present aspect of American affairs is dark and lowering.

The Last Probabilities of War or Peace[1]

THE events of the past week have not settled and do not settle the question of peace or war. We still have to balance dubious probabilities, not to comment upon clear certainties. We still have no decisive intelligence of American opinion, and until satisfactory information is received on that point, all discussions of the subject are wanting in the principal fact and critical *datum*. The general voice of the public has pronounced that war seems less likely than it did last week, and though there may be but a single shade of difference of probability, we concur in the general judgment.

The American Constitution has puzzled most persons in this country since the remarkable course of recent events has attracted a real attention to American affairs, and it has rarely puzzled them more than now. We are in this country used to a Constitution in which the will of the House of Commons, of the popular element in our national polity, is supreme and final. We are used to trace the growth of that Constitution in history, and we consider those times most free when the House of Commons had the greatest, and those times least free in which that House had the least authority. We have, too, been used to hear that in some sense America was a country more free than ourselves, and we naturally anticipated that the body most analogous to the House of Commons would have more immediate influence and more conclusive despotism there than it has here. The surprise was therefore general when we heard that the House of Representatives had passed a resolution commending the act of Captain Wilkes, and yet that such a resolution was not final. If the House of Commons had agreed to such an opinion, we all know how irreversible that opinion would have been.

Nor even in America is such a resolution a matter of inconsiderable importance. The House of Representatives is the lower chamber of their Congress, and is therefore a very just index of common opinion.

[1] This article was first published in *The Economist* for December 21 1861, Volume XIX, pp. 1401–2.

It is composed of average persons representing the ordinary political opinion, not of the more intelligent and educated minority, but of the ordinary rude and practical mass which rules beyond the Atlantic. As a sign of the times, the resolution of the representatives is significant, but its immediate influence is trifling.

The President of America is very much like an English Premier appointed for a term of years. We are all of us familiar with the great power which a prime minister has here; we know that he has great patronage, great power over domestic administration, almost incalculable influence upon foreign policy; but we have no dread of this power. We know that he was appointed, indirectly but effectually, by the representatives of the nation, and that he is *removeable* at their pleasure. The American President is a more popular officer in one sense, because he is appointed by the nation at large; but he is far less amenable to popular influence and control, for he is appointed for a fixed period, during which his discretion is absolute, and, except for treason, he cannot be impeached or removed. The English Premier is a tenant-at-will, but the American President has obtained a *lease for years*.

The result is now most important. Mr. Lincoln can determine the reply which he will give to the despatch of Lord Russell without consulting the House of Representatives, without considering them as a House of very great importance, and only regarding their resolutions as indications of that public opinion to which the ruler of every free state must, from the nature and necessity of his office, pay close and anxious attention. The resolution of the House of Representatives, so far from being conclusive, is scarcely of itself an element in the critical determination of peace or war.

The critical element is the decision of the executive, and, expressed in English phraseology, the probability seems to be that the executive will consult the House of Lords. By the first article of the Constitution, the Senate or upper House is associated with the President in making treaties and in appointing ambassadors. In consequence it has acquired a sort of general supervision of diplomatic matters; it has a permanent committee on foreign affairs which possesses great though undefined influence, and which interferes with the executive to some extent directly, and to a much greater extent indirectly. Theoretically, perhaps, Mr. Lincoln might have instructed Mr. Seward to write an answer to Lord Russell without consulting any other person, but the present probability certainly is that he will not do so.

Mr. Lincoln is a weak man but honest, and, like most honest men, he is cautious. He has shown a disposition on all occasions to avoid a peremptory decision and to keep everything open as long as possible. He has been faithful now to his policy of delay. He has not alluded to the seizure of the *Trent*. It is highly probable, therefore, that in a more or less formal manner he will ascertain the opinion of the diplomatic committee of the Senate, and will reduce (as he has always tried to do) his personal responsibility to a *minimum*, by acting in accordance with the opinion of a respected constitutional authority. Doubtless this is not certain; it is only one possibility out of many; still it has very many chances in its favour, and no very great chance against it.

What the Senate or its committee would say is a most uncertain question too. We hardly know what sort of assembly the Senate will now be. It is composed of representatives from each state (little Delaware sending as many as the 'Imperial State' of New York); and the states of the South, which used to control if not to guide it, are now no longer represented there. On this side the Atlantic no instructed politician will give a confident opinion on the decision of what is practically a new assembly under circumstances wholly novel. But there is a first-rate observation highly favourable to peace. No select committee of sane *Americans can at the present moment wish for war with England.*

There is unquestionably an utter madness among a very large part of the American nation, fostered by long prosperity and by assiduous adulation. They imagine that though they are engaged in a hitherto equal campaign with the South, they can beat the South and England into the bargain. There is a large class of trading politicians, of whom it seems no injustice to say that Mr. Seward is the head, who trade upon this delusion, though they must be too educated to acquiesce or share in it. But if the President is guided by persons who are not mad themselves, and who are not wishing to take advantage of madness in others, he cannot but be anxious for an honourable peace with England.

There are but two possible alternatives for the preservation of peace. Of these, the first and most obvious is, the immediate delivery of Messrs. Mason and Slidell. In this there is nothing dishonourable. If wrong has been done by mistake or inadvertence, there is no shame in setting it right when attention has been drawn to it. We did so before the last war in an analogous case with America herself. In 1808 we unlawfully seized some seamen whom we believed to be British out of the American frigate *Chesapeake*, and as soon as we discovered our error we released the captured persons, and made additional reparation likewise. Surely the Americans may now do what we did then?

The second course is a far less simple and clear one, which will end, as we are persuaded, in the same result, but which is nevertheless encumbered with many intermediate difficulties which will hamper us much before that result is arrived at. We mean a proposal to submit the legality of Captain Wilkes's act to arbitration. Any proposal of this sort will require much caution and consideration before it is accepted. The Americans scarcely (to use a felicitous legal phrase) come into court with clean hands. They have been so overbearing and insolent formerly, that we are entitled to scrutinise with rigid care every part of their policy now. No proposal of arbitration can be listened to which does not emanate from a clear wish to do what is honourable, and a strong anxiety to preserve not only a momentary, but a permanent peace between the two countries. Nor must any vague undefined proposition be submitted to an improper arbitration. An accurate agreement on the point to be referred must be first arrived at, and a fitting arbitrator must also be selected. Such arrangements are always complicated, always difficult, and often end rather in a renewal of the quarrel than in a settlement; still we should be loath to shut the door to *any* possibility of peace. Mr. Lincoln *may* be able to suggest some mode of arbitration which we can honourably accept; and he *may* be permitted to propose it, notwithstanding the wild insanity of a large portion of his country, and notwithstanding the culpable stratagems of some leading politicians who hold high office and are thought to have great influence.

The News from America[1]

THE intelligence we have this week received from America is, on the whole, better than we had any reason to expect. It is not a certainty of peace, but it adds very much to the probability of peace. The great questions to be decided as to the policy of America were two:—First, would there be such a pressure on the Government by the New York mob, other mobs, and the people at large, that it would be unable to exercise its own judgment? Secondly, if it could decide for itself, would the decision be for peace or for war?

The *first* question is now decided, or nearly so. The reception of the English demand in all parts of the Union was not known when our latest accounts were transmitted; but the effect at New York, at Washington, and several other places was known, and if these places may be taken as specimens of the general feeling of the country, as with some allowance they fairly may, the President will be allowed to act for himself. There were no large public meetings to overawe men, and no notice of any such; the tone of the press had changed; the House of Representatives had refused to pledge itself to support Captain Wilkes until the diplomatic committee of the Senate had been consulted. Those who had been loudly unreasonable before were beginning to be much quieter already; those who had been reasonable before, but had been compelled into silence, were beginning to open their lips. On the whole, it seems clear that the Government may act wisely if it will.

Secondly. As to the intentions of the Government, we have no means of speaking confidently as yet. When the last steamer sailed, the *official* demand of England had not been delivered to the President. Lord Lyons had seen Mr. Seward, and had told him what the demand was. But the information was preparatory and conversational, not formal and ultimate. Mr. Seward is understood to have received the communication in a 'good spirit'—to have shown a general disposition

[1] This article was first published in *The Economist* for January 4 1862, Volume XX, p. 1.

to an amicable adjustment—to have expressed no invincible repugnance to the surrender of the commissioners, but yet to have said nothing definite. On the other hand, it is said, though we do not vouch for the accuracy of *this* part of the intelligence, that Mr. Chase had expressed himself favourable to peace at a bank meeting; and the bankers whom he is alleged to have addressed would probably almost require of him to be as pacific as possible. But, nevertheless, as to the intentions of the Government, we are still without any information which can be deemed conclusive and decisive.

Some persons have been inclined to fear that the American government was itself disposed to war, because it has not surrendered the commissioners after the private, but before the formal, communication of the English demand. They think that such an immediate delivery would have been more dignified than a reluctant delivery after consideration and delay, and infer that as Mr. Lincoln has not chosen this course, he does not intend to comply with our demand. But it is dubious whether such an immediate surrender would *now* be very dignified. If Messrs. Mason and Slidell had been released before the requisition of the English Government was known in America, the position of the President and of America would have been undeniably dignified. But there is little difference, if any, between yielding to a formal demand which is avowedly public, and yielding to the same demand informally delivered. Probably the most dignified course at Mr. Lincoln's disposal is a reference of the legal claims of England to some legal adviser—to some court or law officer. If he wishes to surrender the commissioners, he will easily obtain an opinion that they ought to be surrendered.

And there is an additional reason why Mr. Lincoln should not have been in an extreme hurry to surrender Messrs. Mason and Slidell, namely, that he may wish to obtain intelligence of the popular feeling in other parts of the Union besides those which had received the intelligence when our news was sent off. American politicians have been sometimes called, in allusion to a phrase of the puritan times, *waiters upon the people*. Naturally Mr. Seward and his coadjutors would like to hear what the *whole* people felt and thought before they decided on a very delicate, perplexing, and critical subject.

That the American people should change their opinions quickly belongs to their character and to their circumstances. They have not the means of hearing both sides; the press only says what will please them; their politicians only profess what will flatter them. By nature they are impulsive, and in education they are half taught; they are especially subject to passions of opinion; they are almost entirely wanting in ballast to resist them. In consequence, they form their judgments easily and change them as easily.

The Reply of the American Government[1]

AT last we are relieved from the uncertainty which, for the last few weeks, has been hanging over us. The American Government has decided,—not very logically perhaps, but very wisely,—to release on our demand the commissioners whom it had previously detained and imprisoned. So far as the gentlemen themselves are concerned, this is a very tardy and unsatisfactory reparation. They will justly ask: 'Why we were ever incarcerated, if we are now released? Both cannot be right. Either you had a right to capture and detain us, or you had not: if you had, you are wrong in releasing us; if not, as you now say, you were acting tyrannically and illegally in detaining us.' But we are not concerned so much with the Confederate commissioners as with ourselves. We have obtained all which we did ask, all which we could ask, and more than we could venture with any certainty to expect. We requested the release of the commissioners, and they are released. If there were any previous facts which excited our just resentment, or which awakened our solicitude, now those facts should be forgotten. An old proverb tells us not to scrutinise gifts too closely, and under the circumstances we will consider the act of Mr. Lincoln a free gift.

The previous discussions at Washington are not now material. It would appear, however, that the members of the American Cabinet advocated very different opinions, that the President long wavered which he should choose, and that the final result is in the nature of a compromise between them. Those members of the Cabinet who advocated a compliance with the demand of England dwelt, doubtless, on the state of the American finances, upon the expressed opinion of France and of Europe, and, we will hope, upon the plain justice of the case. Those who advocated a non-compliance must have insisted on the previous approval of the act of Captain Wilkes by the Navy Department; upon the tacit endorsement of that approval by the President,

[1] This article was first published in *The Economist* for January 11 1862, Volume XX, pp. 29–30.

who struck out much else from the reports of his subordinates because he disapproved of it, but who did not strike out that; upon the vote of the House of Representatives; upon the actual detention of the prisoners, which was only right if Captain Wilkes was right. They doubtless argued, 'It is mean to relinquish when it is demanded, that which we adopted before it was demanded; it is base to concede under pressure that which we should never have conceded without pressure. It is evident that the out-of-door multitude in many parts of America are strongly inclined rather to blame the tameness than to praise the wisdom of their Government.

The course adopted has been a compromise between these two extreme arguments. The act of Captain Wilkes has been repudiated and disowned, but only from an incidental error in its execution: its principle is entirely justified. The American Government contend, as we are informed, that the *Trent* might and ought to have been taken by Captain Wilkes to New York Harbour, and if so taken she would have been condemned. Mr. Seward, we understand, states as much expressly in his reply to Lord Russell, and dilates on it with care and elaboration. In its consequences this doctrine may be very serious. Mr. Seward's despatch will be a sort of legal manual for American captains; it will give them all which Captain Wilkes sought to obtain by laborious studies in Wheaton and Lord Stowell. If Mr. Seward lays down, as we believe he does, that any mail packet which carries and conveys messengers or couriers from the Confederate states to a neutral power may be seized by Federal cruisers on the high seas, assuredly some will be so seized. The Confederate states will and must send envoys everywhere; our steamers are the great means of transit everywhere. Inevitably some of these steamers will carry some of these messengers. It would be within the doctrine of Mr. Seward, as we understand it, that the packet boat between Boulogne and Folkestone should be captured and taken in tow to New York, because Mr. Slidell or Mr. Mason happened to be on board of her.

We have shown repeatedly that this doctrine is wholly false, and it has been distinctly repudiated by the most important neutral powers. The captain of a mail packet may be *compelled* to take passengers; he is bound both by the law of England and by the law of America to receive all comers. How can he possibly investigate from whence each is coming and whither he is going mediately or immediately. Taking a ticket would become a judicial investigation if this theory were accepted or regarded. 'There is,' says a writer in the 'National Review,' 'another mode of stating the same argument which is even more obvious. Suppose, what may easily happen, that a mail packet has on board her contraband, or possibly contraband, articles belonging to *both* belligerents; suppose that Mr. Adams had been a passenger in the *Trent* as well as Messrs. Mason and Slidell,—would she have been equally liable to confiscation by either the Federal or the Confederate courts? Can a neutral ship, which impartially aids both combatants without asking which is which, or being aware that it is aiding either, be justly subject to confiscation *by* either? The result seems absurd, yet it is inevitably and inextricably assumed by every argument which would justify the condemnation of the mail steamer *Trent* by a court of admiralty.'

If we thought that these doctrines of Mr. Seward were really meant and would be truly acted upon, our joy at the release of the commissioners would be materially mitigated. They seem to us to contain the seeds of so much future dissension, that we could not heartily rejoice at the happy close of the recent dispute. But we are inclined to hope that they may simply be the result of a natural compromise in the American Cabinet. If, as we believe, one party wished to adopt the act of Captain Wilkes both in its mode and in its principle, and if another wished to repudiate that act both in mode and in principle, it is very likely, according to all known habits of conducting business at least in the old world, that one party would yield one-half and the other the other half. The immediate difficulty would be overcome by abandoning the manner of Captain Wilkes's act, and writing a strong letter in favour of its principle; and this, as far as we can learn, seems to have been the actual result.

The moral of all this is very plain and simple. In all future dealings with the American Government, we must ask for what we want, courteously but peremptorily. The evident fact remains. Until they received Lord Russell's letter, they showed no intention of releasing— beyond all question did not intend to release—the commissioners. After they received that letter, the commissioners were at once released. The effect of the Palmerstonian policy is evident, for we have experience of it; that of a refining, hesitating Aberdeenite policy must be conjectured, but it would probably have failed in the principal result. An aged statesman will seldom be able at the extremity of life to confer so signal and so characteristic a benefit on his country.

Shall the Blockade be Respected?[1]

AN impression is rapidly gaining ground among jurists and thoughtful politicians, that the whole code of international law, so far especially as relates to the conflicting rights of belligerents and neutrals, needs thorough investigation and revision. There are many reasons for this. That curious mixture of theory and practice which is loosely called the 'Law of Nations,' is no written or enacted code of indisputable authority, and needing only careful and competent interpretation: it has grown up by degrees in the course of two centuries; partly out of the dogmas of speculative jurists like Grotius and Vattel as to what in their judgment was desirable and right; partly out of the claims of powerful and overbearing belligerents as to what they chose to do and were able to enforce; partly out of the protests of injured and recalcitrant neutrals as to what they were compelled to submit to or were determined to resist; partly out of distinct treaties between particular nations, and having therefore only a local and perhaps only a temporary operation; and, especially of late years, partly out of a series of decisions enunciated by admiralty judges of experience and renown. It was in fact, and is still, a sort of conflicting and fluctuating compromise between judge-made law, and the law of the strongest. Some principles have been universally admitted by the whole civilised world; others by nearly all nations; others again, have remained to this day almost as disputable as ever, the doctrines of one nation having been steadily controverted and resisted by the rest;—but still discussion, practice, and a host of consistent adjudications have introduced something like an approach to order and agreement out of the seething chaos.

The tendency of time and progress has been, as was inevitable, to modify the claims of belligerents both as against each other and against neutrals, and thus to mitigate the sufferings which war inflicts on combatants as on spectators. *Originally*, war meant and involved doing every conceivable injury to the enemy or the enemy's subjects

[1] This article was first published in *The Economist* for January 25 1862, Volume XX, pp. 88–90.

and possessions without the slightest regard to the incidental mischief done to bystanders. *Ultimately,* war may be reduced to a mere conflict between the armies and navies of the combatants, by which neutrals will, directly, be wholly unaffected. We are now in a transition state. The great wars which desolated the early part of this century introduced considerable solidity and much amelioration into international law, but still left several points open to dispute, and several more open to improvement. Considerable modifications, in the interests of commerce and humanity, have been introduced and partially *established* since. Other modifications are still needed, and we trust the present crisis may hasten their discussion and adoption. In the Napoleonic wars, powerful and high-handed belligerents (like ourselves, for example) claimed the right of confiscating enemy's goods in neutral ships and neutral goods in enemy's ships, the right of taking British sailors out of foreign vessels, and virtually (we believe) the right of nominal or paper blockades; and privateering was a recognised and sanctioned practice. By the Treaty of Paris in 1856, nearly all these imperious claims were abandoned formally or practically, both by ourselves and all other nations except the Americans. The neutral flag now covers enemy's goods; neutral goods in enemy's bottoms are exempt from seizure; privateering is renounced and condemned; paper blockades are declared invalid and non-existent; and we should never dream again of taking British subjects out of neutral vessels on the ground of their liability to impressment. In truth, we may say that the only two rights of belligerents *as affecting neutrals* which virtually remain, are blockade, and the search for and confiscation of 'contraband of war' on its way to the enemy's ports. Probably ere long all maritime nations will agree to abandon the second—as not worth the risk of quarrel and collision which it involves, and to modify the first, by some limit to the term for which, even if efficient, it shall be suffered to continue. It is clear that it is a belligerent right of the most sacred, because often the most necessary character, like that of siege and circumvallation. It is almost equally clear that no belligerent could be allowed to blockade the ports of an enemy *for ever,* where access to those ports was of supreme importance to the rest of the world,—as where they constituted the only quarters whence some indispensable article such as tea, cotton, or medicine, for example, could be procured. These, however, are not the questions practically before us now.

We need not, therefore, discuss the point *whether* we should be bound to respect an efficient blockade of the cotton ports of the Confederate states, whatever be the suffering and mischief to ourselves, —nor for *how long*, if not for ever, we ought to endure and respect such blockade. We have always, as our readers know, answered the first question strongly in the affirmative; and, as to the second, we may put it aside as for the present a purely speculative and irrelevant inquiry. The matter now ripe for consideration,—which is much discussed in political and manufacturing circles, which is known to be pressing strongly on the mind of the French Emperor, and which some believe to be also occupying the attention of our own Cabinet,— is, whether, *the blockade being notoriously ineffective and therefore illegal,* we ought not at once to notify to the Federal Government our determination to disregard it, and to our own merchants that they are at liberty to trade with the Southern ports, just as if no blockade had been proclaimed; and that they will be protected in so doing? On every account it is obvious we ought to come to some decision on this matter as promptly as possible. What we do we should do at once; if we determine on doing nothing, that determination should be publicly announced at once.

As to the facts of the case, we understand there can be no doubt. The Americans virtually admit their inability to blockade all the ports by the vandalism (of which more anon) of proceeding to destroy those they cannot adequately watch. But we know that vessels run in and out frequently from most of them; there are almost *regular* ventures from certain West Indian ports to Savannah; and small cargoes get in from time to time all along the coast, and report not having even seen any blockading force. The blockade is quite *inefficient*:—is it in consequence illegal, and *ipso facto* invalid?—We believe there can be no doubt that it is. It was formally declared so at the Congress of Paris; the Americans, though not parties to that Congress or its dicta, had always, in common with other habitual neutrals, protested against paper blockades as unpermissible; and we ourselves, heretofore the great blockaders of the world, had virtually abandoned the pretension even before the Paris declaration. The blockade, therefore, is illegal and invalid, and we are quite entitled to disregard it *if we please.* Shall we do so? Would it be right, wise, and politic to do so? France, we know, would do so willingly. The decision practically rests with England; and the responsibility of that decision is a weighty one. We think our decision ought to be in the negative, and we hope to carry our readers along with us in our reasons.

Our immediate motives for disregarding and annulling the blockade are unquestionably very cogent and very pressing. As long as it exists, we shall obtain no American cotton,—and we have shown in another article how necessary this cotton is to us, and how important to all our interests it is that we should get it soon. It is the daily bread of three counties. The want of it means fearful losses to our manufacturers, actual ruin to many; and, what is far worse, distress, privation, the choice between starvation and the poor rates, to three millions of our most industrious and well-fed operatives. Yet while the ports are invested, even nominally, no cotton will come down to them, partly from fear of its falling into the hands of Federal expeditionists, and partly because the Southerners are resolved to keep it on their plantations till England and France have broken the blockade. With the cessation of the blockade, moreover, there would spring up a very large export as well as import trade between this country and the Confederate states—a trade brisk in proportion to its recent interruption. Those states are denuded of most foreign articles, and the cotton they would send us would be liberally paid for in clothing, sugar, tea, wine, coffee, and cutlery. It is not too much to say that the annulling of the blockade—*which we have a strict legal right to annul*—would make 1862 a year of considerable prosperity to England, instead of a year of almost unexampled adversity—which it now promises to be. It would, to use a colloquial phrase, set our commerce, our cotton manufacture, our railways, and our revenue, *on their legs* again. If it is to be done, it should be done at once, for, as we have once before shown, it will take nearly four months from the date of our decision before the cotton can actually arrive; and if it is *not* to be done, that should be known at once, in order that there may be no intermission in our efforts to obtain the needed raw material from other quarters.

The other motive urged for declaring the blockade null and void is that it would probably terminate, almost immediately, a civil war which is every day becoming more savage and deplorable; which may, if continued, cause the silting up and destruction of all the best harbours of the South; which may end in servile and bloody insurrections; which is devasting the country in which it rages; which is disturbing the commerce of the whole world; and which threatens to involve other nations in its vortex. With the cessation of the blockade would end all prospect of the subjugation of the South, even in the fancy of the Federalists, and the design would be avowedly abandoned. Peace and plenty would in a few months spread their healing influence over both sections of that magnificent, but now distracted land. Certainly these are weighty reasons. Nevertheless they are, to our judgment, outweighed by others. Commercial and material considerations should, we think, give place before political and moral ones.

In the *first* place, our interference will probably be quite unnecessary. Already the leaders of American opinion, and still more the Federal Government, are becoming, not less zealous, but less sanguine in the cause. They are beginning to *realise* in their secret mind that the task they have undertaken is beyond their strength. As long as they believed in the existence of a powerful Union party in the Confederate states; as long as they fancied that the Southerners only wished to make good terms for themselves; as long as they could flatter themselves that their antagonists were not prepared to submit to severe privation and discomfort,—they might not unreasonably indulge in hopes of ultimate success. But all these delusions must be vanishing fast; and the conviction that they have pledged themselves to the *impossible*, is daily gaining ground. Difficulties are thickening around them. Their army is not well disciplined and does not advance; their military chiefs are insubordinate and inharmonious; the expedition down the Mississippi is suspected to be an absurdity; the barbarous plans by which they are endeavouring to supplement their want of real warlike skill and vigour are drawing on them the disgust of the civilised world; and, to crown the whole, the insoluble and *dividing* question, 'What to do with the slaves?' is perplexing and paralysing their action. Then again, the scale of their warfare demands enormous sums of money— *which they have not got*, and *which they cannot get*. They are already in arrears with current payments. With a revenue of twelve millions they are spending one hundred and twenty millions; indirect taxes bring in next to nothing; direct taxes are not even yet voted, much less collected; the loans required are not taken up; and already they have resorted to the desperate, ruinous, and speedily exhausted contrivance of inconvertible paper money. An aggressive war—which theirs is— demands vast expenditure, and they have not the means of spending. Mere want of funds must almost infallibly bring them to a stand in twelve months—probably in six. Is it worth while to encounter the evils of (even lawful) intervention to effect that which circumstances are bringing about so speedily?

In the *second* place, it is most important that peace between the combatants, when it comes, should be permanent and enduring. This it can never be, if it be in any manner or degree the result of foreign interposition. Quarrels that are not *fought out*, are always begun again. Drawn battles—battles stopped by the police—leave the question of the respective strength of the parties undecided and therefore merely postponed. If the United States, after putting forth their full power, are baffled and obliged to acknowledge the independence of the secessionists, they will know that the reannexation they desire is simply impossible and for ever hopeless. If, on the contrary, they are able, even plausibly, to attribute their failure to reduce the Southerners to submission, to any interference of European nations, they will never admit that the dissolution of the Union is an irrevocable and natural termination of the controversy; and under favourable circumstances will be prone to try the enterprise once more.

Thirdly, it is, if possible, still more important that the United States should come out of this conflict with as little unfriendly feeling towards England as possible. There is unfortunately a good deal of standing ill-will towards us among some classes in the Northern states, and under the natural irritation of a desperate civil strife at home, this ill-will has suffered considerable exasperation. But as yet we have done nothing to deserve it. Our conduct has been forbearing and considerate in the extreme; and if our press has spoken out its sentiments with freedom, theirs has been even more sharp and far more hostile; and after all 'hard words break no bones,' and should be forgotten when the sun goes down. In the only two cases in which we have had to *act*,—the recognition of the South as a belligerent, and the demand for the surrender of the captured commissioners,—all sensible Americans already admit that we could have done no less, and that we could not have done that little with more consideration or courtesy. Thus far we have done nothing of which they *could* complain; and when peace is restored they will feel sensible of this, and perhaps grateful for it. But if we were now to disregard and annul the blockade (even if such a step did not bring about a war, which in their excited state of feeling it very probably would), nothing would ever persuade them that the Confederates did not owe their independence to us alone. They would say, and would believe to the end of time, that they were just

356

on the point of conquering the rebels and restoring the Union when England, out of pure avarice and jealousy, stepped in to wrest the victory from their grasp; that we had been treacherous enemies, instead of fair generous neutrals; that it was *we* who had broken up their cherished Union; and that we had dared thus to interpose only because they were embarrassed with another enemy, and had already consented to one humiliation. They would attribute everything to us, and would hate us with insane and unrelenting animosity. Of course this sentiment would be thoroughly irrational and its groundwork utterly unsound; but it would be impossible ever to eradicate it from the national mind. Now, it would be a pity, *if it can be avoided,* to give them even this plausible basis for bad feeling; both because we are naturally anxious to be on truly cordial terms with a nation with whom we shall always have such complicated and extensive business relations, because we sincerely wish them well, and because we have objects, especially those connected with slavery and the slave trade, in which their hearty co-operation will be desirable. It is worth while, therefore, to endure considerable inconvenience and even severe privation for a time, rather than to abandon the hope of an ultimate restoration of kindly feeling between the two people.

Lastly. It would be very undesirable in a case of this kind for our Government to take any steps or to enter on any course of action in which they would not carry the whole country cordially and spontaneously with them—as they did in the late controversy. Now we doubt whether the great body of the British people are yet prepared for any interposition which would *even have the semblance* of siding with, or aiding the establishment of, a slave republic. The social system of the Confederate states is based on slavery; the Federalists have done what they could (untruly and ineffectually enough no doubt) to persuade us that slavery lay at the root of the secession movement, and that they, the Federalists, were hostile to slavery;—and slavery is our especial horror and detestation. It is true that our anti-slavery sentiments, as applied to render distasteful a recognition of the South or any indirect assistance towards its independence, would be both inconsistent and mistaken. We were in amity with the United States, though the whole Union was as much pledged to and as deeply inoculated with slavery as the South can ever be; and we have always continued, almost in a peculiar manner, allied with Spain, though Spain is not only slaveholding but slave-trading. But the real

357

error of the popular sentiment is here:—that every fresh information we acquire and every fresh consideration we give to the subject, makes it increasingly evident that it is the *Restoration* and not the *Dissolution* of the Union that would be the consolidation and perpetuation of negro servitude, and that it is in the independence of the South, and not in her defeat, that we can alone look with confidence for the early amelioration and the ultimate extinction of the slavery we abhor. That this is so we entertain no question; and as earnest emancipationists we hope soon to make this clear to our readers. But it is not clear yet. The majority of Englishmen still think otherwise; and as long as they do so, any intervention on the part of our Government which should place us in a condition of actual opposition to the North, and inferential alliance with the South, would scarcely be supported by the hearty co-operation of the British nation. It should therefore, we conclude, for all these reasons, be avoided if we can avoid it.

Probabilities of a Continuance of the American Civil War[1]

As speculative and philosophical politicians, it is impossible to avoid feeling the intensest interest in the ultimate issue and the contingent consequences of the struggle between North and South. As philanthropists and Christians, it is equally impossible not to deplore the terrible bloodshed and the sanguinary passions which accompany the development of the war,—the mutual animosity of those who ought to be friends, and the mutual devastation wrought by those who ought to be reciprocating each other's commodities and augmenting each other's wealth. But as mere men of business—as practical commercial Englishmen—our more immediate concern lies rather with the duration of the war than with its result. We are more affected by the probability of peace than by its terms. We are more anxious to know when hostilities will cease, than to conjecture which party will come out victorious. Every day that the contest continues inflicts upon us serious distress:—the conditions and compromises by which that contest is brought to a close concern us only indirectly and in the long run. It is natural, therefore, that commercial and moneyed men especially should be desirous of ascertaining what light the recent belligerent movements in America throw on the question whether the war is likely to be a short one or a long one. It is very difficult indeed to see our way; and in dealing with a subject of the details of which we know so little, and with a people whose character we so imperfectly understand, we must speculate very much in the dark; anything like confident conviction is out of the question, and anything like definite prophecy would be singularly rash. Still some points are becoming daily clearer. It is something also to see precisely what are the facts on which the answer we are seeking must depend, even if we are obliged to confess at the same time that we can come as yet to no positive conclusion as to the existence or non-existence of those facts.

[1] This article was first published in *The Economist* for April 26 1862, Volume XX, pp. 450–1.

In the first place, then, the intrinsic superiority of the Federals in wealth and strength—which was never doubted—is made more manifest with every conflict. Their numbers are far greater; their financial resources are essentially much more inexhaustible; and, above all, their command of the sea enables them at once to procure everything they want and to deprive their enemies of all external aid. It was impossible that these advantages should not tell enormously in the long run. At the outset they committed the signal blunder of raising a far greater force than they could train or officer with their existing means, or than they could pay, clothe, and feed without a fearful drain on their funds. But as soon as their first reverses taught them prudence and showed them how deficient and unprepared they were to meet the demands of a prolonged conflict and a resolute and skilful foe, all the singular tenacity, energy, and ingenuity of the national character were called into play. They set vigorously to work to discipline their raw levies and to educate their improvised officers, and by dint of drilling and skirmishing it would seem as if they had now succeeded in bringing up their vast hordes to a very respectable state of efficiency. They certainly fight well, and they do not appear by any means to manœuvre badly. At all events they everywhere go at their work like men who intend to win and have not the faintest doubt that they shall win. Imperfect and doubtful as is much of our information relating to the battle of Pittsburg and the capture of Island No. 10, enough is known to show that both parties fought with indomitable energy, and that on the whole the Federalists were the best managers of the two. Their army is no longer a mob of fiery volunteers. It has evidently become a formidable military force, and will probably improve with every succeeding week and every fresh engagement.

Their finances, too, seem to be more elastic than even most persons on this side of the water ventured to anticipate. The enormous amount of additional paper money which the Treasury was authorised to issue, *has not been issued.* Contractors and others receive 'certificates of indebtedness,' if not for the whole of their claims, at least for a part of their claims, and these are selling at about 96 per cent. The Federalists are not indeed paying their way, but they are getting on wonderfully without paying. It is not easy to say how they manage; but it seems probable they are fighting, marching, carrying, and feeding *on credit.* We hear indeed that the sutlers are making fortunes by advancing money and materials to the soldiers, but we hear of no scarcity of any kind in the camp, nor of any complaints as to arrears of pay. It is true that much may go on of which we do not hear; for the press is controlled not only by the Government, but by the people; and unpleasant facts do not transpire, or are not believed or suffered to gain currency.

But the greatest advantage of all those possessed by the North is that their ports are open and the ports of the South are closed. The whole resources of Europe are available to them. The best munitions of war, the newest artillery, abundance of military clothing, shells and gunpowder in unlimited quantities, can be drawn from the rest of the world as they need them. Their adversaries, on the contrary, are confined in such matters to what they have in store or can manufacture for themselves. Accordingly, there appears to be abundance of everything in the North, and scarcity of everything (except food) in the South. It is in truth, so far, a most unequal contest. If each party had been reduced to the resources of native production, the result might have been very different. As it is, the Federalists have a double advantage. They can still grow rich by trading, and they can import all the means of destroying their enemies. The secessionists, on the other hand, are prevented both from selling their produce and from buying the articles they require for daily use. We do not know whether powder and shot are yet becoming scarce, but certainly clothing, coffee, wine, sugar, butter, and shoes are obtainable only at prices enormously high.

We conclude, therefore, that whenever the two parties meet in actual battle the Northerners must as a rule be victorious. They may encounter particular defeats; they may even sustain disastrous losses; the mismanagement of one general or the greater skill of his adversary may lead to severe temporary reverses. But on the whole, if they fight, the chances are very great that the Southerners must gradually give ground. The *weight of metal* is on the other side. But if they perceive this and accept it, and retreat instead of fighting, the result may be very different. Their adversaries may then be baffled by an extent of territory which they cannot overrun, and by a roadless forest district into which they cannot penetrate with safety. In this case the war *may be a very long one*. Indeed, it is pretty obvious that it *must* be a long one if the Southerners are as resolute as we have been assured they are and as we have every reason to believe. If they are content to play a Fabian and retreating game, to void all pitched battles except where they can take their enemies at an obvious advantage, to retire from the seaboard, and allow the heats and miasmata of the coming summer to fight for them;—if, in a word, their exasperation is great enough, and their powers of endurance patient and tough enough, to induce them obstinately to hold out,—then we confess it seems simply impossible that they should be subdued. *But these are just the conjectural elements of the question.* We have no certain knowledge as to how much and how long they will bear severe privation and the impoverishment of ruined homesteads, an annihilated trade, and the destruction of all the comforts and amenities of life. The Federalists, we are informed, still cling to the conviction that a large Unionist party exists in the South, especially in the great towns; and that as soon as they have obtained possession of several of these this party will arise in strength and insist upon surrender, or at least a compromise. There *may* be such a party: we have not the slightest reason to believe there is; but till we can decide this point, the future must remain uncertain. One thing seems pretty clear—the Northerners, flushed with recent victory and trusting to their unquestionable superiority of resources, are not likely *soon* to offer terms of accommodation;—nor, however willing the more moderate among them might be to compromise the strife, nor, however gladly they might be met by the leaders of the secessionists in listening to such a compromise, does it appear how any arrangement could be come to on any footing except a return to the *status quo*; for the forms of the American Constitution, *still in full force at Washington,* confer on neither President nor Congress the power of negotiating any new conditions of re-union. The tremendous difficulty, therefore, of arranging any terms of peace, even if peace were mutually wished for, will probably be one of the strongest actual causes of a continuance of the war.

To sum up the probabilities of the question in a single sentence:— The *complete* subjugation and prostration of the Confederates appears to offer the only prospect of an early termination of the war;—and such complete collapse on their part could only be the result of very unskilful and impolitic generalship or of very defective powers of resolution and endurance;—and as yet we have seen no symptoms of either of these shortcomings. There is little likelihood that the Federalists, in mid career of victory, will offer any terms of compromise which the South would dream of accepting,—nor, with such singular institutions and such fearfully complicated and momentous points at issue, is it clear how a negotiation, even if both sides or many on both sides yearned for it, *could* practically be set on foot.

Mediation in America[1]

OUR article last week by no means exhausted—indeed, it would not be easy to exhaust—the reasons for hoping that the United States may at length be willing to accept terms of compromise, under the guise of mediation. Every day adds to the number and cogency of the arguments in favour of such a proceeding. We assume—what there exist the strongest grounds for believing—that it is to the Government, to the political leaders, that we have now to address ourselves; and that whatever they determine upon the people, notwithstanding their *bunkum* and bluster, will accept and ratify. Now, these leaders, however bitter and disappointed they may be, can neither be blind to the plain significance of facts, nor insensible to the terrible responsibilities of their position. That position is every day becoming graver, those responsibilities heavier and more alarming, those facts louder, more convergent, and more imperious in their meaning and their tone.

For, first, the war, as it becomes more hopeless on the Federal side, has an ominous but not unnatural tendency to grow more savage and more lawless; and if it continues much longer, will inevitably entail proceedings of such ferocity and wickedness as to stain for ever the Republican name. Already deeds are reported, and there is too much reason to believe have been actually committed, which are a disgrace to the boasted civilisation of our time and of their country. General Butler's acts and proclamations, which have been declared 'infamous' on this side of the Atlantic, have been ratified and applauded on the other. An ovation has been offered at a great meeting at Washington to a Northerner on the *mere supposition* that he was the man who hanged a Southern alderman for hauling down a Federal flag. The Congress has denounced confiscation and death to rebels, and General Pope has legalised plunder and declared that he will execute as traitors all who shall be found violating an enforced oath which he had no right to exact. As a matter of course, President Davis has announced that he

[1] This article was first published in *The Economist* for August 30 1862, Volume XX, pp. 953–4.

will hang in retaliation any of General Pope's officers who may fall into his hands. Already reprisals have begun among the infuriated combatants, and are pretty certain to be repaid with interest. A wounded Federal general has been attacked with his escort, and slain by the Confederates. It is not by any means clear that he was slain in cold blood, or without resistance, or when his helplessness was known; but on the first report of the catastrophe, probably by heated and terrified survivors, a number of secessionists were at once assassinated by the populace near Nashville, though most of them appear to have had no connection whatever with the transaction. Now, it cannot be denied that, if a system of reprisals is established, the whole guilt will lie at the door of the Federal authorities. The insolent absurdity of pretending to regard and treat eight millions of the citizens of free and quasi-independent states as rebels and traitors, is the foundation of the matter, and is utterly unwarrantable and unworthy. If any secessionist citizen, not a spy, or any Confederate prisoner of war, who has not broken his parole, or any Southern individual or civil functionary, shall be hanged on the ground that he is a rebel and traitor and has given comfort and assistance to his fellows,—then we apprehend there can be no doubt that, by every law of morality or of public custom, the Confederates would be perfectly justified in executing Mr. Lincoln, Mr. Seward, or General Butler, if the fortune of war should throw these gentlemen into their hands. Indeed it is by no means clear that General Butler would not be justly liable to military execution independently of such proceedings, as having already transgressed the recognised limitations of legitimate and civilised hostilities. If, therefore, the Federal Government wish to avoid extremities and ferocities and complications which will be inconceivably grievous and dishonouring, they will hasten to terminate the contest while Europe still retains some sympathy with their cause.

Again; if they value the civil liberties of the land—nay, if they value the continued sense of what civil liberty is—they will be anxious to end a state of affairs which is fast extinguishing both. The primary and secondary authorities of the Union, the generals as well as the secretaries of state, are acting as if neither natural rights nor civil law had any longer existence or memory in America. Mr. Seward punishes a citizen who had expressed his sentiments of disgust rather too freely, by ordering him at once to choose between the dagger and the cup,— *i.e.*, between instantaneous imprisonment or being drafted into the army. Yet no law or congressional decree has given Mr. Seward authority thus to supersede all regular magisterial functions and proceedings. Another order from Washington forbids citizens to leave their homes till the militia drafting is completed, and condemns them to military service if they presume to do so. There is no *law* to warrant this; and we may imagine the effect upon a locomotive race like the Americans. A further ukase—as astoundingly despotic as any of the first Napoleon or Nicholas of Russia—which reached us only last week nearly takes away our breath;—for it places under military cognisance, and denounces military punishment against, all who shall *in any way* endeavour to discourage enlistment, or 'shall be guilty of any other disloyal proceeding.' And this proclamation, as far as we can make it out, emanates not from Washington, but from the head-quarters of a general of division. If this be tolerated for an hour, it is obvious that the whole country is virtually under martial law, and the liberties of the freest republic in the world have been suppressed without warrant and without a murmur. We would earnestly pray not only all Northern Americans, but all Englishmen who have hitherto sympathised with their enterprise and admired their character, considerately to weigh the dire significance of these facts—facts which come to us from no hostile sources, and which are related with little surprise and with no disgust by the Federals themselves. To us the proceedings are as amazing as they are ominous and sad.

In the third place, the conscription to which Mr. Lincoln has found himself obliged to have recourse, while it conclusively unveils the decreasing popularity and the increasing necessities of the Federal cause, can scarcely fail immediately to develop a set of consequences at once dangerous and indefensible. The drafting extends to and is to be enforced in all the states to which the Unionist authority reaches, or which are occupied wholly or in part by Unionist troops. Among these are several states of partially or decidedly secessionist proclivities,—as Maryland, Kentucky, Tennessee, and Missouri. In these districts, therefore, the result of the conscription will be to draft by force into the Federal armies numbers who are secessionists at heart or avowedly, and who probably have friends and relations among the Confederate troops. This must almost inevitably entail general and obstinate resistance—to say nothing of the consideration that soldiers so raised must be worse than useless, and would be in fact Confederates in the camp of the Federals. The iniquity, moreover, of compelling such persons to serve is the same as that which has always so revolted every sense of justice both in England and America, when seen in the form of Austrian authorities compelling Italians to serve in the ranks of Italy's oppressors. Practically, however, we apprehend that drafting will be found impossible in the states we have enumerated, and that more troops will be required to enforce it than could be raised by it.

Fourthly. If the war continues, there is much reason to expect that secession may extend by a split among those states which have hitherto comprised the strength of the Union. Pennsylvania is not reliable, and the Western states are beginning to show unmistakable signs of discontent. We are told that Indiana has already by force resisted the conscription. The Eastern and the Western states of the Union have very different interests and feelings. The Western are more anti-slavery than the Eastern; but, except in reference to 'the peculiar institution,' their interests and their characters harmonise rather with the South than with the North. They are agricultural and not protectionist; and if they could be assured of the freedom of the Mississippi, they would have few material inducements for continuing in the Union. Moreover, they are beginning to be conscious that they have furnished more than their fair contingent to the Federal armies; that they have borne most of the sacrifices and have reaped little of the benefits of the war. The debt will be assigned to them in their due proportion; but the money which has caused that debt has been spent, not among them, but almost wholly in the East and North. In consequence, they resent the conscription, and they will resent the visits of the tax-gatherer still more; and there are not wanting indications that the two together may drive them into sullen resistance, if not into actual rebellion. They feel that the eastern section of the Federal Union is not as earnest and sincere as they are in its hostility to slavery; they see that the large bodies of men they have contributed to the Federal armies have been handled feebly and unskilfully; that while their farmers are nearly ruined, eastern contractors and merchants and manufacturers have pocketed enormous gains. The Irish element, again, predominates in the eastern armies, and the German in the western;—and the Irish, and the Germans are not over friendly. If, as seems likely, these various causes of discontent shall combine and culminate and crystallise under the first attempts to carry out the new system of taxation—and nothing is more probable—then the whole Federal power will crumble away; and peace—a disastrous and humiliating peace, because one dictated by the South—will be the unavoidable result. It behoves the Washington Cabinet to be wise in time.

Once more:—It is this fear lest in a short time the fortunes of war may enable the South to dictate terms of peace that makes us especially anxious that mediation should be offered and accepted without delay. If an armistice and proposals for an accommodation be postponed for a couple of months longer; and if, in the course of those two months—as appears highly probable—the Confederates should reconquer New Orleans, drive the Federals out of Tennessee and Missouri, obtain a secession vote in Kentucky, again defeat M'Clellan and again menace Washington,—they will unquestionably be 'masters of the situation,' and any negotiation which may take place for peace must be framed on the basis of a concession of nearly all their original demands. Now, except the reconstitution of the Union by the subjugation of the South, we can scarcely conceive a more disastrous or regrettable result. We were desirous that the South should achieve its independence, because it had a right to do it by every rule of justice and every principle of republicanism; and because in separation, and in separation only, could we discern any hope for the political and moral regeneration of the North. But slavery is so great an evil and so sad a wrong—as an institution it is so fatal to industry, to social progress, to sound views, to real elevation of principle or purpose, that we should grieve to see it enabled to assert or consolidate its empire in any quarter where it is now doubtful or disputed. Now, if the South shall come out of the contest signally victorious and dominant, she will insist on retaining Maryland and Kentucky as well as Texas; and neither Maryland nor Kentucky is really slave in character, or thoroughly tainted and damaged by the spreading cancer of the system, though the prevailing sympathies of both states go with the South. Moreover, any boundary line which gave these states and the whole of Virginia to the Southern Confederacy would be too unjust to the North, and would limit its area so injuriously and unfairly that it could not and ought not to be submitted to, except as a transition measure, or as the issue of a most exhausting defeat. Yet it is plain that if the Confederates so far win the day as to *gain the upper hand*—if they do anything more than merely secure the power of secession—the least they will demand is that every state—or section of state—shall be allowed to decide for itself which of the two republics it will join. In the interests of the North therefore, in the interests of the negro, in the interests of civilisation and humanity at large,—no time should be lost in inaugurating negotiations for a peace. If the Federals wait till the *status quo* instead of the *uti posidetis* must be the basis of accommodation, the consequences may be most disastrous for them and for the world.

Mr. Lincoln's Two Proclamations [1]

THE astonishing absence of statesmanship, and indeed of ordinary political sagacity, which has distinguished the Washington Government from the outset of the civil war, has never been manifested in a more startling or signal shape than in the two manifestoes issued by the President, of which tidings have been brought us by the last mails. He has suspended the writ of *habeas corpus*, and declared martial law throughout the United States with respect to all persons arrested for aiding the rebellion or hindering the draft. He has also proclaimed the emancipation of all slaves in rebel states or belonging to rebels after the 1st of January, 1863. Two more remarkable announcements could scarcely have been made. Two more questionable acts could, in our opinion, scarcely have been committed—or in a more questionable way.

With reference to the first decree, we need not inquire too curiously into the legal right and power of the President to issue it. We apprehend there can be no doubt that the Constitution invested him with no such attributes, and that the Congress has never supplied the deficiencies of the Constitution in this respect, and that it was not competent to do so even if so inclined. We apprehend it is obvious to common sense—and, as we showed some time since, expressly stated in the fundamental act on which all government in America is based—that the writ of *habeas corpus*, being in its very nature a defence and precaution against the encroachments and oppressive proceedings of the executive, *cannot* be arbitrarily set aside by the mere fiat of that executive. If it could be, it would be simply futile and unmeaning, and could afford no protection whatever to the liberty of the subject or the citizen in any land. We apprehend, too, that it is clear the *Federal* Government is not entitled—nay, is expressly disentitled—thus to suspend the operation of *state* law and liberty; and that the Congress even could only do this in certain · *specified* circumstances and within certain *specified* limits.

[1] This article was first published in *The Economist* for October 11 1862, Volume XX, pp. 1121-3.

But we need not dwell upon this part of the question. We may even admit that in crises of imminent and overwhelming public danger, the sovereign—the chief of the executive, whatever may be his style and title—may be right in assuming and exercising powers which do not properly come within his competency, and trust to a subsequent indemnity. He must take care *ne quid respublica detrimenti capiat*—and do what is necessary for this end. But it is obvious at a glance that this decree, taken in conjunction with the appointment of special officers to carry it into effect, virtually amounts to an entire suspension of all civil rights and liberties throughout the *states* by the arbitrary fiat of the *Federal* Government. It places every man's freedom in the power of the Provost Marshal and his deputies, and of any personal enemy who can obtain the ear of these functionaries. Under this proclamation any man anywhere *accused* of the vague and miscellaneous crimes of 'aiding the rebellion or hindering the conscription,' may be seized by any military or civil functionary, imprisoned indefinitely and secretly, and refused all trial and redress (for the suspension of the *habeas corpus* amounts to this and means this),—and with no claim or power to ascertain either the accusation or the accuser. This is plain upon the face of it. The captive need not have *committed* the offence: this could only be ascertained by trial, his right to which is annulled by the proclamation. It is sufficient that he is *charged* with it. The mere rumour, suspicion, or accusation, brought to the ears of any qualified functionary, that he assists rebellion or discourages enlistment— though issuing from a rival in love, from a personal enemy, from an embarrassed debtor—nay, though originating from a pure mistake— empowers that functionary to cast into gaol, and to keep there without investigation or conviction, the most unoffending man, woman, or child, in the whole Union. Nor is this a mere imaginary danger, as the recent inquiry by the Judge-Advocate into the cases of the numbers arbitrarily imprisoned in Fort Warren and Fort Lafayette on the warrants of the Secretary of State abundantly shows.

Now this pseudo-vigorous decree may be necessary; but no necessity for it has yet been shown. It may be silently endured; though we can scarcely anticipate such a degree of submissiveness on the part of wilful freemen or of jealous *state* authorities. Few proceedings can be conceived more calculated to excite resistance in districts where the conscription is already so unpopular as to need such measures to enforce it. It can scarcely be expected that the free citizens of Illinois,

Pennsylvania, or Ohio, will tamely submit to be arbitrarily imprisoned for speaking their mind in reference to a law of which even the original validity is questioned; and their recalcitration is not unlikely to be headed by the governors of the states concerned. If so, another rebellion and another secession may easily be hatched. If Mr. Lincoln endeavours to enforce his decree, the tyranny will exasperate many of his Northern supporters. If he recalls it, the weakness displayed in the whole transaction will disgust them even more.

The proclamation emancipating all slaves in the rebel states after the first day of next year appears more injudicious still. Even those who think that the thing ought to have been done, feel that it has been done at a wrong time and in a wrong way. Both the occasion and the mode are calculated to discredit the motive and impair the effect. The only objects aimed at by the adoption of the emancipation policy must be,— to weaken and bewilder the forces of the South by raising up internal foes, and thus compelling them to detach large numbers of troops to keep peace at home;—to unite and energise the Northerners by adopting a new and higher principle of action;—and to obtain the moral support of Europe by making the war at last an anti-slavery war. But Mr. Lincoln has so contrived his decree as probably to fail in effecting the first of these purposes, and to defeat the two last. Even if the negroes on the Southern plantations were filled with animosity towards their masters, and were ready to rise against them—of neither of which points have we any evidence at all—the proclamation would be either a *brutum fulmen* or a very cruel piece of military tactics. To emancipate slaves whom your proclamation cannot reach or rouse is futile and foolish. To rouse a population whom you could neither aid or protect, merely that they may create a diversion in your favour, is iniquitously unkind and selfish. If the negroes hate their masters as much as the abolitionists assert, then to proclaim emancipation is to let loose ruffianism and vengeance. If, on the other hand, they are for the most part contented and passive, if not attached, then to proclaim emancipation is to waste words on the desert air.

In the second place, we should expect that Mr. Lincoln's proclamation will create the bitterest dissensions among the Federal party, and perhaps paralyse all united action;—nor does the reported adherence of the governors of sixteen states much modify this expectation. It can hardly satisfy the abolitionists, because it neither goes their length nor adopts their principles. It is no declaration against slavery: it is

371

merely a hostile movement against rebels. It is by implication a fresh consecration of the 'peculiar institution,' which it signalises as a privilege too great for the disaffected, and henceforth to be enjoyed only by the loyal. But though the proclamation will not content the abolitionists—who are few—it will effectually disgust and alienate the borderers and the Democrats—who are many. The Unionists in the border states will see at once that, although nominally their slaves are to be secured to them, yet that with the slaves in the planting States proclaimed free, and with the slaves of border rebels all around them actually emancipated, it would be hopeless for them to retain their own permanently or long in contented servitude; and as to the proposed compensation, they have neither any great faith in it nor desire for it. The Democrats of the North, who have never shared in the North-Eastern and the Western condemnation of slavery, but on the contrary have as a rule, till Mr. Lincoln's election, supported the Southerners in almost all political contests, will be alienated by the adoption—clumsy and partial as it is—of a policy to which they have been uniformly opposed. They desire, indeed, to force the South back into the Union, but they have no wish to recover it in a devastated and paralysed condition, with its industry disorganised, its productiveness destroyed, and its wealth (which they fingered and of which so much stuck to their fingers in the process) sapped and swept away. They are scarcely less hostile to abolition than the slaveholders themselves; and we should not be surprised were Mr. Lincoln's proclamation to create a new secession, and effectually to divide that strength on the concentration of which alone the North can rely—we do not say for success but—for escape from ignominious defeat and failure.

Lastly. The proclamation, so half-hearted and inconsistent, far from commanding the moral support of Europe, will alienate what little sympathy for the Northern cause had survived their long series of blunders, boastings, and affronts. Those who are attracted by it must think more of the use which they hope to turn it to, than of the intent or spirit it evinces. The position taken by the President in this decree is so curiously infelicitous, so grotesquely illogical, so transparently *un*-anti-slavery, that we cannot conceive how it could have emanated from a shrewd man and have been countersigned by an educated one. Consider for one instant the ground which Mr. Lincoln has assumed. He hopes, or is supposed to hope, to command the sympathy and applause of the anti-slavery party both in America and England by at last adopting the policy and the shibboleth of 'Emancipation.' And he expects to effect this by the two following singular operations:—He proclaims emancipation to the slaves whom he cannot liberate, and he retains in slavery those whose fate lies within his power. He confirms the servitude of those whom he *might* set free, and he decrees the freedom of those whom neither his decree nor his arm can reach! He does a thing more ludicrously monstrous and inconsistent still:—he enacts that in future the negroes in the slave states shall be free, and that only the negroes in the free states shall be slaves. The North henceforth is to be the only slave portion of the Union. That is, the heinous and hateful institution—to prevent the extension of which and to exonerate itself from the guilt of which we are solemnly assured the Northern section of the Great Republic took up arms—is henceforth to be exclusive privilege of that Northern section, the reserved reward of those who have been loyal to free-soil doctrines and to Federal faith!

The Increased Probability of a Long Duration of the American War[1]

THE various events of which we have news from America by this mail are very important, but the most important tend in a single direction. To the English the most interesting inquiry is how long will this war last. Recent events make it more likely even than before that it will last a long time,—as long or nearly as long as the reign of Mr. Lincoln. There are this week three important new facts which confirm the probability of this result.

First. There is the proclamation of Mr. Lincoln conferring freedom, as he promised, on the slaves in the rebel states. Speculative lawyers raise nice questions as to the legality of this act, but nice points of jurisprudence have no revolutionary efficacy. Nor need we now discuss the moral and philanthropic aspect of the subject: this we have considered at length before. We have now to consider its results. It must prolong the war. It is just the sort of cause which requires some time for its operation. Now that Mr. Lincoln has rightly or wrongly invoked its aid, he is not only justified but bound to wait that aid. He has given freedom to millions of men: he could not at once make a peace consigning them again to slavery. He has asked help from a scattered, unorganised, and distant multitude: he would be foolish as well as wicked if he did not give them time to hear of what he has done for them, to brood upon it in their unformed and slow minds, to act on it in their torpid and tardy manner. There is no fear in the South and no hope in the North of a sudden servile outbreak. But the South fear the desertion of the 'bad slave,' and the North hope for the alliance of the 'good slave.' What the South apprehend is that the most idle, the most worthless, and most dissolute slaves, male and female, will in part shirk work, in part desert, and in part become useless, while it is not possible to apply to them with the usual vigour the usual means of correction. This is especially apprehended of the slaves

[1] This article was first published in *The Economist* for January 17 1863, Volume XXI, pp. 57–8.

in exposed and outlying places on the sea-coast near the Federal armies. There, the disaffected slave will have some means more or less of self-emancipation, and some means more or less adequate of aiding the liberating armies. To avoid this we hear some slaves are being removed into the interior, but then a new danger arises. The 'interior' does not like to have them. After an emancipating decree which all slaves hear of, it is difficult for an owner to retain them in obedience even when isolated from contagion and remote from rumour. But wheresoever distrusted slaves are removed, they are so many missionaries of disaffection. They excite an uneasiness which otherwise would never have been perceptible, but which is difficult to allay when once aroused. The South—at least many persons at the South—we understand, are not comfortable as to the prolonged effect of this proclamation of liberty on men who indeed scarcely know what liberty is, but who have always heard and vaguely believe that it is something good. These apprehensions require time ere they can be verified or dispelled, and Mr. Lincoln would stultify his own act if he did not give them time. The hopes of the North just as much need months for their realisation. They hope that the *élite* of the slaves will exert themselves; that the mass of the slaves will combine; that a vast insurrection will be at length organised;—but how long a time such slow causes must take to produce so immense an effect is evident from the mere statement of them.

The *second* new fact in this week which augments the probability of the prolonged duration of the American war, is the inaugural speech of the new Democratic governor of the state of New York. This is the first time that the Democratic party,—the 'opposition' party to Mr. Lincoln,—have spoken from a seat of office and in a tone of authority. This is the party from whose exertions, if from any exertions, we are to expect an end of the civil war. But they do not seem as yet prepared even to ask for it. Mr. Seymour only tells us he will support the 'Constitution of the Union,' which is the very object for which Mr. Lincoln is at war; he only 'hopes that before the end of his term of service the country would be again great, glorious, and united as it once was.'

In truth, the opposition to a great war is generally an unpopular cause. It is a sort of semi-treason. You seem at all times to side with the enemy, and if the opposition is prolonged you often end by siding with it in reality. Mr. Fox incurred great unpopularity by seeming to rejoice at French victories and to sorrow at English victories; and now that his papers are before us, we know that in the end he did exult in the victories of Napoleon. Mr. Gladstone and Mr. Bright incurred a similar unpopularity during the Crimean war. The popular mind will not make nice distinctions. 'If you are *against* the war, you are *for* the enemy':—that is the natural judgment. Accordingly, in a country like America, where politicians dread unpopularity as if it were leprosy, an opposition party do not like to denounce a war, even though they disprove of and dislike it.

Yet, until some party is bold enough not only to ask but to clamour for, not only to solicit but to insist on, the close of the struggle, Mr. Lincoln and his advisers will probably continue it. It is their war; many of them have grown rich by it, and the rest hope to grow rich. They will not give up the sweets of office and the profits of contracts to the Democrats—to the peace party of the future—without a long and eager contest. They are in possession of the power which for bad motives and for good motives they especially covet, and when attacked, they will contend long and bitterly. As yet they are not attacked at all. The supposed peace party does not dare even to ask for peace.

Mr. Chase's plans, though still, as we have explained elsewhere, complicated by much uncertainty, are evidently intended to serve a party object. The Republicans—the certain war party—have a majority in the present Congress: the Democrats—the possible peace party—have a majority in the elected Congress which will meet next winter. Accordingly, he is asking for borrowing powers to carry him *on to* 30*th June,* 1864,—for £180,000,000. If he succeed, the Democratic Congress will scarcely be able to arrest the war, even if it should wish. It can only stop the supplies, and those have already been granted. It cannot revoke the supplies, for the President would veto it.

Thirdly and lastly. The retaliatory proclamation of Jefferson Davis, which declares General Butler to be a 'felon, outlaw, and common enemy to mankind,'—which reserves for execution the officers of his army when captured,—which hands over all negro slaves to the executive authorities of their respective states to be dealt with according to law, that is to be hanged, or burnt, or flayed alive,—must tend to prolong the war. Each act of threatened cruelty, still more each perpetrated act of cruelty, must embitter that internecine hatred which has passed into a proverb as the peculiar curse and characteristic of

377

civil wars. In the beginning of such wars men fight for an object, real or supposed: in the end they fight because they *have* fought. By the animosities it engenders, a cruel war soon becomes a principal cause of its own continuance.

On these grounds, therefore, we think the present probability to be that the American war will continue perhaps during the entire reign of Mr. Lincoln,—at any rate during by far the greater portion of it.

The True Attitude of the Government of This Country towards the Federal States[1]

THERE has seldom been a more peculiar set of diplomatic relations than that between the Federal states and England at the present time. The natural and reasonable policy of the Federal states was a conciliating and almost apologetic policy towards this country. They were doing us great harm; the blockade of the South which they maintain has ruined many thousands of the most deserving classes among us, and is the one unfavourable feature just now in the general picture of our prosperity. It is inevitable that belligerents should indirectly injure neutrals; war is too great a calamity to be restricted to the mere parties by name concerned in it; the happiness and welfare of all the better part of mankind is so bound up with that of the rest, that it is impossible to injure any one considerable nation without injuring many other considerable nations. Blockades are the particular mode in which a belligerent injures a non-belligerent more plainly and immediately than in any other. Naturally, under such circumstances the combatant nation should be courteous to the non-combatant nation, and should at least give verbal assurances of good-will, at the same time that it inflicts real suffering. This is a policy yet more obvious where the consent of the neutral is essential to the success of the plan of the belligerent; if the success of your strategy depends on the acquiescence of a by-stander, surely you should be civil to that by-stander. Yet the Federal states have never been civil or courteous to England: the habitually unpleasant tone of Washington diplomacy to us has been more unpleasant since the secession of the South even than it used to be. Just at the time when their one effectual method of harming the South might be annihilated at once by a movement of the English fleets, which France has been ready to second and accompany, the Federal states have blustered as they used to bluster when they were

[1] This article was first published in *The Economist* for April 25 1863, Volume XXI, pp. 449–50.

in the height of prosperity, and when the good opinion of England did not vitally concern them.

A short time since, we called the attention of our readers to the re-appointment of Captain Wilkes to the very position in which he nearly caused a war with England in the case of the *Trent*, and to the seizure of the Peterhoff under his orders. And since that time the American minister *here* has assumed to license one or two ships to proceed to the port of Matamoras, thereby implying that no others are trading there with good intentions, and making himself the judge what English trade is to be permitted and what is not. No foreign minister before has ever dreamed of giving permits to English vessels. These are but instances of a general policy. Ever since the commencement of the present disturbances, and indeed before, though no one thought about it—for, while American affairs were prosperous, they were im-material—the Federal Government has been much less than courteous, and not much less than insolent, to England. If the blockade which has ruined our greatest single industry had been an inestimable advantage, they would scarcely be justified in using the tone which they have in fact used.

What is the explanation of this strange policy, and what should be the policy with which we respond to it? The fact is that in consequence of a singular combination of historical accidents,—many of them due to democracy, many to the curious structure of the American Con-stitution, and some to the peculiarities of the Anglo-Saxon race, which is theirs as well as ours,—the Government of the Federal states has fallen into the hands of the smallest, weakest, and meanest set of men who ever presided over the policy of a great nation at the critical epoch of its affairs. The President means well, but he does nothing else well. He was not selected by any competent person or set of per-sons to be the ruler of the destinies of his country at a crisis of revolu-tion: he is the 'accident of an accident' in quiet times: the inexplicable caprice of a forgotten caucus selected Mr. Lincoln as a candidate because no one knew much about him, and therefore scarcely any one could object to him. His ministers are nearly as feeble as he is, without being nearly as good as he is. The whole tradition of Federal politics is a concatenation of paltry arts which their own word 'dodge' and no other will describe. These feeble and mean persons believe that it is a good electioneering expedient, an excellent stratagem for keeping their party in power and office, to subject England to small affronts.

They do not wish war; they had an opportunity for war in the case of the *Trent*, and they made no use of it. They well know that if they cannot conquer the South alone, they cannot conquer the South aided by England; the vulgar American may fancy that he can 'fight and beat' all the world, but no responsible rulers, with the inevitable information of office, before them, can ever believe so. All which the Federal Government wish is to subject England to a few petty outrages which shall flatter their countrymen, but not be really dangerous.

What then, lastly, shall be our policy? It could not by possibility be better explained than in the speech of Lord Russell on Friday night. We must firmly and calmly require that international law shall be enforced, but we must not be led to imitate the aggression of our opponents. We must not exact more than our rights, or exact our rights sooner than accepted law will give them to us. There must be one weight and one measure. When we were belligerents, we laid down rules of law which pressed harshly upon neutrals, and from which neutrals—the Americans among others—suffered. We must not depart from those rules now; we must require what is due, but we must be most careful not to ask for an atom more than is due.

As to the 'licence' which Mr. Adams has proposed to issue, Lord Russell has notified that piece of misconduct to his Government, and he could have done no more. It would have been very harsh to send Mr. Adams his passports for an act which probably was not directed by his Government, and which at any rate *may* not have been so. Mr. Lincoln will be bound to reprimand or recall him.

The case of the *Peterhoff* is more difficult. There is an inherent and universal difficulty in such cases. All of them are adjudicated in courts situated in the capturing country. During the war between England and France, all ships of whatever nation that we seized on the high seas we adjudicated on in our courts, and sometimes upon grounds not entirely acceptable to other nations. So now the American court or courts—for there is an appeal—will have to decide on this capture. If, indeed, it could be shown that there was no *prima facie* ground whatever for the seizure, our Government would be justified in requiring the Government at Washington to anticipate the course of justice and at once to surrender the vessel. But such a negative is very hard to prove. It is nearly impossible to say what may have been other people's reasons for doing anything. We must wait till they tell us. We cannot say with absolute certainty that there were no reasons before Commodore Wilkes's mind which gave apparent plausibility to the legality of seizing the *Peterhoff:* we can say with complete certainty that he has a very strange judgment on such matters, and that after his proved incompetency he ought not to be there to decide them; but we cannot foresee what seeming evidence he may have had. Nor, without proof, must we question the fairness of the American court. It is an inevitable incident of similar litigation that it is tried by a court which may always be accused of leaning to the interest of the country to which it belongs. But we must accept this defect, because it is a necessary defect. We must permit the court to decide, and, unless upon sufficient ground, we must not question its fairness when it does decide.

Lastly. We must be dignified, impartial, and calm. A war with the Federal states would be a great evil to us as well as them; but it would be a great crime likewise if it were engendered by our competent rulers imitating the restlessness and the errors of their incompetent ones.

The Common Sense of International Law

RECOGNITION[1]

THE most recent discussions respecting the American civil war suggest two of the greatest questions with which an international lawyer can occupy himself. The debate on Mr. Roebuck's motion suggests the inquiry under what circumstances ought we to recognise a body of insurgents as an independent state? The ruling of the Chief Baron in the case of the Alexandra induces us to ask what is the legal and the rational limit of the aid which a state professedly neutral may give to a state obviously belligerent? We shall not probably be able to discuss both of these in the present article, but we will at least deal with the first of them, and endeavour to show what are the rules which good sense suggests, and what the doctrines which international law authorises respecting it.

The act of recognition is essentially the act of a neutral. It is almost a judicial act. It amounts to saying this new body politic, though it was yesterday a loose aggregate of mere insurgents which their former government was endeavouring to put down, which probably it will put down, is now a compact and coherent entity which has defined boundaries, which has a sure existence, which the country from which it seceded can never destroy, which is as definite, as palpable, and as certain to continue as other ordinary political existences. Recognition in this sense—its proper sense—is an act of which the *residuary* state—the state seceded from—cannot complain; it has no reference to the cause of the civil war; it implies nothing as to the right of secession; it is prompted by no wish to aid the seceder; it tells the world nothing new; it is only a diplomatic admission of what all the world knows. Two conditions, and two only, are necessary for a just recognition:—

[1] This article was first published in *The Economist* for July 4 1863, Volume XXI, pp. 732–3.

first, that the future existence—not only the present momentary life, but the indefinite future continuance of the new state—should be really and truly certain; next, that the recognising state has no sinister by-thought which warps its judgment. A recognition from partiality to the insurgents—a premature recognition while the existence of the seceding state is as yet insecure and unreliable—is a good *casus belli* to the residuary state against the recognising state.

This will be easily seen very clearly. Every act of recognition which does not conform to those rules is an act of *intervention,* and every one admits that intervention is a good *casus belli.* Intervention on behalf of rebels or seceders is an act of evident hostility to the state which the insurgents wish to leave. It is perhaps avowedly done for their benefit, and it certainly does benefit them: it is perhaps avowedly designed to injure the state seceded from, and certainly does injure it.

But recognition, if not impartial, and if the success of the insurrection be still dubious, is exactly of this sort. It is a help to the insurgents, and a hindrance to their former government. It is a deviation from neutrality, for it aids one belligerent at the expense of the other; it may be an act of intervention of the most effective kind, for it may turn opinion and credit, upon which the sinews of war largely depend, in a particular direction; it may influence the success of the rebellion at the most critical moment, by giving to it pecuniary strength, and by taking from its enemies pecuniary strength.

It is only when the event of a struggle is substantially decided, or when there is no armed contest going on of an important kind or with any sort of equality, that recognition can be really neutral; for it is only then that it can bring no valuable aid to one belligerent or do no great harm to the other belligerent. Such was the doctrine laid down by the late Sir George Cornewall Lewis, who was, beyond other men, qualified to form an opinion on such a subject, and it is supported by all the best authorities on international law.

Now, if such be the law regulating recognition, the application of it to the case of the Confederate states is very clear. You have only to hear the pleadings of the advocates for it,—of Mr. Roebuck or Mr. Spence. They say recognition will put an end to the civil war, and the cessation of the war is a plain good to England. This is only saying in other words 'we will aid the insurgent states against their old government: the two parties being at present fighting with some approach to equality, we will interfere so as to destroy that equality:'

the present undecidedness of the struggle is to be our reason for stepping in to decide it, and there cannot be, according to the principles laid down, a worse reason: it is the exact reason why we should not step in.

It is, indeed, most probable that the result of the war will be the independence of some of the seceding states. *The Economist* is the last organ which is likely to depreciate that probability, or to explain it away. When almost all writers, including nearly every influential one, were unanimous in treating the movement in the Gulf states as a local and a transitory discontent, we were bold enough to predict that it would cause a permanent dissolution of the Federal Union. But though this is the *most* probable issue of events, we cannot say that it is the only possible or fairly probable solution. Many other events are, to use a slang phrase, 'on the cards': that is, are among these reasonable contingencies which a prudent person in ordinary life would take account of. As neutrals, we cannot recognise the Confederacy while it only *may* be independent, while its independence is only one event in a host of probabilities, while it is only, in Paley's celebrated phrase, 'one guess among many': if we do so, we help it to become independent; we make that particular solution of events more likely than it was before. As neutrals, we can only recognise a new state when it *must* be independent, for then we can neither aid the acquisition of that independence or prevent it.

And although it has long been most probable that some of the Southern states will succeed in establishing their independence, it is still very uncertain which of them will. 'Is the South,' it has been well asked, 'to include the Mississippi and New Orleans? If so, what is to become of its *de facto* independence, while the Federal gunboats hold the former and a Federal army is in possession of the latter?' And this is very material. When we recognise a state we do not recognise an unknown quantity: we recognise it precisely because it is a *de facto* power of known extent and known boundaries. If we cannot tell with some decent approximation where the new state we recognise begins and ends, we shall be in much difficulty, for there will be large tracts of country—a great debatable land belonging to no one; and if any English people are injured there, we cannot tell from which government, whether from the seceding state or the residuary state, we are to demand redress.

It is, too, very dubious whether the effect of recognition would not be to prolong the war which it is sought to terminate. The most natural termination would be caused by the decline of the warlike spirit in the North, and the intervention of England would more than anything else excite and fan this spirit just when all other events and the evident diminution in the probability of success ought to weaken it.

Mere recognition would, therefore, when the subject is examined, be a breach of international law, without even the base merit of a corresponding advantage. It would not shorten hostilities; it would get us no cotton; it would not relieve our manufacturing districts. If we chose to intervene by war, to break the blockade, to create the 'South' as we created Belgium and as we created Greece, we should at least gain much. But the objections to this course are so many and so obvious, that no one even proposes it.

The Invasion of the Federal States [1]

WE do not profess to be military prophets, we could not as civilians undertake to foretell what would be the result of General Lee's recent movements even if the actual position of his troops, their number, and that of his enemies, were completely set down before us. That amateur generalship which excels in anticipation has never been permitted to *The Economist*. On the present occasion, the place and the strength of the Federal and of the Confederate forces are so uncertain that it might well stagger a professional critic even to explain the precise present without predicting the distant future. Our object at present is much more limited. It is to draw attention to the consequences of a single fact which is itself not entirely confirmed, but which, if it be confirmed and developed, may develop itself into very important consequences.

It would appear that this invasion in force of the Federal soil, and this threatening of the Federal capital have not called out any of the extreme enthusiasm, have excited none of the fury, have awakened none of the national thrill which such great events were, it would seem, likely to excite. There have been specific allegations of apathy against Pennsylvania and others, but there has been no praise of any one for zeal. The attack on the sacred spot in which alone, by the Constitution and the law, the Government of the Federal states is legal, excites none of that alarm, consternation, or overwhelming interest which in most countries an attack upon the capital and seat of government would excite. The Federal states seem to look on, we do not say placidly or calmly, but still without zeal, without an excess of military enthusiasm, without passion, while their capital is in danger, and the soil of their country is polluted. When first Fort Sumter was attacked, a nerve of exquisite feeling thrilled through the country: there is nothing like that now.

If this intelligence should be confirmed it may have considerable

[1] This article was first published in *The Economist* for July 11 1863, Volume XXI, pp. 757–8.

consequences. Suppose the Confederates should remain masters, if not of Washington, say of any considerable extent of Federal territory. Surely this would be the best illustration of the hopelessness, the unreasonableness, the folly of the war, that can be conceived. The North set out to conquer the South, all sensible and calm critics predicted failure, though not such utter and wretched failure as we have seen, but the North went on; it said it would conquer the South. Suppose it now appears that it cannot hold its own—that some of the soil of the union is without hope or help in the hands of the disunionist. What greater practical refutation can be expected? Mr. Cobden once asked the protectionist if they must run their head against a wall before they can be convinced; might we not ask Mr. Lincoln the same question?

The practical importance of some patent, popular, incontrovertible refutation of the Federal cause can only be understood by considering it in connection with the peculiarities of the Federal character as circumstances have made it, and their constitution expresses it. In two respects we should especially consider this. First, the present revolution has developed and exemplified what was for the most part unknown in Europe,—the *bureaucratic* character of the American people. Their President is their head for a fixed term, and by law it is very difficult to alter his policy during that time. The Congress have only the extreme remedy: the final penalty of constitutional states, the power of refusing the supplies; their legislature has no minor, gradual, applicable method of controlling the executive; there is nothing equivalent to a vote of want of confidence in this country. During the period of Mr. Lincoln's administration there is scarcely any means of effectually controlling his policy or of arresting the war. Secondly, even as to the choice of his successor, there is a vast difficulty. The constitution of the United States concentrates the selection of their four years' future policy upon a single trial,—upon the presidential election. For months before the period this great event is computed, calculated, and watched for; for months beforehand each party which as a chance of success considers only how this chance may be made more, and how the chances of its antagonists may be made less. We have often explained, and it is well known, how each of the contending parties select for their candidate not the best and highest, but the most unexceptional and least *deterrent* person they can find. A nearly unknown man, like Mr. Lincoln or Mr. Pearce is a better candidate than a known statesman, because there is less in him that can be objected to. For precisely the same reason they like an unobjectionable policy. A great party does not months before-hand like to stake its existence on a bad 'ticket,' as the phrase goes, upon an unpopular, though very likely a just, policy. Now, a peace policy until a war is flagrantly hopeless is always an unpopular policy: it is a sort of petty treason, a siding with the enemy, an admission that the cause of patriotism and feeling is hopeless, and must be relinquished. Until there is some signal, unmistakable catastrophe we have no great faith in any great party in the United States being willing to stake their success as a party on so insecure, so deterring, so injudicious a foundation as a plain peace policy. It would give their opponents a monopoly of the sentiment of patriotism and of the national passion; and how strong these are, especially with the lower and less wise classes we all know. So long as the mass of the people in the Federal states can think and wish to think the conquest of the South possible and advisable, we do not believe the democratic or any party will dare explicitly at a presidential election to avow a contradictory policy. It is a wretched consequence of a bad constitution that a political party is obliged to make its programme for years in advance; and of necessity it issues a pleasing prospectus, a flattering prophecy, not a grave and homely policy suited to the wants and subject to the difficulties of the pressing hour.

It is but a speculation, not the result, of such operations as are going on near Washington. No inference from such vague information as alone has reached this country can be more than a speculation, but it would at least make a peace party possible in the North if the South could hold so much of the North as to prove by *effectual* evidence that the true object of the war, that the conquest of the South, was itself impossible.

America[1]

THE late news from America has been of a very mixed character, with respect both to what we expect to be the result of the American civil war, and what we wish to be the result of it. The end which has ever been wished for by us has been one singularly different from that desired by the zealots for the Federals, or the zealots for the Confederates. We could produce rather strong invectives from our contemporaries who entirely sympathise with the Federals, charging us with Confederate predilections, and equally strong invectives from our contemporaries on the opposite side charging us with Federal sympathies. What we have always wished is—

First. That the South should be independent. We desire that the unwilling people of the South should not be forced into a union with the North which they dislike and hate. We *know* that a restoration of real union, of voluntary union by arms is impossible. We wish that the North should never be enabled by conquest to attempt a tyrannical, a forcible, an unreal reunion; we wish to save the North from the danger of military pre-eminence, as well as the South from the disgrace and pain of military subjugation.

Secondly. Though we wish the South to be independent, we wish it to be weak. We have no sympathy with, we most strongly condemn, the fanatics at the South who have hoped, and perhaps yet hope, to found a great empire on the basis of slavery. We do not believe that predial slavery such as exists in the slave states is a possible basis for a good and enduring commonwealth; and we have no words to express our abhorrence of the notion which the advocates of the South, *in* the South, advance so freely—that it is the only good basis of a commonwealth. We wish that the area of slavery should be so small, that, by the sure operation of economical causes, and especially by the inevitable exhaustion of the soil which it always produces, slavery should, within a reasonable time, be gradually extinguished.

[1] This article was first published in *The Economist* for August 1 1863, Volume XXI, p. 941.

Thirdly. For obvious reasons, we wish that these results should be obtained as soon, and that civil war should cease as soon, as possible.

If we compare the recent news with these fixed wishes as with a sort of standard, the result is plain. First. We shall rejoice at the reduction of Vicksburg and of Port Hudson by the Federal armies. The best mode of confining slavery within fixed limits is the conquest by the North of the line of the Mississippi. If that great river could bound slavery on the west, and sea on the east, its extinction could not be delayed for very many years—not longer, probably, than it would be desirable that so great and pervading a social change should be delayed. The gradual and felt approach of such an event is almost as great a benefit as the event itself.

But we must regret the defeat of General Lee's invasion of the North. If, as we not long since proved at some length, the South had been able to acquire and retain a considerable portion of Northern territory, the North *could* not have believed that it was possible for it to conquer the South. The war would have ceased for the simplest of all causes,—from the winning of such a success on the part of the weaker combatant as would have shown the arrogant aim of the stronger claimant to be untenable. But now every such hope is at an end. The victory of General Meade must tend to prolong the war for a considerable period. While Mr. Lincoln remains in office, as we have often shown, there was little hope for any peace. Until there seems no longer any possibility of military success, until the people of the North in general, and by a great majority, admit the conquest of the South to be impossible, we do not believe that the Democratic party or any other party will stake their hopes of success upon an avowed and declared policy. They would incur a great and obvious risk of defeat if they did so. The mention of a peace, which is thought to be degrading during a war which is thought to be glorious, must always be unpopular, and is apt to be deemed a sort of treason. For a long period to come, the North will now have a sufficient store of plausible hope, and while that is the case in a country like America, where the spirit of electioneering is the spirit of politics, no great peace party will ever be possible.

We do not think that the riots at New York materially modify these conclusions. They show the extreme unpopularity of the conscription in that city, the weakness of the municipal government, the disposition of the Democratic state governor to temporise with a

Democratic mob rather than to support a Republican Federal administration. But they hardly show more than this. They do not prove Mr.
Lincoln to be unable to raise for a considerable time many men and
some money. In New York he may not enforce the conscription, but
elsewhere he can and will; and while a war government has sufficient
men, sufficient money, and plausible hope, any peace is beyond
probability.

The feeling of a calm observer of these great events will, therefore,
we believe, be a very mingled one. He will rejoice at the prospect of
limiting the area of slavery, but he will regret the stimulus given to the
warlike passion of the North, the prolongation of the civil war, the
continuance also of suffering in Lancashire, and the opportunity which
has been given to the people of New York to expose the weakness of
their municipal government, their hatred of the negro, and their
turbulence.

Prospect of Peace in America[1]

THE position of affairs at the present moment in more than one quarter is critical, and calls for unusual caution. We take the opportunity of laying before our readers a few considerations which deserve to be carefully weighed by all men of business.

Expectation, long disappointment, in the end tires out;—and is apt to tire out just at the wrong moment. For some time after the commencement of the Civil War in America most of us were inclined to believe that it would soon be over. Some fancied that the South would be immediately overpowered; some, that the mercantile and money-making spirit of the North would soon enforce peace even on an unwilling administration; some, that the passion in which the war began would speedily wear itself out and be replaced by the shrewd and calculating sense which is usually supposed to reign there: some that, as taxes would not be paid and foreign loans could not be obtained, the very means of making war would rapidly come to an end. But as months and years rolled on, as the troops levied swelled from 70,000 to 700,000, as the debt increased from £50,000,000 to £350,000,000, as gold rose from par to 150 pm., as one loan and one army succeeded another, as men and money were both lavished with unexampled profusion, and yet neither men, nor money, nor zeal, nor passion, seemed to be exhausted, and as, in the North at least, a certain air of prosperity seemed to be preserved and even to increase through all,—observers began to despair of a change and to declare that they could see no reason why the war should not last for many long years yet. A few months ago, this was the general impression; and both at home, in the east, and in the west, men were risking their capital and basing their speculations on the assumption that no change was to be looked for, for at least some time to come.

Recently, however, several indications have been noticeable by unimpassioned spectators which justify a doubt whether the end may

[1] This article was first published in *The Economist* for September 7 1864, Volume XXII, pp. 1165–6.

not be much nearer than we have got into the habit of supposing. As we explained last week, the difficulties of ascertaining what is really the national sentiment in America on the subject of the war are very great, and even when ascertained the difficulties in the way of carrying out that sentiment into action are by no means small. Still, looking at all the aspects of the political horizon, we cannot but think that an early termination of this disastrous war is nearer and more probable than a short time ago the most sanguine of us were able to believe.

In the first place, a presidential election is at hand,—an election which habitually agitates and convulses the whole country—an election which for the time turns every one into a politician, and which may fairly be expected to restore to every one that practical freedom of speech, thought, and action which for a considerable period has been suspended. It is undeniable that Mr. Lincoln's administration has given satisfaction to no one. Its notorious and unprecedented corruption has disgusted the lovers of public purity and decency; its numerous acts of illegal and stupid tyranny have alienated the lovers of liberty and constitutional right; its military incapacity has disgusted all;—while its inconsistent, timid, and tentative proceedings on the slavery question have alarmed and offended the Democratic masses, without having given confidence or satisfaction to the hearty abolitionists. A change of persons, if not an entire change of party, would seem to be imminent;—and a change of this sort and degree is usually pregnant with many other changes. Nor does it seem clear how Mr. Lincoln's and Mr. Seward's successors can alter the action of the Government except *in the direction* of peace; for certainly the war cannot be prosecuted with more vigour, though it may well be prosecuted with more skill, than heretofore.

The Democratic party—Mr. Lincoln's great antagonists—have always been inclined towards terms of accommodation, though clinging to the Union (professedly at least) as earnestly as the Republicans. Their sympathies originally were with slavery and with the South and it is from them that the cry for peace and negotiation has arisen whenever it has been able to make itself heard. If they can only get hold of a hustings watch-word—an electioneering 'platform'—which, without surrendering the dream of *The Union,* shall offer a prospect of ending the war there is every reason to believe that they will run their opponents hard. Now, the notion of a convention of states to discuss terms of *accommodation* (not of *separation*) which has lately been much ventilated, does offer such watch-word and 'platform.' It is, moreover, in accordance with an express provision of the Constitution, and as such has for Americans a strength and an attraction of its own. It is a fair demand; it is a reasonable demand; it is a demand which may be honestly and cordially joined in by thousands whose ulterior hopes and designs are as wide as the poles asunder, but who all flatter themselves that the convention can be made to issue in the realisation of their own desires. Now, it is difficult to suppose that, if such a convention once meets and proceeds actually to *discuss* terms of accommodation, the war will ever be allowed to break out again. Passion will have had time to subside; men will have had leisure to estimate aright the dreadful amount of waste and destruction—destruction of other things besides life and money—which the war has occasioned; and parties will have been brought side by side and face to face in other relations than in battle array. Northerners bent on the reconstruction of the Union, Southerners bent on the establishment of their independence, may alike call out for a convention, each party hoping to make its own views prevail therein;—and others neither fanatically Federal nor fanatically Confederate may also join in the demand, fancying that it will not be wholly impossible in such an assembly to devise some *tertium quid* which shall satisfy both sections. Already some such conception has been dimly shadowed out in the shape of two separate republics, or it may be three, united in a federal bond. The scheme may be a wild one, an unreal one, an unworkable one; but it may, nevertheless, be eagerly accepted as a compromise by antagonists, both weary of conflict, but both too proud to admit failure or defeat.

One fact, we apprehend, is certain,—that the more thoughtful spirits of the North, both in the east and in the west, are sick and weary of the war. Some few are courageous enough to say this openly: many admit it frankly in private. The repeated failures of successive generals and armies to penetrate to Richmond; the small effect produced on the resolution or strength of their antagonists by even the most decided Federal successes, such as those of Vicksburg and New Orleans: the unflinching determination of the South in spite of the disappointment of all their hopes of foreign assistance—even the most indirect; and the increasing cost and difficulty of finding recruits to fill up the vacancies in their ranks caused by unprecedented slaughter, disease, and desertion,—these things have slowly forced on the minds of all who are not too passionate either to observe or think, the conviction that they are engaged in a hopeless task, and that the South cannot and will not be conquered. They have been silent hitherto, feeling that they did not like to speak till they were sure, that if they had spoken in the full height of popular frenzy they would have spoken in vain, and that in fact it would have been dangerous as well as well as useless to speak. But now the presidential election is bringing about a crisis when they may speak with the certainty of being heard, and when to be silent would be cowardly and criminal.

But besides all this, people generally—the contractors and political adventurers excepted—are getting staggered at the prospect before them. Mr. Chase's retirement, after having added three hundred millions to the national debt and not one million to the national revenue; the alarming balance sheet last presented to the public; the renewed loans and paper issues of Mr. Chase's bewildered successor at the Treasury; and gold at 250,—are circumstances which make most men serious, though they may not make sanguine men despond. Other ominous symptoms, moreover, are beginning to show themselves, which warn patriots to beware and pause while it is yet time. The Western states are discontented; they have lost their lucrative trade with the South, they have incurred heavy expenses, they have contributed large forces to the struggle,—and they see no result from all their efforts and their sacrifices,—while hearing that thousands at Washington and New York have grown rich by the war which has made them poor. Others are murmuring that it was the New England states that dragged the Republic into the struggle, and are asking whether the Union might not be reconstructed without *them*. Nay some, in their new-born eagerness to end the crisis, are even heard to speculate aloud whether the South might not be enticed back into the bosom of the old connection by a surrender or a concession of everything the want of which or the fear of which originally led to separation. There are, it is said, thousands who would thankfully take back the slaveholders at the cost of expelling the abolitionists.

The great fact, however, which more than all the rest points to the probability of peace is that now, for the first time, *people are beginning to speak of it,*—to speak of it as a thing very desirable and not at all impossible—a thing which may perhaps be arrived at in more ways than one—a thing which a good citizen may hint at and even boldly discuss without being gagged, stoned, or sent to Fort Lafayette. We all know how language and sentiments of this sort spread; how thousands, who have *thought* thus all along, dare to echo words which at last they hear from other mouths; and above all, when once the realisation of a hope long secretly dreamed of appears to be within reach, how ready in a marvellously short time men become to secure that realisation on conditions which a month or two earlier they would have scouted as monstrous and inadmissible. As soon as the people of the North shall proclaim that they truly wish for peace, if peace can be procured on fair and honourable conditions, and shall agree to an armistice, and shall either appoint commissioners or summon a convention to consider terms,—we do not believe that *any* difficulty as to those terms will be suffered to lead to a renewal of the war. We believe that a convention once met, *for the purpose of accommodation*, will not separate without having effected that purpose, on some basis, and in some fashion, and by some compromise,—even though the basis be unsound, even though the fashion be unprincipled, even though the compromise be hollow and transparent;—perhaps even though the condition be the re-consecration of slavery, the secession of New England, or the establishment of two independent republics with a Union for foreign policy between them. Anything, in fact, will do as the nominal foundation for a peace passionately longed for and determined on beforehand.

Negotiations for Peace[1]

EARLY in the week the public mind was again much excited by the prospect of a speedy termination of the American conflict. A few moments given to a calm consideration of the difficulties that lie in the way of any terms of accommodation might have sufficed to moderate the fears of some and the hopes of others; but it was certain that Mr. Lincoln and Mr. Seward had actually gone to Fort Monroe to meet the Vice-President of the Southern Confederacy and two of his colleagues for the avowed purpose of seeing whether negotiations were practicable; and this was so much more decided a step towards arrangement than any that had yet been taken, as fully to warrant the impression that the affair 'looked like business,' and that something *might* come of it. The envoys have met, and separated; and though the American papers are still full of speculation on the subject, nothing has been announced, and the general belief is that nothing has been done.

It would much modify the sensitiveness of the mercantile mind in this country if we were thoroughly to represent to ourselves the difficulties attendant on each of the various bases which it is imaginable might be adopted as the starting point for negotiating terms of peace or accommodation. It is clear no doubt that, for some reason or other, there has been just of late a more decided inclination on the Federal side, if not on both sides, to try and ascertain if it were possible to find any terms on which a treaty could be set on foot, than had hitherto been manifested. What this reason may be,—whether Mr. Lincoln thinks the South so completely beaten and down-hearted that it would be willing to return to the Union if the way back could anyhow be smoothed,—or whether he is really staggered and uneasy at the state of his finances,—or whether he can have in truth, or can think he has, any ground for fearing a European intervention,—we have no means of knowing. But the fact remains that he appears

[1] This article was first published in *The Economist* for February 18 1865, Volume XXIII, pp. 190–1.

actively willing, if not anxious, to negotiate; and, however explained, it is a significant fact enough. But what can be the *basis* of a negotiation?

In ordinary wars between ordinary nations, peace can at any time be cooked up easily enough, as soon as both parties really wish for it, or as soon as one party wishes for it strongly and is willing to pay for it handsomely. A little territory given up, or a heavy indemnity consented to, or an advantageous commercial treaty arranged, can usually pave the way to a decent compromise, the worsted party of course, conceding the most. But in the present instance, *compromise* would seem out of the question. When each party is fighting for a distinct and positive purpose and principle, compromise means surrender. The South might have had peace at any moment since the commencement by abandoning their object,—*viz.*, independence. The North might have made peace at any moment by abandoning their object,— *viz.*, the maintenance of the Union. Is it supposed that either of these surrenders is to be the basis of the negotiations now attempted to be set on foot?

(1.) Peace may be made on the principle of the South avowing itself beaten, and consenting to re-enter the Union on such conditions as its conquerors may grant. We have no doubt the Federal leaders would be disposed to make these terms as easy as they could, but does any one fancy the South to be so shattered, or divided, or disheartened as thus to surrender at discretion? It is certain there are no signs of this as yet,—so that supposition may be put aside. (2.) Peace may be inaugurated by the North consenting to the independence of the South, on condition of limiting that independence to the states now actually held by the Confederacy, *i.e.*, to East Virginia, the Carolinas, Georgia, Alabama, and perhaps Florida, thus permitting a dissolution of the Union on condition that only a small portion shall be rent away? But are there any of the slightest indications, that the North is ready to dream of such a surrender of its cherished aim and fancy which would still leave slavery standing and the Union thus severed? And would not this be about the most unwise condition of peace for both parties?—inasmuch as it would at best but postpone the final subjugation of the South and the ultimate victory of the North, leaving only an armed truce and a perpetual menace to fill up the interim before the inevitable drama was played out. Thus there seems not the faintest rational ground for anticipating that negotiations could be based upon the surrender by either belligerent of the very object for which it entered into, and has hitherto persisted in, the war. The North are not likely to forego the hope of maintaining the Union intact, or restoring its former integrity, just at the moment when, for the first time, there has seemed a reasonable prospect of realising their ambitious and patriotic vision. The South are not likely to give up *their* object,—to surrender at once independence and property,—their freedom *and* their slaves,—while it is still in their power, hard hit as they have been and exhausted as they no doubt are, to save one at least—and that the dearest—of their aims, by voluntarily sacrificing the other;—to secure their independence by liberating and arming their slaves. It would seem as if they could have no motive for seeking peace on a basis which would leave them not only baffled and defeated, but utterly ruined and denuded. If their cherished institution and their valid property *must* be sacrificed (they may well argue), let them and not their enemies claim the merit and reap the benefit of the surrender.

But there are two other *conceivable* bases on which negotiations might, it is suggested, be set on foot. The Confederates might (3) return to their allegiance on condition of amnesty, equal rights, blended debts, and restored property,—in a word, a re-construction of the Union, with slavery as it stood before secession. A while ago, there is no doubt the North, by an immense majority, would have conceded such terms at once. Even now, probably, most persons would be *disposed* to grant them, if they could. Some even would prefer them to universal emancipation and unconditional surrender. But are such terms any longer possible? In the first place, it is not easy to see how Mr. Lincoln *could*, without actual infamy, consent to the re-establishment of slavery where his abolition proclamation has reached, and where his troops have occupied the territory and set free the negroes,—or to the continuance and guarantee of it as of yore in the regular slave states. Two years since, perhaps even eighteen months since, such a scheme seemed the most natural, and would certainly have been the most popular and welcome solution of the difficulty, but too much has been said and done to make it admissible with honour now. In the second place, how, even if accepted, could such a scheme be made to work? Which are to be considered as slave states, and which as free? In which category are to be classed Louisiana, Mississippi, Missouri, and Tennessee? How could 2,500,000 slaves get on—*factionner*, as the French say—with 1,500,000 free blacks on the other side of nearly every frontier river or imaginary line? How little could either party hope to profit by a compromise so discreditable to both? The North would get back their Union shattered, embittered, enfeebled, and disgraced; and the South would get back their 'domestic institution' mutilated, impaired, impoverished, and doomed. But, in the third place, *could* such a compromise be consented to by the North? Is not the abolition party far too strong, too resolute, and too sanguine to suffer it? Would not a Southern secession, healed in such a fashion, be a certain signal for a New England secession almost as difficult to heal or crush?

(4.) It has been hinted more than once in American journals, that the two combatants have reached that pitch of excoriated and infuriated temper, that they could arrange their own differences on the general basis of animosity to everybody else. It is said, and by some the notion evidently finds favour, that the South might well surrender something of its grand scheme of imperial independence, and the North some of its passion for the Union and its dislike for slavery, for the sake of being once more in a position to warn or drive every European people off transatlantic soil. The proposed federation of the British North American colonies, the establishment of the Mexican Empire under Maximilian, and the late extravagant rumour of the cession of some important provinces adjoining the southern frontier of the United States to France, have, it is said, combined to convince both belligerents that foreign nations are profiting by their dissensions, and that, unless they can adjust their quarrel speedily and unite as one people against the rest of the world, their cherished idea—cherished by both alike—of having the entire continent to themselves must be definitively abandoned. 'And what,' it is asked, 'in comparison with this grand idea, are minor questions of internal administration and the negro's future? Is there no contrivance by which the South may have her independence, and yet the Union be preserved, and the Great Republic be again the pattern, the hope, the terror to all other nations that she once was? Why, as we had before thirty-three sovereign states, can we not have now two sovereign federations, free and independent, united together, as regards all foreign action, by one indissoluble bond, and more capable than ever, when thus fused in a new crucible, of once more giving the law to Europe?' Such is the idea which at this moment is unquestionably exciting the brains of many of the least worthy and the most American on both sides of the Potomac; and, knowing how excitable the American mind is on the subject of empire and exclusive possession of a continent, we should not like to pronounce too confidently on the extent to which such feelings may operate in making negotiators on both sides (if ever negotiations are begun) anxious to come to terms, if by any contrivance, any gloss, any compromise, accommodation should appear possible. Two remarks only we would make on such a basis for peace: —First. That, considering the ineradicable differences of character and temper between North and South, to say nothing of those differences of interest which must continue to prevail till the true principles of economic science are understood in America,—we should feel little confidence in the permanent agreement as to views of foreign policy between the two sections of such a great republic, unless fortified and fixed by hostile action against others or hostile pressure from without. Secondly. That the rest of the world could not look with much favour or anticipated comfort on the formation of a new power thus motived and thus clenched,—a power whose two fundamental rules of action and *raisons d'être* would be, to defy its neighbour, and to annex its neighbour's land.

The Assassination of Mr Lincoln[1]

THE murder of Mr. Lincoln is a very great and very lamentable event, perhaps the greatest and most lamentable which has occurred since the *coup d'état*, if not since Waterloo. It affects directly and immensely the welfare of the three most powerful countries in the world, America, France, and England, and it affects them all for evil. Time, circumstances, and agent have all conspired as by some cruel perversity to increase the mischief and the horror of an act which at any moment, or under any circumstances, would have been most mischievous and horrible. It is not merely that a great man has passed away, but he has disappeared at the very time when his special greatness seemed almost essential to the world, when his death would work the widest conceivable evil, when the chance of replacing him, even partially, approached nearest to zero, and he has been removed in the very way which almost alone among causes of death could have doubled the political injury entailed by the decease itself. His death destroys one of the strongest guarantees for continued peace between his country and the external world, while his murder diminishes almost indefinitely the prospects of reconciliation between the two camps into which that country has for four years been divided. At the very instant of all others, when North and South had most reason to see in his character a possibility of reunion, and to dread the accession of his inevitable successor, a Southerner murders him to place that successor in his chair, gives occasion for an explosion of sectional hate, and makes a man who has acknowledged that hate master of armies which can give to that hate an almost limitless expression in act. At the very moment when the dread of war between the Union and Western Europe seemed, after inflicting incessant injury for four years, about to die away, a murderer deprives us of the man who had most power and most will to maintain peace, and thereby enthrones another whose tendencies are at best an unknown quantity, but who is sure, from

---

[1] This article was first published in *The Economist* for April 29 1865, Volume XXIII, pp. 495–6.

inexperience, to sway more towards violence than his predecessor. The injury done alike to the North, to the South, and to the world, is so irremediable, the consequences of the act may be so vast, and are certainly so numerous, that it is with some diffidence we attempt to point out the extent of the American loss, and the result that loss may produce.

The greatness of the American loss seems to us to consist especially in this. To guide and moderate a great revolution, and heal up the wounds created by civil war, it is essential that the Government should be before all things strong. If it is weak it is sure either to be violent, or to allow some one of the jarring sections of the community to exhibit violence unrestrained, to rely on terror as the French convention, under a false impression of its own dangers, did, or to permit a party to terrorise, as the first ministry of Louis XVIII did. The 'Reign of Terror' and the 'Terreur Blanc' were alike owing, one to an imaginary the other to a real weakness on the part of the governing power. There are so many passions to be restrained, so many armed men to be dealt with, so many fanatic parties to convince, so many private revenges to check, so many extra legal acts to do, that nothing except an irresistible government can ever hope to secure the end which every government by instinct tries to attain, namely, external order. Now, the difficulty of creating a strong government in America is almost insuperable. The people in the first place dislike government, not this or that administration, but government in the abstract, to such a degree that they have invented a quasi philosophical theory, proving that government, like war or harlotry, is a 'necessary evil.' Moreover, they have constructed a machinery in the shape of states, specially and deliberately calculated to impede central action, to stop the exercise of power, to reduce government, except so far as it is expressed in arrests by the parish constable, to an impossibility. They have an absolute parliament, and though they have a strong executive, it is, when opposed to the people, or even when in advance of the people, paralysed by a total absence of friends. To make this weakness permanent they have deprived even *themselves* of absolute power, have first forbidden themselves to change the Constitution, except under circumstances which never occur, and have then, through the machinery of the common schools, given to that Constitution the moral weight of a religious document. The construction of a strong government, therefore, *i.e.* of a government able to do great acts very quickly, is really impossible, except in one event. The head of the executive may, by an infinitesimal chance, be a man so exactly representative of the people, that his acts always represent their thoughts, so shrewd that he can steer his way amidst the legal difficulties piled deliberately in his path, and so good that he desires power only for the national ends. The chance of obtaining such a man was, as we say, infinitesimal; but the United States, by a good fortune, of which they will one day be cruelly sensible, had obtained him. Mr. Lincoln, by a rare combination of qualities—patience, sagacity, and honesty—by a still more rare sympathy, not with the best of his nation but the best average of his nation, and by a moderation rarest of all, had attained such vast moral authority that he could make all the hundred wheels of the Constitution move in one direction without exerting any physical force. For example, in order to secure the constitutional prohibition of slavery, it is absolutely essential that some *forty-eight* separate representative bodies, differing in modes of election, in geographical interests, in education, in prejudices, should harmoniously and strongly co-operate, and so immense was Mr. Lincoln's influence—an influence, it must be remembered, unsupported in this case by power—that had he lived, that co-operation, of which statesmen might well despair, would have been a certainty. The President had, in fact, attained to the very position— the dictatorship—to use a bad description, required by revolutionary times. At the same time, this vast authority, not having been seized illegally, and being wielded by a man radically good,—who for example really reverenced civil liberty and could tolerate venomous opposition,—could never be directed to ends wholly disapproved by the ways of those who conferred it. It was, in fact, the authority which nations find it so very hard to secure, which only Italy and America have in our time secured,—a good and benevolent, but resistless temporary despotism. That despotism, moreover, was exercised by a man whose brain was a very great one. We do not know in history such an example of the growth of a ruler in wisdom as was exhibited by Mr. Lincoln. Power and responsibility visibly widened his mind and elevated his character. Difficulties, instead of irritating him as they do most men, only increased his reliance on patience; opposition, instead of ulcerating, only made him more tolerant and determined. The very style of his public papers altered, till the very man who had written in an official despatch about 'Uncle Sam's web feet,' drew up his final inaugural in a style which extorted from critics so hostile as the *Saturday Reviewers*, a burst of involuntary admiration. A good but benevolent temporary despotism, wielded by a wise man, was the very instrument the wisest would have desired for the United States; and in losing Mr. Lincoln, the Union has lost it. The great authority attached by law to the President's office reverts to Mr. Johnson, but the far greater moral authority belonging to Mr. Lincoln disappears. There is no longer any person in the Union whom the Union dare or will trust to do exceptional acts, to remove popular generals, to over-ride crotchetty states, to grant concessions to men in arms, to act when needful, as in the *Trent* case, athwart the popular instinct.

2. The consequences of this immense loss can as yet scarcely be conjectured, for the one essential datum, the character of the President, is not known. It is probable that that character has been considerably misrepresented. Judging from information necessarily imperfect, we have formed an *ad interim* opinion that Mr. Johnson is very like an average Scotch tradesman, very shrewd, very pushing, very narrow, and very obstinate, inclined to take the advice of any one with more *knowledge* than himself, but unable to act on it when opposed to certain central convictions, not oppressive, but a little indifferent if his plans result in oppression, and subject to fits of enthusiasm as hard to deal with as fits of drunkenness. Should this estimate prove correct, we shall have in the United States a government absolutely resolved upon immediate abolition, whatever its consequences, foolish or wise according to the character of its advisers, very incapable of diplomacy, which demands above all things knowledge, very firm, excessively unpopular with its own agents, and liable to sudden and violent changes of course, so unaccountable as almost to appear freaks. Such a government will find it difficult to overcome the thousand difficulties presented by the organisation of the states, by the bitterness of partisans, or by the exasperated feelings of the army, and will be driven, we fear, to over-come them by violence, or at least to deal with them in a spirit of unsparing rigour. It is, therefore, we conceive, *primâ facie* probable that the South will be slower to come in, and much less ready to settle down when it has come in, than it would have been under Mr. Lincoln; and this reluctance will be increased by the consciousness that the North has at length obtained a plausible excuse for relentless severity. It will also be much more ready to escape its difficulties by foreign war. Beyond those two somewhat vague propositions, there are as yet too few data whatever for judgment. Least of all are there data to

decide whether the North will adhere to the policy of moderation. Upon the whole we think they will, the average American showing in politics that remarkable lenity which arises from perfect freedom, and the consequent absence of fear; but he is also excitable, and it is on the first direction of that excitement that everything will depend. If it takes the direction of vengeance, Mr. Johnson, whose own mind has been embittered against the planters by family injuries, may break loose from his Cabinet; but if, as is much more probable, it takes the direction of over reverence for the policy of the dead, he must coerce his own tendencies until time and the sobering effect of great power have extinguished them. He is certainly a strong man, though of rough type, and the effect of power on the strong is usually to soften.

The fall of Richmond and its effect upon English Commerce[1]

The fall of Richmond is one of the most striking events of modern history. On the one side the great hopes of the Confederates, their equally great efforts, the sympathy they have gained in Europe: on the other side, the undaunted courage of the Federals, their refusal to admit, even to their imagination, the possibility of real failure,—their accumulating power, which for many weeks past has seemed to concentrate like a gathering cloud about the capital of their enemies, give to the real event the intense but melancholy interest that belongs to the catastrophe of a tragedy. It is impossible not to feel a sympathy with the Confederates. There is an attraction in vanquished gallantry which appeals to the good side of human nature. But every Englishman at least will feel a kind of personal sympathy with the victory of the Federals. They have won, as an Englishman would have won, by obstinacy. They would not admit the possibility of real defeat; they did not know that they were beaten; or, to speak more accurately, they knew that though they seemed to be beaten they were not: they felt that they had in them latent elements of conclusive vigour which, in the end, they should bring out, through they were awkward and slow in so doing. We may alter, perhaps, to suit this event, the terms which, in one of the greatest specimens of English narrative, the great English historian describes on a memorable occasion the conduct of Rome. 'But there are moments when rashness is wisdom, and it may be that this was one of them; panic did not for a moment unnerve the iron courage of the American democracy, and their resolute will striving beyond its present power created, as is the law of our nature, the power which it required.'

But leaving history to deal in a becoming manner with the imaginative aspect of this great event, let us look at its present aspect in a business-like manner. The details of it are yet uncertain, and any

[1] This article was first published in *The Economist* for April 22 1865, Volume XXIII, pp. 461–2.

conclusive judgment on minute results would be absurd. But, as far as we know, what does it amount to, and what will be its result?

It used to be said that Richmond was not essential to the Confederacy; that it was a nominal and accidental capital; that it was not even the original capital; that Virginia was but an outside state in a Confederacy with a vast interior; that even if this superficial outwork was lost, the war could be indefinitely protracted; that the fall of this exterior fortification would have scarcely affected the resistance of the provinces, upon which everything depended. And at the outset of the war when these words were used, they were doubtless substantially true. Subsequent events have in many respects confirmed them, and have in few tended to contradict them.

But now the case is altered. The loss of an outer fortification does not impair the resisting faculty, when it is lost early in the day—when its defenders have not spent upon it the resources which are needful to defend the citadel. It still appears to be true, that if sometime since when the Confederacy had three armies unbroken—when no hostile army had penetrated their interior—when their organisation was as yet intact, its Government had retired from Richmond, the war would not have ceased on the evacuation. The task of pursuing three armies retiring in a vast and friendly country by converging lines would certainly have been difficult, and might not have been successful. Loose bodies of insurgents, if such there were, would then have had large armies upon which to support their accessory operations. But now the Confederacy have no such armies. What Lee may have saved, what Johnston may still command, we do not know; but we may say without fear that they are incalculably less than the armies of the Confederacy a year ago, that they cannot maintain as compact bodies even a defensive and retiring conflict with the eager armies of the North.

But without organised armies, can the Confederates be defended by loose insurgents and guerilla warfare, acting alone and without support? We believe that history affords no countenance to such an idea. A guerilla warfare requires the aid either of disciplined forces or of inaccessible territory. The history of the Spanish war shows conclusively that the guerilla resistance of the nation would have been useless without the regular resistance of the English army under the Duke of Wellington; the Spaniards enabled him to effect more with fewer troops, but they did little themselves. A territory like Arabia, a mountain chain like the Caucasus, can be defended by a few bodies of men with little discipline as well as by many more with discipline. Nature does so much that *any* sort of human force is sufficient to complete it. But the territory of the Confederacy though vast is penetrable: it is not a fortress, it is only a battle-field; it is a country in which a martial population, aided by effective armies, may well resist an invading enemy; but it is also a country from which even the most martial population may be brushed off with ease by diffused and disciplined forces.

Even under the most favourable circumstances a guerilla warfare by a nation of slaveowners must have unusual difficulties. The slaves cannot be relied on as a native peasantry can be relied on. It is said that Sherman on his march through Georgia always had good information regularly brought by negroes. We do not vouch for this as a fact, but it illustrates our meaning as an example. It is impossible that the existence of a slave class, which is not a part of the nation, which requires to be kept down by the nation, should not always be an impediment to the rising of the nation; and especially so in this case, when the invading army proclaims liberty to those slaves. We cannot expect a protracted guerilla resistance from a nation which has neither an inaccessible territory, nor a regular army, nor an attached peasant population.

But if the Confederacy cannot long defend itself, if the civil war must soon come to an end, what will be its effect on us? The war itself disturbed us much in its origin and much by its continuance, will it also disturb us much by its cessation?

It is undeniable that the fall of Richmond, such as we have ascertained it to be, would have been of disastrous consequences to several branches of English commerce if it had happened six months ago. When cotton and its substitutes were weakly held at extravagant prices, the sudden occurrence of so great a catastrophe must have caused of itself many failures. So many slow and steady agencies all tending to produce a fall of price were then operating, that the addition of a single one of a striking nature might have produced lamentable results. A great panic in one class of articles would in a sensitive state of the commercial world have produced a semi-panic in other articles. But *now* the case is different. Prices have greatly fallen. Whether they may have reached their lowest point exactly may be argued, but they have fallen so low that no great further drop is possible or likely.

Many weak holders have been cleared away, and the nominal price in consequence is firmer and more real than the nominal price of six months since. The peculiar circumstances affecting cotton we explained in an elaborate article last week. We showed that even on the assumption that 'the civil war in America must be near its close,' there was no ground for thinking that cotton would experience a further fall, but rather a probability that the present fall had been too great and too sudden to be permanent. In fact, as so often happens, the effect of the defeat of the South has been *discounted*; the result of the expectation has been as great, if not greater, than the result of the event.

There is another circumstance of great importance. The world is getting 'short of clothes,' and especially of good clothes. When the war broke out great stores of cotton goods were found to be lying in warehouses at Manchester and elsewhere, and many persons were eager to raise the common cry of over-production; they fancied there was something anomalous and out of place in so vast an accumulation. But Mr. Cobden, with that *real* perception of the facts of commerce which characterised his mind, immediately said, 'No, there is no unnecessary accumulation, except in one or two particular markets, as India and China, and in other exceptional cases; we have not more goods on hand than we ought to have.' In reality, a very considerable accumulation of stored manufactures is an attendant condition, an inevitable consequence, of the present vast and delicate division of labour. When everybody is working for everybody, everybody is injured by the mischances of everybody. An English middle class consumer is fed and clothed by an immense multiplicity of labourers; their numbers are considerable, and they are of several kinds. If any one important species of these labourers is impeded, we risk the loss of some article of prime necessity. But we *insure* against it. We keep a stock of each durable article so considerable that we have much to last for a long time, even if the means of producing it have by some casualty suddenly stopped. Some people say the world ought always to have 'two years' stock' of clothes on hand, and now we have nothing like it.

The effect of this will be very remarkable. When the American war broke out we *had* two years' stock on hand, and we lived on that till other sources of supply were opened and made effectual. The existence of that supply *insured* us then; its *non*-existence will insure us now. As we return to a usual and normal state of things, we shall tend to recur to our regular and habitual accumulation. We have not only now to clothe the world—we have to clothe it and something more. We have to make up our stock; to again create the guarantee fund, which shall insure us against any new calamities—against some deprivation of supply as sudden and as unlikely as an American civil war would have seemed five years ago. At that time any one who had prophesied the actual history of those five years would have been deemed a lunatic: our stored resources saved us then, and we must store them up again now to use them in like manner.

And this additional demand will gradually carry off an additional supply—especially if, as is likely, the clothes made with cheap material be better than the clothes made with dear material. There will be a capital demand for cotton and other goods, if once it is understood that the end is attained, that the bottom is reached, that the trader nearest the consumer—the small shopkeeper—had better supply himself at once. The small shops of the world are now only half supplied; if they once take to supplying themselves, the demand will be great.

As far, therefore, as the producing power of America is concerned, we do not think its revival, even if it should occur very rapidly, would derange our market, or affect us except beneficially. Nor, as far as its consuming power is concerned, can we expect much from the conclusion of the war. Some sanguine persons fancy that we shall at once have a vast trade with the United States the moment they are reunited—the moment the war stops. But there is no ground for so thinking either as respects the South or the North. *Some* additional trade with both, of course, there will be, but not enough to affect Lombard street—to alter the demand for the *capital* of England. First, as to the North, its tariff cripples to an incredible extent all commerce with it. It has been spending largely and recklessly. It has been borrowing largely and recklessly. It has been misusing its currency. The repentance after these errors will be a time of *strait* and difficulty, and though under good management its splendid national resources are quite sufficient to cope with this difficulty, yet the difficulty is real and considerable. The *additional* immediate trade which we shall have with the North will not be of the first magnitude—will not affect the money market.

Nor will the trade with the South. The South is disorganised, and must long be disorganised. What the fate of its peculiar civilisation may be we cannot yet say, for there are no data, and any conclusion is only 'one guess among many,' one notion a little better perhaps than others, but without any solid ground of evidence. But so much is evident that great changes are in store for the South,—that it must pass through a social revolution,—that during the revolution it will not buy *as* it used to buy,—that after the revolution tastes will have changed, and it will not buy *what* it used to buy.

On the whole, therefore, the conclusion is, that though the catastrophe of the American war seems likely to happen more suddenly and more strikingly than could have been expected, yet its principal effect will have been already anticipated, and it will have less influence on prices and transactions than many events of less considerable magnitude.

The Reconstruction of the Union[1]

W E have of late abstained from writing about America, partly because
the subject is a painful one and partly because it is so obscure. Our
information as to what is going on there is very imperfect and fragmentary, very confusing and contradictory, and often quite unreliable.
Out of the multitude of obscure and perplexing statements that come
over to us, however, we may collect a few facts about which there
exists no doubt. One of these is that the degree of ruin and destitution
which prevails over the chief portion of the Southern states surpasses
anything that had been imagined. It exceeds anything that can be
accounted for by the devastation committed by the Federal troops,
merciless and extensive as this was; for it exists in districts and over
vast areas where the Federal troops never penetrated. It cannot be
accounted for, except in a very limited degree, by the disorganisation
of industry, the flight of a large portion of the labouring population,
the abandonment of plantations, and the general interruption to
ordinary agricultural occupations. This does much no doubt in four
years, but there is something beyond what this alone would explain.
Property appears rather to have vanished than to have been destroyed.
The wealthiest men seem now to be actually destitute. Those who
were worth hundreds of thousands, not to say millions, of dollars
before the war, can scarcely now find means of subsistence for themselves and their families. Numbers who used to be in more than easy
circumstances are now desperate solicitors for aid from Northern
friends to enable them to live from day to day. Stocks of food and
other necessaries of life have disappeared; seed-time has been neglected,
and harvests are in consequence alarmingly scanty. It is in fact a case
of absolute *want*, prevailing over nearly a whole country. The Federal
authorities are in many districts called upon to provide rations not
only for masterless negroes but for destitute and starving whites;—
and how long this state of things may continue it is impossible to

[1] This article was first published in *The Economist* for September 16 1865, Volume XXIII,
pp. 1113–4.

foresee. The truth is that the efforts made by the South to conquer their independence were even more stupendous and exhausting than any one imagined. The expenditure of life and capital was enormous; each state sent its last dollar and its last man; and the conflict was not given up till the means of further resistance were literally at an end. The completeness of their prostration is shown in the general admission, that, though their feelings of hostility are as bitter as ever, they are absolutely without power to give effect to them. There is not the faintest attempt at a guerilla warfare, or the remotest whisper of any renewed insurrection, either soon or at any future time. The most zealous Southerners confess that their defeat has been complete and crushing; and they can do nothing but submit to the terms imposed upon them by the conquerors, and prepare by political management and intrigue to recover, indirectly and by degrees, an influential if not a predominant place in the re-constructed Union.

It seems clear that slavery as an institution, as it existed, that is, before the war, as a legalised and recognised status, is at an end. This result appears to be accepted, avowedly and formally, by the Southerners themselves. In fact, it may be considered as the condition on which alone the President allows them to re-organise themselves and re-enter the Union, and as such they have submitted to it. They will attempt, no doubt, and may to some extent succeed in evading or neutralising the full results of the admission by indirect measures, more or less insidious, oppressive, and unwise. But they are evidently not going to contest the point openly or in force. Meanwhile, however, the accounts which reach us of the condition of the unhappy negroes, and the treatment they meet with on all sides, are deplorable and painful in the extreme. Liberated from their old masters and unable to find new ones for themselves,—helpless with the helplessness natural to men who have never been taught or allowed to initiate or arrange their own actions, and not knowing how to set about any work which is not prepared for them and ordered to them,—calling, therefore, for support and aid upon those who conferred this impoverishing freedom upon them, but calling for the most part in vain, because their liberators, with the best will in the world, simply *cannot* provide sustenance or organise employment for such vast and sudden numbers,—little inclined to labour at all, as might be expected, because labour in their minds is associated with slavery and liberty with idleness,—despised and not loved (to say the least) by the great mass of the Northerners,

and actually detested by the Irish,—hated at once with the mortification of defeat and the bitterness of destitution, by those to whom they
were a short time ago both slaves and wealth,—and exposed, therefore,
on all sides to ill-treatment and neglect against which, and the consequences of which, nothing short of ubiquitous omnipotence could
effectually protect four millions of suddenly emancipated serfs,—these
unhappy victims of philanthropy and civil war are dying, we are told,
by thousands; numbers are shot on the slightest provocation or from
sheer brutality by the miscellaneous ruffians who abound there; numbers more sink under disease and famine; numbers emigrate north-
ward, to fare no better; the law does not protect them; the civil
authorities will not; the military authorities cannot. The Federal Government is evidently doing its best to discharge its duty to the poor
freedman, as Major Howard's interesting though not very hopeful
account recently published made clear enough; but the task is beyond
their powers;—and what will be the fate of the liberated slaves when
re-organisation shall have been completed and state rights shall begin
to be re-asserted, it is more easy than agreeable to conjecture. The
difficulties might be got over, perhaps, were Southern proprietors
wiser and better than ordinary masters, and emancipated negroes less
ignorant and wilful than ordinary men; but as it is, we fear, they will
task even American capacities beyond their strength and range.

The third point that is clear amid the general obscurity is that those
were right who prophesied that the worst difficulties of the Federals
would commence after the war was ended, though the difficulties
experienced are not precisely of the kind that were anticipated. There
does not appear to be much need of *keeping down* the South by military
force;—the work of subjugation and defeat was too effectually done
for that to be required generally, or to demand a large force in the
few districts where it may be required. But there is the difficulty of
having an entire population *on hand* in one form or another; of having
a dissolved society to re-organise; of having to perform this task
through the instrumentality of men who are for the most part hostile,
recalcitrant, and sinister in their designs; of being compelled to commit the practical management of political details to a conquered people
who act with a different design and pull towards a different end from
their conquerors. President Johnston appears to have deliberately,
and perhaps wisely, adopted the principle of leaving the work of
reconstruction in the several conquered states to the loyal or quasi-

loyal citizens of those states. Possibly he could scarcely do otherwise. But in the meantime, as nearly the whole of the citizens profess to be loyal, fully admit the fact of their total discomfiture, and readily take the proffered oath of allegiance, the function will practically fall into the hands of those who, though accepting the Union and perhaps in a manner reconciled to it as an inevitable fate, yet hate the North as bitterly as ever, and think of nothing but recovering by politics the ascendancy which they have lost by war, and who though, accepting the abolition of slavery in name, have no idea of allowing it as a complete, genuine, and unresisted fact,—who intend still to make the negro work, whether he likes it or not, and, though prepared to pay him for his labour, purpose to pay him at a rate determined by themselves. Two great and knotty questions, therefore, still remain for solution before the difficulties of reconstructing the Union can be at all considered to be got over, and both these are complicated and perplexing ones, on which the greatest difference of opinion prevails even among zealous Northerners, and which will probably be found to involve some extensive constitutional innovation. The first is, whether the Federal Government must not retain in its own hands, or enact or assume if it do not possess, the power of disallowing any *state* law or ordinance which would clash with or defeat its purposes,— a claim which would almost seem to be necessary at this crisis, but which would be a complete extinguisher to the still popular doctrine of state rights, and would in effect reduce the several state governments to the position of colonial or provincial legislatures. The second is, whether in order effectually to protect the negro, it will not be essential to insist on negro suffrage. This, again, would be an equal invasion of the constitutional idea of state rights—each state having, and having always exercised, the indisputable privilege and power of determining its own electoral franchise. Now, of course, the Southern states—even that portion of the population of them which is deemed loyal—have not the slightest notion of admitting either of these claims, and in their objections they will be sustained by a very large proportion of the Northern people, especially the old Democratic party, who are anything but friendly to the negroes, and who are little inclined to increase the powers or the ascendancy of the Federal Government. Both questions are full of difficulty:—the one proceeding would at a stroke convert a confederation into an indivisible republic, and make the United States a sort of democratic Empire with one elective head;

and the other would confer a substantive, and it might at times prove a *deciding*, influence over the policy of the country upon a race whom the mass of the people dislike, whom all except a few despise, and whom not even their friends and admirers profess to believe are *yet* fit for the franchise. Moreover, a new and curious question arising out of the emancipation proclamation has just been laid before the President by a committee of Boston abolitionists, which must be grappled with at once. This was ably and clearly explained in the *Spectator* of last week; but, in common with the two other questions we have just named, it is too important to be discussed at the end of an article.

Vast, however, as are the difficulties which lie before the Americans, ere their country can again assume a normal and settled condition, it cannot be denied that they are applying themselves to their work with their usual earnestness and energy, and we have no doubt they will accomplish it far more speedily than any other nation could do. Their power of recovery is absolutely wonderful. Scarcely six months have elapsed since the virtual termination of the war by Lee's surrender, and of that time much was unavoidably lost by the transfer of supreme power into fresh hands in consequence of Lincoln's assassination and Mr. Johnston's accession to the presidential throne. Yet in those few months how much has been effected! A large proportion of the troops have been disbanded; hundreds of vessels have been taken out of commission and laid up in ordinary; the work of reconstruction has already made considerable progress in several of the Southern states as far as mere political arrangements go; industry is beginning to raise its head by degrees in some of the districts, and cotton is gradually filtering down into the Gulf ports; while in those provinces which have escaped the ravages of war—that is, nearly the whole north and west—the discharged soldiers are slowly returning to fill up the deficiency in population which had been severely felt, and labour and enterprise are re-assuming all their former energy. In a couple of years, we have little doubt, the *external* appearance of things throughout the Union will be nearly what it was before the war. Below all this there will, of course, be traceable the scars of wounds that can never be altogether healed; and also, we would hope, the net result of lessons which will never be forgotten.

The Contending Policies in the United States[1]

THE President's message, alike in that part of it which seems to us sound and in that part of it which seems to us utterly unsound, is a very remarkable testimony to the vigour of what we may call political superstition in America,—a political superstition which has been valuable enough in its time, as the history of the war itself shows, but the time for which has certainly passed, though neither the so-called conservatives nor the so-called radicals of the Union appear to know that it has passed. The message, as regards its larger policy, may be divided into two sections. In the one, Mr. Johnston insists that the Union has never (theoretically) been broken at all,—that the rebellion was legally nothing in the world from beginning to end,—that the war was fought by the North in defence of the thesis that the Union could not be divided,—and that the victory of the Union troops was, in fact, a triumph for the logical proposition that the Union is indissoluble. Hence, says Mr. Johnston, the rebel states never were out of the Union. If they never were out of the Union, they are now in the Union. If they are now in the Union, they should be entitled to the privileges of the Union,—that is, they should have the free organisation of their own state constitutions and their full representation in Congress;—which, as Mr. Johnston, after the manner of Euclid, proves, was to be demonstrated. And he draws the very indisputable inference that the recent legislation of Congress has been hostile to the one object for which, according to this mode of putting it, the battle of the civil war was fought, namely, the maintenance of the Union, and ought accordingly to be repealed. After getting thus far, Mr. Johnston criticises the counter-legislation by which Congress has thwarted what he conceives to be the true policy,—the legislation which has forced negro suffrage on the rebellious states, by making their acceptance of it the price of their re-admittance. He points out, with a good deal of

[1] This article was first published in *The Economist* for December 21 1867, Volume XXV, pp. 1442–3.

vigour, that the negroes are unfit for the electoral duties imposed upon them; that they have only just been released from a degrading bondage, which is the worst of all preparations for political power; that if they are to have this right of suffrage forced upon them, it must be, at present, in opposition to, and against the will of, their old masters the whites of the South; that their suffrage can, therefore, only be secured by military authority, imposed contrary to the Constitution, and at great expense to the country, on the Southern states; that if left to themselves the negroes could, by no possibility, hold their ground against the practised organising habits of the whites; and that, therefore, what Congress is really fighting for is, an unconstitutional guarantee for negro government in states where negro government will never be accepted by the most intelligent part of the community, and where, moreover, it *ought* not to be accepted even if it could.

Now we confess that in this latter part of his message we agree as heartily with Mr. Johnson as against congress, as we agree with Congress as against Mr. Johnson in holding that it is mere pedantic word-fencing to try and make believe that the Union has never been divided, and in declining to build the new legislation of to-day on so absurd and unreal a figment. But in *both* the opposite programmes, that of Mr. Johnson and of the radical party alike, we recognise the overwhelming influence of a most potent traditional superstition. Mr. Johnson makes a sort of idol of the Constitution; declines to recognise that the Constitution did not prevent a war; forgets to observe that as it did not prevent a war before it had ever been defied, it is irrational to suppose it can prevent conflict for the future now that it has most effectually, and for a period of several years, been defied; and, in fact, preaches to the North the positive duty of adopting the ostrich's policy of burying its head in the sand, and ignoring the destruction that awaits it. Indeed, the President evidently thinks that destruction itself should be heartily welcome, if it only springs legitimately from the Constitution. If the result of the President's policy were—as it could scarcely help being—that the South would come back into the Union to destroy the Union, would begin by repudiating the debt incurred for its own subjugation, go on by repealing all the recent legislation of Congress in favour of the emancipated slaves, and re-imposing in every Southern state the actual supremacy of the white caste, at the cost both of all civil and criminal justice to the negro and of every institution tending to educate and raise him in the social scale,—we say, if this were the result of the President's policy, Mr. Johnson would evidently be not only satisfied but more than satisfied. He would say that it was the fruit of the Constitution and of state rights and anything that was the fruit of the Constitution and of state rights must inevitably be pure good. In a word, Mr. Johnson makes a mere fetish idol of the Constitution. He puts the Constitution above all the objects for which the Constitution was created,—ignores facts, however imposing, which are, unfortunately, not reconcilable with the legal construction of this particular document,—deduces from that document various inferences which are not consistent with existing facts, and yet wants to give these inferences all the weight and authority of actual facts,—and altogether conducts himself as if the Constitution had not been made for Americans but rather Americans for the Constitution.

If the radical party are free from this grave superstitious error of Mr. Johnson's, they fall into one almost as grave of their own. As they cannot help seeing the failure of the Constitution to provide a remedy for their recent difficulties, they have fallen back a step on the celebrated declaration of independence, and try to get out of that great aboriginal document of their history what they fail to extract from the organic statute of their Government. In the declaration that all men are born free and equal, they imagine that they have a supplement to the Constitution, and one in which they can find a cure for their recent troubles. And, accordingly, the only idea Congress seems to have had in its recent legislation has been, apparently, the attempt to incorporate the idea of the equality of the negro and the white in the constitutions of those Southern states which have given so much trouble from their attempt to found on slavery a new society and a new polity. And had the development of a sufficient practical equality—equality of men before the law, *i.e.*, equality in a civil and political sense—been the *ultimate aim* of their legislation and administration for the beaten states, nothing could have been wiser. But like the President attempting to elevate the purely theoretic Union of a paper constitution into a fact, the radicals attempted to elevate the purely theoretic equality of all men in a paper declaration of independence into a fact, and, apparently, supposed they should be able to *make* it a fact without the preparation and growth of any historical institutions. President and radicals alike seem to have been sheerly unable to recognise that, to a certain extent, they had no law and no precedent to go upon,—that they had to begin again, without the help of any documentary and legal basis from which to start. The documentary superstition was strong in both alike. For a long time,—and most fortunate for the Union it is that this was so,—all the Unionists agreed to regard the Constitution as a sacred quasi-divine document which the secessionists had blasphemed. In that idolatrous state of mind Mr. Johnson still appears to linger. The radical party of the country have gone one step further than Mr. Johnson. They have realised that the Constitution has, for a certain purpose at least, broken down. But even they have not been able to realise that they need to create something wholly unprovided for at the time of the formation of the Constitution, and must abandon the idea of setting up any machinery which will go of itself. The prerequisite of all such constitutional machinery—a society not utterly divided against itself, but able to work together in unity— does not yet exist at the South. Mr. Johnson ignores this, and wants so to ignore it as to throw all the power into the hands of those who caused the rebellion, and who still hate the Union. The radicals equally ignore this, and want to throw all the power into the hands of the negroes. Either policy seems to us founded on a grave error and superstition, and to be at issue with existing facts; and both alike seem due to the incapacity of Americans to conceive that there is any state of society to which the much admired political expedients of the infant Republic are not in any way adapted.

To our minds, it seems plain that while it would be pure absurdity to give back, on foolish technical grounds, the full political power of the South into the very hands which formerly overthrew the Union, and which would now, if they could, defeat the policy absolutely needful to restore, strengthen, and perpetuate it, it would be very nearly as foolish to commit the reconstruction of political life at the South to a mass of uninstructed, ignorant, almost barbarous, freedmen. Besides, as Mr. Johnson justly observes, it cannot be done without military authority to support the negro ascendancy; and, with military authority once asserted there, you might establish a government over both the contending elements alike,—a government, the only object of which would be to guard civil order and equal justice in the courts of law without any respect for colour, and to avoid the necessity of extemporising a wretched pretence of political life, for which, as yet, there are no sufficient elements consistent with the safety of the Union. The loyal element at the South is not instructed, and the instructed element is not loyal. The natural and, as we believe, just inference is, that society should be allowed to recast itself for some years to come, during which all the opportunities of a good primary education should be extended to the negroes,—nay, if necessary, forced upon them. In that way, neither the mischiefs of a restoration of the old *régime*, nor the hardly less mischiefs of the compulsory imposition of a new *régime* that would, by its ignorance and incapacity, bring freedom and equality into permanent disrepute, need be incurred. Military government may sound an arbitrary and dangerous precedent for a republic to adopt. Still, it is not by sound but by sense that the Americans should be governed, and our complaint of them is precisely this—that they are at present far too apt to be led by mere formula, and not by the inherent reason of the matter. Where society is divided into two inter-necine sections, the elements of political self-government, except by one section at the expense of the other, do not exist. The true policy is, then, to dispense with self-government, to keep strict order, to form and protect institutions administering impartial justice *and imparting impartial education,* and to trust to the healing influence of time gradu-ally to build up a society in which self-government would again become possible. This is the policy from which the radicals shrink, because it sounds arbitrary, and which Mr. Johnson, in the insanity of his idolatry for the Constitution, denounces. But it is the only policy truly adapted to the situation; and we cannot help hoping that when the narrow-minded influence of the present President has ceased to exert its impeding influence, the majority in Congress will open their eyes to the fact that the policy of forcing-on negro supremacy in the South has been a mistaken one, and that the attempt to restore republican institutions there has been, and is, premature.

Juan Prim

Introductory note

Juan Prim (1814–1870) was born at Reus, Otalonia, in Spain. He served in the volunteers of Isabella II, and became a lieutenant-colonel in the Carlist war. Opposed to the dictatorship of Espartero he was exiled in 1839. He was elected deputy for Tarragona in 1843, defeated Espartero and entered Madrid in triumph. The regent Maria Christina made him major-general and Count of Reus. The Prime Minister Narvaez, however, sentenced him to six years' imprisonment for his part in the uprising in 1843. The sentence was never executed, and Prim remained in exile in France and England until 1847. On his return he was made captain-general, under an amnesty. He was elected to the *Cortes* in 1854; in 1856 he was promoted lieutenant-general, and in 1860 was made a marquis. Prim was a member of the opposition to Narvaez, and at his death in 1868, Prim and Serrano raised the standard of revolt at Cadiz. After a short campaign Serrano was elected regent and Prim was made president of the council and a marshal. He was assassinated in 1870.

Marshal Prim[1]

THE want of interest felt by the general public of Europe in the details of the assassination of Marshal Prim is a very remarkable, and, as far as we know, an unprecedented fact. His death was of course telegraphed all over Europe, and was regarded in some ways as an event of the first importance; but there was little or no curiosity to learn the details of the catastrophe,—none of those long telegrams, full of nothing, which would have followed any other crime of the same kind, and extraordinarily little sympathy expressed, except for King Amadeus who had not been shot. Europe apparently cared only about the results of the event, and but little about the event itself—a sure proof that it was but little interested in the personality of the sufferer. And Europe, as is usually the case, was right, for apart from his position, there was very little to interest mankind in Marshal Prim. That position was without doubt exceptional. Marshal Prim was probably the only perfect example of the interrex, of the king who is not king and never means to be king, ever seen in the modern world. He ruled a very great country with an unbroken success as dictator for two years, and yet he never regarded himself as one of the possible candidates for the permanent sovereignty. For two years there has practically been in Spain no law but Marshal Prim's will; throughout that period he has objected to any *régime* except the royal, and yet it seems clear that he had no intention of putting the crown upon his own head, that he honestly regarded himself as a mere dictator *ad interim*, bound to carry out a specific change in the destinies of his country. That is a strange position, and it is not rendered less strange by the entire absence of genius in the man who occupied it. We desire to speak kindly of Marshal Prim, for his murder was a disgrace to the party which either organised or allowed it; but it is probable that no man so entirely an ordinary man, no man so completely without a following created by himself, ever occupied so lofty a position. It is

[1] This article was first published in *The Economist* for January 7 1871, Volume XXIX, pp. 5–6.

of course difficult, if not impossible, thoroughly to estimate a man whose secret history has yet to be written; but Marshal Prim appears to us to have been merely a good officer, a trustworthy general of division, distinguished from other good officers mainly by this—an exact and somewhat unusual comprehension of his own capacities. His earlier life was passed as an officer believed to be of ability, who shifted from party to party as a new party rose to power, but who was so little of a partisan that in shifting he lost no respect, and none of the military confidence of his subordinates. In the short and not very important war between Spain and Morocco he behaved remarkably well, finding, during a momentary confusion, an opportunity for the display of his most exceptional faculty—one, however, which he shares with many soldiers—bravery of the kind which increases as the danger grows more imminent. Mankind in general, not being brave, values bravery very highly; and there is no doubt Marshal Prim possessed the quality in its supreme degree,—the degree in which it is exceptional—that he was brave to the point at which a man is more of a great man in extreme danger than he is when quietly seated in a room. In the intrigues which followed this war Prim displayed no especial quality, except that of commanding the confidence of soldiers; nor in the revolution or in the interregnum, was he ever more than the good general of division; but then he was the good general of division, and not the indifferent one. Having driven out his mistress—whom he hated as, on the whole, a discreditable head for the Spanish Army— his idea was to maintain military order until a new sovereign or commander-in-chief could be discovered, and he never interested himself much about any other point. No revolutionary government was ever quite so wanting in originality. General Serrano and Admiral Topete had assisted him, so General Serrano and Admiral Topete were to have great offices—any offices, in fact, they liked, provided they left the Army in the hands of Prim. Civil appointments were given pretty much as it happened. Foreign affairs took their chance, except in so far as they involved military considerations, in which case the Marshal took them into his own hands. As for internal government he regarded it as most officers regard internal government. A king was usual and necessary, so he sought for a king. *Cortes* were usual, so *Cortes* were elected. Freedom was popular, so, as far as was consistent with the Marshal's notions of order, freedom was allowed. As we understand, he never interfered much with any manifestation of opinion until opposition showed itself in the form he understood—in insurrection in the streets of some city, and then he put it down, with shot and steel if he could, if not, with shell, differing from other officers only in this—that he would go any length, would actually batter down any city of Spain rather than not secure the victory. As he was a really good officer, thoroughly trained and full of experience, and opposed to untrained men, he always succeeded; and when he had succeeded, he went quietly on again without any additional bitterness. The true grievances of Spain seem never to have struck him. The true wants of Spain never particularly moved him. There was to be order till the historic system was rebuilt, and at any sacrifice he obtained the order he recommended. He did not originate anything, or make any experiments, or engage in any desperate intrigues, but just went on as a good general officer would, intent on his idea of maintaining the tranquillity of his district. That he succeeded is due to the fact that he *was* a good officer, that he could secure ordinary military obedience, and that, this secured, his force was adequate to its work.

There are but two original points in Marshal Prim which lift him out of the ruck of continental second-rate generals. The first was a certain indifference to anything out of the range of his ideas, which enabled him to leave a good deal of power to men whom most military dictators would have interfered with, such as his civilian colleagues; and the second, as we have said, was a clear idea of the ultimate limit of his own pretensions. He was competent to be a chief administrator under a king, but he was not competent to be king himself. Most men in his position would have sought the crown, but he did not; on the contrary, he, being a Spanish officer at heart, most probably thought himself unworthy of it. It is clear from his ultimate action that the rather ridiculous speech, in which he described his resistance to his wife's importunities urging him to be king, was only over frank, that his efforts to find a sovereign were genuine enough, that he really thought he could *make* a king, and ought to make one out of the right wood, and in the regular well-understood way. He was vastly ambitious but his ambition was only to be supreme under the King—the regular ambition of every Englishman, modified by the history of the country, by the fact that in Spain the road to power lies through revolutions, and not through parliamentary votes.

The third and last peculiarity of Prim's mind was in one way a special, in another a very common, one. Such of our readers as have come in contact with soldiers or sailors of experience have probably noticed their remarkable proclivity to a kind of political speculation wholly apart from their usual lines of thought. The grim admiral, whom nobody may oppress, is often an outrageous Tory; the steady general, full of the ideas of the service, is often an earnest radical. Neither would bear genuine ultra-toryism or full-grown radicalism, but the speculative side of their minds tends towards absolute conclusions on one side or the other. Prim was a man of that kind. He laboured to rebuild the throne, but he earnestly thought and openly said that some day or other the throne would be condemned as surplusage; that republicanism was the creed of the future; that some day or other, 'when there were republicans in Spain,' the republic would be established there. His belief was quite honest, though it had, except as a speculative theory, next to no meaning, and its expression gave rise to a vague idea spread throughout Europe, that Marshal Prim had ideas which might bear fruit, that he was not quite understood, that he might yet take a course very much at variance with anything expected of him. That belief gave a certain piquancy and impression of uncertainty to his actions; but he had all the while no ideas of the kind, no more intention of establishing a republic than Sir De Lacy Evans, who in theory was heartily on that side, but in practice would have fought for her majesty like a zealot. Marshal Prim accepted the republic for a century or two hence, and meanwhile intended monarchy; and the contrast between his belief and his single speculative doubt probably produced the disappointment and eagerness for revenge which led to his lamentable end. The republicans thought of him as a statesman who had cheated them, whereas he was only a very good officer, who thought that at present things should go on as usual, but fancied that some hundreds of years hence it might be possible and advisable to do without a king.

Louis Adolphe Thiers
Introductory note

Louis Adolphe Theirs (1797–1877) was born at Marseilles. He studied law at Aix, and then went to Paris, where he began to contribute to the *Constitutionnel*. From 1823–7 he was engaged in writing his *History of the French Revolution*. In 1830 he was a founder of *National*, a new opposition newspaper, and was a radical supporter of the new dynasty. He became Minister of the Interior in 1832, and grew much less radical. He changed office frequently, but remained in the Government for four years, and eventually became President of the Council and virtually Prime Minister. In 1840 after a period of opposition he became President of the Council and Foreign Minister, but resigned after six months. He now began his *History of the Consulate and Empire*, which occupied him for more than a decade. Under the Republic he became a conservative republican, and was much criticised for such inconsistency of conduct as voting for Louis Napoleon as President. In 1863 he re-entered political life as deputy for a division of Paris, and for the next seven years was the leader of the anti-imperialists in the chamber. He helped to stir up the war of 1870 through his continual reference to the loss of French prestige in current affairs. After the collapse of the Empire he was chosen as deputy by more than twenty constituencies, of which he selected Paris, and was elected by the Assembly Chef du Pouvoir Exécutif. In August 1871 he was elected President of the Republic. Strong opposition to him was inevitable, as he was a man of great determination and inflexible opinions. In 1873 regulations were proposed and carried to restrict the executive and parliamentary powers of the President. An interpellation was called for, which the President construed as a vote of want of confidence, and, though on a different formal issue, a vote of the kind was carried. Thiers resigned, though he continued to sit in the Assembly, and from 1876, until his death in 1877, in the Chamber of Deputies.

M. Thiers[1]

THE character of the present President of the French Republic is remarkable perhaps mainly for this, that he is the first ruling man who has appeared of his own kind. Should the idea of hereditary power perish in Europe, as many unprejudiced observers think it will, and should that idea be replaced by a system of election regulated mainly by great cities, as is again extremely probable, our children may see many men like him; but he is as yet the only man of his kind who has risen to supreme power over a great country. No American President has been in the least like him, and he is perhaps, of all men who ever attained *quasi*-regal power, the one who differs most entirely in all the characteristic features of his intellect from an ordinary king. He is indeed, in modern history, the only instance of a man essentially *litterateur* who has risen to independent power—power, we mean, beyond that a member of a cabinet—the only man whose inner belief has been that the policy of a great country could be successfully directed by mere brain, by a mind acting on its own impulses, without guidance from national feeling, or party feeling, or steady flow of well understood political thought. The son of a locksmith, without a personal follower in France, the claim of M. Thiers, in his own eyes, to rule that country is that he is the ablest man in it; that he, best of all men, can meet the difficulties of the hour by the expedients of the hour; can best foresee, and devise, and persuade, and guide. There is no trace of the sovereign about him, none of the sovereign's dignity, or reticence, or belief in other things than ability; and yet he has all the self-confidence, the latent but immovable self-conceit—using the word in no depreciatory sense—which Prince Bismarck is said to have once declared to be the first characteristic of the great sovereign caste. He really thinks himself competent to rule by force of his own mental power and nothing else; is in fact a journalist on the throne, with all the merits, and, except perhaps one, all the defects we should expect

[1] This article was first published in *The Economist* for March 30 1872, Volume XXX, p. 384.

from a man in that singular position. He has, to begin with, the journalist's intellectual fearlessness; frames a policy, or maintains a plan, exactly as he would if he had only to maintain his convictions on paper; when opposed trusts to his power of persuasion, of oratory, of logic, but displays at the same time a strong and separate will, which, mainly because it is so entirely self-derived, so completely independent of any force existing outside his own mind, imposes strongly on those with whom he comes in contact. M. Thiers, for instance, has no military experience, and extremely little knowledge of finance; but it is quite likely that his view of military reorganisation, and his notion of financial policy, may prevail, just as under certain circumstances it is quite likely that the view of an editor of *The Times*, or of any man of exceptional literary hold over the electors, might prevail in England. The definiteness and systematic clearness apt to belong to men who are advising without responsibility, pertain to all to M. Thiers's views, and frequently give his policy an appearance of strength to which it is not entitled. When he says, for example, that France must 'rally Catholicism' to her, or that 'he will lean on no party,' or that 'nothing is possible except the republic,' he seems to be laying down the bases of a policy, whereas he has probably never even thought, but how to make his brilliant epigrams *work*, or considered the immense mass of opposing forces which will impede the realisation of ideas so clear, so far reaching, and so independent of the practical necessities of political life.

It is, we believe, this literary tone of mind, this habit of thinking about a subject as if he were going to speak a speech or write an article about it, and not as if he were going to deal personally with the men and the interests involved, which gives M. Thiers his exceedingly serviceable courage. For example, he believes, probably rightly, that the French army needs training in camp, and he has accordingly kept it in camp all the winter, thereby provoking extreme, and it may be even dangerous, discontent among the soldiers. The usual kind of ruler, knowing how weak a provisional government must be, would have hesitated to do that; would have feared sickness and unpopularity and opposition; but M. Thiers gave the order as readily as he would have made a speech recommending it, and his act therefore creates the impression of security and power usually attaching only to the acts of long-established governments. He is quite assured in his own mind that this is the right thing to do, and does it with as little hesitation as if great administrative acts no more involved consequences than clever speeches or stinging newspaper articles; as if somebody else than himself were to take the actual responsibility. He has, in fact, the confidence not of the statesman, but of the *litterateur*, and with a dangerous crisis on hand, drives down to a hostile assembly with the cheeriest conviction that, once on his feet, he shall soon convince everybody that he is in the right. This kind of political courage, though not the real article, has much of its effect, more especially in M. Thiers, whose powers, though essentially literary, are in their way quite real, and who possesses one qualification not often found in that kind of man. He can do business. He may not comprehend the facts accurately, as in this matter of finance, but the moment he has determined on his line, he can give the needful orders, select the needful men, set the machine going in fact in the direction in which he wishes it to go. This capacity makes it much more easy to him to carry out his views than it would be, for example, to a man like M. Emile de Girardin to carry out his, and relieves him of his greatest danger—the opposition of professional men who do not consider his policy so much as his ability to give the orders they want, and understand their practical representations. He does not stumble over details, he is insatiably industrious, and he therefore succeeds in governing as a purely literary man would not do. This faculty may keep him in his place for years, and that will be an advantage to his country, which needs rest; but it will not enable him to realise those epigrammatic ideas which with him stand for policies. We do not think he will be speedily overthrown, but we suspect France and Europe will find that many of his objects will be as much and as little attained as that announced by Canning, when exactly in M. Thiers' manner he announced, after acknowledging the Spanish-American republics, that he 'had called a new world into existence to redress the balance of the old.' That sounded like statesmanship, as M. Thiers' ideas often do, and was, like many of those ideas, not a policy, but only a political epigram.

François Pierre Guillaume Guizot
Introductory note

François Pierre Guillaume Guizot (1787–1874) was born at Nîmes. In 1812 he took the chair of modern history at the Sorbonne and although he took no active part in politics at this time, was closely connected with leading Liberals, who at the first restoration secured for him the post of secretary-general of the Ministry of the Interior. He was secretary-general to the Ministry of Justice from 1815–16, and a director at the Ministry of the Interior from 1819–20. At this period Guizot was one of the leaders of the *Doctrinaires*, monarchists who believed in a *juste milieu* between absolutism and democracy. When reaction was at its height after the murder of the Duc de Berri, in 1820, Guizot was deprived of his offices and until 1828 his course of lectures was interdicted. He became one of the Liberal opposition to the government of Charles X. Guizot published numerous works at this time, among them his *Histoire des origines du Gouvernement Représentif*, 1828. In 1830 Guizot was elected by Lisieux to the Chamber of Deputies, and retained that seat all his political life. He was now a Conservative and an ardent supporter of Louis Philippe; for the next eighteen years he was a foe of democracy. In the government of Marshal Soult he was the Minister for Public Instruction, and established and organised primary education. He revived the branch of the Institut de France which Napoleon had suppressed, the Académie des Sciences Morales et Politiques. In 1840 he became Ambassador to London, and later took the portfolio for foreign affairs and eventually assumed the ostensible rank of prime minister. He sought to restore good relations with other powers, particularly with England, and to unify the conservative party. After the fall of the monarch in 1848 he escaped to England. He eventually returned to France and settled down to literature, publishing many books on French and English history. He died in 1874.

M. Guizot[1]

THE announcement of the death of M. Guizot will take the minds of many back to the cold February evenings in 1848, when London, long used to political calm, was convulsed by a new excitement, when we heard cried in rapid succession, 'Resignation of Guizot,' 'Flight of Louis Philippe,' 'Proclamation of the Republic,' and when the present chapter of European politics began. M. Guizot lived to see many events and many changes, but none which restored him to pre-eminence, or which made him once more a European personage. His name was never cried in the London streets again. M. Guizot was in most respects exactly the opposite of the common English notion of a Frenchman. There floats in this country an idea that a Frenchman is a light, changeable, sceptical being, who is fond of amusement, who is taken with childish shows, who always wants some new thing, who is incapable of fixed belief on any subject, and on religion especially. But Guizot was, on the contrary, a man of fixed and intense belief in religion, who was wholly devoted to serious study, who probably cared as little for the frivolous side of life as any human being who ever lived, who was stiff in manner and sedate in politics to a fault. A puritan born in France by mistake is the description which will most nearly describe him to an ordinary Englishman, for he had all the solidity, the solemnity, and the energy of puritanism, as well as some of its shortcomings. And it is very natural that such should be his character, for he came of a Huguenot family, who really were French puritans. The French national character is much more various than it is supposed to be according to common English ideas, and the serious stern variety which M. Guizot represents is one of the most remarkable.

Indeed, in the special peculiarity which coloured his political life, he was a most characteristic Frenchman. He represented their excessive propensity to political fear. As we all know, a principal obstacle to good government in France is a deficiency in political courage. At the

---

[1] This article was first published in *The Economist* for September 19 1874, Volume XXXII, pp. 1129–30.

present moment a very considerable part of the nation are inclined to return to the Empire—not that they are attached to the Empire, not that they do not see its defects, not that they are not ashamed of its end, but because they are so impressed by the difficulties of making any other strong government that their heart fails them. They want something which will save them from the *Commune*, and they are disposed to run back to what saved them from the Commune before without any sufficient inquiry whether a better safeguard cannot be found, or whether this one will be effectual. The excess of their apprehension obscures their eyes and distorts their judgment. Guizot had no partiality for the Empire or for anything like the Empire, but nevertheless his whole political life rested on a similar feeling and aimed at a similar end. He, too, was frightened at revolutionary excess; his father perished in the first revolution. He was born in 1787, and consequently began his intellectual life about 1800, just when the reaction against the revolution was the strongest, when its evil was most exaggerated, and when its good was most depreciated. A strong, serious, unoriginal mind—and such was [2] M. Guizot's—which receives such penetrating impressions early in life generally holds them on, in one shape or another, till the end, and so in this case. Guizot was devoted through life to what he called the 'Conservative' policy; he was always endeavouring to avert revolution; he was incessantly in dread of tumult: he saw attack and commotion everywhere. But he had no notion what was the real counterforce in France to the revolutionary force. We now know from experience that that force, though it calls itself the force of numbers, can be controlled by appealing to numbers; that the peasant proprietors, who are the majority in France, hate nothing so much and fear nothing so much; that they think revolution may take from them their property, their speck of land, their 'all' and, therefore, they will resist revolution at any time and on any pretence, and will support any power which they think can prevail against it. But Guizot did not perceive this great force. His great *recipe* for preventing revolution was not by extending the suffrage but by restricting it. He did not see that the masses in France having property of their own were only too likely to be timid about property. His scheme was to resist revolution by keeping the suffrage so high that it included only a few in the towns, that it scarcely included any of the masses in the country. He proposed to found the throne of

---

[2] The original article has 'as' but I have substituted 'was'.

constitutional liberty on a select *bourgeoisie*—few in number, moderate in disposition, easily conciliated by their interests. The revolution of 1848 might have been evaded if he had been willing a little to extend the suffrage, but he would not extend it. The proposals then made for so doing seem now trivial and unimportant, but Guizot sincerely believed that they would ruin the country; sooner than grant them he incurred a revolution. He was so perturbed by the excessive dread of revolution that he could not see what was the true power with which to oppose it, that he threw away a mighty power, that he relied solely on a weak one, that he caused the calamity he was always fearing.

It is this great misfortune which will always colour any retrospect of M. Guizot's career and render it a melancholy one. In many minor ways he accomplished much good. As a minister of public instruction he did much—much, perhaps, which no other man at that time could have done—for education in France. When Ambassador in England he did much to prevent a war which was then imminent, and which M. Thiers would have hurried on; through his whole career, by a lofty scrupulosity, he did much to raise the low level of morality in French public life. As an orator he had great triumphs at the tribune, though his eloquence is too little business-like and too academical for our English taste. But notwithstanding these triumphs and these services, his political career must ever be held to be a complete failure, for he failed in the work of his life—in the aim he had specially chosen as his own. His mission—he would have accepted the word—was to avert revolution, and he caused revolution. Nor is the failure one which was slight in its effects or which history can forget. On the contrary, every page of present French politics bears witness to its importance. No French republic and no French monarchy can now have nearly as much strength or nearly as much chance of living as the monarchy of July had, which Guizot destroyed.

Of his literary productions this is not the place to speak. Nothing can be more unlike ordinary Parisian literature than they are. That literature generally reminds its readers of the old saying, 'That the French would be the best cooks in Europe if they had got any butcher's meat.' Of French cookery nothing can be more libellous; but of much French literature it would be quite true to say that the writers would be the first in Europe if they only knew anything about their subject. The power of expression has been cultivated to an extreme perfection, but unfortunately the writers have neglected the further task of finding anything true and important to say. But M. Guizot's works are the reverse of all this. A work of more solid erudition than the 'History of French Civilisation' was never written by a German professor, and few Germans have ever written anything so accurately matured, and so perfectly mastered. In this respect he contrasts admirably with his great rival. There used to be a story—a just story in the main we believe—of a critic who betted that he would find five errors in any five pages of Thiers' great history of the Revolution. Even his warmest admirers indeed have never contended that M. Thiers had a scrupulous love of truth, was a careful collector of evidence, or a fine judge of it when collected. But M. Guizot was all three. The labour expended on his books must have been very great, and much more than it would be now, for he has himself helped his successors certainly to arrive at his own conclusions with greater ease, and perhaps also to arrive at improved conclusions.

From our peculiar view, as an economical statesman, M. Guizot has, we are sorry to say, no title to respect. He and his fellow ministers under Louis Philippe left it to the Empire to improve the material condition of the French people. He did little to promote railways, and he objected to the English treaty of 1860 because it was an approach to Free-trade, because it would enable 'the English manufacturers, after an English commercial crisis, to export their goods to France and to swamp the French manufacturers.' The real principles of Free-trade had never penetrated into his mind, any more than into the minds of Louis Philippe's other ministers, and partly on that account France now looks back to the time of the Empire as to the 'golden age' of wealth and industry, and not to the time of the free monarchy.

We are sorry to have to write so much of blame of one whose character all Europe respected, and some of whose virtues were so valuable to France. But it is one perhaps painful consequence of pro-longed old age that a man's character at death is estimated with perfect partiality. Those who most hated him and those who most loved him are mostly passed away or superseded in the scene of affairs. And if, as in M. Guizot's case, the good which he did was mostly one of temporary moral impression, and the evil which he caused one of lasting political result, there will be always more blame than praise to say. The impalpable virtues can hardly be described and are mostly forgotten, but the indelible consequences of the political errors are fixed on the face of the world; they cannot be overlooked, and they must be spoken of.

King Leopold I of the Belgians
Introductory note

Leopold I of Belgium (1790–1865) the fourth son of Francis, Duke of Saxe-Coburg Saalfeld, was born at Coburg in Germany. In 1816 he married Charlotte, daughter of George IV of England. After her death in 1817 he continued to live in England. In 1831 he was elected King of the Belgians, and accepted the throne after first assuring himself that he had the support of the great powers. For the first eight years of his reign he had to contend with the hostility of William I of Holland, until the differences between the two countries were settled by the Treaty of the Twenty-four Articles, in 1839. From then until his death he was the administrator of the newly formed kingdom. In 1848 the Belgium throne remained unshaken despite the revolutionary atmosphere on the continent. Leopold I died at Laaken in 1865.

King Leopold[1]

KING LEOPOLD, of Belgium, who died on Sunday, was for thirty years an international cabinet minister. The unique character of that position, without precedent except in the annals of the papal court, would of itself be sufficient to explain the immense interest felt by Europe, and especially by the highest class in Europe, in the tidings of his death, but the event derived additional importance from a fact little noticed by the public. An international cabinet minister has become more than ever necessary, and there is no other who possesses the requisite combination of qualities and position. Englishmen, who rarely study foreign politics with any attention, are scarcely aware of a new and very curious difficulty which, on the Continent, besets all international questions. The rule of individuals is not ended, but it has gradually been limited by another seldom exercised but when exercised quite irresistible kind of sway. Despite constitutions, and charters, and assemblies, and other arrangements tending to divide power, about a dozen persons still possesss the initiative of great political action on the Continent. If two persons in Prussia, or one in France, or three in Italy, or one in Austria, or two in Russia have made up their minds, the act on which they have made it up is nearly certain to be attempted, and very likely indeed to be carried through. But they are subject to this restriction, that the act to be accomplished must be at least tolerable to their own peoples, and all other peoples to be affected by it. For example, if the Emperor of the French, the King of Prussia, and Count von Bismarck, had made up their minds to divide Belgium, armies would move, war would begin, and a great political epoch would commence. But the three persons who possess this tremendous initiative understand perfectly well that though popular forms will not stop them, it is needful, in order to succeed, to know what the European world would feel in the event of their taking action. Kings are now in the position of strong cabinet ministers, who

[1] This article was first published in *The Economist* for December 16 1865, Volume XXIII, pp. 1520–1.

can do or refuse to do almost anything, but who are obliged, never-theless, to form an idea whether their action or refusal of action will be acceptable to the country. It is possible, therefore, for an adviser who knows them, and the other great politicians, and the different peoples, and who can speak with some of the frankness of an equal, and who is trusted as only equals ever are trusted, to give most effective and weighty counsel either for or against the contemplated movement. Only a king could do this, and only a king personally neutral, and only a personally neutral king who was, and was known to be, a man of great judgment, serene intellect, and disinterested character. Such a man was Leopold, and he had therefore among the small knot of gentlemen who really govern Europe just the kind of influence which a strong minister, say Sir Cornewall Lewis, has in the Cabinet of a single nation. This influence was always exerted, if not in favour of peace and freedom, at least of order and moderation, of temperance in demand and forbearance in resistance, and its loss is as real a calamity to Europe as the loss of Sir Cornewall was to England. How great that loss was none but ministers know, and how great this loss none but kings, who can seldom find an adviser who knowing all the points is neither interested nor a subject. Their peoples can know it only through an induction, but then the induction is a very strong one. No one would deny that it is important to restrain the Emperor of Austria from rashness, or the King of Prussia from untimely aggression, or the Emperor of the French from giving the rein to 'ideas,' or our own sovereign from holding out too long against a public wish, and King Leopold by his exceptional position had, and exercised, very much such a power of restraint. It is said, for example, that a letter from him warning his connection, the Kaiser, not to invade Piedmont arrived just too late, and though the story may, like most such stories, be entirely baseless, it illustrates exactly the value of his position. The Kaiser, who would listen to nobody else, might have listened to him, and immense misfortunes to Austria would have been averted. The death of such a man is a serious event, more especially as he cannot be replaced. There does not now exist a human being who could write a letter to every great sovereign in Europe with a certainty that his words would be weighed as those of a wise king, friendly to the person addressed.

That is a great loss, and it is the greater because the great personal authority of King Leopold served to conceal, or rather to neutralise, one of the many territorial difficulties now existing in Europe. He ruled a state which statesmen have for many years thought ought to be kept neutral, which is greatly coveted by a very powerful people, which is quite incapable of self-defence, and yet which, in the judgment of many persons of authority, *must* be kept independent. King Leopold did keep it independent. It is as certain as any thing in politics can be, that as long as he lived the 'Belgian question' would never arise, and it is not certain that his son can keep it from arising. Now the Belgian question may mean very little indeed—the voluntary resolution of a few provinces, now forming one little kingdom, into parts of three bigger kingdoms,—but it may also mean that most appalling of conceivable calamities a general European war, perhaps the one event the possibility of which shakes the fortitude of cool and experienced statesmen. The mere revival of a question to which so monstrous a possibility attaches is of itself an evil, and a great evil, and with King Leopold's death it does revive. People often say that the lives of individuals cannot now-a-days involve such immense results, because the world has passed beyond the era of dynastic wars, but that is only partially true. No king can now undertake a war of conquest because he chooses, but almost any king can restrain his people from undertaking one which *they* choose; and the influence of King Leopold helped to make kings willing to use that veto in the case of Belgium. The influence of individuals was once greatly overrated, but the tendency is now too much in the other direction, as any one will see who looks through the interminable papers about the late Danish war. King Frederick being a legitimate dynast other legitimate dynasts did not like to attack him; but when he died they attacked his successor, and nearly succeeded in creating a general war. We may see the same occurrence from almost the same cause in Belgium, or we may not. The probability is we shall not, for existing things always like to continue existing, and Belgium cannot well cease to exist without the consent of the Belgian people, but no one worthy of attention would deny that the possibility of seeing it has been increased by King Leopold's death. He was a very able man, and his son is not very able; he was very moderate, and his son is tinged with a faith of all others least favourable to moderation; he had enormous personal weight, and his son has none at all. It is possible to overrate the importance of such differences, but *quantum valeant* they are losses to a kingdom which cannot afford to lose anything, which is always in peril of its existence, and which cool-headed men still greatly desire should continue.

For all these reasons, we deeply regret King Leopold, who, more-over, was a good friend to England, and a statesman of a sort very rare and very valuable among kings. He was, perhaps, the only one in Europe who clearly saw—what by-and-by many will be compelled to see—that an able sovereign who wants power can get it without killing people, or shutting up assemblies, or punishing free speech, or imped-ing free life in any way. Let the form of government be what it may, it must be carried on by a limited number of persons, and if the form is monarchical, these persons must listen to what the king has to say. If what he says is, on the whole, the best thing said, they must adopt it, and with an able king it is very likely to be the best thing. No minister has his freedom from party bias, or his experience, or his intercourse with powerful persons abroad, or his knowledge of both parties, or generally his indifference to minor points. These are immense in-tellectual advantages, and, when coupled with the mysterious hold kings have over the masses of their subjects, give him quite as effective a dictatorship as most sensible politicians would desire. In 1848, King Leopold had to tell his people that, if they liked, he would resign, but all the same, during the seventeen following years no party in Belgium could pass an Act of which he heartily disapproved, and he once or twice carried measures opposed to the wishes, and even the wills, of all Belgians save the members of the Chamber. He had convinced the latter, and, that accomplished, was a good deal more powerful than most absolute monarchs. Such an example could not fail to find imita-tors, and the death of such a king is the loss not only of a great security, but of a very good and effective example.

Count Camillo Benso di Cavour

Introductory note

Camillo Benso di Cavour (1810–1861) was born at Turin, son of the
Marchese Michele Benso di Cavour. He was trained at the military
academy at Turin and was commissioned a lieutenant. In 1835 he
visited France and England, where he gained impressions that strengthened his view that a constitutional monarchy was a better form of
government than republicanism or absolutism. In 1847, at the time of
the reforms effected by Charles Albert, King of Sardinia, Cavour
founded the newspaper *Il Risorgimento*, and urged the King to grant a
constitution. He advocated war against Austria in 1848 when the first
hostilities broke out. Cavour won a seat in the Chamber in the election
in June 1848, but lost it the following year. After a disastrous defeat
at Novara in March 1849, Cavour favoured making peace with Austria,
and on his return to parliament in July, he supported the ratification of
the Treaty of Milan. In 1850 Cavour entered the D'Azeglio cabinet as
Minister of Agriculture, and later also held the Ministry of Finance.
In 1852 as a result of an arrangement with the leader of the left centre,
a 'connubio' was made with the right centre, which gave Cavour a
parliamentary majority and he became Prime Minister. Between 1852
and 1859 he effected a series of reforms in tariffs, finance, the army, and
relations with the Church. Recognising the need for French and British
support in Piedmont's struggle against Austria, Cavour brought
Piedmont into the Crimean War on their side in 1855. In 1858 Napoleon III met Cavour secretly, and an agreement was made to drive
Austria completely out of Italy. A treaty was drawn up and signed in
1859 proposing to annex Parma, Modena, Lombardy and Venetia to
Piedmont, and promising an Italian independence dominated by the
constitutional kingdom of North Italy. France was to receive Nice and
Savoy. An Austrian ultimatum to disarm precipitated the war. In
July 1859, after the battle of Solferino, Napoleon arranged a preliminary peace, in disregard of his compact with Cavour. Cavour
immediately resigned. He was called back to power in January 1860,

and in March negotiated the Turin Treaty. Savoy and Nice were to go to France, in return for which the Emperor acquiesced in the annexation of the central states to Piedmont. When Garibaldi undertook his expedition against the kingdom of Naples, Cavour negotiated with both Francis II, the Bourbon King at Naples, and with Garibaldi, to whom he sent some help, so that he would profit whether Garibaldi lost or won. When Garibaldi had conquered Sicily and crossed to the mainland, Cavour felt that intervention by the regular army was necessary, and it was sent South to complete the defeat of Francis II and occupy Naples. On the way it destroyed the papal army at Castelfidardo, so that Umbria and the Marches were annexed as well as Sicily and Naples, leaving only Venetia still an Austrian territory, and Rome the only papal territory. A new parliament was summoned representing all the new regions, and in March 1861 Victor Emmanuel was proclaimed King of Italy. Before Cavour could realise his plans to annex Rome and make it the capital of Italy, he died at Turin in June 1861.

The Death of Count Cavour[1]

THE foremost statesman in Europe,—the man whose life was of the highest political value to the world, and second only in *importance* to that of the Emperor of the French,—is no more. The death of Count Cavour is felt to be an event of the same unspeakable moment, though, as it seems to Englishmen, of exactly opposite tendency, with that which so suddenly snatched away the late Czar in the middle of the Crimean war. The death of Nicholas was the death-blow of the aggressive policy in Russia; and the enemies of Italy will no doubt dare to hope that the removal of the great leader of Italian regeneration will prove a catastrophe as fatal to the hopes which he inspired, and the far-sighted policy by which he advanced with sure and equal step to their realisation. But the parallel is utterly delusive. Count Cavour was the leader of an advancing age, and did but represent a moral force which secured for his country the sympathy of all advancing nations, and the fear or respect of even the most retrograde. The power by which he worked was not his own, and does not die with him. Nicholas, on the other hand, represented a policy which belonged to the past rather than to the present; with strong unflinching determination he strove to stem the tide of European opinion, and he rallied for this purpose the forlorn hope of Russian barbarism. For his death, therefore, there was no remedy;—the power by which he had worked was dwindling fast even beneath his hands, and faded rapidly away when he was struck down. He restored and represented a dying tradition; Count Cavour created and represented a new spring of national pride and hope which will constitute the tradition of unborn generations.

The events of his short but crowded political career, which extended only over eleven years,—and the most important part of it during which he was Prime Minister only over nine,—have been too often recapitulated within the last two days to need formal narration here.

[1] This article was first published in *The Economist* for June 8 1861, Volume XIX, pp. 619–20.

Those years of his life in which the political character is chiefly formed were passed in England: he did not return to Piedmont until he was 32 years old; and hence it has been the greatest pride of English statesmen to point to Count Cavour's wonderful success as in some sense a graft taken from a British stock. Nor is it mere national egotism to believe this. It was his clear-sighted financial creed, and a great financial speech in 1850, which first introduced him to power; and he had learned his political economy from Adam Smith. It was a speech on ecclesiastical jurisdiction, expressing his deep conviction that all Churches should be zealously restrained from interference with secular affairs, which first gained him extensive popularity in Italy;—and such a Church he had seen in England and England alone. It was his steady belief in a constitution worked by the natural aristocracy of a country, but yet in close connection with the popular mind, which gave him an instrument at once sufficiently powerful and sufficiently under control to carry out his great designs; and such a constitution he had seen only in England.

Yet, though England may have supplied him with political prin-ciples suited to his needs, it certainly could not have given him the consummate power with which he used them. Probably no English statesmen that ever lived would have exhibited, under such circum-stances, so striking a combination of audacity and tact,—of course to incur a great risk, and sagacity in measuring what risk would be too great,—of equal power to strike, and to hold back his own supporters from striking, according to the circumstances, as Count Cavour. No statesman known to history has ever counted the cost of such great dangers with so cool and strong a mind. He was as strong in defeat as in success. It was nearly the first act of his political career, after the great disaster of Novara, to urge the duty of cordially strengthening Charles Albert's government instead of indulging in useless recrimina-tions. And his first great venture as a minister was so contrived as to be a cordial to the Italian spirit,—a stimulant to the exhausted hopes of a long oppressed nation. The master-stroke of forcing Sardinia into a favourable comparison with Austria by sending an army to the Crimea, while Austria remained sullen and passive in the principalities, gained him even far more power at home than abroad, because it raised the hopes and animated the national pride of Italy. Nor was it Count Cavour's fault if he was subsequently obliged to wound that national spirit in the equivalent rendered for the aid of France. Had

England been willing in 1856 to unite with France and Sardinia in resolutely curbing the influence of Austria in Italy, the same great result might possibly have been obtained without the same humiliating price. It is well known that Count Cavour applied, and applied in vain, to England for a counterweight to the influence of France,—and that the great debt of exclusive obligation afterwards incurred, was incurred in consequence of our refusal to interfere.

But neither in sending a Sardinian contingent to the Crimea, nor in the negotiation of the French alliance, did Count Cavour display so happy a combination of sagacity and daring, as in the occupation of the Umbrian Marches last year, and the summons to the Pope to dismiss his foreign auxiliaries. Had Garibaldi been permitted to push on into the Roman territory, the revolution would have passed beyond the control of Sardinia, and an anarchy risked which would have brought down either an Austrian or an extended French intervention. Had Sardinia prohibited Garibaldi's movement upon the Roman territory, as she did the further movement upon Venetia, the unpopularity incurred would have probably overthrown the Sardinian ministry and seriously risked the Sardinian leadership. The reasons for the movement were urgent and weighty, but the danger confronted was enormous. The Pope was driven to extremities,—Austria had a new and almost unanswerable excuse for marching to his aid, since the moral logic of the step would certainly have justified quite as well the invasion of Venetia,—and the ultramontane party in France was irritated into an opposition so vindictive, that it was far from certain whether the Emperor might not be obliged to withdraw his countenance. It cannot be doubted that in discriminating the true moment to defy the Pope and take the formal guidance of the Neapolitan revolution, Count Cavour gave proof of the rarest and highest statesmanlike genius. He had before him a problem in which all the alternatives seemed equally menacing. He instinctively chose for his country the solution which involved danger indeed, but no humiliation,—not the loss of that leadership which had been, during so many months of Garibaldi's enterprise, in partial abeyance; and the resolve raised him to a place in the nation's affections of which he can now never be deprived.

That such a statesman should be cut off while Rome is still in the hands of France, and Venetia still in the hands of Austria, is more than tragic,—for in tragedy the intertwining threads are all cut together,—but here the country's need continues, though the man who could best satisfy it is gone. In no one else can the same powers be found united;—the capacity for ruling rightly, and the capacity for convincing a free people that they are ruled rightly;—the power to win the confidence of an Italian parliament as no one else could win it, and the power to use the authority so gained as no one else could use it. No English statesman except Pitt has ever gained a power so nearly equivalent to a dictatorship as Count Cavour has exercised for the past nine years over the growing state of Sardinia. Nor is such a combination of practical sagacity and intellectual sagacity,—of the passion that sways, the reasoning that guides, the strength that retains, and the humour that fascinates men,—often seen combined in the same person. Ricasoli, Minghetti, Ratazzi, all seem dwarfed beside the great intellect and will which have so recently been put forth in all their power, not only to grasp new conquests, but to restrain his countrymen from snatching at the inaccessible. But that firm faith in the destinies of his country expressed in his last hour by the dying statesman has been sown by him in so many Italian hearts that it will be impossible for them to despond. It was the last crowning triumph of his life to reconcile all the great men who had assisted him in the glorious work. And now, though in the bitterness of their loss, when they look at Rome and Venetia, many may feel inclined to echo the melancholy old words of patriotic despondency, 'The harvest is past, the summer is ended, and we are not saved,'—they will not allow themselves to doubt that the same power which raised up Count Cavour for his work, and engraved its purposes on the marvellous triumphs of his short administration, will find instruments noble enough to complete what he has so nobly begun.

Giuseppe Mazzini

Introductory note

Giuseppe Mazzini (1805–1872) was born at Genoa. He studied law at the University of Genoa, but very early devoted himself to the cause of Italian unity. He joined the Carbonari but was betrayed, imprisoned and exiled to France, where in 1831 he formed the society 'Young Italy'. Its objects were to liberate Italy from foreign and domestic tyranny and to unify it under a republican government, and these objects were to be achieved through education and revolt where necessary. Mazzini was deported from France to Switzerland, and from Switzerland to England. While in exile he organised or assisted in numerous conspiracies: he was concerned in an uprising in Piedmont in 1833; in 1834 there was an unsuccessful attempt to emancipate Savoy, in 1844 he aided the Bandiera brothers in Calabria; and he was involved in uprisings in Lombardy between 1852–3, and in Leghorn and Naples in 1857. Although none of these attempts succeeded, Mazzini believed that they were in themselves valuable, for resolute action by a few might effect an invincible popular uprising. Mazzini served as a triumvir of the Roman Republic in 1849, after the withdrawal of Pope Pius IX from Rome, but the Republic was crushed by French arms and Mazzini escaped to London. After several expeditions he was sentenced to death in Italy in 1857, for complicity in revolutionary outbreaks. He retreated again to London where he edited a new journal, *Pensiero e Azione*. He was elected by Messina to the Italian parliament in 1865, but refused to take the oath of allegiance and never assumed his seat. In 1866 he was granted an amnesty and the death sentence was removed. He was again expelled from Italy in 1869 for having conspired with Garibaldi. He spent his last years trying in vain to organise the working people on a democratic basis. He regarded the unification of Italy which Cavour had achieved as a travesty of his hopes, and died, disappointed, at Pisa in 1872.

Mr. Stansfeld and Signor Mazzini[1]

It is impossible to deny that the Junior Lord of the Admiralty has come out of the recent personal attacks upon him, *àpropos* of the Greco affair, somewhat damaged by the encounter. It is equally clear to us that this result is substantially an unjust one, and that the damage incurred is due solely to the want of tact and skill by which his, Mr. Stansfeld's, defence was so signally marked. We believe he had a perfectly good case, had he known how to put it forth with fitting boldness and candour. Throughout the whole debate only Mr. Bright and Mr. Forster said the right thing or took the right tone; and in one point even Mr. Forster's spirited defence of his friend was weak, and we think mischievous. Originally the facts of the case were very simple; the allegation was very narrow; and the culpability involved in all that any one really believed or entertained for a moment, absolutely *nil*.

The charge was brought, or rather the insinuation made, in the accusing speech of the Public Prosecutor in France, whose pleasure and duty it is, notoriously, to make matters look as bad as possible against the prisoner and his friends. One of the Prosecutor's chief aims was to connect Mazzini with Greco's plot. In this attempt, as we all know, he signally failed. Greco's intercourse with Mazzini was of a date much earlier than this affair; the supposed complicity of Mazzini rested on the sole assertion of Greco, and is denied positively by Mazzini, and we presume no one will believe Greco in such a matter in preference to Mazzini. The only scrap of *evidence* consists of two fragments of letters *asserted* by the Procureur-Imperial, but not proved, to be in Mazzini's handwriting, and with no date affixed. The sole connection of Mr. Stansfeld with the matter was the inference of the Procureur, a perfectly legitimate one under the circumstances, that the writer of these fragments discovered on Greco's person, *whoever he might be*, desired him to address letters, *at some time or other*, to the house in which Mr.

[1] This article was first published in *The Economist* for March 26 1864, Volume XXII, pp. 382–3.

461

Stansfeld lives. (The other statement of the Procureur, that Mr. Stansfeld had been in 1857 the banker of the Tibaldi conspiracy fund, was made on no authority, sustained by not a tittle of evidence, and fell to the ground at once as a mere loose slander, for which no one believes there was ever the slightest shadow of foundation.)

Unhappily, Mr. Stansfeld did not confine himself to a simple and indignant denial of the remotest knowledge of either the Greco plot or the Tibaldi fund, and to a frank acknowledgment that he had allowed Mazzini to receive letters at his house under cover to him or under feigned names,—and *a bold justification and explanation* of the reason why he had done so. Instead of this, Mr. Stansfeld not only launched out into praise of Mazzini's character—which as an attached friend of many years he was right and generous in doing,—but proceeded to expound Mazzini's views, and to declare that Mazzini shared his own detestation of the doctrine that political assassination was ever a warrantable act—which he need not have done, and which he could not do with safety or without rashness.

Mr. Stansfeld is guilty, has been found guilty, has admitted that he is guilty, of two—and only of two—things—*first*, of loving and admiring Mazzini personally, and *secondly*, of protecting Mazzini's correspondence by allowing it to be addressed to his house:—*In neither of these things* is there anything to be ashamed of, any guilt or anything needing apology or deprecatory exculpation. (When Mr. Stansfeld took office indeed, the matter was somewhat changed, and official proprieties then would suggest that he should have requested Mazzini to obtain the needed security through some other friends. This he appears to have done, though we are not exactly informed *when*.) There is nothing to be ashamed of in being Mazzini's friend. He is, in our opinion, a very wrong-headed, perverse, mischievous man;— a man with whose views of Italian liberty and the means by which it can be best promoted we entirely disagree;—a man who, by his extreme republican notions and his extravagant and absurd ideas of the efficacy of mere popular and insurrectionary enthusiasm as against or instead of regular armies and constitutional organisation, has (we believe) done more harm to his country than his influence in keeping up the fanatic longing for unity and independence among the people has done good. We consider that he has often been a dreadful mar-plot, that his misguided fanaticism has sacrificed many valuable lives, that he values unity far too much and civil liberty far too little. If we had been Cavour, and Mazzini had urged the republican party to oppose and counter-work the constitutional struggles in 1859 and 1860 (as at one time there was reason to fear he would do), we should have hanged him without scruple, though with regret, as a dangerous enemy (though not an intentional one) to his country's cause. But with all this, we should be no more ashamed of Mazzini's personal friendship, than of that of Kossuth, or Mr. Bright, or Daniel O'Connell, or Garibaldi, or Louis Blanc,—or any other patriot, whom we hold to be in the main earnest and sincere, though in our opinion, and to our ceaseless indignation and condemnation, perverse, misguided, and very mischievous. Mr. Gladstone hit the exact truth when he had the courage to say that, however mistaken and injudicious and *exalté* we might deem Mazzini to be, every one who knows him will agree that he has all the virtues as well as all the faults of an enthusiast, and that both his patriotism and his general tone of character have something about them of singular purity, devotion, and disinterestedness. A man's political views may be utterly wrong-headed, and yet he may be a fascinating and a noble character.

Whether Mazzini would maintain that political assassination is ever justifiable, we do not know. We should be sorry to vouch for him on this head,—or to shriek at him as a detestable villain if he does hold that doctrine. *We* do not hold it. We, in common with nearly all English thinkers, and with the better portion of continental ones, have at last found out that such acts of violence are nearly always impure in motive, that they are intellectually irrational, that politically they are blunders, that they are with the rarest exceptions indisputable crimes, and that it is for the good of the world that they should be held up to signal condemnation. But when we reflect that in this country nearly every boy who goes to a public school and nearly every young man who goes to the university, is brought up, if not to honour and worship and make idols of Brutus and Harmodius and Aristogiton, the tyrannicides of old, at least to defend and respect them as pure patriots and martyrs; that up to the age of 24, the right and duty of political assassination, as exemplified in those noble characters, is to say the least an open question with the ingenuous youth of England; and that it is not till we escape from our instructors and come forth to think and act in life that we throw off this perilous and false doctrine,—then we do say that the enormous and *mysterious* horror expressed by so many members of Parliament, who have themselves gone through this peculiar phase of hero-worship, is ludicrously misplaced and can scarcely be sincere. And further, we are not quite sure that any, even of those gentlemen, who remember and will duly weigh the case of the Emperor Paul I. of Russia, will be inclined to argue that there can be *no* case in which the removal by secret violence of an incurable and unmanageable brute may become a defensible necessity.

We say, then, that the member for Halifax need not be at all ashamed of his friendship for Mazzini, and was right and manly to avow it. We go further, and we concur with what was said by Mr. Bright in his generous and manly speech on the subject, that we should not be disposed to think very highly of the love of liberty, or the regard for justice, or the hatred of oppression and of wrong, of any Englishman who has not sympathised with the cause of Italy and the efforts of Italian patriots, and whose sympathies, at all events in early youth, did not carry him to the very verge of aiding those men and joining in those efforts:—fortunate if those generous and youthful impulses never led him to become the unintentional assistant of outraged and maddened exiles whose nature was not scrupulous and whose means were not unexceptionable;—fortunate, also, if his ardent sympathy with a great and noble cause never brought him into connection with patriots less pure and less noble than Mazzini.

And now one word as to the second charge against Mr. Stansfeld— namely that he gave to M. Mazzini's correspondence the protection of his address and name. Have we forgotten—above all have honourable members who sit on the Opposition side of the House forgotten—*why Mazzini's correspondence comes to need this abnormal protection?* Have the events and the discussions of February and March, 1845, passed from their memory? Have they forgotten that it then came to light that Mazzini's letters had been, at the suggestion of foreign powers, habitually opened at the English Post Office; that information gleaned from those letters of a wild plot (*which Mazzini endeavoured to prevent*) was conveyed to the Austrian Government; and that in consequence of that information the unhappy conspirators were seized, several slain in fight, and nine, including the Brothers Bandiera, executed in cold blood? After this, and remembering this, where is the liberal Englishman, where the friend of Italy, where the lover of justice, who would not feel prompted to do all he could to secure Mazzini's correspondence from future official violation abroad? And who would blame men for yielding to those promptings? And how did it happen that, remembering this, even Mr. Stansfeld's friends joined in condemning the use he had permitted his friend (when he was not yet in office) to make of his house? And, still more curious, how was it that during the whole course of the discussion, no one referred to those very questionable proceedings in 1844 and 1845, which rendered it necessary, in order to protect English official honour and Italian patriotic lives, that Mazzini's correspondence should be carried on under feigned names and at the addresses of personal friends?

Mazzini[1]

THE death of Mazzini means the suppression of a great political force which had latterly been used, certainly not for unworthy, but for impossible, and therefore anarchical ends, but which undoubtedly had revivified the political life of Italy, and furnished the raw materials of which the great political strategy of Count Cavour was able to make such wonderful use. Cavour without Mazzini would have been an engineer without a supply of force. Mazzini without Cavour would have been a great force without any guarantee for its successful organisation.

And yet Mazzini was by no means like Garibaldi—a man without political sense and judgment. He was a sort of half-way house between 'the inspired idiot' of Caprera and the wily diplomatist of Turin. Mazzini had a very great and powerful governing mind. His personal influence over young men was something rarely paralleled. When he could choose his own instruments, and choose such as were susceptible of being impressed by his own ardent enthusiasm, he was a man of very rare administrative power. The Association of Young Italy bore wonderful testimony to his extraordinary capacity for diffusing his own disinterestedness and his own faith in national life and unity, with even thrilling intensity, through a widely-spread network of political societies. More than this, his administration of Rome during the dangerous months in which the triumvirs ruled it in 1849 was, as everybody who has heard the details of it admits, a perfect marvel of sagacity and moderation. Mazzini's administrative power was indeed very great when he could act through men whose loyalty to himself he had secured by possessing them with his own patriotic idealism. His lofty and just, if deeply prejudiced, type of character was wonderfully rich in personal insight, and in days of great national enthusiasm and danger such as befel Rome during his administration, he had every advantage for displaying his highest qualities. It was only when he had to act with men of equal power with himself, but possessed with radically different notions of political equity and patriotic duty, that

[1] This article was first published in *The Economist* for March 16 1872, Volume XXX, pp. 323–4.

Mazzini failed. He was an idealist who could allow generously for the deficiencies and selfishness of the people so long as he was not asked to work himself through the lower order of motives. In Rome his magnanimity of policy, and his tolerance for the beliefs which he held to be dangerous superstitions, excited the admiration even of conservative statesmen like Lord Palmerston. But Mazzini, like all men whose belief is essentially of the ardent religious type, could not endure to appeal to the low worldly motives and the self-indulgent impulses or 'such creatures as we are in such a world as the present.' His horror of the adroit arts of statesmanship was profound. He could bear to labour for the debased and the ignorant, for selfishness and vice, but he could not bear to take its opposition into account when considering what he ought to do. He was, it is said, in 1849 offered the premiership by Charles Albert, on condition that he should give up his larger schemes for Italy, and get the republicans of Lombardy (then for a moment conquered from Austria) to accede to the surrender of Lombardy to the Piedmontese king. He refused, and would have thought himself for ever degraded if he had acceded to the idea, and he at least would have been *really* debased by the compromise, for his life was lived in the ideal world, and if he was not to preach a united and glorified Italy, he was nothing. Yet it was a weakness, and a great weakness, in his character, that he could hardly conceive of the honesty of statesmen who took a very different and far more historical view of Italian progress, who were content to develop the only popular monarchy of the peninsula into an Italian monarchy, and to do so by degrees, pausing for long intervals to wait for better opportunity and stronger aid. That to him was no better than the worldly wisdom of an apostle sent to preach a gospel to a great race, who should have accepted a rich bishopric offered him on condition of his ceasing to stir beyond a particular province, and should have settled down in it to enjoy the world instead of invading and conquering it. Mazzini was quite statesman enough to know that Italy could not in a moment, no nor in many years or generations, even approach the type of his own ideal republic, that she must for many generations be more or less swayed by the historical conceptions of the past, and that the less abrupt and violent the change of outward form proposed, the more chance of stability there would be. He knew this so well that while throwing his own influence most enthusiastically into the republican scale, he more than once offered to leave Italy to decide for herself on the new form of government, when once she should be free and united, and in a position to judge calmly of her own wishes. Yet this concession was really formal, and was nothing but the sacrifice made by his own strong prepossessions to his intellect. Mazzini might have known, and somewhere deep down in his mind probably did know, that this sort of concession was perfectly empty, that you cannot hold-over these sort of questions till a nation is ready to decide them— that the pretence of holding them over gives a shock to 'the historical consciousness' of the people, that you must work with the constitutional materials you have, without throwing the slur on them of proclaiming to the whole people that they are but provisional and liable to a speedy repudiation.

The truth was that Mazzini's own historical sense was completely at issue with his religious or politico-religious convictions, and that the latter were too strong for the former. Had he been wise he would have accepted in his latter days the rôle of a political teacher rather than a practical intriguer. Italy had won, under the certainly by no means stainless political character of Victor Emmanuel and his statesmen, a far larger measure of unity and freedom than anyone but a fanatic had any right to hope for. To improve the standard of political faith in Italy, to disseminate higher ideas of freedom, purer notions of political duty and manliness, might have been left to Mazzini, in spite of his accepting the actual *régime*, as any practical politician would have accepted it in his place. But Mazzini could not bear to admit that 'the logic of facts' is one of compromise, which must admit very mixed motives if it will win anything at all in the sphere of practice. He almost created the force which did so much to regenerate Italy; but in Italy itself he could not endure to admit that the regeneration was full of alloys, and that Italy remained only an earthly country in very decidedly earthly moral conditions. He almost undid,—at any rate he did his best to undo,—the great good he had done, because he could not recognise in its his own ideal. In England, in France, in Germany, his political conceptions were far soberer and saner; there he could bear to see that perfection was impossible, and that even imperfection must not be too often disturbed if the imperfect elements were to be lessened. But in Italy he was a dreamer—a dreamer even in his creative work—and still more a dreamer when he tried to destroy what he himself had created because it did not shadow forth to his exacting eyes any of the beauty and glory of his own dream.

Cardinal Antonelli

Introductory note

Cardinal Antonelli (1806–1876) was born at Sonnino in Italy. He was ordained deacon but not priest, and was created a cardinal by Pope Pius IX in 1847. In 1848 he became the Governor of the papal states, which were then for the first time established under a democratic constitution. After his own and succeeding governments had fallen amidst a state of revolution, he planned the flight of the Pope to Gaeta, where he was made Secretary of State. After the return of the Pope to Rome in 1850 he was officially appointed Secretary of State, and placed in general control of the Government of the papal states until their elimination in 1870. It was Cardinal Antonelli's policy to retain the good will of the French Government and of Napoleon III, as he believed that this was the only way of preserving the Pope's temporal sovereignty over central Italy during the growing movement for Italian unity. France had maintained a garrison in Rome since 1850, and Cardinal Antonelli looked to it for protection. He was opposed to any quarrels, even religious ones, with France, and tried to resist the raising of a papal army. From 1870 until his death in 1876, Cardinal Antonelli was in charge of the Pope's relations with foreign governments.

Cardinal Antonelli[1]

WE have never been able to feel, or even entirely to understand, the
sort of loathing admiration for Cardinal Antonelli usually expressed
by both the Liberal and Protestant worlds. Among Englishmen in
particular, he has been accepted as the embodiment of the priestly
wiliness, which of all bad qualities they hate most; but while he was
never a priest, having for some unknown reason abstained from taking
full orders, there is no proof that he possessed any supernatural
degree of wiliness. The secret memoirs of the period will one day tell
us much more about him; but, subject always to their future revela-
tions, Cardinal Antonelli does not strike us as a very remarkable
man, but only a rather belated specimen of a class of statesmen once
very common in Europe, and especially common in the annals of the
Roman Church—men who thought that the best way to protect
states, and great organisations of all kinds, was to alter as little as
possible, to divide their dangerous enemies, and to exert as much
influence as possible over important and hostile individuals. He believed, in fact, in intrigue, at a time when more than intrigue was
needed for the safety of his charge—the temporal power—and even
in intrigue he did not succeed very well. He neither destroyed, nor
defeated, nor paralysed any great enemy of the Papacy; on the contrary, he alienated a great many possible allies. It was of the highest
importance to the temporal power to show that the Papacy could—
allowance being made for its ideas—govern the States of the Church
very well, and Cardinal Antonelli governed them very badly—so
badly as to excite in the States themselves great discontent, and in
Europe a deep contempt for clerical maladministration. It was of the
greatest importance to the Papacy to recognise that new powers had
arisen in the world stronger than kings, courts, or armies, and to the
last Cardinal Antonelli thought that to win the favour of kings,
courts, and armies was to succeed, and did not win it. He might easily

[1] This article was first published in *The Economist* for November 11 1876, Volume
XXXIV, pp. 1312-3.

have made an alliance with the Russian Government, and he only exasperated it; he might repeatedly have arrived at a *modus vivendi* with Cavour, and he only resisted him; he made the support which Napoleon III. was forced to accord to the Vatican a galling annoyance to him, and he irritated the new power—Germany—into measures undistinguishable from persecution. It may be said, of course, that much of his failure was due to his master, the Pope, a man of a very peculiar, though intelligible character, but Cardinal Antonelli had the Pope's full confidence, and if possessed of the qualities with which he was credited, he ought to have been able to manage an old gentleman whom he quite understood, and who was not so able as himself. No one can produce a despatch from Cardinal Antonelli of a first-rate kind, one which altered events or modified the policy of rulers, or produced any impression except of a certain adroitness and polish in its writer. The Cardinal had no doubt great tenacity, but it was only because he desired always the same object, and thought always it could be obtained in the same way, and therefore held obstinately to his line, which very often was not a wise one. It is very difficult to doubt, for instance, that an abler man could have saved the estates of the Church in Spain, or have enabled Francis of Naples, to keep his kingdom, when Cavour wished not to take it, or have made some quiet agreement with a politician so little moved by religious rancour as Prince Bismarck. As far as we can see, Cardinal Antonelli, with all his polish and his charm of manner and his supposed worldly wisdom, never acquired any influence of any sort over any dangerous person, not even over sovereigns who, like King Victor Emmanuel, sincerely believed in the spiritual danger of a conflict with the Papacy, or, like the Queen of Spain, was heartily and honestly devoted to the Church. As we read him he was a man of fine manners, much knowledge of persons, great patience, and some ability in intrigue, who never quite understood the times in which he lived, or the comparative strength of forces in motion, or the real views of the statesmen whom he had to manage. He was obliged always to wait upon events, and therefore never controlled them. It is certain, to give concrete instances of his want of foresight, that he thought the Austrians would defeat the French in 1860, that he believed the French would defeat the Germans in 1870, and that he did not expect the final entry of the Italians into Rome. He was as habitually wrong in his political forecasts as Maria Theresa's adviser, Kaunitz, whom in many other respects he so greatly resembled. His failures to win may not have been his fault, for the forces against him were overwhelming, but his failure to foresee, with the immense machinery of Rome to help him in foreseeing, unquestionably throws doubt on his claim to be a statesman of any high order.

Cardinal Antonelli is regarded in England as having been an exceptionally bad man, but there is very little evidence that he was one. As Secretary of State in an absolute monarchy, he was callous to the personal suffering of revolutionists, Voltairians, and other enemies; but he was no more callous than Prince Gortschakoff, or M. Rouher, and was not in any degree blood-thirsty. He probably rather disliked killing people when imprisoning them would do, and certainly acted as if he did. A worldly wise man, of elegantly luxurious tastes, he was first minister of a Church which has become ascetic, and was naturally supposed to be a hypocrite; but there is no proof of that either. He probably thought about his Church much as Lord Eldon thought about his, and never questioned or examined its spiritual claims at all. There it was, and his business was to defend it; and he did defend it, as well as he knew how, hating its open enemies, for instance, with a most sincere heart. He did not take part in theological discussions. He avoided taking full orders. He never pretended to be devout or ascetic, or spiritually-minded, or anything else except devoted to the Holy See, and he was devoted. That he did not live up to the precepts of his Church is likely enough, though Roman gossip is very malignant; but neither did Philip the Second, or many another most sincere believer. It is said he stole a fortune, and he clearly possessed one which he could not have inherited; but it is most probable that he only managed cleverly the great perquisites which, by immemorial custom, flowed into his hands, and was only to blame for want of disinterestedness, and not for peculation. If he would have taken bribes millions would, from time to time, have been poured into his lap. The nepotism of which he was accused was of no immoderate kind, and there is no more reason why a Cardinal should not promote his relations than why an English bishop should not give livings to his sons-in-law. It is much better not to do it, but it is not a crime. The personality of the Cardinal for good and evil has, in fact, been exaggerated by English opinion, and it is very doubtful if his decease will leave any important blank in the Council which, whenever the Pope is not personally moved by religious, or, at all events, pietistic emotion, controls the Roman Church. It certainly will not suffer greatly, for Cardinal Antonelli, whatever his good qualities, wanted that even balance among them which is probably, in this world, the cause of good luck. He never succeeded in anything, not even in managing the master who promoted and trusted him, and the affairs of the Holy See will probably go on with less friction because Cardinal Antonelli is away. Nothing can be worse for a Church in difficulties than to be represented in external affairs by a man whom his enemies believe to be a marvel of wiliness and guile, except perhaps to be represented by a man who is so esteemed without any good reason other than his smooth immovability. Nothing fetters the Catholic Church in England and other Protestant countries like the belief in the underhandedness of its managers, and in Cardinal Antonelli's case the whole world thought of the Pope's foreign secretary as English bourgeoisie think of every Jesuit.

Henry Crabb Robinson

Introductory note

Henry Crabb Robinson (1775–1867) was born at Bury St. Edmunds, the youngest son of a tanner. He was educated at private schools, and was then articled to an attorney at Colchester. Between 1800–2 he travelled in Germany and Bohemia, where he met Goethe and Schiller. He became correspondent for *The Times* at Altona, then foreign editor, and from 1808–9 special *Times* correspondent in the Peninsula. He was a barrister of the Middle Temple and a leader of the Norfolk Circuit, from which he retired in 1828. He was a founder of the Athenaeum Club and of University College, London. Acquainted with many and very various notable persons of his day, his *Diary* and *Letters* record his dealings with them. Crabb Robinson died in London in 1867.

Henry Crabb Robinson[1]

PERHAPS I should be ashamed to confess it, but I own I opened the
three large volumes of Mr. Robinson's memoirs with much anxiety.
Their bulk, in the first place, appalled me; but that was by no means
my greatest apprehension. I knew I had a hundred times heard Mr.
Robinson say that he hoped something he would leave behind him
would 'be published and be worth publishing.' I was aware too—for
it was no deep secret—that for half a century or more he had kept a
diary, and that he had been preserving correspondence besides; and
I was dubious what sort of things these would be, and what—to use
Carlyle's words—any human editor could make of them. Even when
Mr. Robinson used to talk so I used to shudder; for the men who have
tried to be memoir-writers and failed are as numerous, or nearly so,
as those who have tried to be poets and failed. A specific talent is as
necessary for the one as for the other. But as soon as I had read a little
of the volumes, all these doubts passed away. I saw at once that Mr.
Robinson had an excellent power of narrative-writing, and that the
editor of his remains had made a most judicious use of excellent
materials.

Perhaps more than anything it was the modesty of my old friend
(I think I may call Mr. Robinson my old friend, for though he *thought*
me a modern youth, I *did* know him twenty years)—perhaps, I say,
it was his modesty which made me nervous about his memoirs more
than anything else. I have so often heard him say (and say it with a
vigour of emphasis which is rare in our generation even than in his),—
'Sir, I have no literary talent. I cannot write. I never *could* write anything, and I never *would* write anything,'—that being so taught, and
so vehemently, I came to believe. And there was this to justify my
creed. The notes Mr. Robinson used to scatter about him—and he

[1] DIARY, REMINISCENCES, AND CORRESPONDENCE OF HENRY CRABB ROBINSON, BARRIS-
TER-AT-LAW, F.S.A. Selected and edited by Thos. Sadler, Ph.D. In three volumes.
London, 1869. 36s. This essay was first published in the *Fortnightly Review* for August 1
1869, Volume VI, pp. 179–88. An abridged edition of Crabb Robinson's diary was
published by the Oxford University Press in 1967, edited by Derek Hudson.

was fond of writing rather elaborate ones—were not always very
good. At least they were too long for the busy race of the present
generation, and introduced Schiller and Goethe where they need not
have come. But in these memoirs (especially in the Reminiscences and
the Diary—for the moment he gets to a letter the style is worse)
the words flow with such an effectual simplicity, that even Southey,
the great master of such prose, could hardly have written better.
Possibly it was his real interest in his old stories which preserved
Mr. Robinson; in his letters he was not so interested and he fell into
words and amplifications; but in those ancient anecdotes, which for
years were his life and being, the style, as it seems to me, could
scarcely be mended even in a word. And though, undoubtedly, the
book is much too long in the latter half, I do not blame Dr. Sadler,
the editor and biographer, for it, or indeed blame anyone. Mr. Robinson had led a very long and very varied life, and some of his old
friends had an interest in one part of his reminiscences and some in
another. An unhappy editor intrusted with 'a deceased's papers,'
cannot really and in practice omit much that any surviving friends
much want put in. One man calls with a letter 'in which my dear and
honoured friend gave me advice that was of such inestimable value,
I hope, I cannot but think you will find room for it.' And another
calls with memoranda of a dinner—a most 'superior occasion,' as they
say in the north—at which, he says, 'There was conversation to which
I never, or scarcely ever, heard anything equal. There were A. B. and
C. D. and E. F., all masters, as you remember, of the purest conversational eloquence; surely I need not hestitate to believe that you will
say something of that dinner.' And so an oppressed biographer has to
serve up the crumbs of ancient feasts, though well knowing in his
heart that they are crumbs, and though he feels, too, that the critics
will attack him, and cruelly say it is his fault. But remembering this,
and considering that Mr. Robinson wrote a diary beginning in 1811,
going down to 1867, and occupying thirty-five closely-written volumes, and that there were 'Reminiscences' and vast unsorted papers,
I think Dr. Sadler has managed admirably well. His book is brief to
what it might have been, and all his own part is written with delicacy,
feeling, and knowledge. He quotes, too, from Wordsworth by way
of motto—

> A man he seems of cheerful yesterdays
> And confident to-morrows; with a face

Not worldly minded, for it bears too much
A nation's impress,—gaiety and health,
Freedom and hope;—but keen withal and shrewd:
His gestures note,—and hark his tones of voice
Are all vivacious as his mien and looks.

It was a happy feeling of Mr. Robinson's character that selected these lines to stand at the beginning of his memoirs.

And yet in one material respect—in this case perhaps the most material respect—Dr. Sadler has failed, and not in the least from any fault of his. Sidney Smith used to complain that 'no one had ever made him his trustee or executor;' being really a very sound and sensible man of business, he felt that it was a kind of imputation on him, and that he was not appreciated. But some one more justly replied, 'But how could *you*, Sidney Smith, expect to be made an executor? Is there any one who wants their "remains" to be made fun of?' Now every trustee of biographical papers is exactly in this difficulty, that he cannot make fun. The melancholy friends who left the papers would not at all like it. And, besides, there grows upon every such biographer an 'official' feeling—a confused sense of vague responsibilities—a wish not to impair the gravity of the occasion, or to offend any one by levity. But there are some men who cannot be justly described quite gravely; and Crabb Robinson is one of them. A certain grotesqueness was a part of him, and unless you liked it you lost the very best of him. He is called, and properly called, in these memoirs Mr. Robinson; but no well-judging person ever called him so in life. He was always called 'old Crabb,' and that is the only name which will ever bring up his curious image to me. He was, in the true old English sense of the word, a 'character;' one whom a very peculiar life, certainly, and perhaps also a rather peculiar nature to begin with, had formed and moulded into something so exceptional and singular that it did not seem to belong to ordinary life, and almost caused[2] a smile when you saw it moving there. 'Aberrant forms,' I believe naturalists call seals and such things in natural history; odd shapes that can only be explained by a long past, and which swim with a certain incongruity in their present *milieu*. Now 'old Crabb' was (to me at least) just like that. You watched with interest and pleasure his singular gestures, and his odd way of saying things, and muttered, as if to keep up the recollection, 'And *this* is the man who was the friend of Goethe, and is the

---

[2] The *Fortnightly* (p. 181) has 'moved' for 'caused'.

friend of Wordsworth!' There was a certain animal oddity about 'old Crabb' which made it a kind of mental joke to couple him with such great names, and yet he was to his heart's core thoroughly coupled with them. If you leave out all his strange ways (I do not say Dr. Sadler has quite left them out), but to some extent he has been obliged, by place and decorum, to omit them, you lose the life of the man. You cut from the negro his skin, and from the leopard his spots. I well remember poor Clough, who was then fresh from Oxford, and was much puzzled by the corner of London to which he had drifted, looking at 'old Crabb' in a kind of terror for a whole breakfast time, and muttering in mute wonder, and almost to himself, as he came away, 'Not at all the regular patriarch.' And certainly no one could accuse Mr. Robinson of an insipid regularity either in face or nature.

Mr. Robinson was one of the original founders of University College, and was for many years both on its senate and council; and as he lived near the college he was fond of collecting at breakfast all the elder students—especially those who had any sort of interest in literature. Probably he never appeared to so much advantage, or showed all the best of his nature, so well as in those parties. Like most very cheerful old people, he at heart preferred the company of the very young; and a set of young students, even after he was seventy, suited him better as society than a set of grave old men. Sometimes, indeed, he would have—I do not say some of his contemporaries, few of them even in 1847 were up to breakfast parties, but persons of fifty and sixty—those whom young students call old gentlemen. And it was amusing to watch the consternation of some of them at the surprising youth and levity of their host. They shuddered at the freedom with which we treated him. Middle-aged men, of feeble heads and half-made reputations, have a nice dislike to the sharp arguments and the unsparing jests of 'boys at college;' they cannot bear the rough society of those who, never having tried their own strength, have not yet acquired a fellow-feeling for weakness. Many such persons, I am sure, were half hurt with Mr. Robinson for not keeping those 'impertinent boys' more at a just distance; but Mr. Robinson liked fun and movement, and disliked the sort of dignity which shelters stupidity. There was little to gratify the unintellectual part of man at these breakfasts, and what there was was not easy to be got at. Your host, just as you were sitting down to breakfast, found he had forgotten to make the tea, then he could not find his keys, then he rang the bell to have them searched for; but long before the servant came he had gone off into 'Schiller-Goethe,' and could not the least remember what he had wanted. The more astute of his guests used to breakfast before they came, and then there was much interest in seeing a steady literary man, who did not understand the region, in agonies at having to hear three stories before he got his tea, one again between his milk and his sugar, another between his butter and his toast, and additional zest in making a stealthy inquiry that was sure to intercept the coming delicacies by bringing on Schiller and Goethe.

It is said in these memoirs that Mr. Robinson's parents were very good-looking, and that when married they were called the handsome couple. But in his old age very little regular beauty adhered to him, if he ever had any. His face was pleasing from its animation, its kindness, and its shrewdness, but the nose was one of the most slovenly which nature had ever turned out, and the chin of excessive length, with portentous power of extension. But, perhaps, for the purpose of a social narrator (and in later years this was Mr. Robinson's position) this oddity of feature was a gift. It was said, and justly said, that Lord Brougham used to punctuate his sentences with his nose; just at the end of a long parenthesis he *could*, and did, turn up his nose, which served to note the change of subject as well, or better, than a printed mark. Mr. Robinson was not so skilful as this, but he had a very able use of the chin at a conversational crisis, and just at the point of a story pushed it out, and then very slowly drew it in again, so that you always knew when to laugh, and the oddity of the gesture helped you in laughing.

Mr. Robinson had known nearly every literary man worth knowing in England and Germany for fifty years and more. He had studied at Jena in the 'great time,' when Goethe, and Schiller, and Wieland were all at their zenith; he had lived with Charles Lamb and his set, and Rogers and his set, besides an infinite lot of little London people; he had taught Madame de Staël German philosophy in Germany, and helped her in business afterwards in England; he was the real friend of Wordsworth, and had known Coleridge and Southey almost from their 'coming out' to their death. And he was not a mere literary man. He had been a *Times* correspondent in the days of Napoleon's early German battles, now more than 'seventy years since;' he had been off Corunna in Sir John Moore's time; and last, but almost first it should have been, he was an English barrister, who had for years a considerable business, and who was full of picturesque stories about old judges. Such a varied life and experience belong to very few men, and his social nature—at once accessible and assailant—was just the one to take advantage of it. He seemed to be lucky all through; in childhood he remembered when John Gilpin came out; then he had seen— he could not hear—John Wesley preach; then he had heard Erskine, and criticised him intelligently, in some of the finest of the well-known 'state trials;' and so on during all his vigorous period.

I do not know that it would be possible to give a better idea of Mr. Robinson's best conversations than by quoting almost at random from the earlier part of these memoirs:—

At the Spring assizes of 1791, when I had nearly attained my sixteenth year, I had the delight of hearing Erskine. It was a high enjoyment, and I was able to profit by it. The subject of the trial was the validity of a will— Braham *v.* Rivett. Erskine came down specially retained for the plaintiff, and Mingay for the defendant. The trial lasted two days. The title of the heir being admitted, the proof of the will was gone into at once. I have a recollection of many of the circumstances after more than fifty-four years; but of nothing do I retain so perfect a recollection as of the figure and voice of Erskine. There was a charm in his voice, a fascination in his eye, and so completely had he won my affection that I am sure had the verdict been given against him I should have burst out crying. Of the facts and of the evidence I do not pretend to recollect anything beyond my impressions and sensations. My pocket-book records that Erskine was engaged two and a half hours in opening the case, and Mingay two hours and twenty minutes in his speech in defence. E.'s reply occupied three hours. The testatrix was an old lady in a state of imbecility. The evil spirit of the case was an attorney. Mingay was loud and violent, and gave Erskine an opportunity of turning into ridicule his imagery and illustrations. For instance, M. having compared R. to the Devil going into the Garden of Eden, E. drew a closer parallel than M. intended. Satan's first sight of Eve was related in Milton's words—

> Grace was in all her steps, heaven in her eye,
> In every gesture dignity and love;

and then a picture of idiocy from Swift was contrasted. But the sentence that weighed on my spirits was a pathetic exclamation—'If, gentlemen, you should by your verdict annihilate an instrument so solemnly framed, *I should retire a troubled man from this court.*' And as he uttered the word *court,* he beat his breast and I had a difficulty in not crying out. When in bed the following night I awoke several times in a state of excitement approaching fever—the words '*troubled man from this court*' rang in my ears.

A new trial was granted, and ultimately the will was set aside. I have said I profited by Erskine. I remarked his great artifice, if I may call it so; and in a small way I afterwards practised it. It lay in his frequent repetitions. He had one or two leading arguments and main facts on which he was constantly dwelling. But then he had marvellous skill in varying his phraseology, so that no one was sensible of tautology in the expressions. Like the doubling of a hare, he was perpetually coming to his old place. Other great advocates I have remarked were ambitious of a great variety of arguments.

About the same time that I thus first heard the most perfect of forensic orators I was also present at an exhibition equally admirable, and which had a powerful effect upon my mind. It was, I believe, in October, 1790, and not long before his death, that I heard John Wesley in the great round Meeting House at Colchester. He stood in a wide pulpit, and on each side of him stood a minister, and the two held him up, having their hands under his armpits. His feeble voice was barely audible. But his reverend countenance, especially his long white locks, formed a picture never to be forgotten. There was a vast crowd of lovers and admirers. It was for the most part pantomime, but the pantomime went to the heart. Of the kind I never saw anything comparable to it in after life.

And again—

It was at the Summer Circuit that Rolfe made his first appearance. He had been at the preceding Sessions. I have a pleasure in recollecting that I at once foresaw that he would become a distinguished man. In my Diary I wrote, 'Our new junior, Mr. Rolfe, made his appearance. His manners are genteel; his conversation easy and sensible. He is a very acceptable companion, but I fear a dangerous rival.' And my brother asking me who the new man was, I said, 'I will venture to predict that you will live to see that young man attain a higher rank than any one you ever saw upon the circuit.' It is true he is not higher than Leblanc, who was also a puisne judge, but Leblanc was never Solicitor-General; nor, probably, is Rolfe yet at the end of his career. One day, when some one remarked, 'Christianity is part and parcel of the law of the land,' Rolfe said to me, 'Were you ever employed to draw an indictment against a man for not loving his neighbour as himself?'

Rolfe is, by universal repute, if not the very best, at least one of the best judges on the Bench. He is one of the few with whom I have kept up an acquaintance.*

* 'Since writing the above, Baron Rolfe has verified my prediction more strikingly by being created a peer, by the title of Lord Cranworth, and appointed a Vice-Chancellor. Soon after his appointment, he called on me, and I dined with him. I related to Lady Cranworth the anecdote given above, of my conversation with my brother, with which she was evidently pleased. Lady Cranworth was the daughter of Mr. Carr, Solicitor to the Excise, whom I formerly used to visit, and ought soon to find some mention of in my journals. Lord Cranworth continues to enjoy universal respect.—H.C.R. 1851.'

Of course, these stories came over and over again. It is the excellence of a reminiscent to have a few good stories, and his misfortune that people will remember what he says. In Mr. Robinson's case an un-skilled person could often see the anecdote somewhere impending, and there was often much interest in trying whether you could ward it off or not. There was one great misfortune which had happened to his guests, though he used to tell it as one of the best things that had ever happened to himself. He had picked up a certain bust of Wieland by Schadow, which it appears had been lost, and in the finding of which Goethe, even Goethe, rejoiced. After a very long interval I still shudder to think how often I have heard that story; it was one which no skill or care could long avert, for the thing stood opposite our host's chair, and the sight of it was sure to recall him. Among the ungrateful students to whom he was so kind, the first question always asked of anyone who had breakfasted at his house was 'Did you undergo the *bust*?'

A reader of these memoirs would naturally and justly think that the great interest of Mr. Robinson's conversation was the strength of the past memory; but quite as amusing or more was the present weakness. He never could remember names, and was very ingenious in his devices to elude the defect. There is a story in these memoirs:—

I was engaged to dine with Mr. Wansey at Walthamstow. When I arrived there I was in the greatest distress, through having forgotten his name. And it was not till after half an hour's worry that I recollected he was a Unitarian, which would answer as well; for I instantly proceeded to Mr. Cogan's. Having been shown into a room, young Mr. Cogan came—'Your commands, sir?'—'Mr. Cogan, I have taken the liberty to call on you in order to know where I am to dine to-day.' He smiled. I went on: 'The truth is, I have accepted an invitation to dine with a gentleman, a recent acquaintance, whose name I have forgotten; but I am sure you can tell me, for he is a Unitarian, and the Unitarians are very few here.'

And at his breakfasts it was always the same; he was always in difficulty as to some person's name or other, and he had regular descriptions which recurred, like Homeric epithets, and which he expected you to apply to the individual. Thus poor Clough always appeared—'That admirable and accomplished man. You know whom I mean. The one who never says anything.' And of another living poet he used to say: 'Probably the most able, and certainly the most consequential, of all the young persons I know. You know which it is. The one with whom

I could never *presume* to be intimate. The one whose father I knew so many years.' And another particular friend of my own always occurred as—'That great friend of yours that has been in Germany— that most accomplished and interesting person—that most able and excellent young man. Sometimes I like him, and sometimes I *hate* him. You,' turning to me, 'know whom I mean, you villain!' And certainly I did know; for I had heard the same adjectives, and been referred to in the same manner, very many times.

Of course a main part of Mr. Robinson's conversation was on literary subjects; but of this, except when it related to persons whom he had known, or sonnets to 'the conception of which he was privy,' I do not think it would be just to speak very highly. He spoke sensibly and clearly—he could not on any subject speak otherwise; but the critical faculty is as special and as peculiar almost as the poetical; and Mr. Robinson in serious moments was quite aware of it, and he used to deny that he had one faculty more than the other. He used to read much of Wordsworth to me; but I doubt—though many of his friends will think I am a great heretic—I doubt if he read the best poems; and even those he did read (and he read very well) rather suffered from coming in the middle of a meal, and at a time when you wanted to laugh, and not to meditate. Wordsworth was a solitary man, and it is only in solitude that his best poems, or indeed any of his characteristic poems, can be truly felt or really apprehended. There are some at which I never look, even now, without thinking of the wonderful and dreary faces which Clough used to make while Mr. Robinson was reading them. To Clough certain of Wordsworth's poems were part of his inner being, and he suffered at hearing them obtruded at meal times, just as a high churchman would suffer at hearing the collects of the Church. Indeed, these poems were among the collects of Clough's Church.

Still less do I believe that there is any special value in the expositions of German philosophy in these volumes, or that there was any in those which Mr. Robinson used to give on such matters in conversation. They are clear, no doubt, and accurate, but they are not the expositions of a born metaphysician. He speaks in these memoirs of his having a difficulty in concentrating his 'attention on works of speculation.' And such books as Kant can only be really mastered, can perhaps only be usefully studied, by those who have an unusual facility in concentrating their mind on impalpable abstractions, and an uncommon inclination to do so. Mr. Robinson had neither; and I think the critical philosophy had really very little effect on him, and had, during the busy years which had elapsed since he studied it, very nearly run off him. There was something very curious in the sudden way that anything mystical would stop in him. At the end of a Sunday breakfast, after inflicting on you much which was transcendental in Wordsworth or Goethe, he would say, as we left him, with an air of relish, 'Now I am going to run down to Exeter Street to hear Madge. I shall not be in time for the prayers; but I do not so much care about that; what I do like is the sermon; it is so clear.' Mr. Madge was a Unitarian of the old school, with as little mystical and transcendental in his nature as any one who ever lived. There was a living piquancy in the friend of Goethe—the man who *would* explain to you his writings—being also the admirer of 'Madge;' it was like a proser, lengthily eulogising Kant to you, and then saying, 'Ah! but I do love Condillac; he is so clear.'

But, on the other hand, I used to hold—I was reading law at the time, and so had some interest in the matter—that Mr. Robinson much underrated his legal knowledge, and his practical power as a lawyer. What he used to say was, 'I never knew any law, sir, but I knew the practice. . . . I left the bar, sir, because I feared my incompetence might be discovered. I was a tolerable junior, but I was rising to be a leader, which I was unfit to be, and so I retired, not to disgrace myself by some fearful mistake.' In these memoirs he says that he retired when he had made the sum of money which he thought enough for a bachelor with few wants and not a single expensive taste. The simplicity of his tastes is certain; very few Englishmen indeed could live with so little show or pretence. But the idea of the gross incompetence is absurd. No one who was so ever said so. There are, I am confident, plenty of substantial and well-satisfied men at the English bar who do not know nearly as much law as Mr. Robinson knew, and who have not a tithe of his natural sagacity, but who believe in themselves and in whom their clients believe. On the other hand, Mr. Robinson had many great qualifications for success at the bar. He was a really good speaker: when over seventy I have heard him make a speech that good speakers in their full vigour would be glad to make. He had a good deal of the actor in his nature, which is thought, and I fancy justly thought, to be necessary to the success of all great advocates, and perhaps of all great orators. He was well acquainted with the petty technicalities which intellectual men in middle life in general cannot learn, for he had passed some years in an attorney's office. Above all, he was a very thinking man, and had an 'idea of business'— that inscrutable something which at once and altogether distinguishes the man who is safe in the affairs of life from those who are unsafe. I do not suppose he knew much black-letter law; but there are plenty of judges on the bench who, unless they are much belied, know very little either—perhaps none. And a man who can intelligently read Kant, like Mr. Robinson, need not fear the book-work of English law. A very little serious study would have taught him law enough to lead the Norfolk circuit. He really had a sound, moderate, money-making business, and only a little pains was wanted to give him more.

The real reason why he did not take the trouble I fancy was that, being a bachelor, he was a kind of amateur in life, and did not really care. He could not spend what he had on himself, and used to give away largely, though in private. And even more, as with most men who have not thoroughly worked when young, daily, regular industry was exceedingly trying to him. No man could be less idle; far from it, he was always doing something; but then he was doing what he chose. Sir Walter Scott, one of the best workers of his time, used always to say that 'he had no temptation to be idle, but the greatest temptation, when one thing was wanted of him, to go and do something else.' Perhaps the only persons who, not being forced by mere necessity, really conquer this temptation, are those who were early broken to the yoke, and are fixed to the furrow by habit. Mr. Robinson loitered in Germany, so he was not one of these.

I am not regretting this. It would be a base idolatry of practical life to require every man to succeed in it as far as he could, and to devote to it all his mind. The world certainly does not need it; it pays well, and it will never lack good servants. There will always be enough of sound, strong men to be working barristers and judges, let who will object to become so. But I own I think a man ought to be able to be a 'Philistine' if he chose; there is a sickly incompleteness about people too fine for the world, and too nice to work their way in it. And when a man like Mr. Robinson had a real sagacity for affairs, it is for those who respect his memory to see that his reputation does not suffer from his modesty, and that his habitual self-depreciations—which, indeed, extended to his powers of writing as well as to those of acting—are not taken to be exactly true.

In fact, Mr. Robinson was usefully occupied in University College business, and University Hall business, and other such things. But there is no special need to write on them in connection with his name, and it would need a good deal of writing to make them intelligible to those who do not know them now. And the greater part of his life was spent in society where his influence was always manly and vigorous. I do not mean that he was universally popular, it would be defacing his likeness to say so. 'I am a man,' he once told me, 'to whom a great number of persons entertain the very strongest objection.' Indeed he had some subjects on which he could hardly bear opposition. Twice he nearly quarrelled with me: once for writing in favour of Louis Napoleon, which, as he had caught in Germany a thorough antipathy to the first Napoleon, seemed to him quite wicked; and next for my urging that Hazlitt was a much greater writer than Charles Lamb—a harmless opinion which I still hold, but which Mr. Robinson met with this outburst: 'You, sir, YOU prefer the works of that scoundrel, that odious, that malignant writer, to the exquisite essays of that angelic creature!' I protested that there was no evidence that angels could write particularly well, but it was in vain, and it was some time before he forgave me. Some persons who casually encountered peculiarities like these, did not always understand them. In his last years, too, augmenting infirmities almost disqualified Mr. Robinson for general society, and quite disabled him from showing his old abilities in it. Indeed, I think that these memoirs will give almost a new idea of his power to many young men who had only seen him casually, and at times of feebleness. After ninety it is not easy to make new friends. And, in any case, this book will always have a great charm to those who knew Mr. Robinson well when they were themselves young, because it will keep alive to them the image of his buoyant sagacity, and his wise and careless kindness.

End of Volume IV

INDEX*

Note: III, IV indicate volumes; ed. after a page number indicates that a subject is mentioned in an editorial introduction to a section of the text; bis indicates two separate references to a subject on one page.

* Two indices are provided, one general and the other to Bagehot's epigrams (p. 521)

BAGEHOT, WALTER—*cont.*
15 *ed.*, 17–24 *ed.*
posthumous fame uncertain, *III*
23–4 *ed.*
quotation, use of, *III* 35 *ed.*
sense of history, *III* 33–6 *ed.*
sense of life, *III* 39 *ed.*
BAGEHOT, WALTER: Opinions by,
mentioned or quoted on
Althorp, *III* 27 *ed.*, 32 *ed.*, 37 *ed.*
Bolingbroke, *III* 34 *ed.*
breaking egg, *III* 37–8 *ed.*
Byron, *III* 39 *ed.*
conservatism, 19th century
cowardice, *III* 26–7 *ed.*
dullness, *III* 29 *ed.*
fame, reputation, *III* 38 *ed.*
Harley, *III* 26 *ed.*, 27 *ed.*
Hazlitt, *III* 36 *ed.*
importance of property, education,
III 31 *ed.*
Industrial Revolution, *III* 34 *ed.*
intellectual things trivial, unworthy,
III 39 *ed.*
Robert Lowe, *III* 29 *ed.*
Lord Lyndhurst, *III* 35 *ed.*
Macaulay, *III* 35–6 *ed.*
mass man, 'monotony', *III* 27–8 *ed.*
Louis Napoleon, *III* 30–1 *ed.*
passage of time, *III* 33 *ed.*
Peel, *III* 28 *ed.*, 34 *ed.*
Pitt, *III* 29–30 *ed.*
reading old letters, *III* 33 *ed.*
Reform Act, 1832, *III* 27 *ed.*
sense, nonsense, *III* 39 *ed.*
Adam Smith, *III* 32 *ed.*
James Wilson, *III* 32–3 *ed.*
BAGEHOT, WALTER: Tributes to
Matthew Arnold, *III* 38 *ed.*
W. W. Rostow, *III* 24 *ed.*
Ballot, Parliamentary elections, J. S.
Mill on, *III* 543
Barrington, Mrs. Russell, on
Bagehot's interest in Louis
Napoleon, *IV* 15 *ed.*
Belgium, possible French invasion,
1850's, 1860's, *IV* 70, 124–5

Bellingham, John, *III* 247
Benjamin, Judah P., *IV* 222
Bentinck, Lord George, *III* 493, *IV*
65
Béranger, Pierre Jean de, *IV* 56
Bismarck, *IV* 21 *ed.*, 117, 123–4,
161, 174
Birmingham, *III* 163
Blanc, Louis *IV*, 32, 42
Blockade of Confederate States'
ports, *IV* 182 *bis ed.*, 250–1, 257
effects on cotton trade, *IV* 267–70
reasons for and against
disregarding the blockade, *IV*
353–8
Board of Trade, statistical
department, *III* 526
Bolingbroke, Henry St. John, 1st
Viscount, *III* 42 *ed.*
Bagehot quoted on, *III* 34 *ed.*
Bolingbroke, Henry St. John, 1st
Viscount: Career
father, *III* 45
boyhood, grandparents, *III* 45–6
marriage, *III* 47
enters Commons, *III* 47–8, 49
exploits anti-Hanoverian prejudice,
III 52–3
exploits feeling against possible
French war, 1700, *III* 53–4
Secretary of War, *III* 57
retires for 3 years, *III* 57–8
Secretary of State, Leader of
Commons under Harley, *III* 63,
64
in charge of peace negotiations
with France, Treaty of Utrecht,
III 64, 65–72
reactions to, criticisms of Treaty
in England, *III* 68, 70–2, 73,
76, 77, 80
leaves Commons, obtains peerage,
III 72, 73
inability to form policy concerning
Anne's successor, *III* 74–6
distrusted by Anne and Tory
party, *III* 76–7, 78

Brougham and Vaux, Henry Peter
Brougham, Baron: Career—*cont.*
"manages" the King, dissolution
of Parliament, *III* 182–4
administrative career ends, leader
of Opposition, *III* 184–5
Brougham and Vaux, Henry Peter
Brougham, Baron:
Characteristics
aggressive, impulsive, *III* 171–2
agitator, *III* 165–78, 196–7
aristocratic opinions, *III* 196
conspicuous labour, verve, *III*
173
'devil', mischievous excitability,
III 178, 196–7
easy anger, *III* 172, 196–7
energy, Titanic, *III* 198
enterprising intellect, wholeness
of vision, *III* 176
'manager', manipulator of men,
III 174, 182–4
memoirist, *III* 193, 198
oratory rough and ready, manly,
III 176, 186–7, 188, 189
readiness to act, *III* 173–4
speeches dull to read, *III* 188
unselfishness, *III* 172–3
use of nose as punctuation mark,
IV 481
vehemence in speeches, *III* 189,
190, 197
versatility, *III* 159, 191, 196, 197,
368
want of judicial qualities, *III*
181–2, 197
want of sensitive judgement,
nature, *III* 177–8
want of thinking, deliberating
intellect, *III* 177, 186–8,
190–1, 198
Brougham and Vaux, Henry Peter
Brougham, Baron: Interests
classical Greek oratory, *III* 188–9
education, popular, *III* 168–9, 192
law reform, *III* 169–70, 185–6
physical science, *III* 191

Brougham and Vaux, Henry Peter
Brougham, Baron: Works
Discourse, ancient oratory, *III*
188–9
Political Philosophy, III 190–1,
197–8
Speeches, III 189–90
Statesmen of George III, III 193,
198
Brougham and Vaux, Henry Peter
Brougham, Baron: Writings
quoted on
economic conditions, England,
1814–15, *III* 166–8
Lord Castlereagh, *III* 168
Brougham and Vaux, Henry Peter
Brougham, Baron: Tributes to,
criticisms of quoted
Canning, *III* 170–1
Lord Cockburn, *the Harangue, III*
190
Lord Holland, *III* 174
Francis Horner, *III* 182
Sir James Mackintosh, *III* 174
The Times, III 379
Sir Nicholas Tindal, *III* 180
Brougham and Vaux, Henry Peter
Brougham, Baron: Popular
sayings about, quoted by
Bagehot
all in a fume, III 189
most misinformed man, III 191
Buccleugh, Duke of, *III* 96, 107–8
Buchan, Alastair, biography of
Bagehot, *The Spare Chancellor,
IV* 180 *bis* ed., 182 ed., 193 ed.
Buchanan, James, *IV* 214, 228 *bis*,
239, 278
Buckle, Henry Thomas, *III* 86, 93
Buckstone, J. B., *III* 179
Bull Run, battle of (Manassas
Junction), Aug. 1861, *IV* 184
ed., 265–6, 272, 274, 275, 276
Bunsen, Baron, work on Egyptian
history, *III* 386–91
Burke, Edmund, *III* 134, 135, 145,
237, *IV* 134

Church of England—*cont.*
Gladstone's theory concerning,
III 434–6
Civil Service, Civil Servants, no
connection with Parliament
after 1832, *III* 228
Clarendon, George William
Frederick Villiers, 4th Earl,
III 524–8
Cleon, *III* 270
Clive, Lord, *III* 495
Clough, Arthur Hugh, *IV* 480, 484,
485
Cobden, Richard, *III* 250, 284–5 *ed.*
appearance, impression as speaker,
III 293–4
controversy with Delane, *III* 287
Corn Laws, success in repeal of,
III 284 *ed.*, 288, 290, 291, 295
energetic, original thought, *III*
296–7
Free Trade, interest in, *III* 284 *ed.*,
287–8, 291, 293, 295
French treaty, *III* 291
irritability, failure to influence
events, 1860's, *III* 291
man of business, *III* 295–6
on dissolution time for English
parliaments, *IV* 171
on Sir Robert Peel, *III* 268, 294–5
on Peel's sliding-scale method,
repeal of Corn Laws, *III* 185
opinion of Palmerston, *III* 280
oratory clear, to the point, *III* 296
playfulness, *III* 293
political outsider, *III* 287–8, 290–1
sensitiveness, *III* 294–5
simplicity in speeches,
'unadorned eloquence', *III*
290, 291
suggestive, animated temperament,
III 289–90
unique character, *III* 297
wanting in discretion, wide
culture, *III* 290, 296–7
Cobden, Richard: Tributes to,
quoted

Disraeli, *III* 295
James Wilson, *III* 289, 297
Cochrane, Provost, *III* 93–4, 116
Cockburn, Lord, anecdote on
Brougham, *the Harangue*, *III* 190
Cockburn, William, Dean of York,
III 264–6
Coleridge, Samuel, *III* 267, 392, *IV* 37
on Southey, *III* 402
Commerce *see* Trade
Confederate States of America:
attitude of Louis Napoleon, *III*
104, 107, 108
threatening attitude of Southern
states, Jan. 1860, *IV* 195–6
attitude to secession from Union,
Jan. 1861, *IV* 201–9
dependence on Northern States
for funds, *IV* 206
possible relationship with Britain
after secession, Jan. 1861, *IV*
211–14
possible future of Southern
states after secession, Jan. 1861,
IV 223–5
aggressive, pre-planned nature of
secession movement, *IV* 227–31,
260, 304, 318–19
new constitution, improvements
on old one, *IV* 235–6
Gregory's motion to Commons to
recognise Confederacy, April
1861, *IV* 242–4
no possibility of good issue for
provoked war, *IV* 248
territorial space, stubborn temper
making for difficult invasion
campaign by Federalists, *IV*
261–3
pretensions confirmed by battle
at Manassas Junction, Aug. 1861
(Bull Run), *IV* 265
belief in English, French
intervention to break
blockade, *IV* 268, 354
advantages to Confederate troops
in retreating, *IV* 361–2

INDEX

Education, popular, *III* 157 *ed.*,
168–9, 192, 299, 300
Eldon, Lord, *III* 124, 162, 178, 180,
195–6, 234, *IV* 473
believed himself intended victim
of Bellingham, *III* 247
quoted, on being an agitator, *III*
165
Toryism natural, excusable in,
III 234
Elections, United States *see* President,
United States, election of
Electoral college, U.S. Constitution,
IV 279
Elizabeth I, *III* 428
Elliot, Sir Gilbert, *III* 228
Emancipation Proclamation
(Lincoln's), Oct. 1862, *IV*
186–7 *ed.*, 190 *ed.*, 371–3, 375–6
Emerson, Ralph Waldo, *III* 418
England, economic, political, social
conditions, 1810's, *III* 159–68,
210–11, 212–13
Englishmen as politicians, *III* 202–3
Erskine, Thomas, *IV* 482–3
Everett (American diplomatist),
paper on Monroe Doctrine, *IV*
95–9
Examination systems, education,
III 88
Expenditure, national, Britain:
after 1815, *III* 163
Henry Fawcett on, *III* 537–8
J. S. Mill on, *III* 543
Exports, export trade, Britian, boom,
bubble, 1814, *III* 166–7
Eyre, Edward John, *III* 560–5

Factory system, Lancashire, *III* 249
Fawcett, Henry, *III* 534–8
Federal government, United States,
Hamilton's plan for, *IV* 287–90
Fenianism, *III* 548
Finance *see* Credit; Currency
Fitzwilliam, Lord, *III* 138
'Fixity', French desire for, *IV* 23
ed., 169–70, 175–6, 441–2, 443

Flogging, J. S. Mill on, *III* 544
Foreign affairs, J. S. Mill on, *III*
543
Foreign Enlistment Act, 1819
(Britain), *IV* 187 *ed.*, 251–2
Forster, William Edward, *III* 308,
467–8, *IV* 461
determination not to recognise
Southern Confederacy, *IV* 244
Fort Pickens, *IV* 237
Fort Sumter, *IV* 230, 241
Fox, Charles James, *III* 71, 134, 135
145, *IV* 39
coalition with Lord North, *III*
136–9, 141–2
exulted in Napoleon's victories
IV 376–7
on dull, able speaker, *III* 395
on his oratory, *III* 422
quoted, on Burke, *III* 242
France, French:
fear of, prejudice against in
England, 17th, 18th centuries,
III 50, 53–4, 55, 58
general economic condition in
1750's, *III* 98–104, 116–17
no trade with Britain, 18th
century, *III* 145
weakened by Spanish Succession
war, *III* 63, 64–5, 67
for Second Empire period *see*
especially entries under
Napoleon III
see also National character, French
Fraud, unsuccessful, successful,
III 491
Fréderick, King of Denmark, *IV* 449
Frederick, King of Prussia, position
as head of army, *IV* 22 *ed.*, 155,
157–9
Freedom, civil rights, suppressed in
United States, 1861–2, *IV* 320,
364–5
Free trade, Protection, *III* 93, 112,
117
Bright's interest in free trade,
III 299

499

Gladstone, William Ewart:
Characteristics—*cont.*
eager interest, energy, love of
labour, *III* 418–19, 421, 425–6,
477
expenditure, dislike of, *III* 438
expositor of his time, not original
intellect, *III* 438
good sense, sympathy with newly
developing influences, *III* 435–6,
451
influence in politics, *III* 429
lack of moderation, unsteady
intellectual history, *III* 433–6
oratory, bad effects, disorganising
impulse of, *III* 429–33
oratory, greatness of, in
Parliament, *III* 419–25
Oxford man, creed, *III* 416–17,
418, 434
pacifism, Christianity, *III* 421–2,
439
popular orator, Greenwich speech
III 461–4
scholastic intellect, *III* 426–9, 433
unpredictable actions, contrary to
own interest, *III* 471
unpredictable actions, uncertainty
about his career, *III* 415–16
Gladstone, William Ewart: Writings,
speeches quoted on
Irish Home Rule, *III* 457
oratory of adaptation, *III* 423
Royal supremacy in ecclesiastical
affairs, *III* 427–9
speech on reform, Manchester,
1865, *III* 443
Gladstone, William Ewart: Works
Chapter of Autobiography, A, 1868,
III 451–5
Church and State, 1838, *III* 434,
451–4, 462
Homer, III 416, 418–19, 431
Ritualism and Ritual (essay), 1874,
III 471–5
Gladstone, William Ewart: Opinions
on by others

Christian, morbid, *III* 422
good Christian, atrocious pagan,
III 436
Homeric criticism, 'cared about
sons of Priam', *III* 477
unrivalled Parliamentary
statesman (Lord Russell),
III 478
violent reformer, *III* 468–9
Glasgow, trading city, 1750's,
III 92–4, 104, 116
Godolphin, Lord, *III* 57 *bis*, 59
Gordon, George William, *III* 560 *ed.*,
563, 564, 565
Gorham, Rev. Cornelius (Gorham
case), *III* 427–9, 435 *bis*
Goschen, George Joachim, *III* 467,
566 *ed.*, 567, 569
Government, centralised, principles
of, *III* 253–5
Graham, Sir James, on Palmerston,
III 277
Grand Alliance, 1701, *III* 56
betrayed, disunited by
Bolingbroke's secret
negotiations, *III* 66–8
Grant, Ulysses S. *IV* 189 *ed.*
Granville, Lord, *III* 468, 517
on John Bright, *III* 304
Graves, Samuel Robert, *III* 530–3
Greco plot, *IV* 461 *bis*, 462
Greeks, classical, *IV* 51
Grenville, George, *III* 132
Greville, Charles, *III* 216
Grey, Sir George, *III* 370
Grey, Lord, *III* 147, 179, 218, 230
465
Grote, George, on J. S. Mill, *III*
556–7, 558
Grote's *History of Greece, III* 403
Guizot, François Pierre Guillaume,
IV 56, 440–4

Habeas Corpus Act suspended,
England, *III* 164, 211
Habeas Corpus, suspension of by
Lincoln, Oct. 1862, *IV* 369–71

Hamilton, Alexander, *IV* 287–90
Hamilton, Sir William, *III* 89, 558
Hampden, Dr., *III* 435, 435 note
Hanover, House of:
    chosen as heirs to English Crown,
        III 52, 74–5, 81, 225–6
Hardy, Gathorne, *III* 317, 320, 498,
    509
Hare, Thomas, *III* 229
Harley, Robert, Earl of Oxford, *III*
    56, 59–63
    Bagehot quoted on, *III* 26 ed., 27 ed.
    conscience in use of public money,
        III 77–8
    man of business, *III* 61
    master of intrigue, *III* 61–2, 75
    moderate in politics, *III* 52, 60–1,
        72, 75, 77
    no directing ability, *III* 64
Harper's Ferry, Virginia, *IV* 196, 245
Hayter, Sir William, *III* 425
Hazlitt, William, *III* 36–7 ed.
    Bagehot quoted on, *III* 36 ed.
    opinion of, quoted by Bagehot,
        IV 73
    quoted on popular education, *III*
        192
Henley, Joseph, *III* 536, 536 note
Herbert, A. P., *III* 28 ed.
Herschel, Sir John, *III* 557, 557 note
Hindostan, *IV* 82
History, as passing of time, *III* 43
Holland, Lord:
    quoted on Brougham as publicist
        for election, *III* 174
    quoted on Lord North, *III* 133
Holy Alliance, *III* 156 ed., 160, 168,
    209
Horner, Francis, on Brougham, *III*
    182
Houghton, Lord, *III* 295
Household suffrage, *III* 223, 318–19,
    497, 508
House of Commons:
    Irish members, *IV* 296
    Leader of, qualifications for
        position, *III* 219

middle class predominancy in,
    reasonableness of sovereign
    authority, *IV* 301
power in relation to Lords, *III*
    248–9
see also Parliament, Britain
House of Lords:
    case for abolition, possible danger
        of institution, *III* 514–15
    constitution, unfixed number of
        members, *III* 216–17
    Gladstone on popularity of, *III* 464
    power in relation to Commons,
        III 248–9
    power in 1860's, *IV* 93
House of Representatives:
    and Captain Wilkes, *IV* 339, 343
    immediate influence unimportant,
        IV 339–40
Howard, Major, account of measures
    to relieve distress of freed
    slaves, *IV* 421
Hume, David, *III* 89 *bis*, 90 *bis*, 111,
    116, 433
    literary style of, *III* 105–6
    quoted on Charles Townshend,
        III 96–7
Huskisson, William, *III* 145, 214,
    332 *bis*
Hyde Park riots, *III* 508

Imperialism, Bonapartism:
    after Louis Napoleon's death,
        IV 165–72, 173
    guarantee of "fixity" of
        government, *IV* 169–70, 172,
        177
Imperialism, Louis Napoleon's
    government, faults of, *IV* 129,
    131
Income tax, Britain, *III* 163
    attempt to raise, 1816, *III* 166
    Gladstone's use of, *III* 431–2
Indemnity, Acts of, *IV* 311–12
India:
    cotton trade with Britain, 1850's,
        1860's, *IV* 216

Macaulay, Thomas Babington, Lord
—*cont.*
correspondence with Gladstone,
1839, *III* 451, 452
on parliamentary statesmen, *III* 289
on Pitt, *III* 152, 155
quoted, on Calvinism, *III* 110
quoted, on debating, *III* 257–8
Mackintosh, Sir James, *III* 169
quoted, on Brougham as
manipulator of men, *III* 174
quoted, on Members for
working-class constituencies,
III 224
quoted, on suffrage, *III* 219
quoted, on union of England and
America, 1823, *IV* 95
quoted, on unreformed House of
Commons, *III* 268
MacMahon, Marshal, *IV* 170–1
Madison, James, quoted on danger
to Constitution in difference of
opinion between classes of
states, North and South, *IV* 293
Manassas Junction, battle of (Bull
Run), Aug. 1861, *IV* 184 ed.,
265–6, 272, 274, 275, 276
Mansfield, Lord, *III* 105
Marlborough, John, 1st Duke of:
commander in wars, 1701–13
III 56–7, 58–9
dismissed, *III* 63
Marmontel, Jean François, quoted
on Quesnay, *III* 103–4
Marrast, *IV* 46
Masham, Mrs. (Miss Hill), *III* 59,
62, 63 *bis*, 76, 77–8
Mason, James M., *IV* 182 ed., 183 ed.,
341, 344, 348, 349
Mass man, 'monotony' *III* 230
Bagehot quoted on, *III* 27–8 ed.
results of reform, Parliamentary
representation, *III* 225
Maximilian, Archduke, *IV* 85–8
Maynooth College, *III* 434–5, 445,
452 *bis*, 453, 454
Mayo, Lord, *III* 498

Mazzini, Giuseppe, *IV* 84, 460–5,
467–9
character of, *IV* 462–3
Meade, General George Gordon, *IV*
392
Mediation, recognition, American
Civil War:
by Britain, *IV* 184–6 ed.
by Napoleon III, *IV* 185 ed.
necessary at once for humane and
political reasons, Aug. 1862,
IV 363–8
Melbourne, Lord, *III* 184, *IV* 62
Mexico, Mexican Empire, 1863,
IV 20 ed., 27 ed., 85–8, 326
French invasion, *IV* 27 ed., 96–7,
98–9, 104
Middle classes, Britain, *III* 164, 165
after Napoleonic war, 1815, *III* 162
liberal ideas of, 1830, *III* 178
manufacturers, business men,
III 249–50
middle-class eloquence in
Commons, reformed Parliament,
III 269–70
representation before and after
1832, *III* 222, 223–4, 225
see also Capitalists, manufacturers
Mill, John Stuart, *III* 112, 394, 395,
540 ed.
contagious enthusiasm, *III* 558
excitability, susceptibility,
III 547–8
on his cultivation of a persuasive
style, *III* 94
on Irish land tenure, *III* 548–53
political faith, confession of,
III 542–6
Mill, John Stuart: Works
*Examination of Sir W. Hamilton's
Philosophy, III* 558
*Principles of Political Economy,
III* 555–6, 557, 558
System of Logic, III 555–7, 558
Mill, John Stuart: Opinion about,
quoted by Bagehot, *Tom Hughes
bound up with Ricardo, III* 548

Radicals, radicalism, *III* 161
  and Liberal Party, *III* 538
  differences with J. S. Mill,
    III 542–5
Radnor, Lord, *III* 330, 342
Railway mania, 1840's, James
    Wilson's writings, *III* 342
Railways:
  introduction into India, *III* 345
  Palmerston on, *III* 280–1
Raynouard, Monsieur, *III* 379–81
Record, The, III 246
Reform Act, Bill, 1832, *III* 200 *ed.*,
    268, 269, 299
  Bill proposed, *III* 215
  crisis, state of public mind,
    III 178–9
  obstacles to passing, Parliament,
    William IV, *III* 215–17
  old system of representation,
    changed by Act, *III* 219–25
  old system's variety, advantages,
    III 224, 225–8
  posterity's view of Act, *III* 201–2
  results of Act, changed powers of
    representation, *III* 224–5, 229–30
Reform Act, 1867, *III* 201, 229, 491,
    508
Reform Bill, 1866, *III* 300
Reprisals, atrocities in American
    Civil War, *IV* 363–4
Revenue, controlled by Commons,
    III 72–3
Ricardo, David, *III* 112, 115
Richmond, Duke of, *III* 320
Richmond, Virginia, fall of, *IV* 189
    ed., 413–14
Ritualism, Gladstone on, *III* 471–5
Robinson, Henry Crabb:
  as barrister, *IV* 486–7
  as literary critic, *IV* 485
  as metaphysician, *IV* 485–6
  literary style, *IV* 477–8
  memoirs quoted, *IV* 482–3
Robinson, Henry Crabb:
  Characteristics
  breakfast parties, *IV* 480–1

  conversations, anecdotes, *IV* 482–6
  facial features, use of chin, *IV* 481
  forgetfulness, friends' names,
    IV 484–5
  grotesqueness, animal oddity,
    IV 479–80
  'old Crabb', *IV* 479–80
  vigorous intolerance on some
    subjects, *IV* 488
Robinson, Henry Crabb: Opinions
    writings quoted on
  A. H. Clough, *IV* 484
  Thomas Erskine, *IV* 482–3
  Hazlitt's inferiority to Lamb,
    IV 488
  his ability as lawyer, *IV* 486
  his ability as writer, *IV* 477
  his intolerance, *IV* 488
  Madge (Unitarian preacher),
    IV 486
  Baron Rolfe, Lord Cranworth,
    IV 483
  John Wesley, *IV* 483
Rockingham, Lord, *III* 134–5, 142
Roebuck, John Arthur, on
  recognition of Confederacy,
    IV 383, 384–5
  quoted on Brougham and
    dissolution of Parliament,
    III 182–4
Rolfe, Baron (Lord Cranworth),
    IV 483
Rollin, Ledru, *IV* 70
Roman Catholic Church, *III* 427,
    IV 58–60, 471, 473–4
Roman Catholic party, France,
    IV 109, 127
Romance language, Sir George
    Lewis on, *III* 379–81
Romans, Roman Empire, national
    character, *IV* 51
Rome, French occupation, 1860's,
    IV 109, 127
Romilly, Sir Samuel, *III* 169
  quoted on effects of French
    Revolution on reform
    movements, *III* 208–9

Slavery—*cont.*
not the true issue between Union
and Confederacy, 1861, *IV*
233–5, 276, 316–18
new anti-slavery laws not
supported by main secessionists,
IV 243
Northern English manufacturers'
determination not to recognise
Southern Confederacy, *IV* 244
English public opinion concerning
slavery, and reasons for not
intervening in Federal
blockade, Jan. 1862, *IV* 357–8
Lincoln's proclamation emancipating
all slaves in Southern states,
Oct. 1862, *IV* 371–3, 375–6
slave population a hindrance to
guerrilla warfare in a defeated
country, *IV* 415
freed slave population of Southern
states beyond help, powers of
Federal Government after Civil
War, *IV* 420–1
see also Negroes
Slidell, John, *IV* 182 *ed.*, 183 *ed.*,
341, 344, 348, 349
Smith, Adam, *III* 84 *ed.*, *IV* 456
Bagehot quoted on, *III* 32 *ed.*
Smith, Adam: Career
boyhood, Glasgow University,
III 87–8
exhibitioner to Oxford, *III*
88–90
elected Professor, Glasgow
University, *III* 91–2
studies practical applications of
wealth, revenue in Glasgow,
III 92–4
tutor to Duke of Buccleugh,
III 96–8
publishes *Wealth of Nations*,
III 105–7
commissioner of customs, *III*
108–9
prevented from further writing,
III 108–9

death, *III* 109
Smith, Adam: Characteristics,
Interests
absentmindedness, *III* 85–6, 108,
113
bonhomie, *III* 97
business matters, inability in,
III 108
England, knowledge of,
sympathy with, *III* 89–90,
116
free trade, authority on, *III* 112,
295
Greek, knowledge of, *III* 89
love affairs undocumented,
III 111–12
oratory, lecturing, gift for, *III*
90–1
political economy, founder of,
III 112
religion, attitude to, *III* 110–11
strongminded, adaptable, *III*
104–5
Smith, Adam: Writings quoted on
French revenue laws, *III* 99–100
Oxford University, *III* 88
Smith, Adam: Works
Lectures on Justice (destroyed),
III 87
*Some Considerations Concerning
the First Formation of
Languages*, *III* 87
Theory of Moral Sentiments, The,
III 86–7, 94–6, 105
Wealth of Nations, The, *III* 88,
130
anachronisms in, *III* 106–7
beginnings, first ideas of, in
lectures, *III* 119
lessons of, *III* 118–19, 295
part of much larger scheme,
III 86–7, 118
power of persuasive argument
in, *III* 94, 110
style, *III* 105–6
success of, reasons for, *III*
114–17

Smith, Adam: Works—*cont.*
  treatment too interesting,
    popular for subject,
    criticism answered by
    Bagehot, *III* 110, 115
Smith, Sydney:
  as executor, *IV* 479
  on quickness, *III* 376
  on the abstract in Scotland, *III* 93
  quoted, on Lord Eldon, Chancery,
    III 162
  quoted, on Perceval, *III* 246
  quoted, on political economy,
    III 330
Snell Foundation, Glasgow, Oxford,
    III 88, 90
Socialists, Socialism, in France,
    IV 40–2
  fear of in 1851 revolution, *IV* 32–4
  transportation of Socialists to
    Cayenne, Jan. 1852, *IV* 42–3,
    78
  dislike of parliamentary
    government, *IV* 133–4
  possible republican experiment
    after 1870, *IV* 148–50
Society for the Diffusion of Useful
    Knowledge, *III* 192
Socrates, *IV* 51
Somerset, Duchess of, *III* 76
South Carolina, attitude after
    secession, Dec. 1860, *IV* 201–2,
    203–4, 219
South, Confederate states *see*
    Confederate States of America
Southey, Robert, *III* 402
Spain, Spanish Empire, in 1700's,
    III 53, 55, 64–5, 67, 69
Spanish America, Canning's policy
    for republican states, 1823,
    IV 95–6
Spanish Succession, War of 1701–13,
    III 56, 64–5
Spectator, The, accusations, alleged
    English lack of sympathy with
    slavery abolitionists, *IV* 316,
    321

Spencer, John Charles, 3rd Earl *see*
    Althorp, John Charles Spencer,
    Viscount
Stanhope, Philip Henry, 5th Earl, as
    historian, *III* 123–4
  quoted, on Mr. Coke's declining
    to stand, *III* 142
  quoted, on Sir George Lewis,
    Martello towers, *III* 375–6
Stansfeld, Sir James, *IV* 461–5
Statesmen:
  as advocates, debaters, British,
    III 257–61, 437, 572
  commonplace ideas of, *III* 244–5
  constitutional, parliamentary
    III 242, 253, 257–61, 276, 281,
    289
  defects of, British, *III* 288–9
  ease, fixity in money matters,
    British, *III* 567–9
  knowledge of great statesmen
    necessary to England, *III* 440
  theorising of French politicians,
    political writers, *IV* 60–1
  see also Assembly, French; House
    of Commons; Parliament,
    Britain
Stephen, James, *III* 166 note
Stephens, Alexander, *IV* 243
Story, Justice, on election
    machinery, U.S. President,
    IV 302–3
Stowe, Harriet Beecher, *IV* 315–16,
    317, 318
Stowell, Lord, quoted on popular
    education, *III* 169
Strikes:
  Henry Fawcett on, *III* 538
  J. S. Mill on, *III* 544
Style, literary, *III* 105–6
Suffolk, Lady, *III* 82
Suffrage, Britain *see* Parliamentary
    representation
Suffrage, France:
  Guizot's restrictions, high
    bourgeois suffrage, 1840's,
    IV 442–3

Union, United States of America
—*cont.*
attitude to Mexico, 1863, *IV* 86, 87
attitude towards U.S. of Louis
Napoleon, 1863, *IV* 108
colonies, colonial background,
IV 284–5
Sir George Lewis on, March
1861, *III* 403
plebiscite, use of, *IV* 139
State and Federal powers, 1860's,
III 458
want of variety in political life,
national character, *IV* 97–8, 99
Union, United States of America,
and Civil War, *IV* 196–9
divided front on slavery issue,
Jan. 1860, *IV* 196–9
disruption of Union unwelcome
to Northerners, reasons,
IV 205–7
possible relationship with Britain
after secession of Southern
states, Jan. 1861, *IV* 213–14
attitude to secession, Jan. 1861,
IV 219–23
attitude, Feb.–Mar. 1861,
undetermined, *IV* 229–31
true issue between Union and
Confederacy not slavery but
control over government of
Union, *IV* 233–6
border slave states, importance of
their actions Feb.–Apr. 1861,
IV 229, 237–8, 241–2, 245,
247–8
ultimate Union victory forecast
by Bagehot, *IV* 246–7, 361–2
closer union, stronger Federal
Government forecast by
Bagehot as result of war,
IV 247–8
anger of Federalists towards
England, June, Sep., 1861,
IV 259–60, 315–22
victory in war but not success in
coercion of Southern states

forecast by Bagehot, *IV* 261–3,
296–7
disruption of Union more
inevitable after battle at
Manassas Junction, Aug. 1861
(Bull Run), *IV* 265–7, 275–6
disruption of Union welcome to
Bagehot, reasons, *IV* 326–8
breakdown in military and
administrative system, late 1861,
IV 335–6
military, financial difficulties of
war, *IV* 355–6
Bagehot's desire to establish good
relations with Union after war
IV 356–7
superiority, advantages of
Federals in war, *IV* 360–1
threat of split in Union between
East and West over
conscription, taxation, *IV* 366–7,
398
Government policy of subjecting
England to small affronts,
IV 379–82
invasion by Confederates under
Lee, 1863, possible political
consequences, *IV* 387–8, 389,
392
idea of convention of states to
discuss terms of accommodation,
possible end of war, Aug.–Sep.
1864, *IV* 396–7, 399
financial position, 1864, *IV* 395,
398
danger of warlike attitude to
Europe after Lincoln's
assassination, *IV* 407–8, 410
need for control over legislation
of states during reconstruction
of Union, *IV* 422–3
Johnson's attitude to Union as
indissoluble, never broken by
rebellion, Dec. 1867, *IV* 425–7
see also Constitution, American;
Lincoln, Abraham; President,
United States; Secession; Slavery

Useful Knowledge Society, *III* 192
Utrecht, Treaty of, 1713, *III* 55,
65–8, 69–72, 73, 76, 77, 80

Vergniaud, Pierre, *III* 187–8
Vicksburg, Missouri, fall of, *IV* 189
ed., 392, 397
Victor Emmanuel, King of Italy,
IV 453 *ed.*, 469, 472
Victoria, Queen:
hereditary, divine right, *III* 49–50
John Bright's loyalty to, *III* 318
Virginia:
attitude towards slavery, 1861,
IV 204–5
secession, April, 1861, *IV* 245

Wages, English manufacturing
districts, post-1815, *III* 161
Walpole, Sir Robert, *III* 73, 81, 163,
IV 39, 51
concerned only with present
problems, *III* 149
landed gentleman, fitted for
administration, *III* 249
on dishonesty in ministers, *IV* 115
on gratitude for patronage, *III* 141–2
unsensitive nature, *III* 68
Washington, rumoured Confederate
invasion, April 1861, *IV* 241–2,
246
Wealth of Nations, The, see Smith,
Adam: Works
Weguelin, Mr. *III* 346
Wellesley, Lord, *III* 375
quoted, on Peel, *III* 262–3
Wellington, Duke of, *III* 160, 215,
264
as a 'character', *IV* 38
influenced by James Wilson's
economic arguments, *III* 332
quoted, on Brougham's use of
great seal, *III* 182
quoted, on Peel, *III* 263
unpopularity of, unsuccessful
legislation, *III* 214
Whigs, Whig party, *III* 71, 212,

236, 257
as close combination of political
intelligence, through select
constituencies, *III* 226
choice of Hanover as heirs to
crown after Anne, *III* 52, 74
impeachment of Dr. Sacheverell,
1710, *III* 62
Reform Bill crisis, 1832, *III* 179
see also Liberals, Liberal party
Wilberforce, William:
elected M.P. for Yorkshire, *III* 142
on Brougham's versatility, *III* 191
on Pitt, *III* 128
Wilkes, Captain Charles, *IV* 182
ed., 330–1, 337, 339, 342, 343,
347–8, 349, 380, 382
Wilkes, John, *III* 195
William III, *III* 51, 55–6
William IV:
causes confusion over Reform
Bill, *III* 217
'managed' by Lord Brougham,
III 182–4
turns out Lord Melbourne's
ministry, *III* 231
Wilson, James (father-in-law to
Bagehot), *III* 322 *ed.*, 323 note
Bagehot quoted on, *III* 32–3 *ed.*
Indian saltpetre, export duty,
IV, 236
quoted, on Cobden, *III* 289, 297
Wilson, James: Career
boyhood, education, *III* 323–4
partner, hat manufacturers,
III 324–5
owner of business, 1831, *III* 325–6
marriage, 1832, *III* 325 note
loss of capital, investment failure,
1837–9, *III* 326–8
pamphlet, speeches on Corn
Laws, 1839, 1840's, *III* 328,
330, 332–8
pamphlet *The Revenue*, 1841,
III 338–41
founds *The Economist*, 1843,
III 330, 341–2

Wilson, James: Career—*cont.*
M.P. for Westbury, 1847, 1852,
III 342–4, 346
Joint Secretary, Board of Control,
1848, *III* 344–6
Financial Secretary to Treasury,
1853, *III* 346–51
refuses offers of different posts,
1855, 1856, *III* 351–2
M.P. for Devonport, 1857, *III* 352
Vice-President, Board of Trade,
1859, *III* 352
Financial Member, Council of
India, 1859, *III* 352–4
economic measures, India,
1859–60, *III* 354–9
illness, death, *III* 359–61
Wilson, James: Characteristics
active temperament, *III* 324, 329
animation, naturalness of manner,
355
appearance, *III* 361
as master of Socratic art of
inquiry, *III* 345–6
as writer on economics subjects,
III 330–42
business, transacting ability,
III 325, 328, 329, 330–2
convincing arguments of,
economics, *III* 332, 342
efficiency, accuracy, intelligibility,
III 347–9
fair-mindedness, *III* 345
iron constitution, great capacity
for work, *III* 341, 350
judgement even, consistent,
III 349–50
memory, accurate and detailed,
III 349

moral character, common sense
approach, *III* 361
private life, *III* 362
sanguine temperament, *III* 328–9
shyness, reticence, *III* 361–2
thoroughness, *III* 324
work with subordinates cordial,
encouraging, *III* 362 note
Wilson, James: Tributes to, *III* 362–4
Sir George Lewis, *III* 377
Windham, William, on popular
education, *III* 168–9
Women's suffrage:
John Bright not in favour of,
III 317, 319–20
J. S. Mill on, *III* 542–3
Wordsworth, William, *III* 255,
IV 480, 485
quoted, in relation to Crabb
Robinson, *IV* 478–9
quoted on French Revolution,
1830, *III* 214
Working classes, England:
enfranchisement of, *III* 224,
299–300
impoverishment, disaffection,
post-1815, *III* 161, 211
Northern England, effects of
Federal blockade of Confederate
ports, *IV* 215–17, 267–8, 321
Working classes, peasantry, France,
IV 27 ed., 105–6, 113, 131, 162
support for Louis Napoleon in
voting of, *IV* 81, 142

Yancey, William Lowndes, *IV* 243
York, Dean of (William Cockburn),
quoted, on Peel's scrupulousness,
III 264–6

INDEX TO BAGEHOT'S
EPIGRAMS

INDEX TO BAGEHOT'S EPIGRAMS

Volcano, edge of (Sir George
  Lewis), *III* 378

Whig ministries, low-church
  bishops, *III* 179
Wilson, James, animated man,

inanimate subjects, *III* 236
World, wiser than any philosopher,
  III 393

Youth, illusions pass away, *III* 127